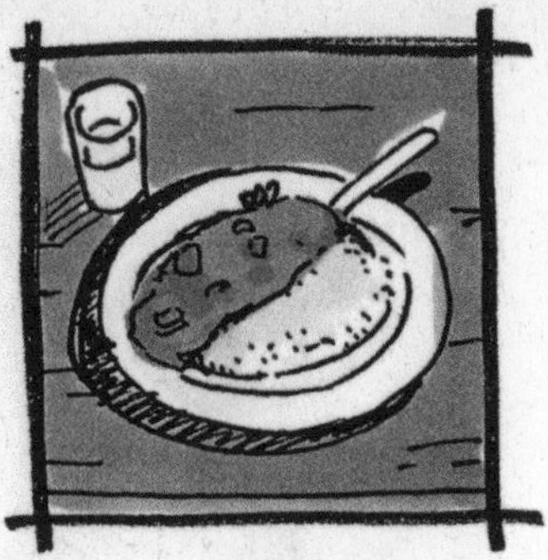

Curry rice or rice curry... I have no idea what the difference is...

—*Masashi Kishimoto, 2006*

岸本斉史

Author/artist Masashi Kishimoto was born in 1974 in rural Okayama Prefecture, Japan. After spending time in art college, he won the Hop Step Award for new manga artists with his manga **Karakuri** (Mechanism). Kishimoto decided to base his next story on traditional Japanese culture. His first version of **Naruto**, drawn in 1997, was a one-shot story about fox spirits; his final version, which debuted in **Weekly Shonen Jump** in 1999, quickly became the most popular ninja manga in Japan.

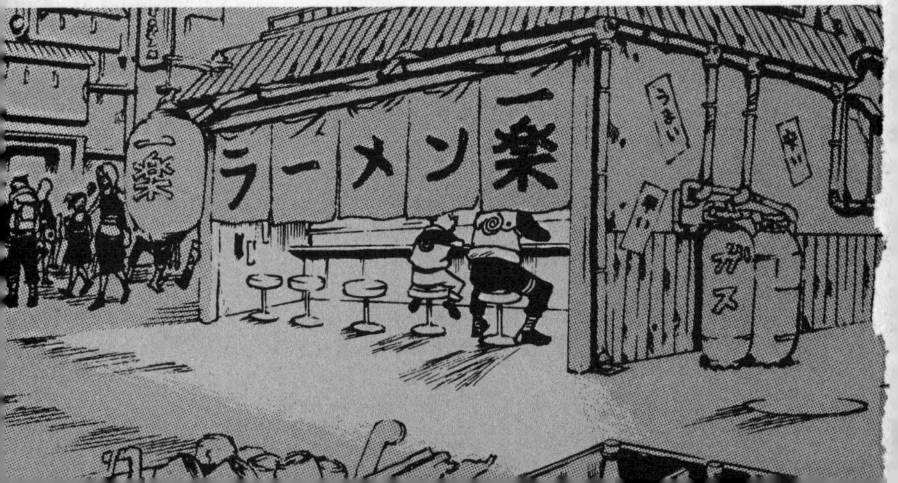
一楽
ラーメン一楽

NARUTO VOL. 35
The SHONEN JUMP Manga Edition

STORY AND ART BY MASASHI KISHIMOTO

Translation/Mari Morimoto
English Adaptation/Deric A. Hughes & Benjamin Raab
Touch-up Art & Lettering/Sabrina Heep
Design/Sean Lee
Editor/Joel Enos

Editor in Chief, Books/Alvin Lu
Editor in Chief, Magazines/Marc Weidenbaum
VP, Publishing Licensing/Rika Inouye
VP, Sales & Product Marketing/Gonzalo Ferreyra
VP, Creative/Linda Espinosa
Publisher/Hyoe Narita

NARUTO © 1999 by Masashi Kishimoto. All rights reserved. First
published in Japan in 1999 by SHUEISHA Inc., Tokyo. English translation
rights arranged by SHUEISHA Inc. The stories, characters and incidents
mentioned in this publication are entirely fictional.

No portion of this book may be reproduced or transmitted in any form
or by any means without written permission from the copyright holders.

The rights of the author(s) of the work(s) in this publication to be so
identified have been asserted in accordance with Copyright, Designs and
Patents Act 1988. A CIP catalogue record for this book is available from
the British Library.

Printed in the U.S.A.

Published by VIZ Media, LLC
P.O. Box 77010
San Francisco, CA 94107

SHONEN JUMP Manga Edition
10 9 8 7 6 5 4 3 2 1
First printing, February 2009

www.viz.com

RATED T FOR TEEN

PARENTAL ADVISORY
NARUTO is rated T for Teen and is recommended
for ages 13 and up. This volume contains realistic
and fantasy violence.

ratings.viz.com

THE WORLD'S
MOST POPULAR MANGA
SHONEN JUMP
www.shonenjump.com

SHONEN JUMP MANGA EDITION

NARUTO

VOL. 35 THE NEW TWO

STORY AND ART BY
MASASHI KISHIMOTO

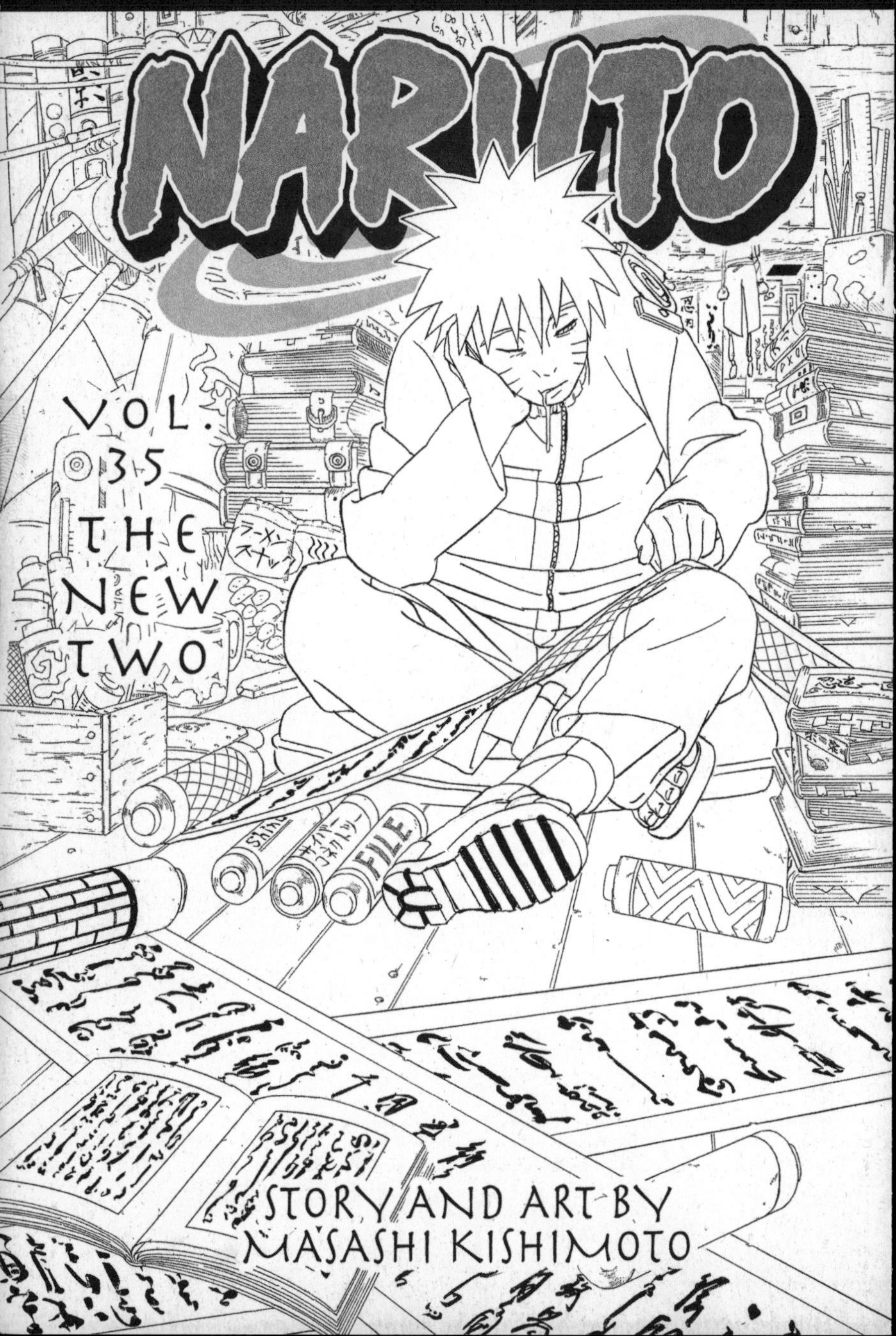

FILE

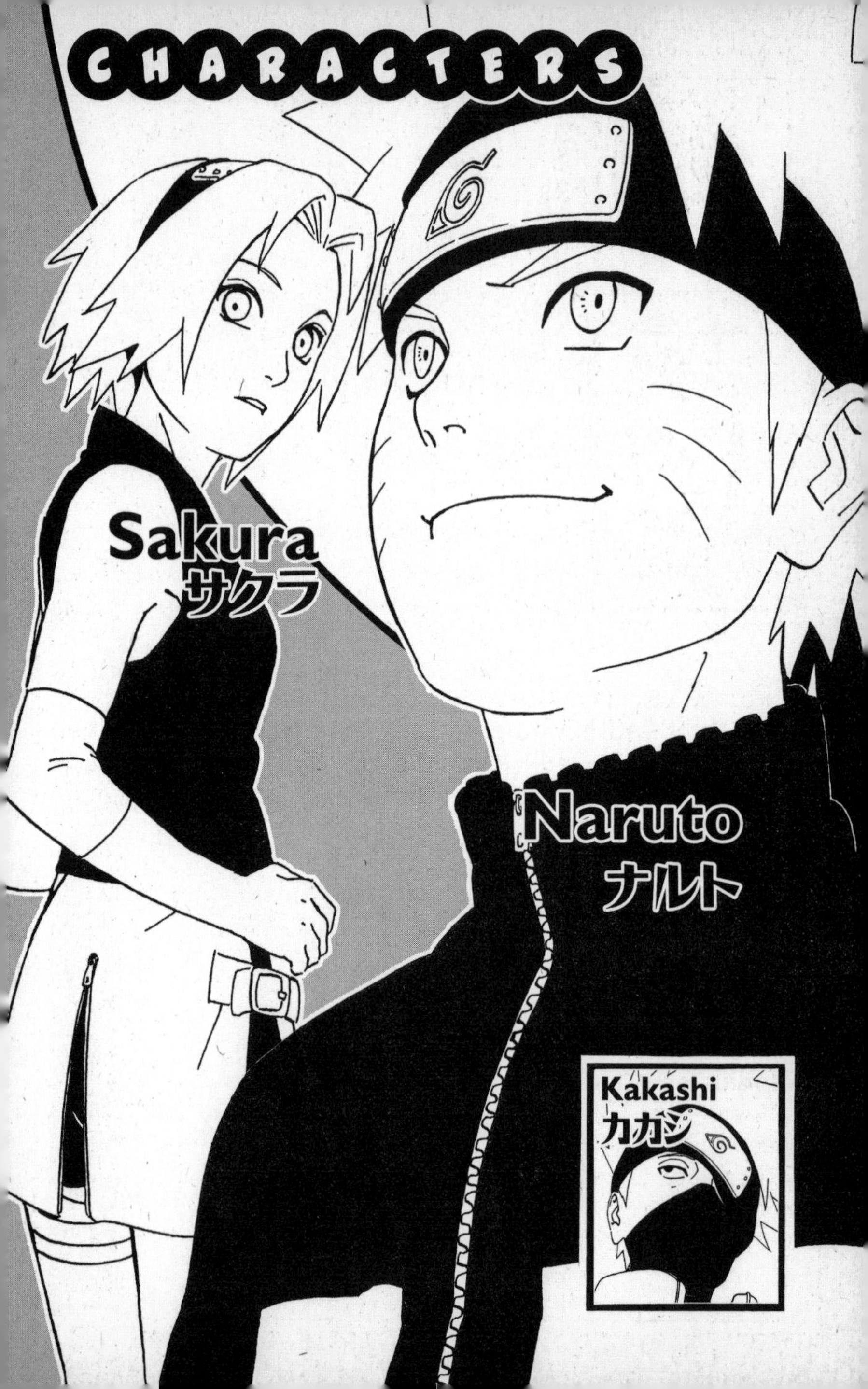
CHARACTERS
Sakura
サクラ
Naruto
ナルト
Kakashi
カカシ

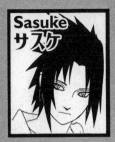

Sasuke
サスケ
Tsunade
綱手
Sai
サイ
Asuma
アスマ
Shikamaru
シカマル
Yamato
ヤマト

The Story So Far...

Team Kakashi's mission to rescue Uchiha Sasuke from the sinister Orochimaru continues! While Captain Yamato's doppelganger searches for the villain's secret hideout, Naruto and Sakura pore over Sai's mysterious picture book and finally learn the truth about their treacherous teammate's troubled origin...

Sai, meanwhile, remains in the company of Orochimaru where he at last comes face to face with Sasuke. But the young man he meets bears little to no resemblance to Naruto's friend of the past. Gone are any traces of the light that was once inside him. All that remains is a being of darkness bent on destruction...

Team Kakashi finally infiltrates Orochimaru's lair and goes toe to toe with Sasuke. Now more powerful than ever, he leaves his former friends in the dust, picking up the pieces of their failed mission...

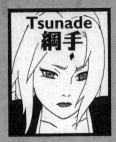

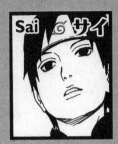

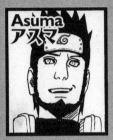

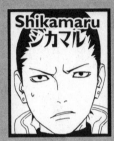

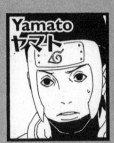

CONTENTS

NARUTO

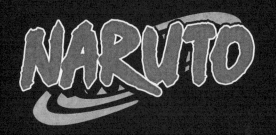

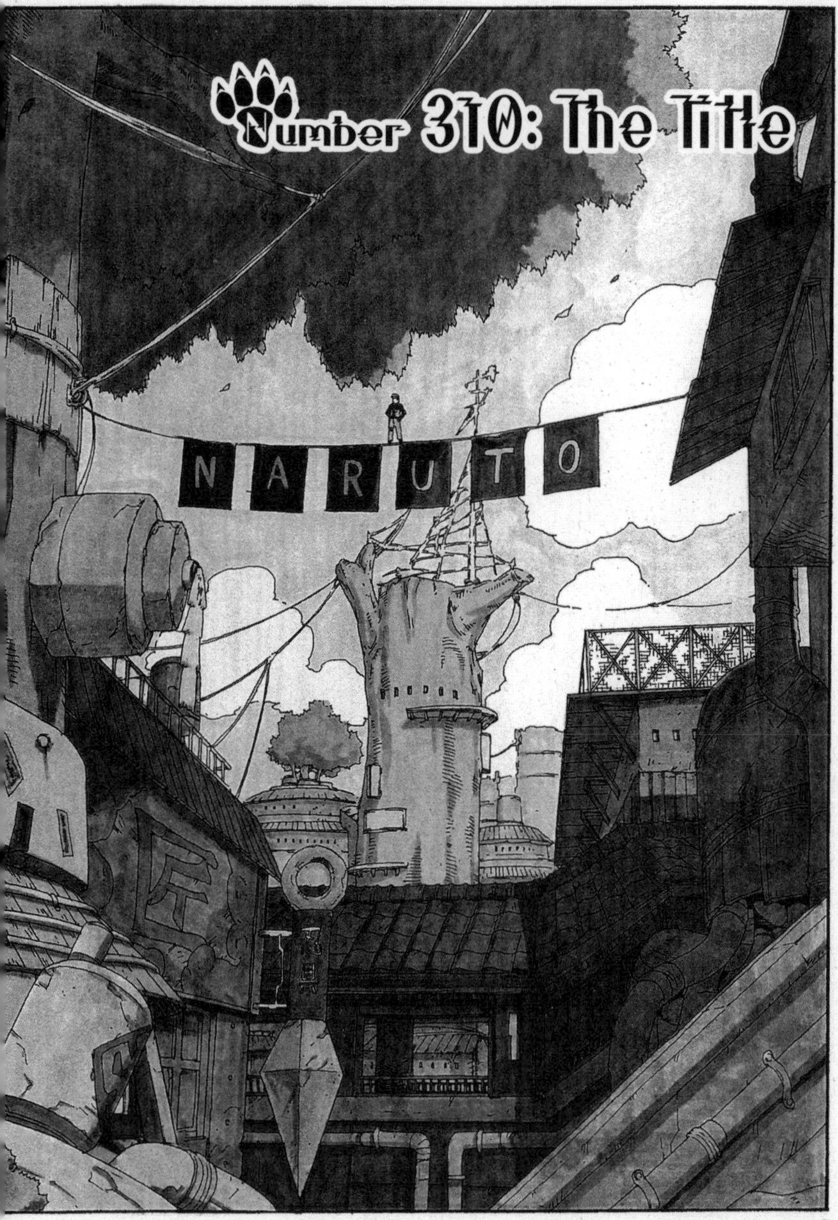
Number 310: The Title
NARUTO

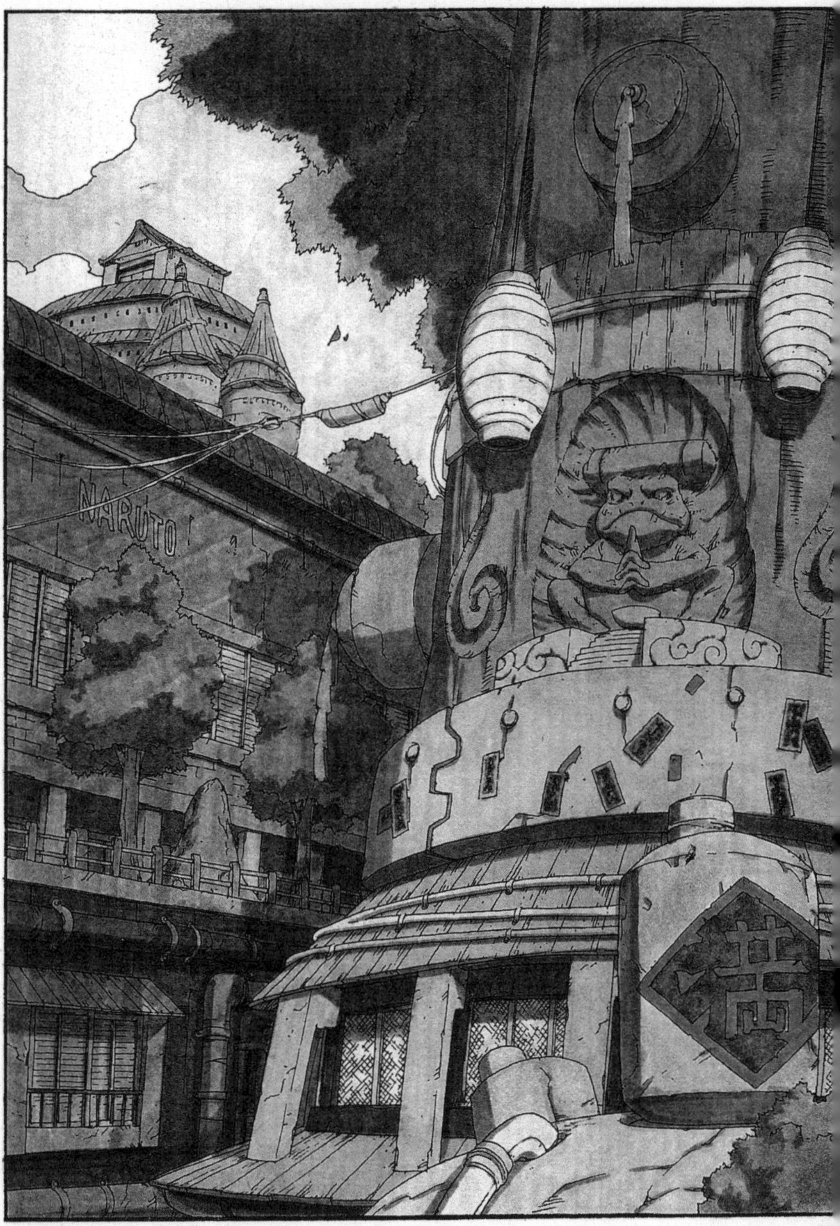
NARUTO

NARUTO

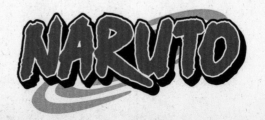

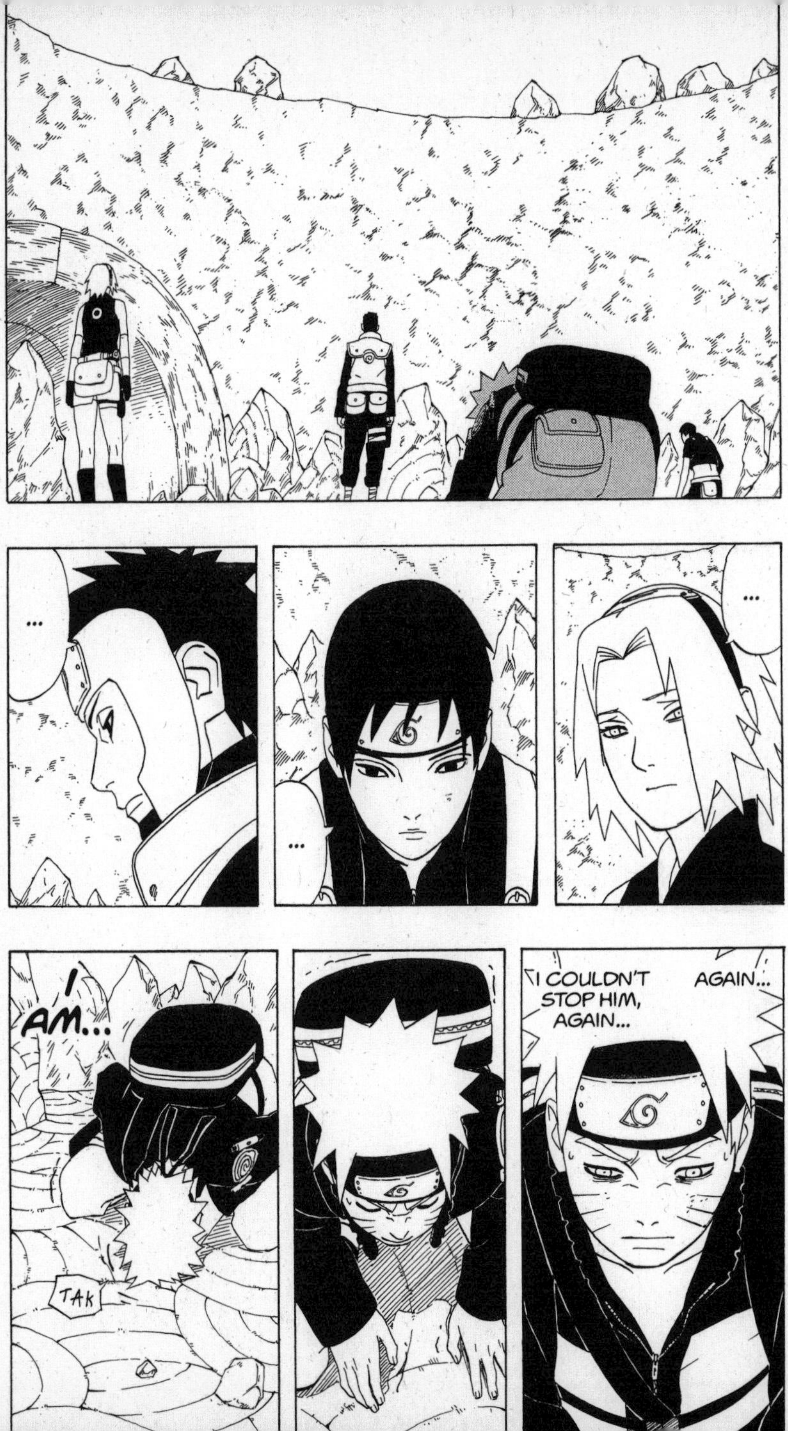
...
...
...
I COULDN'T STOP HIM, AGAIN...
AGAIN...
I AM...
TAK

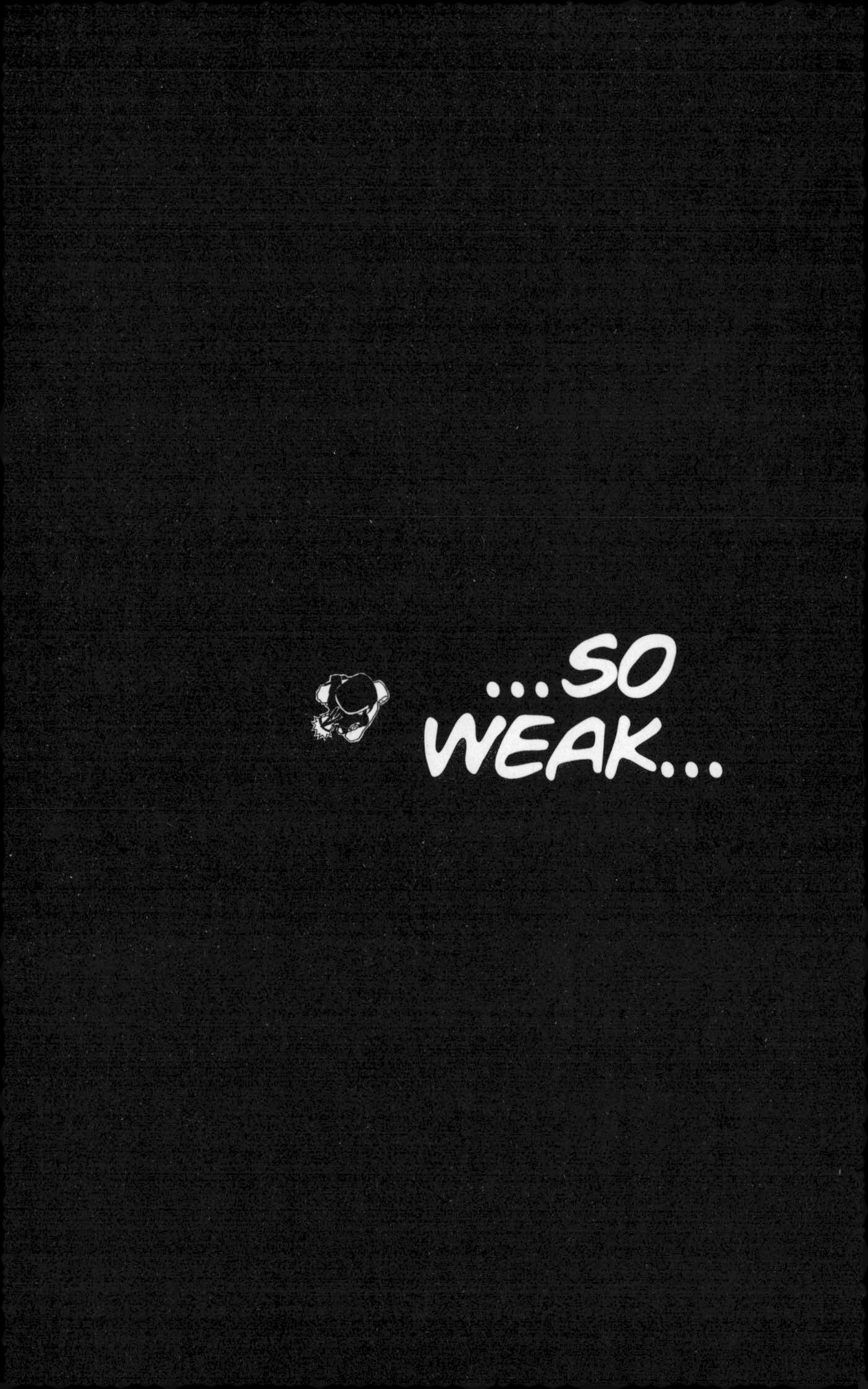
...SO WEAK...

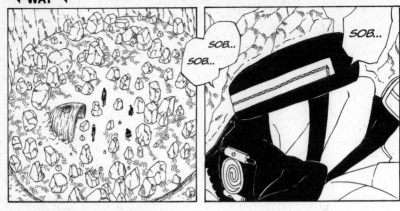

READ THIS WAY

SOB...

SOB...

SOB...

...

CRY-ING...

...

...WON'T MAKE SASUKE COME BACK, NARUTO.

...

...

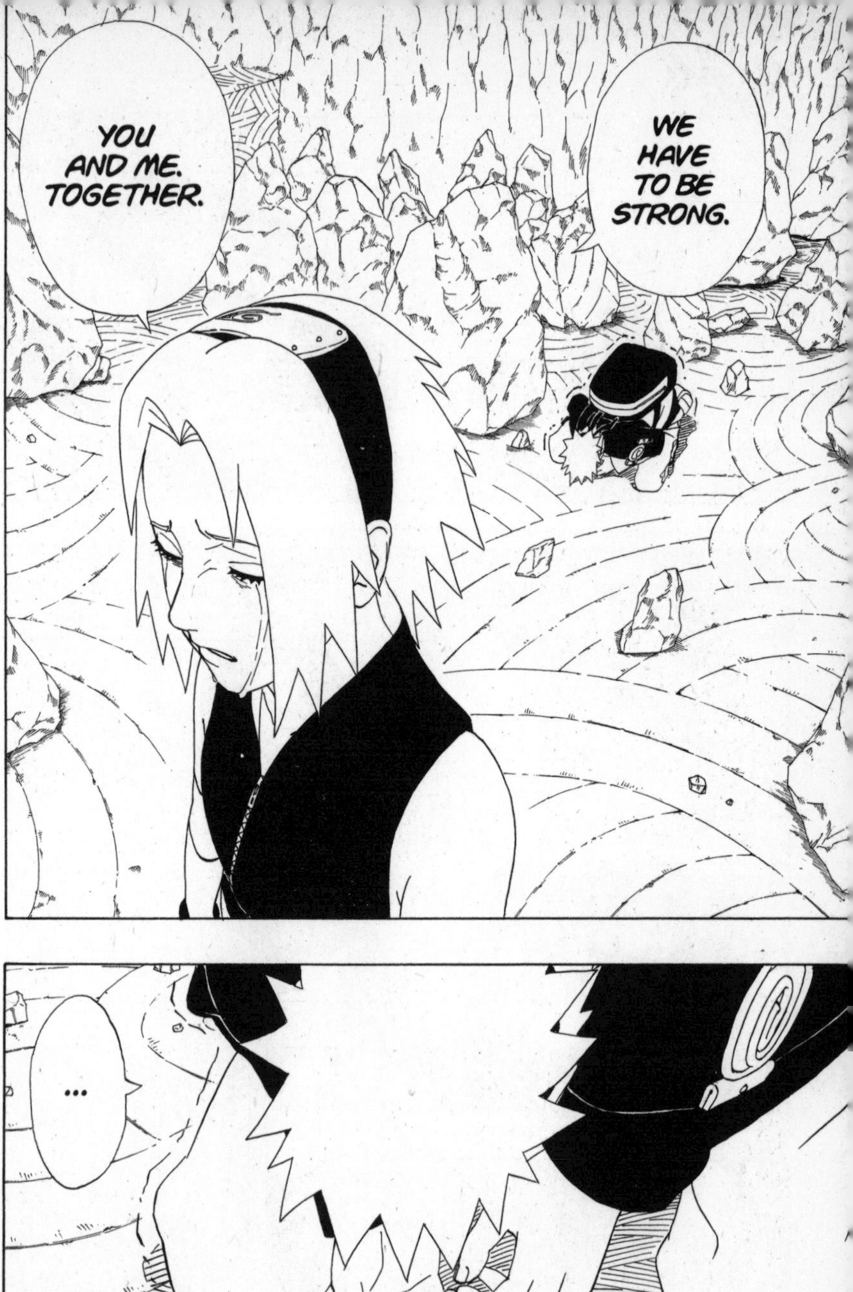
WE HAVE TO BE STRONG.
YOU AND ME. TOGETHER.
...

READ THIS WAY

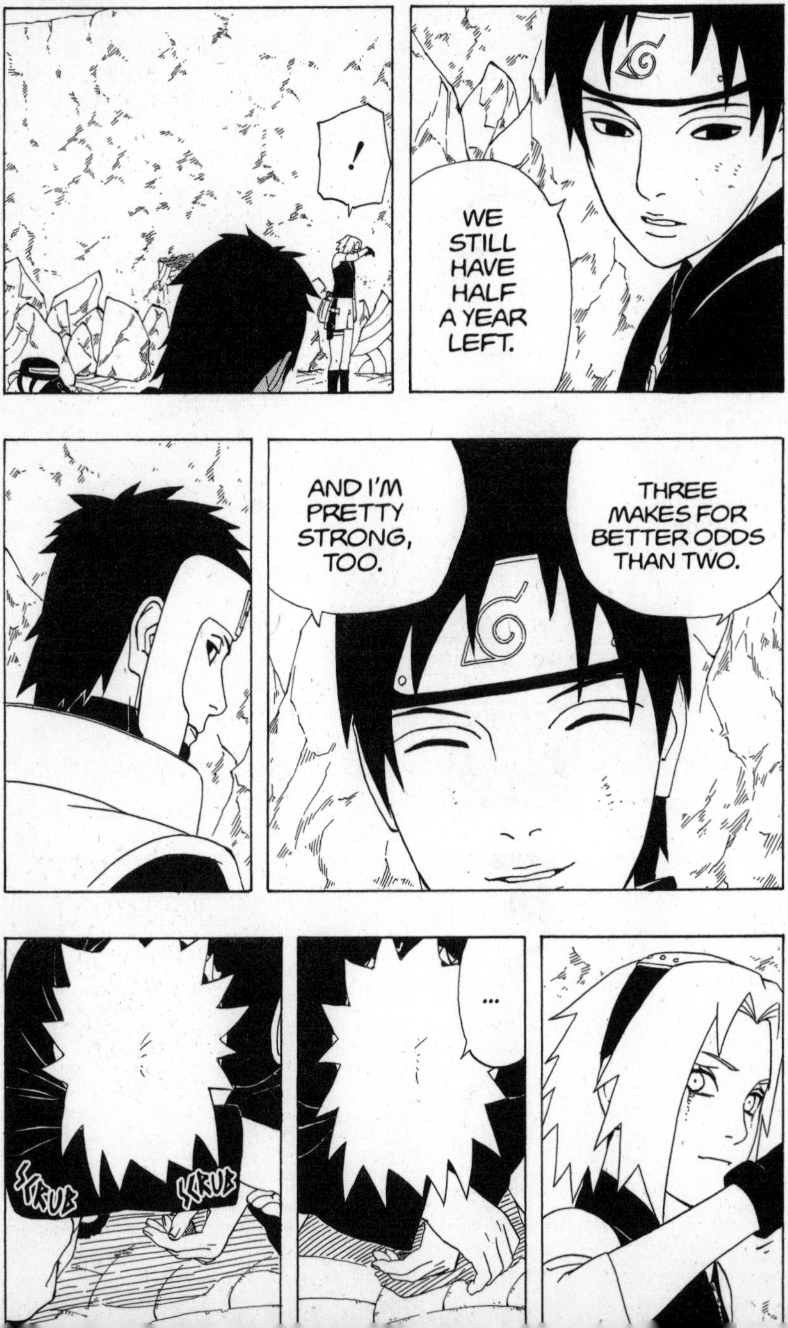
WE STILL HAVE HALF A YEAR LEFT.
!
THREE MAKES FOR BETTER ODDS THAN TWO.
AND I'M PRETTY STRONG, TOO.
...
SCRUB
SCRUB

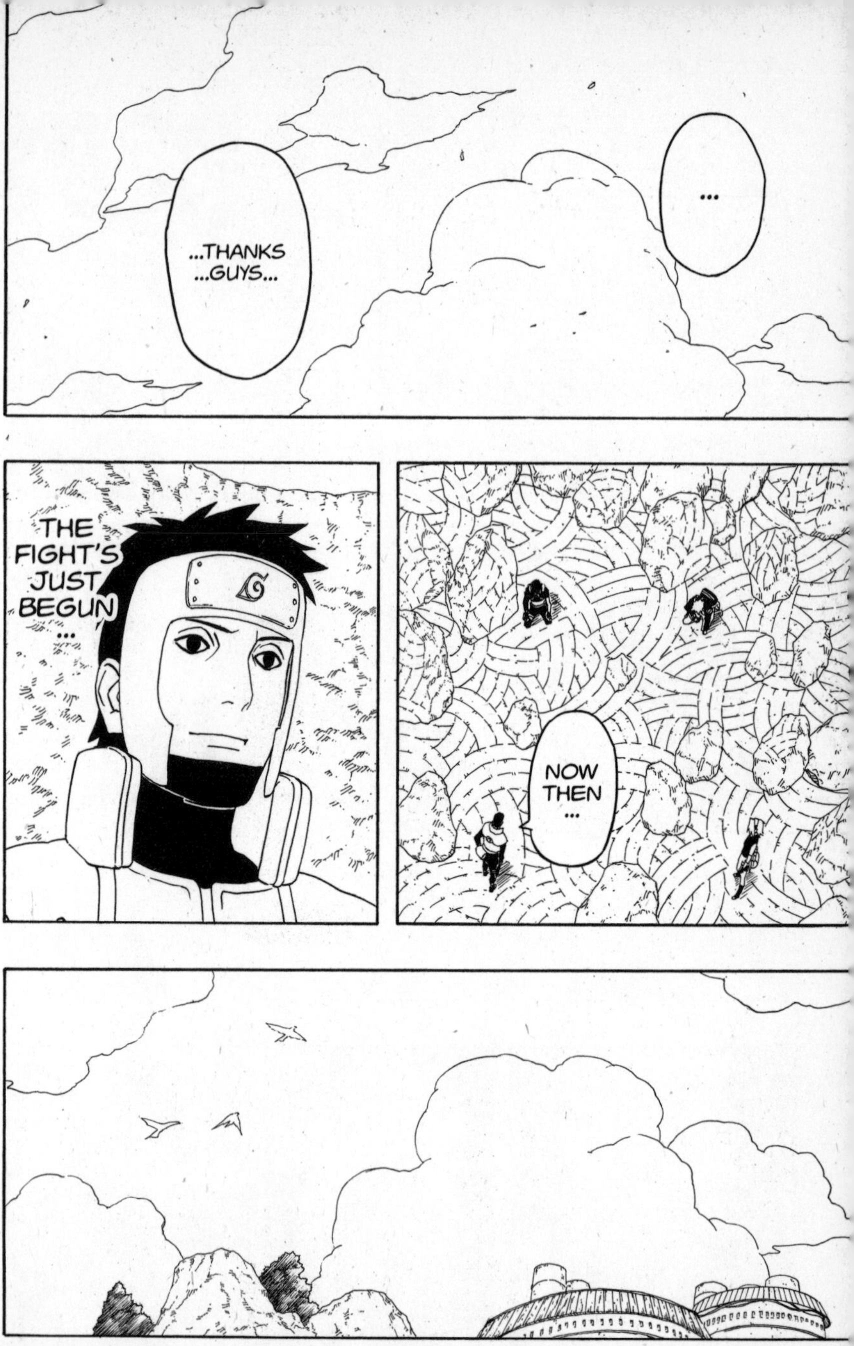
...
...THANKS ...GUYS...
NOW THEN ...
THE FIGHT'S JUST BEGUN ...

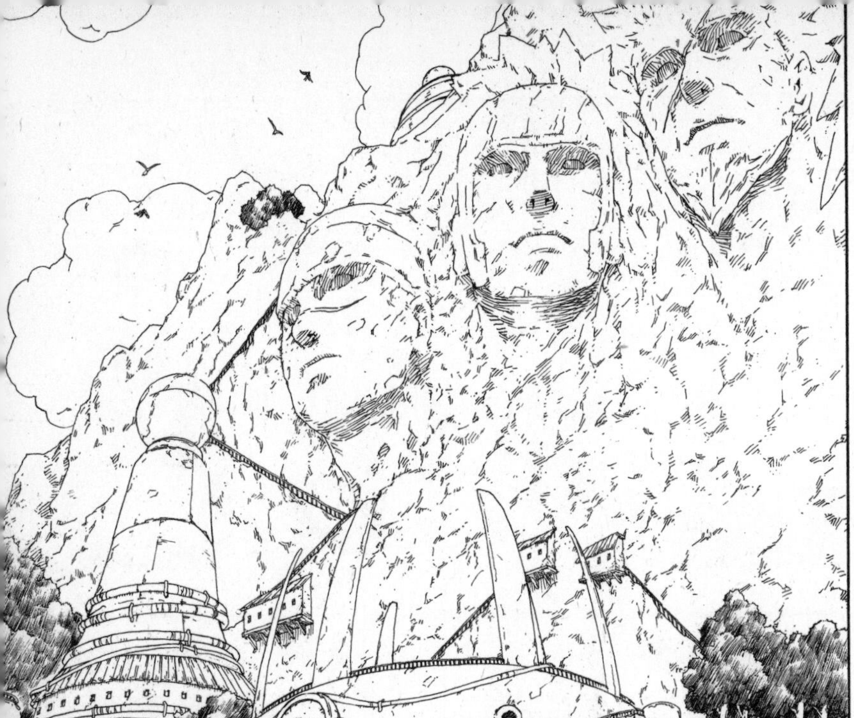
火

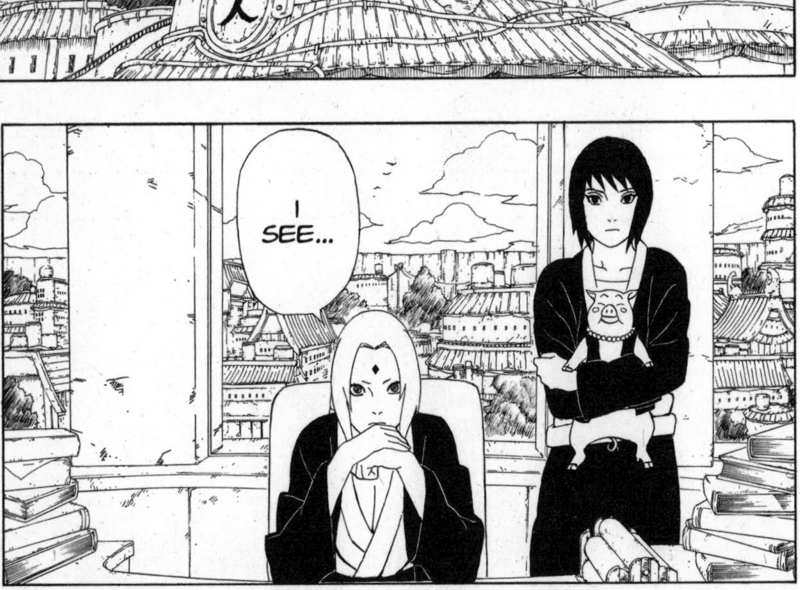
I SEE...

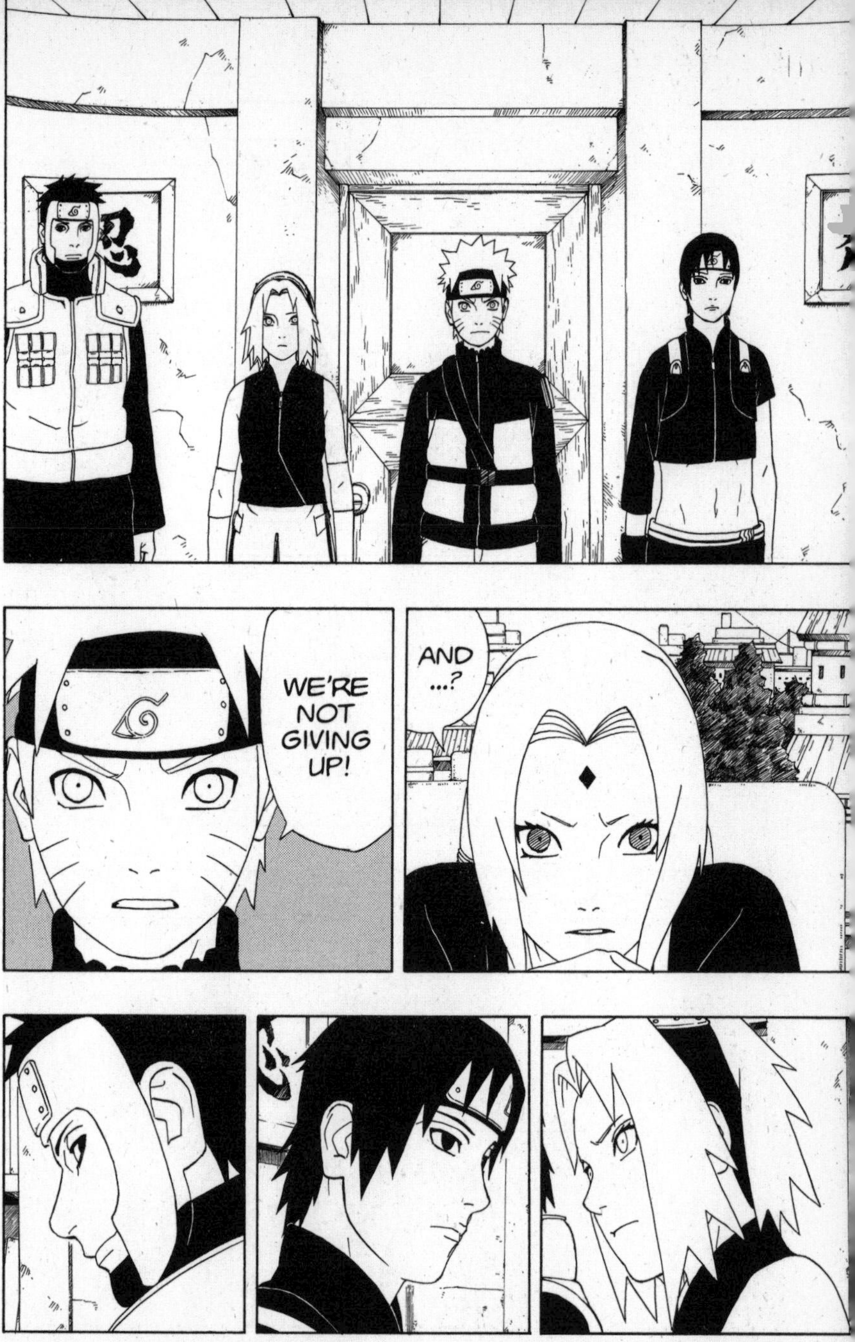
AND ...?
WE'RE NOT GIVING UP!

READ THIS WAY

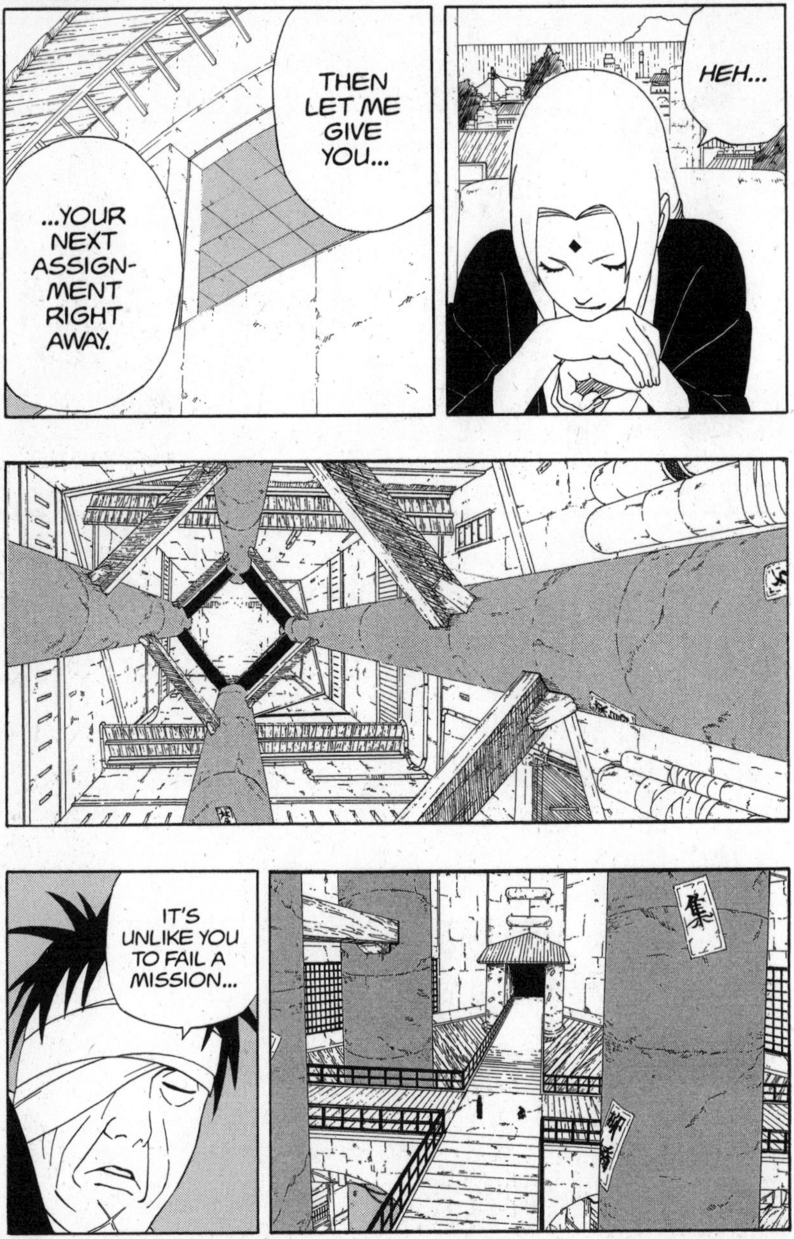
HEH...
THEN LET ME GIVE YOU...
...YOUR NEXT ASSIGNMENT RIGHT AWAY.
IT'S UNLIKE YOU TO FAIL A MISSION...

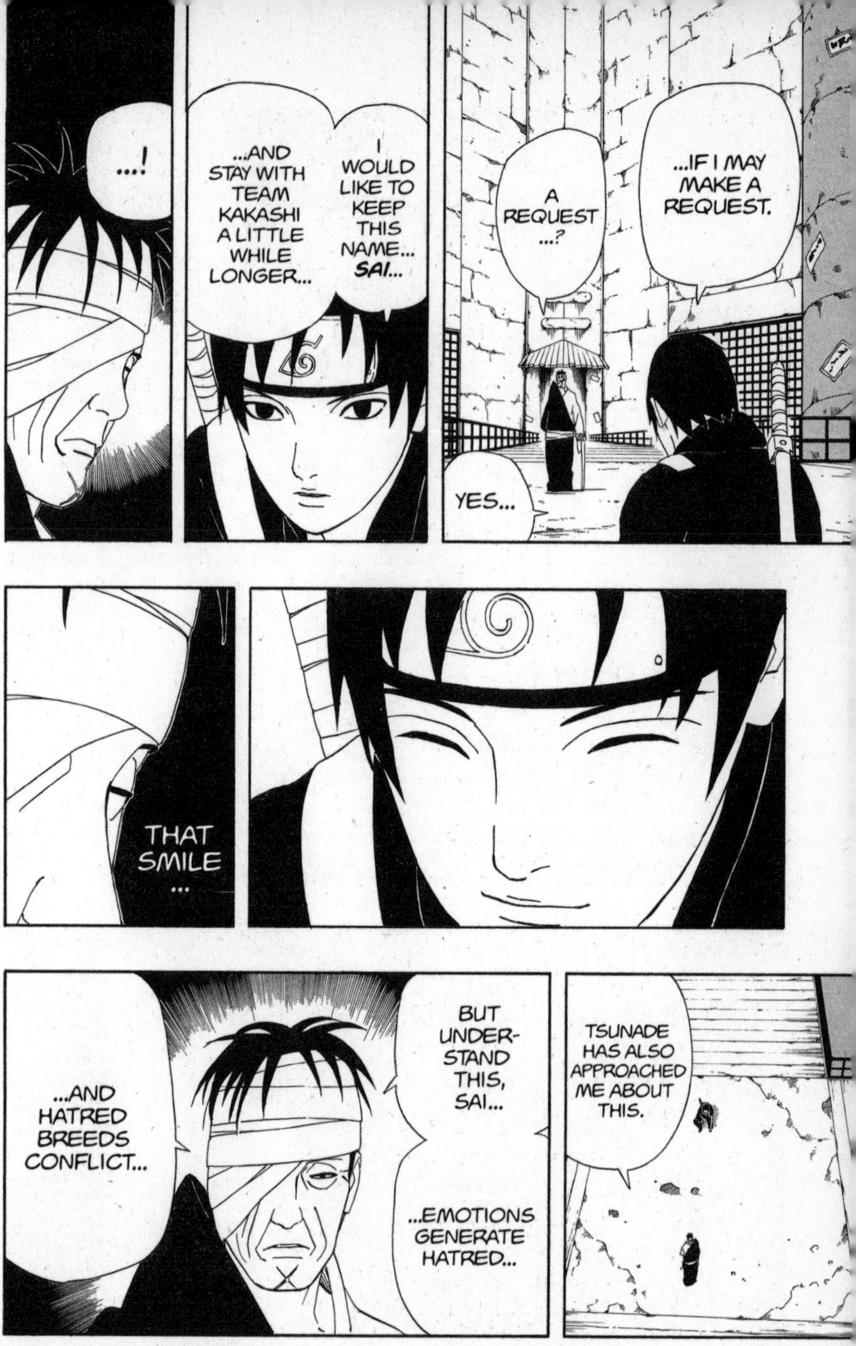

...IF I MAY MAKE A REQUEST.
A REQUEST ...?
YES...
I WOULD LIKE TO KEEP THIS NAME... **SAI**...
...AND STAY WITH TEAM KAKASHI A LITTLE WHILE LONGER...
...!
THAT SMILE ...
TSUNADE HAS ALSO APPROACHED ME ABOUT THIS.
BUT UNDER-STAND THIS, SAI...
...EMOTIONS GENERATE HATRED...
...AND HATRED BREEDS CONFLICT...

READ THIS WAY

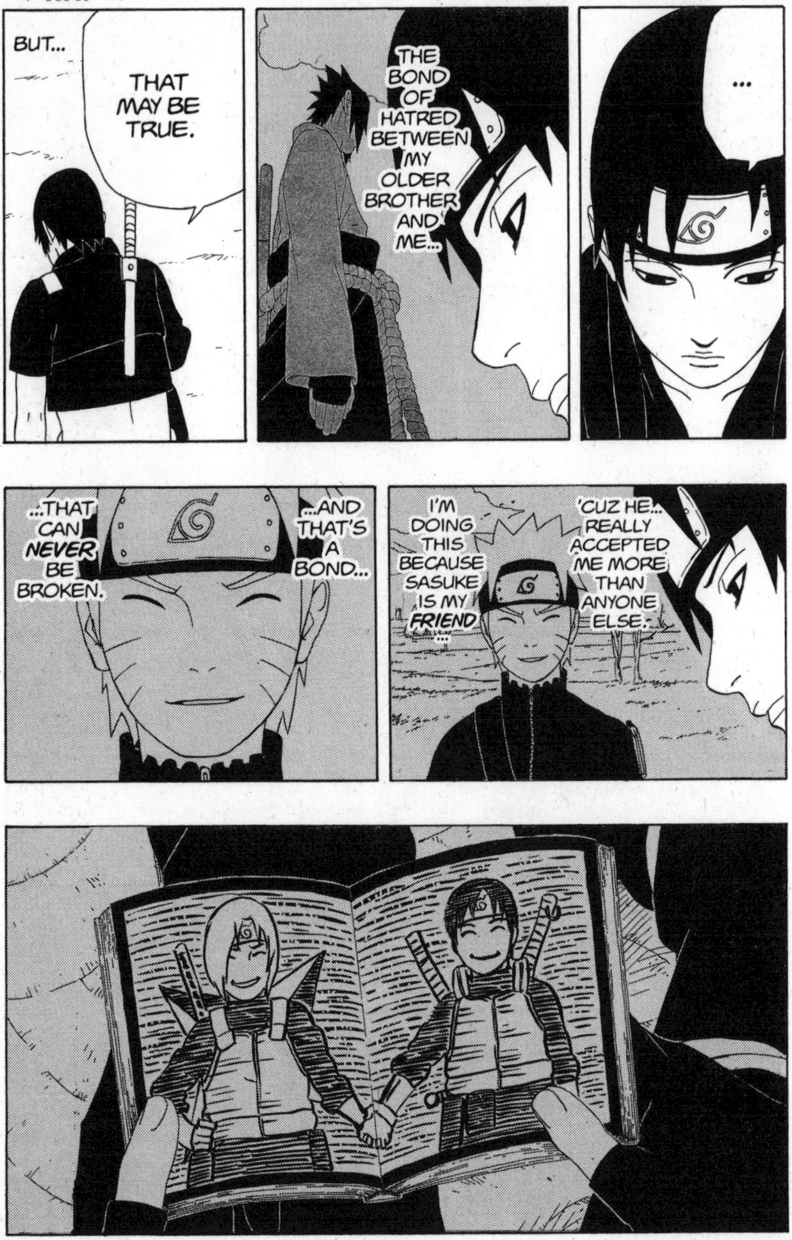
...
THE BOND OF HATRED BETWEEN MY OLDER BROTHER AND ME...
BUT...
THAT MAY BE TRUE.
'CUZ HE... REALLY ACCEPTED ME MORE THAN ANYONE ELSE.
I'M DOING THIS BECAUSE SASUKE IS MY **FRIEND**...
...AND THAT'S A BOND...
...THAT CAN **NEVER** BE BROKEN.

YOU KNOW WHAT THE WORD *COMRADE* MEANS?

(COMRADE)

REACH

...I DO? AS A MATTER OF FACT...

22

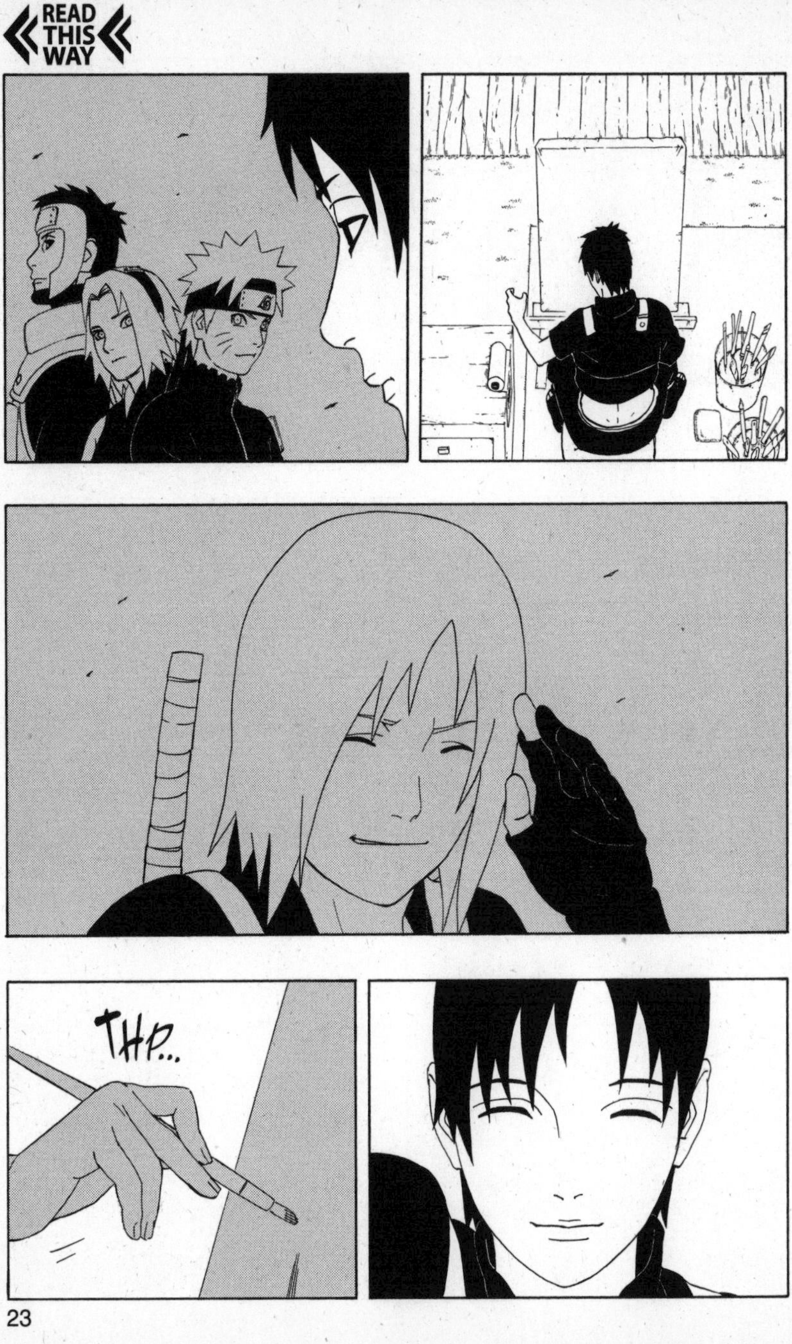
READ THIS WAY
THP...

HEY!

SAI!!

WE'RE MEETING TO GO OVER OUR NEXT MISSION!

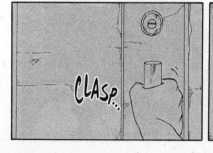

CLASP...

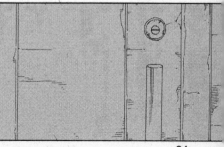

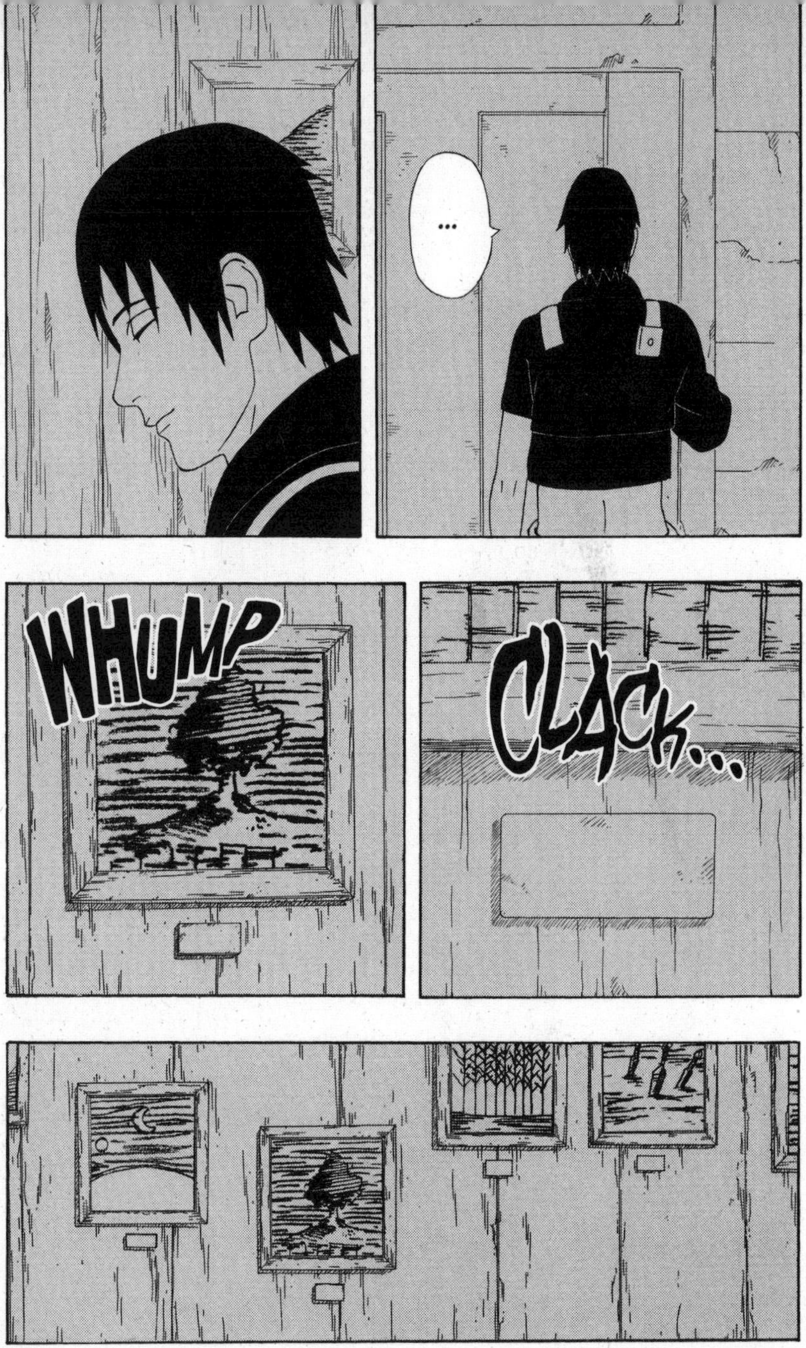
...
CLACK...
WHUMP

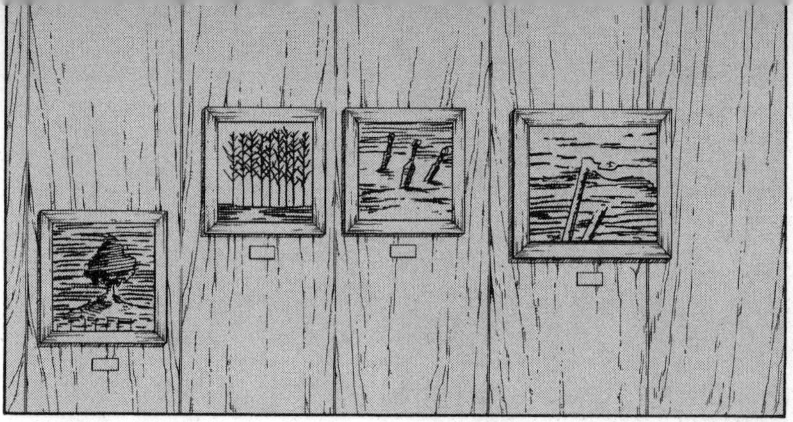

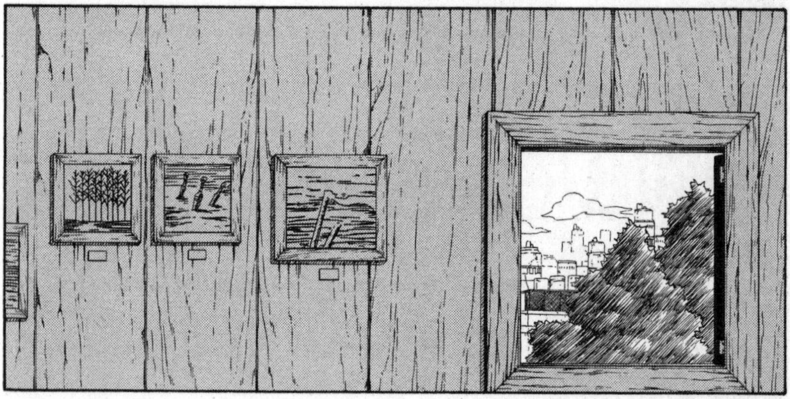

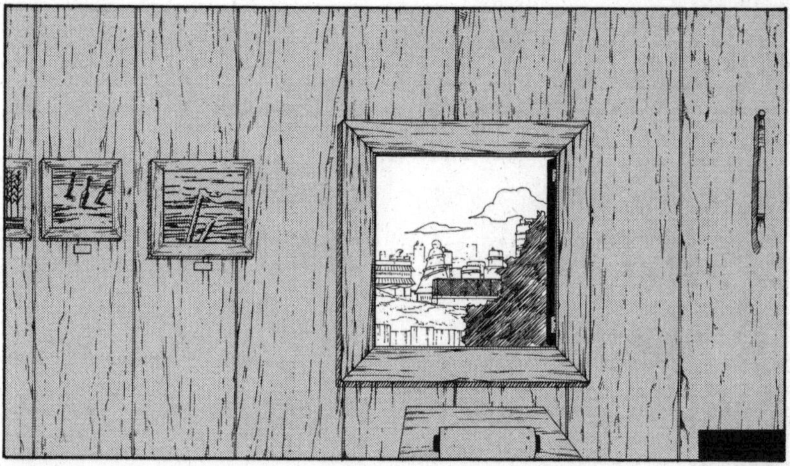

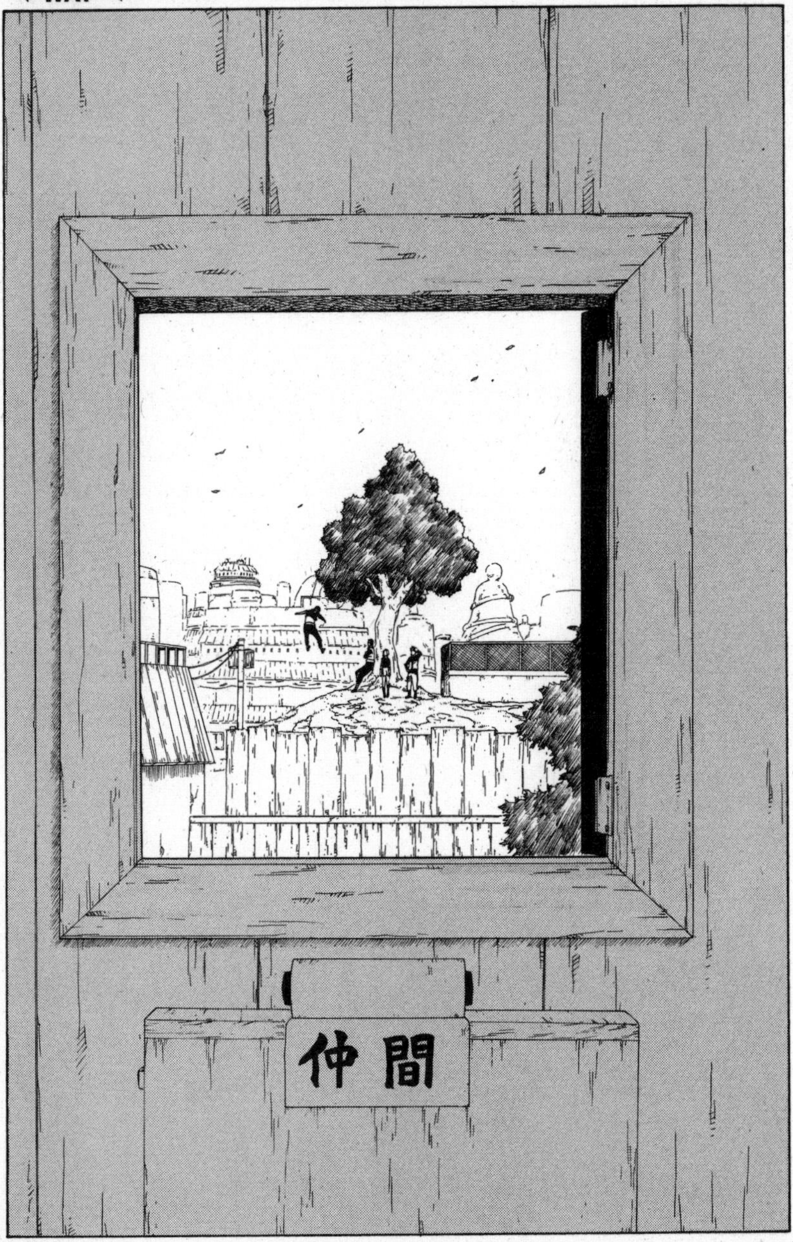
仲間

Number 311: Nicknames

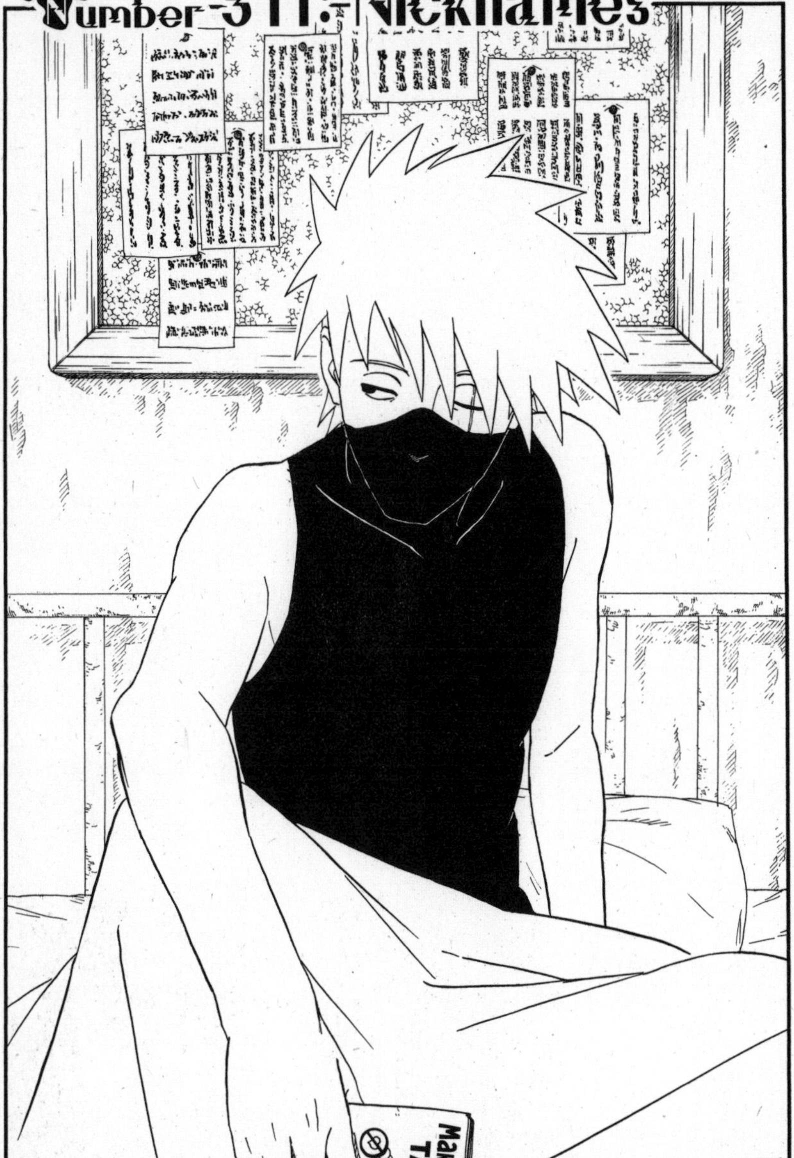
Make-Out TACTIC

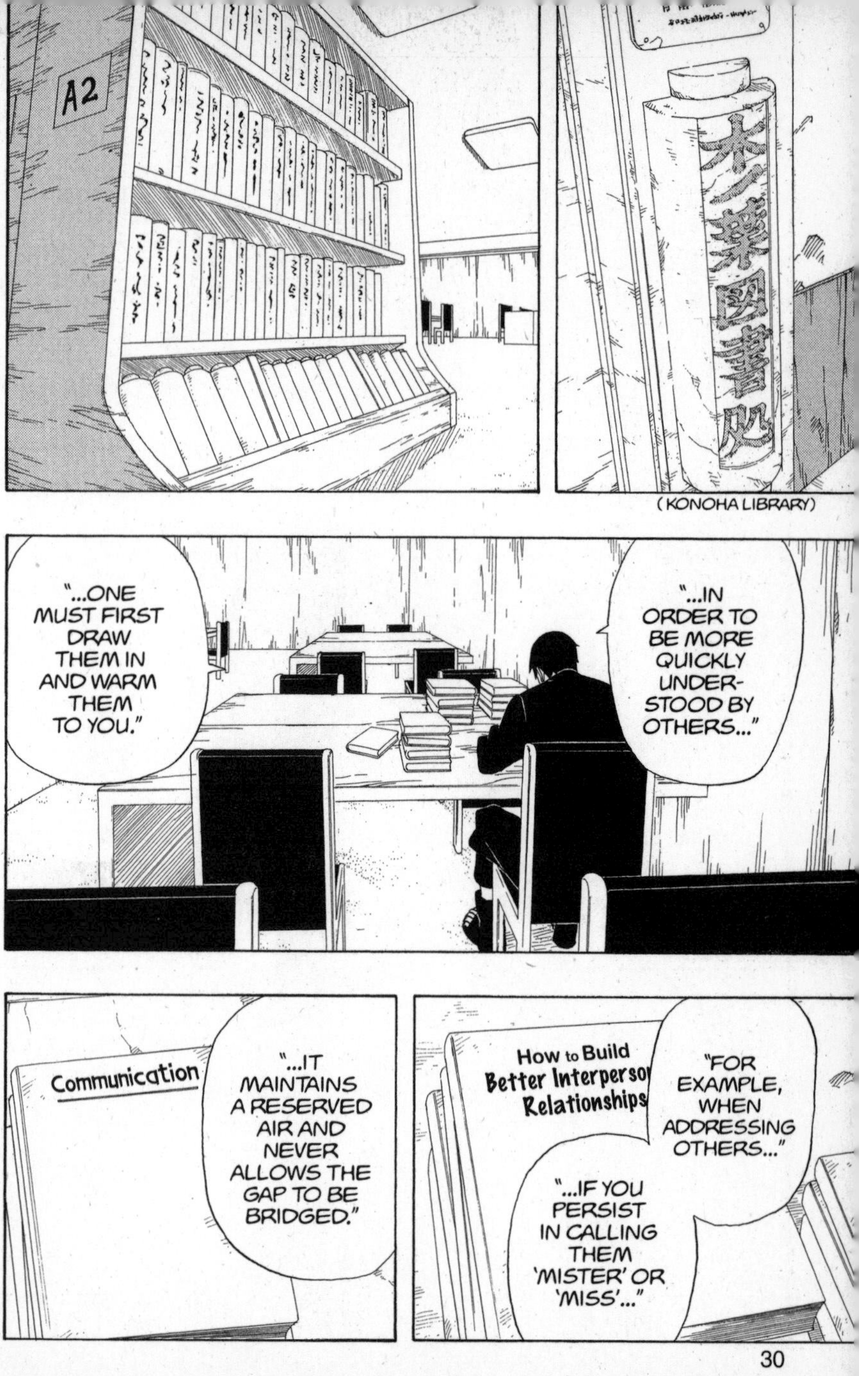
木ノ葉図書館
(KONOHA LIBRARY)
A2
"...IN ORDER TO BE MORE QUICKLY UNDER-STOOD BY OTHERS..."
"...ONE MUST FIRST DRAW THEM IN AND WARM THEM TO YOU."
How to Build Better Interperso Relationships
"FOR EXAMPLE, WHEN ADDRESSING OTHERS..."
"...IF YOU PERSIST IN CALLING THEM 'MISTER' OR 'MISS'..."
Communication
"...IT MAINTAINS A RESERVED AIR AND NEVER ALLOWS THE GAP TO BE BRIDGED."

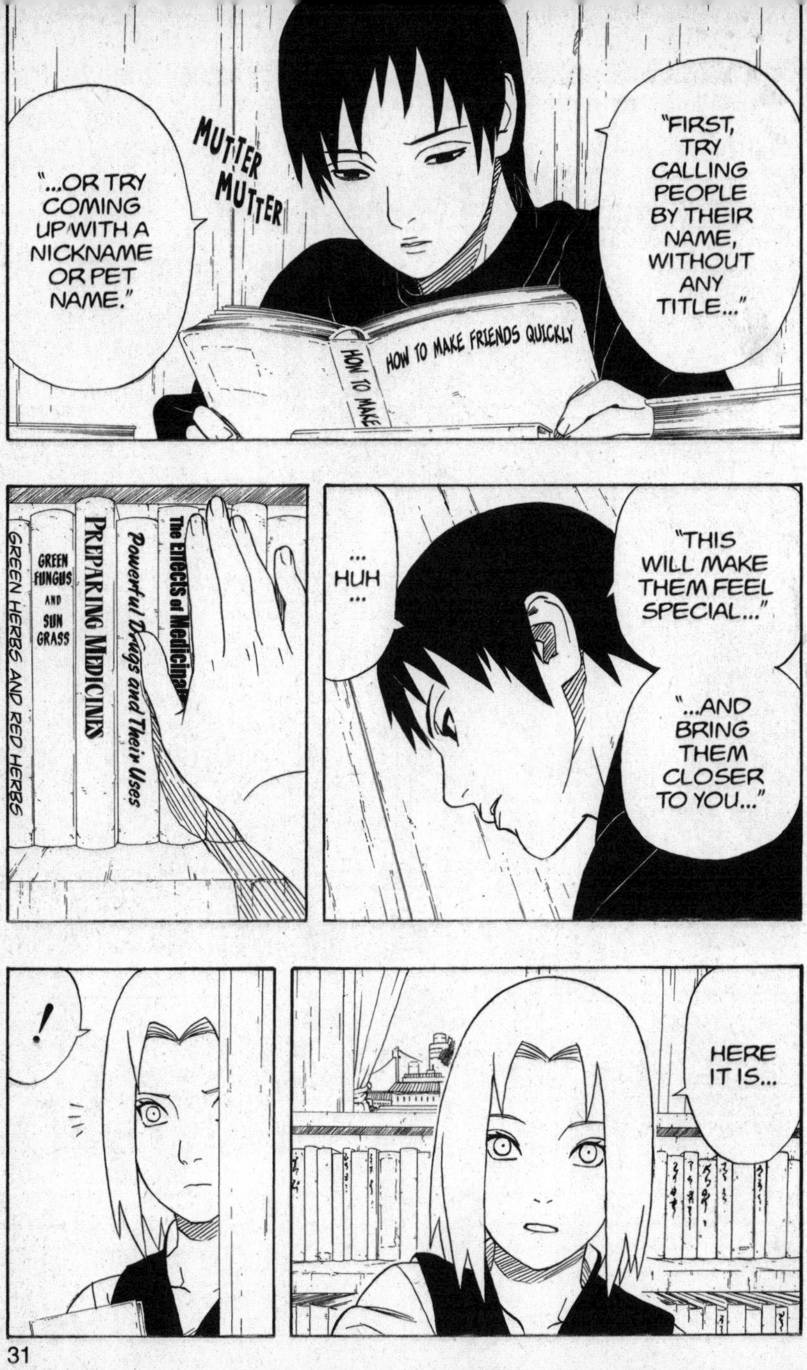

"FIRST, TRY CALLING PEOPLE BY THEIR NAME, WITHOUT ANY TITLE..."
MUTTER MUTTER
HOW TO MAKE FRIENDS QUICKLY
HOW TO MAKE
"...OR TRY COMING UP WITH A NICKNAME OR PET NAME."
"THIS WILL MAKE THEM FEEL SPECIAL..."
"...AND BRING THEM CLOSER TO YOU..."
... HUH ...
The Effects of Medicina
Powerful Drugs and Their Uses
PREPARING MEDICINES
GREEN FUNGUS AND SUN GRASS
GREEN HERBS AND RED HERBS
HERE IT IS...
!

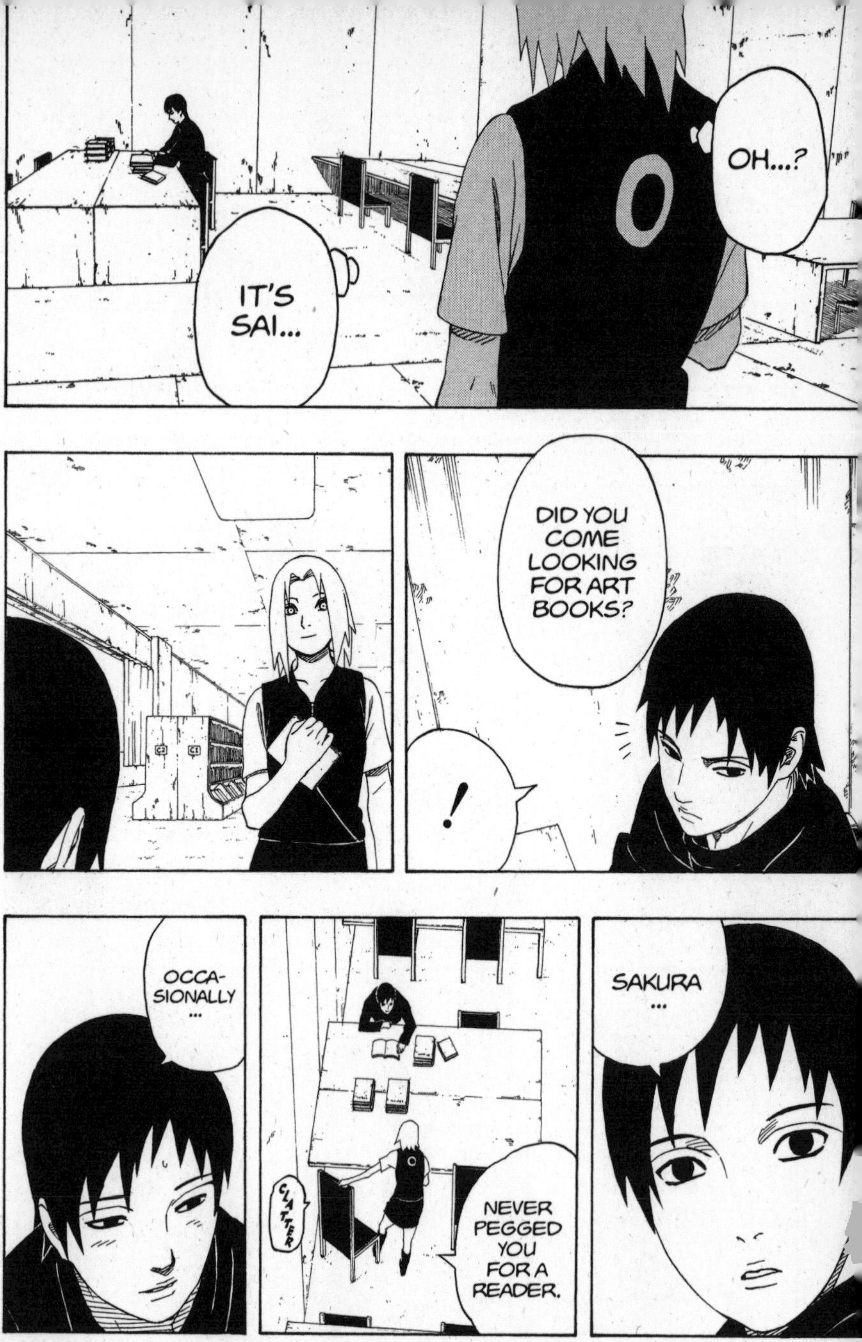
OH...?
IT'S SAI...
DID YOU COME LOOKING FOR ART BOOKS?
!
SAKURA ...
CLATTER
NEVER PEGGED YOU FOR A READER.
OCCA-SIONALLY ...

READ THIS WAY

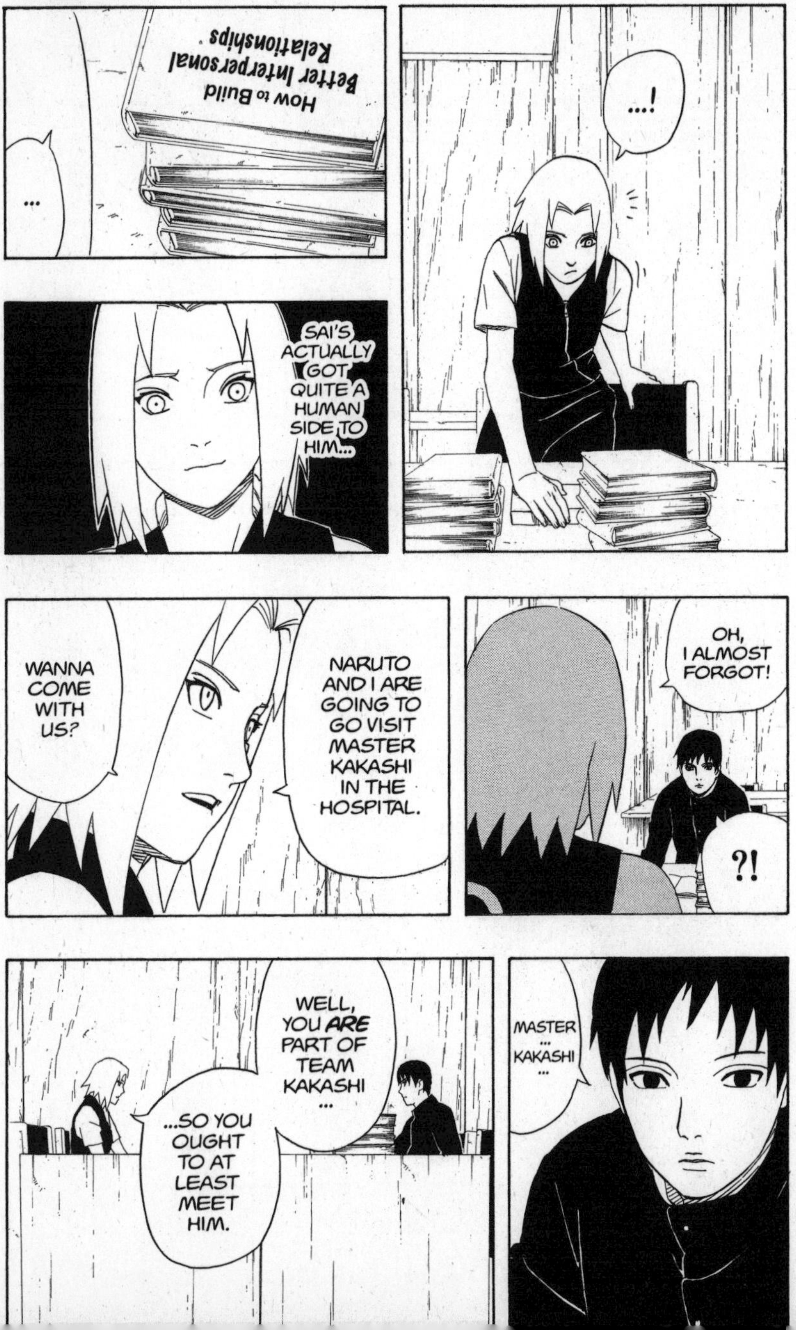
...!
How to Build Better Interpersonal Relationships
...
SAI'S ACTUALLY GOT QUITE A HUMAN SIDE TO HIM...
OH, I ALMOST FORGOT!
?!
NARUTO AND I ARE GOING TO GO VISIT MASTER KAKASHI IN THE HOSPITAL.
WANNA COME WITH US?
MASTER ... KAKASHI ...
WELL, YOU **ARE** PART OF TEAM KAKASHI ...
...SO YOU OUGHT TO AT LEAST MEET HIM.

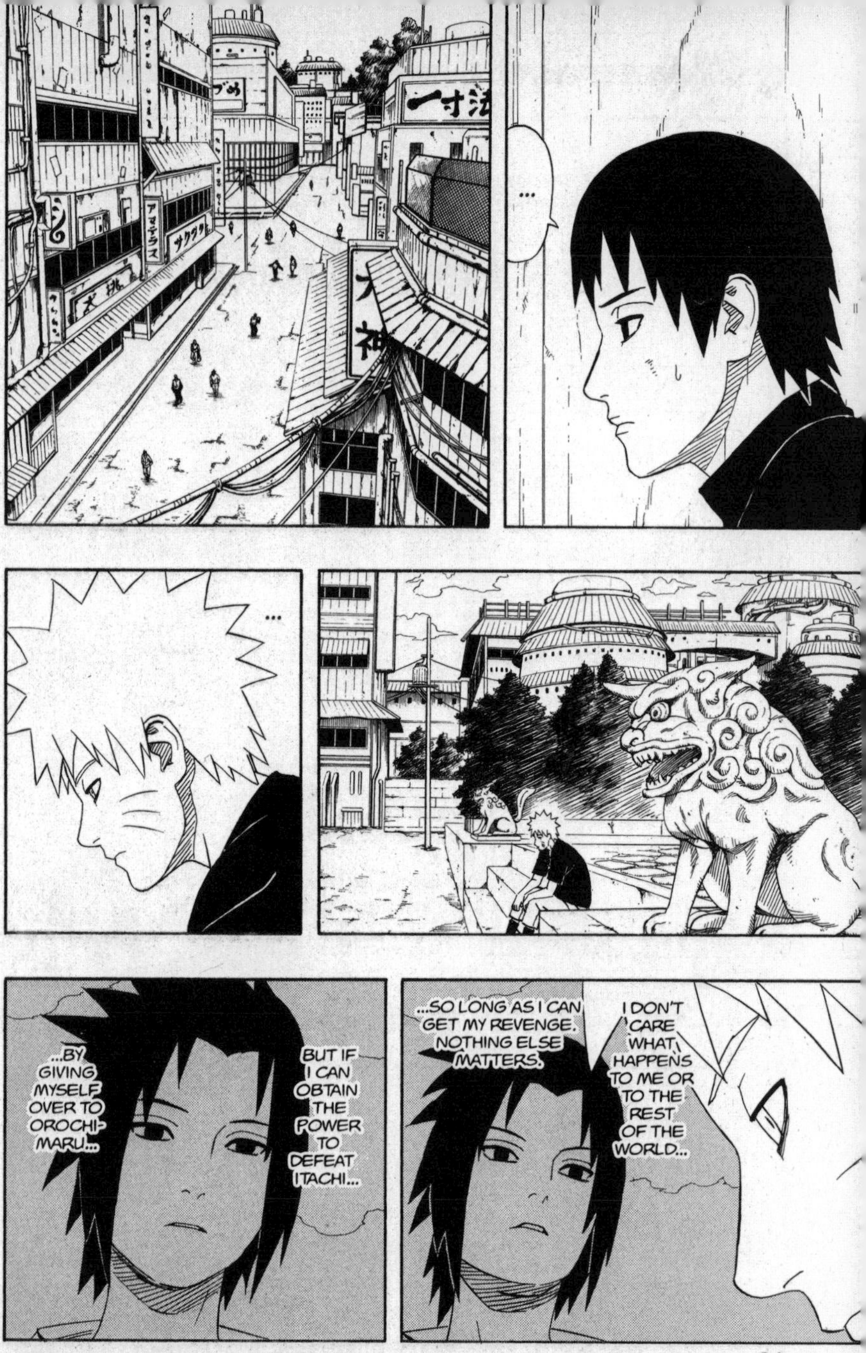
...
...
I DON'T CARE WHAT HAPPENS TO ME OR TO THE REST OF THE WORLD...
...SO LONG AS I CAN GET MY REVENGE. NOTHING ELSE MATTERS.
BUT IF I CAN OBTAIN THE POWER TO DEFEAT ITACHI...
...BY GIVING MYSELF OVER TO OROCHI-MARU...

READ THIS WAY

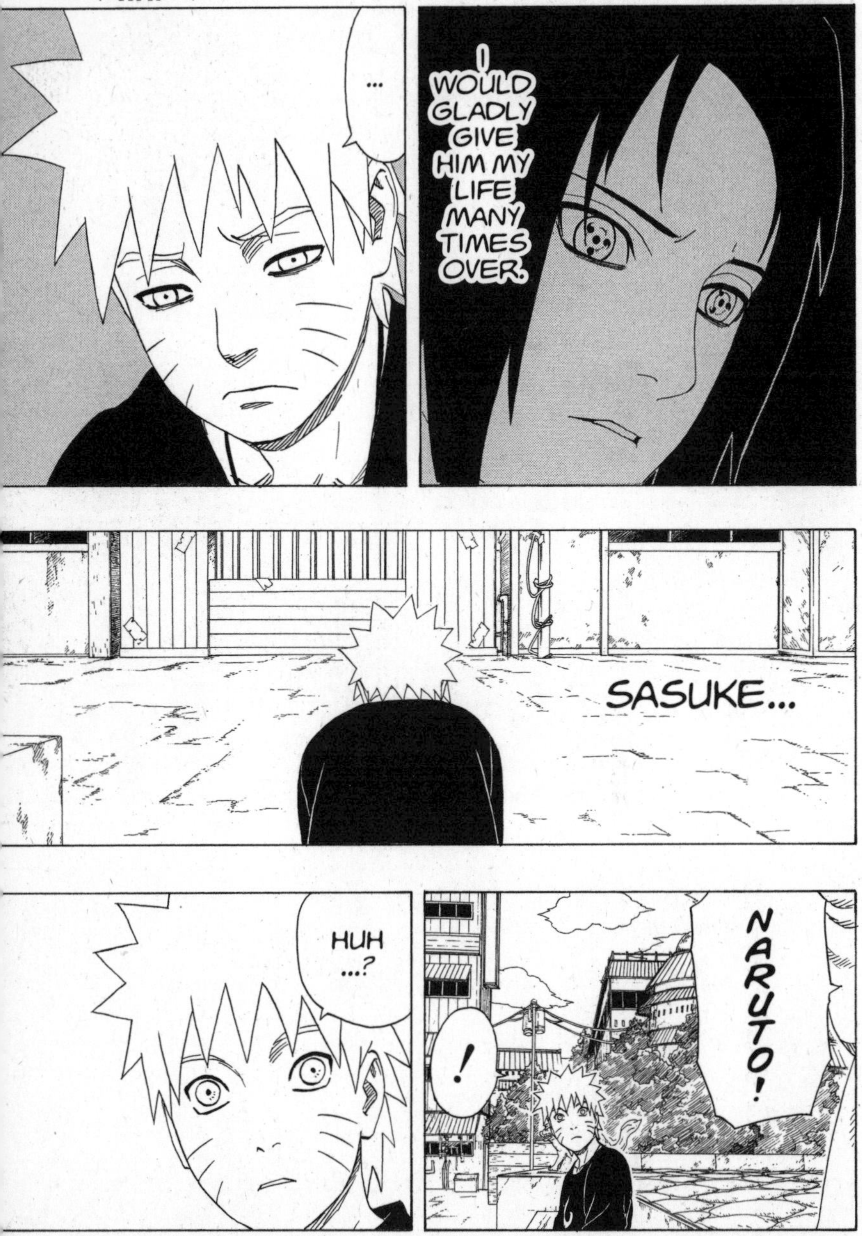
I WOULD GLADLY GIVE HIM MY LIFE MANY TIMES OVER.
...
SASUKE...
NARUTO!
!
HUH ...?

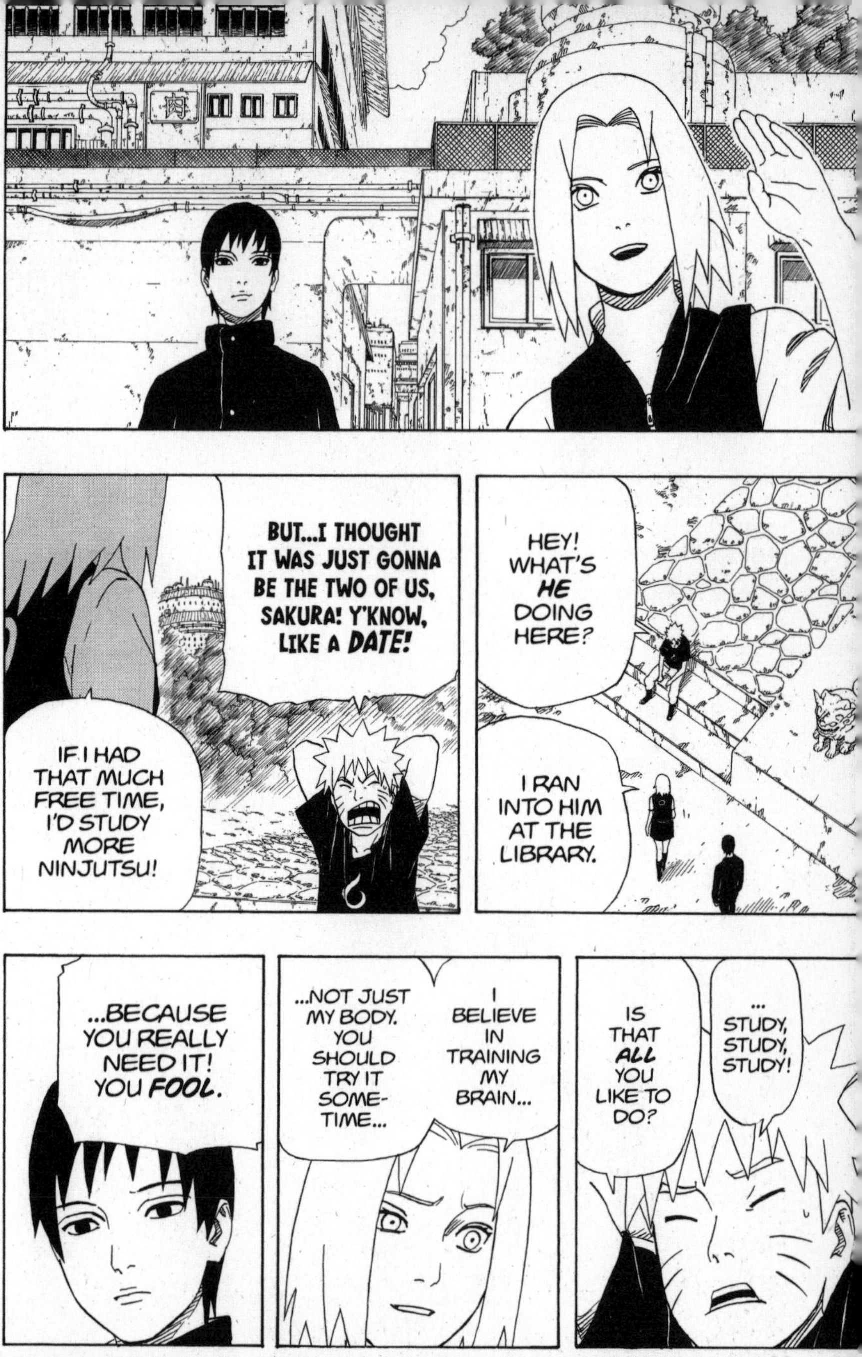

HEY! WHAT'S *HE* DOING HERE?
I RAN INTO HIM AT THE LIBRARY.
BUT...I THOUGHT IT WAS JUST GONNA BE THE TWO OF US, SAKURA! Y'KNOW, LIKE A *DATE!*
IF I HAD THAT MUCH FREE TIME, I'D STUDY MORE NINJUTSU!
... STUDY, STUDY, STUDY!
IS THAT *ALL* YOU LIKE TO DO?
I BELIEVE IN TRAINING MY BRAIN...
...NOT JUST MY BODY. YOU SHOULD TRY IT SOME-TIME...
...BECAUSE YOU REALLY NEED IT! YOU *FOOL*.

READ THIS WAY

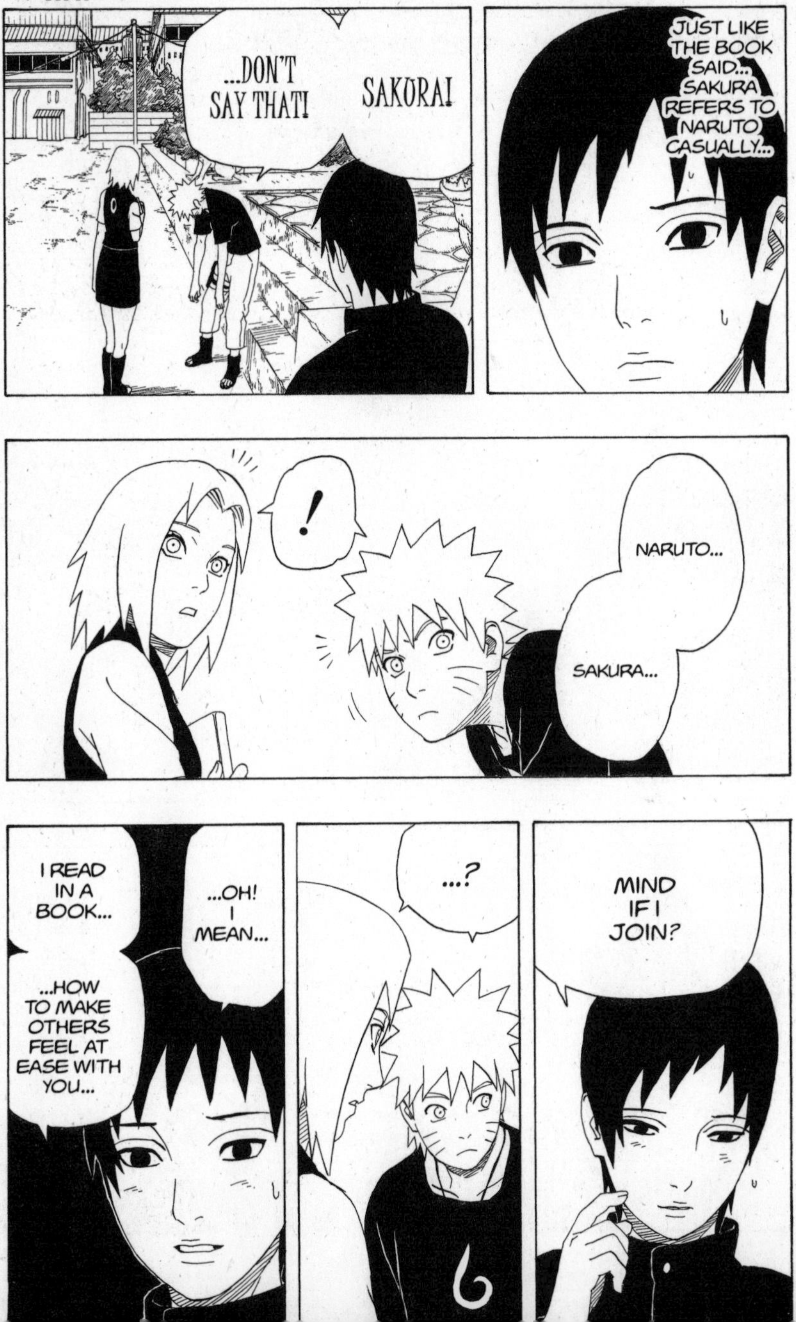
JUST LIKE THE BOOK SAID... SAKURA REFERS TO NARUTO CASUALLY...
SAKURA!
...DON'T SAY THAT!
NARUTO...
SAKURA...
!
MIND IF I JOIN?
...?
...OH! I MEAN...
I READ IN A BOOK...
...HOW TO MAKE OTHERS FEEL AT EASE WITH YOU...

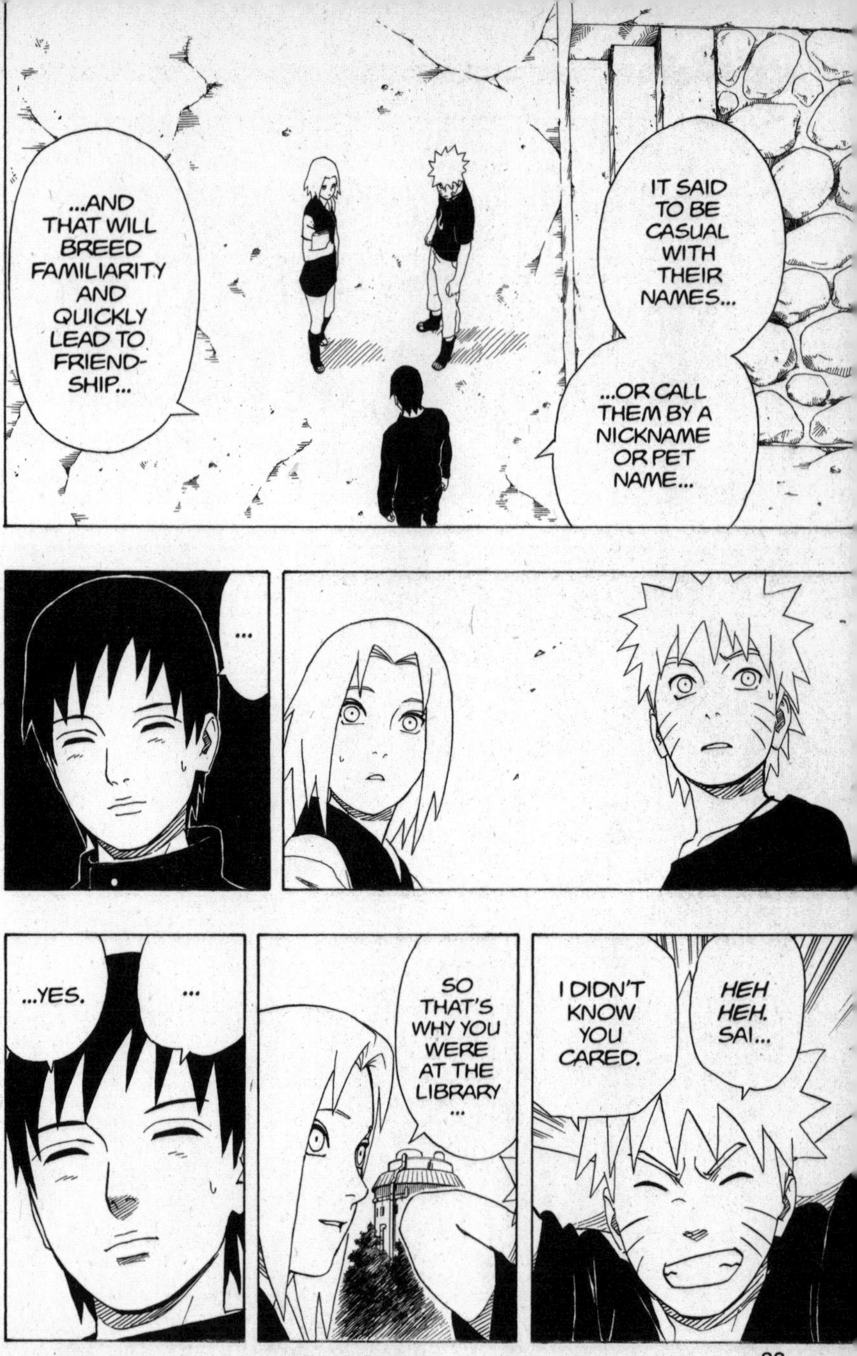
IT SAID TO BE CASUAL WITH THEIR NAMES...
...OR CALL THEM BY A NICKNAME OR PET NAME...
...AND THAT WILL BREED FAMILIARITY AND QUICKLY LEAD TO FRIEND-SHIP...
...
HEH HEH. SAI...
I DIDN'T KNOW YOU CARED.
SO THAT'S WHY YOU WERE AT THE LIBRARY...
...
...YES.

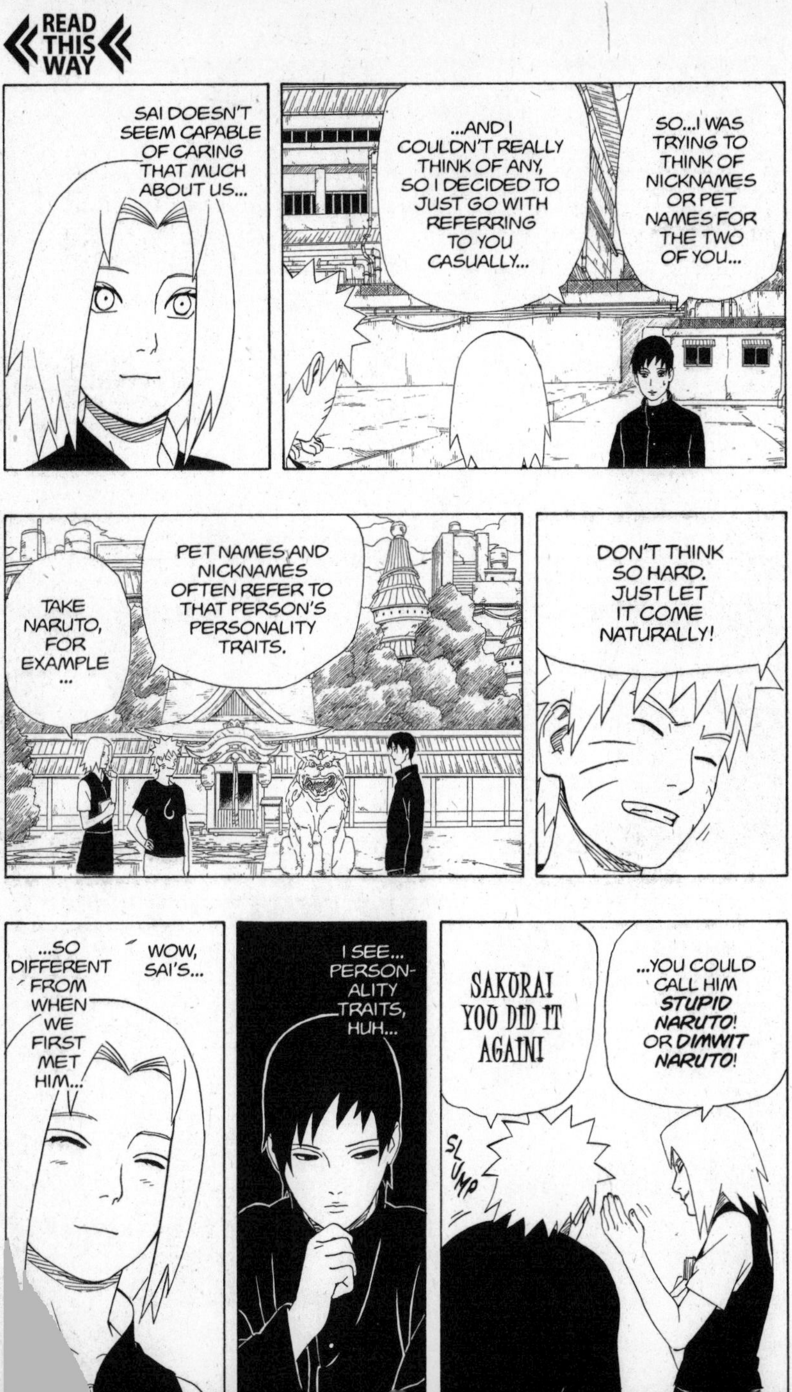
READ THIS WAY
SO...I WAS TRYING TO THINK OF NICKNAMES OR PET NAMES FOR THE TWO OF YOU...
...AND I COULDN'T REALLY THINK OF ANY, SO I DECIDED TO JUST GO WITH REFERRING TO YOU CASUALLY...
SAI DOESN'T SEEM CAPABLE OF CARING THAT MUCH ABOUT US...
DON'T THINK SO HARD. JUST LET IT COME NATURALLY!
PET NAMES AND NICKNAMES OFTEN REFER TO THAT PERSON'S PERSONALITY TRAITS.
TAKE NARUTO, FOR EXAMPLE ...
...YOU COULD CALL HIM *STUPID NARUTO*! OR *DIMWIT NARUTO*!
SAKURA! YOU DID IT AGAIN!
SLUMP
I SEE... PERSONALITY TRAITS, HUH...
WOW, SAI'S...
...SO DIFFERENT FROM WHEN WE FIRST MET HIM...

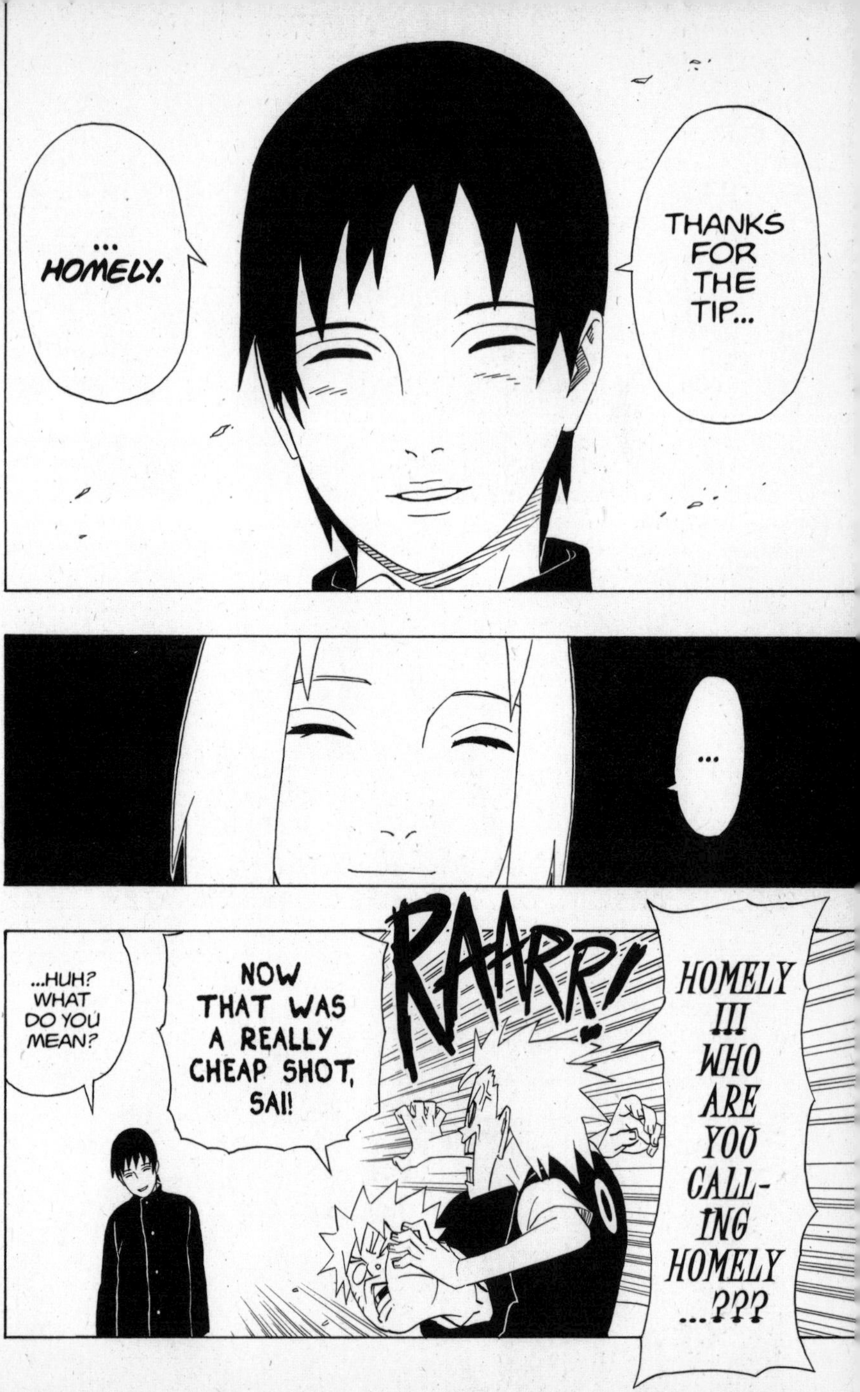
THANKS FOR THE TIP...
...HOMELY.
...
HOMELY!!! WHO ARE YOU CALLING HOMELY...???
RAARR!
NOW THAT WAS A REALLY CHEAP SHOT, SAI!
...HUH? WHAT DO YOU MEAN?

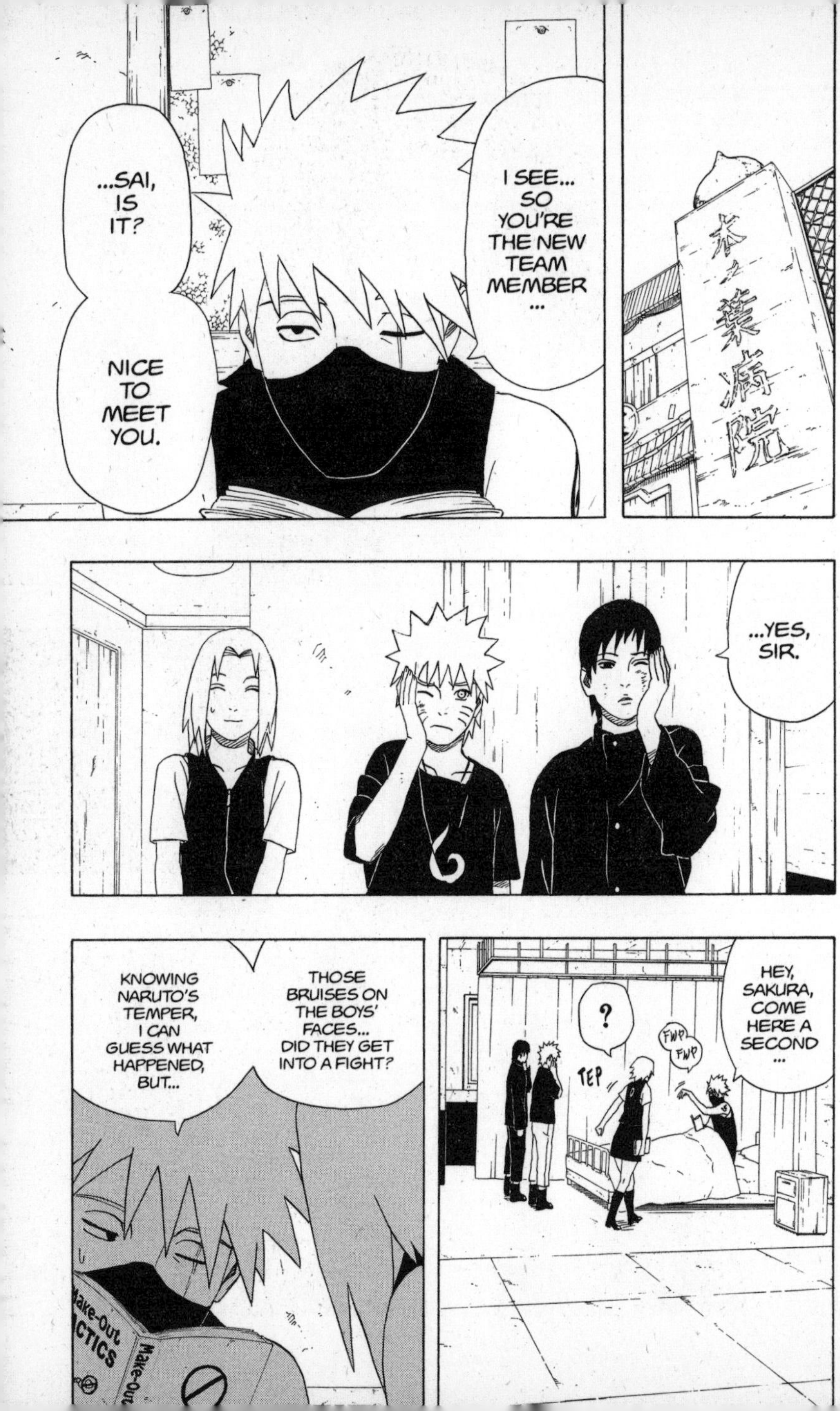

木ノ葉病院
I SEE... SO YOU'RE THE NEW TEAM MEMBER...
...SAI, IS IT?
NICE TO MEET YOU.
...YES, SIR.
HEY, SAKURA, COME HERE A SECOND...
FWP FWP
?
TEP
THOSE BRUISES ON THE BOYS' FACES... DID THEY GET INTO A FIGHT?
KNOWING NARUTO'S TEMPER, I CAN GUESS WHAT HAPPENED, BUT...
Make-Out

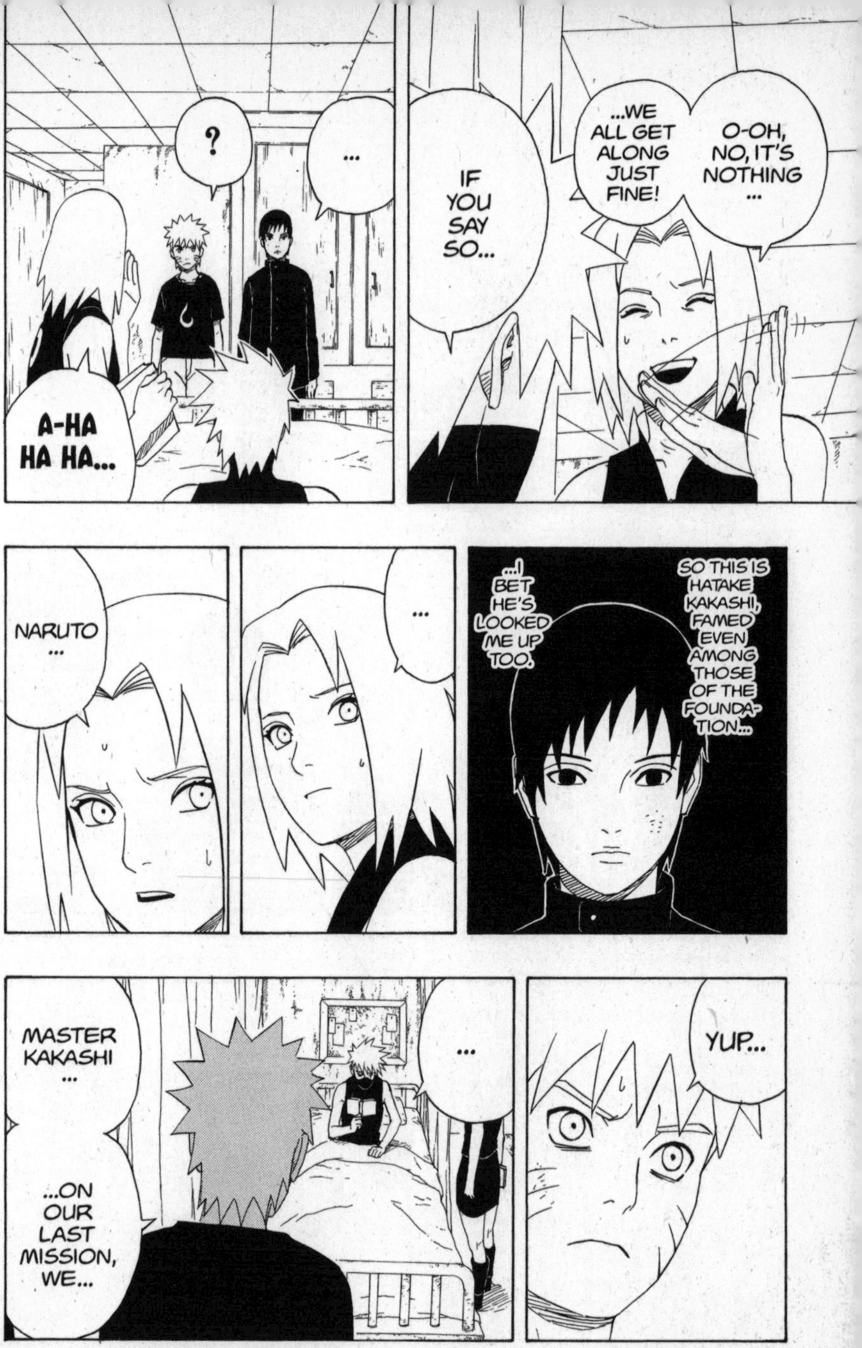
O-OH, NO, IT'S NOTHING ...
...WE ALL GET ALONG JUST FINE!
IF YOU SAY SO...
...
?
A-HA HA HA...
SO THIS IS HATAKE KAKASHI, FAMED EVEN AMONG THOSE OF THE FOUNDATION...
...I BET HE'S LOOKED ME UP TOO.
...
NARUTO ...
YUP...
...
MASTER KAKASHI ...
...ON OUR LAST MISSION, WE...

READ THIS WAY

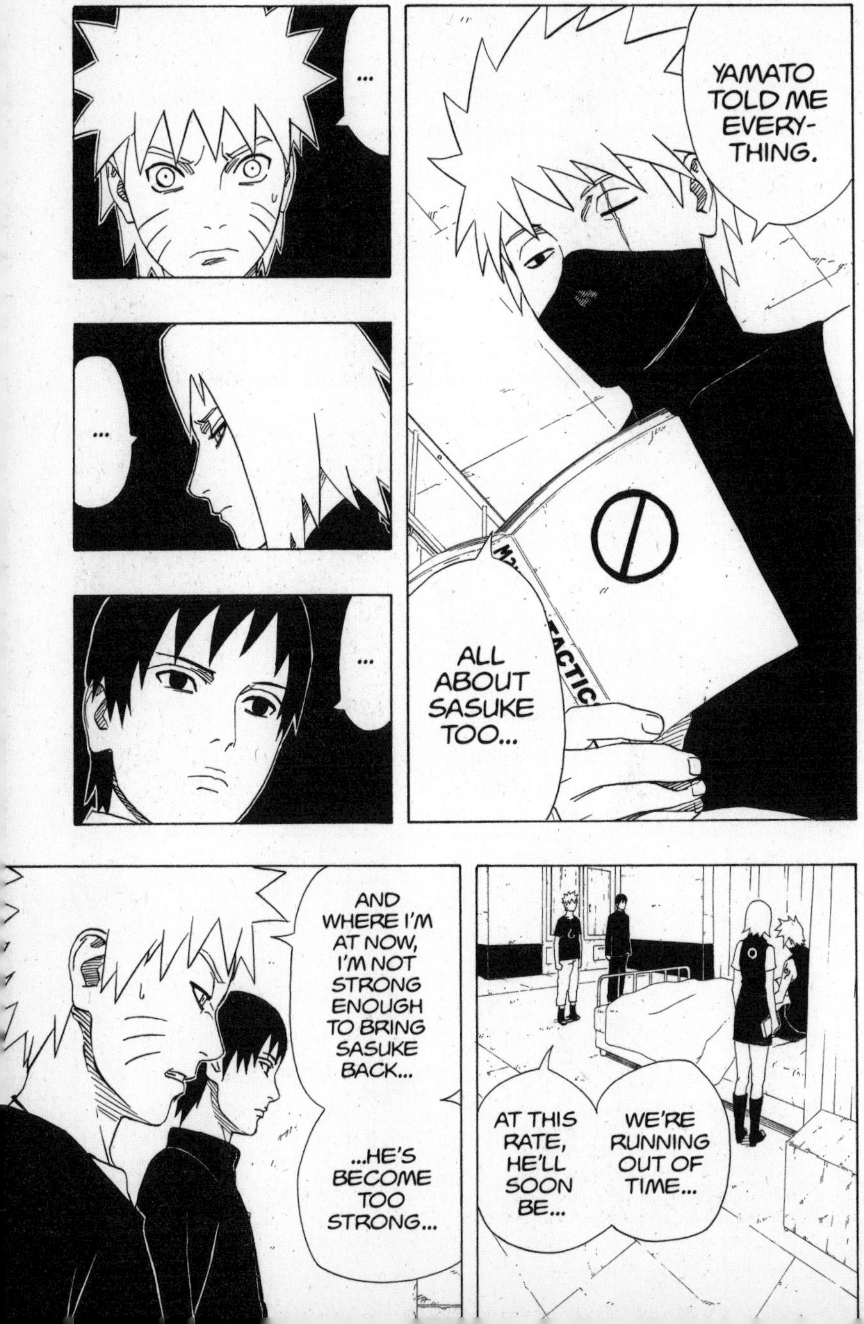

YAMATO TOLD ME EVERY-THING.
ALL ABOUT SASUKE TOO...
...
...
...
WE'RE RUNNING OUT OF TIME...
AT THIS RATE, HE'LL SOON BE...
...HE'S BECOME TOO STRONG...
AND WHERE I'M AT NOW, I'M NOT STRONG ENOUGH TO BRING SASUKE BACK...

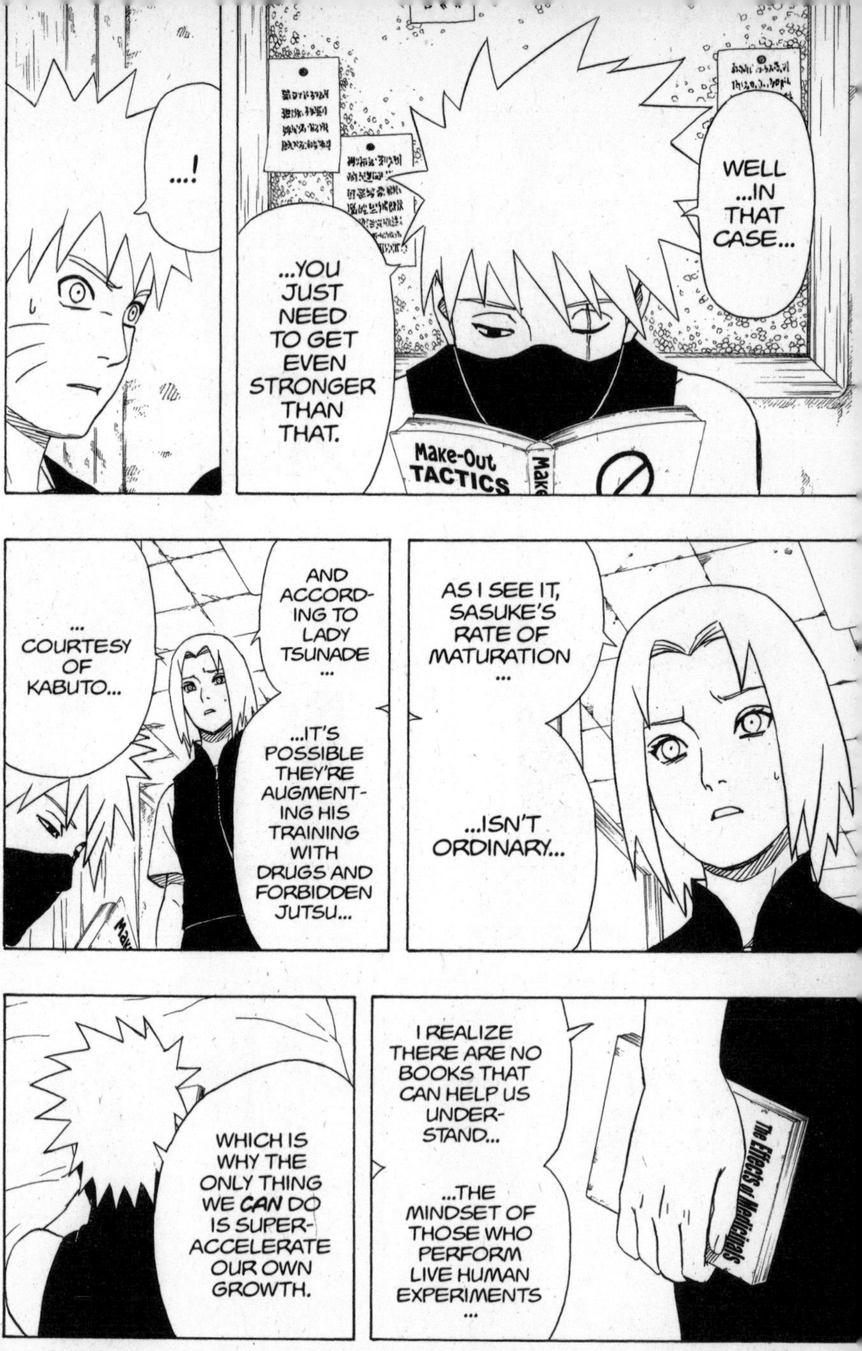
WELL ...IN THAT CASE...
...YOU JUST NEED TO GET EVEN STRONGER THAN THAT.
Make-Out TACTICS
...!
AS I SEE IT, SASUKE'S RATE OF MATURATION ...
...ISN'T ORDINARY...
AND ACCORD-ING TO LADY TSUNADE ...
...IT'S POSSIBLE THEY'RE AUGMENT-ING HIS TRAINING WITH DRUGS AND FORBIDDEN JUTSU...
... COURTESY OF KABUTO...
I REALIZE THERE ARE NO BOOKS THAT CAN HELP US UNDER-STAND...
...THE MINDSET OF THOSE WHO PERFORM LIVE HUMAN EXPERIMENTS ...
The Effects of Medicinals
WHICH IS WHY THE ONLY THING WE *CAN* DO IS SUPER-ACCELERATE OUR OWN GROWTH.

READ THIS WAY

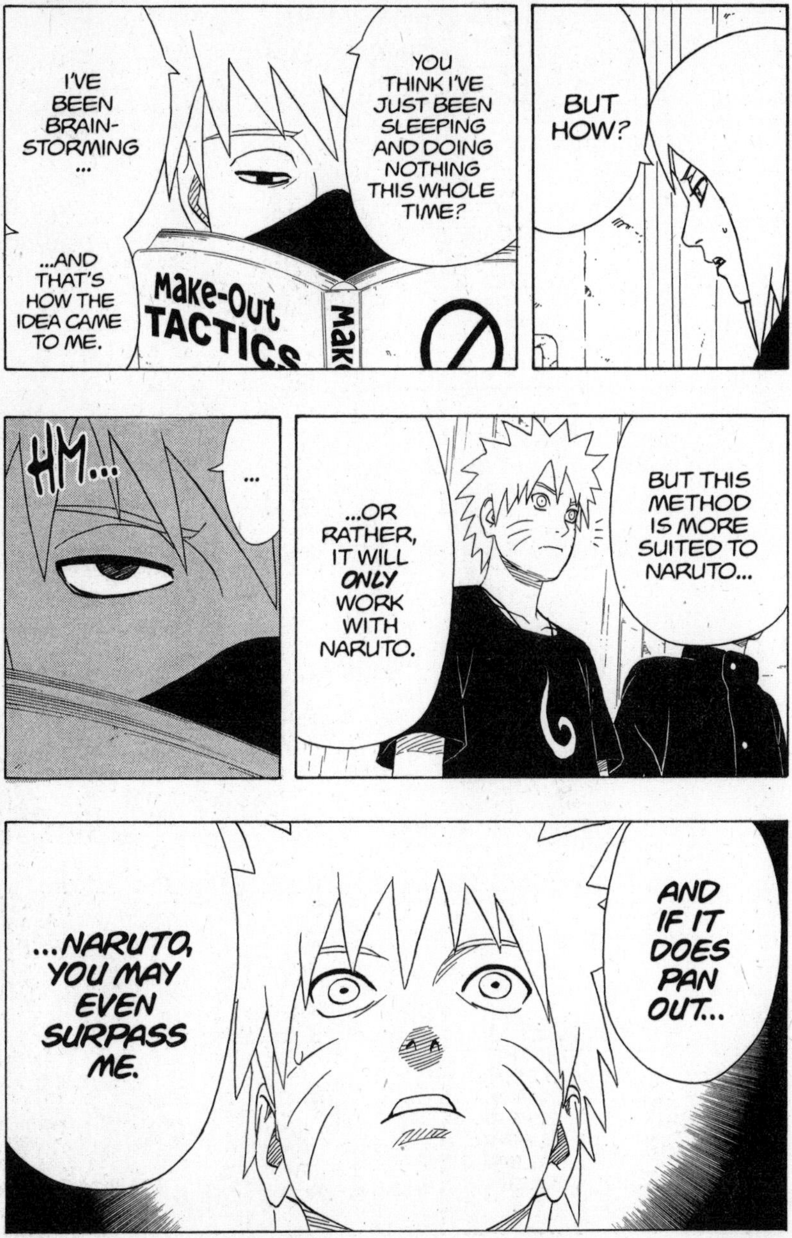
BUT HOW?
YOU THINK I'VE JUST BEEN SLEEPING AND DOING NOTHING THIS WHOLE TIME?
I'VE BEEN BRAIN-STORMING ...
...AND THAT'S HOW THE IDEA CAME TO ME.
Make-Out TACTICS
BUT THIS METHOD IS MORE SUITED TO NARUTO...
...OR RATHER, IT WILL ONLY WORK WITH NARUTO.
...
HM...
AND IF IT DOES PAN OUT...
...NARUTO, YOU MAY EVEN SURPASS ME.

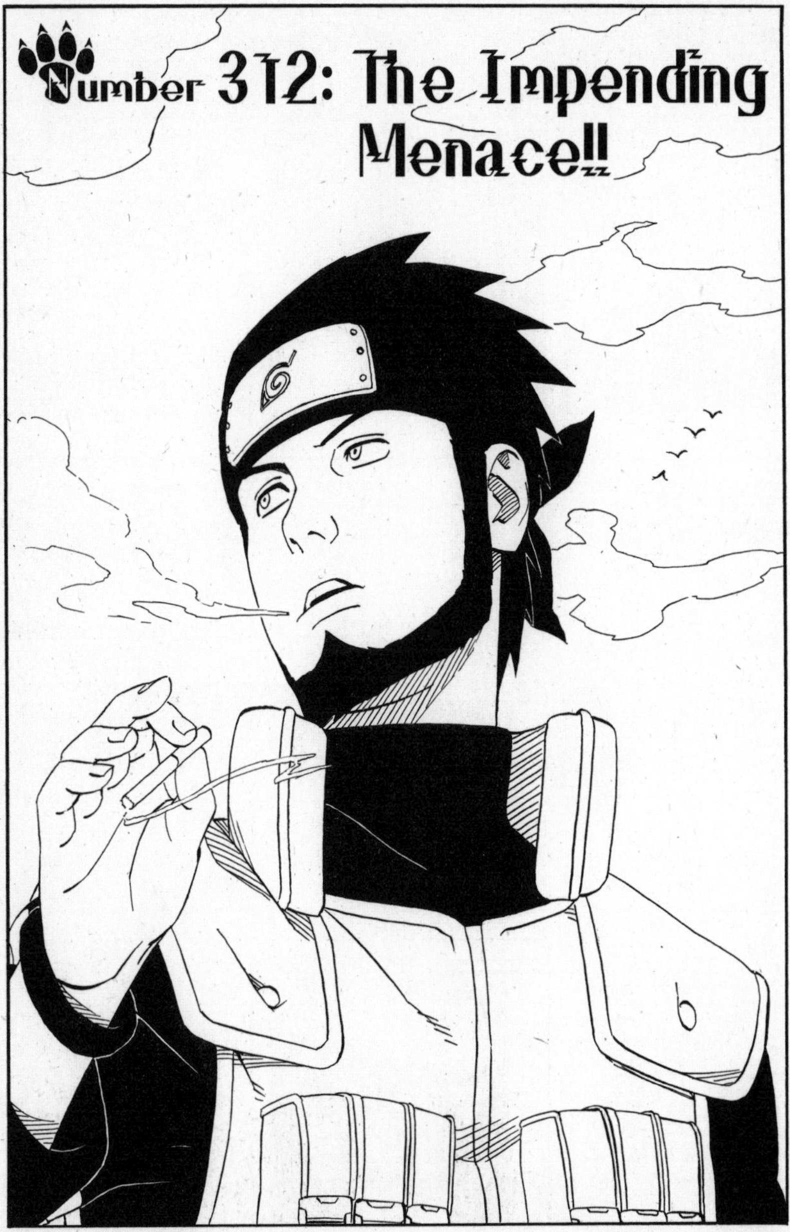
Number 312: The Impending Menace!!

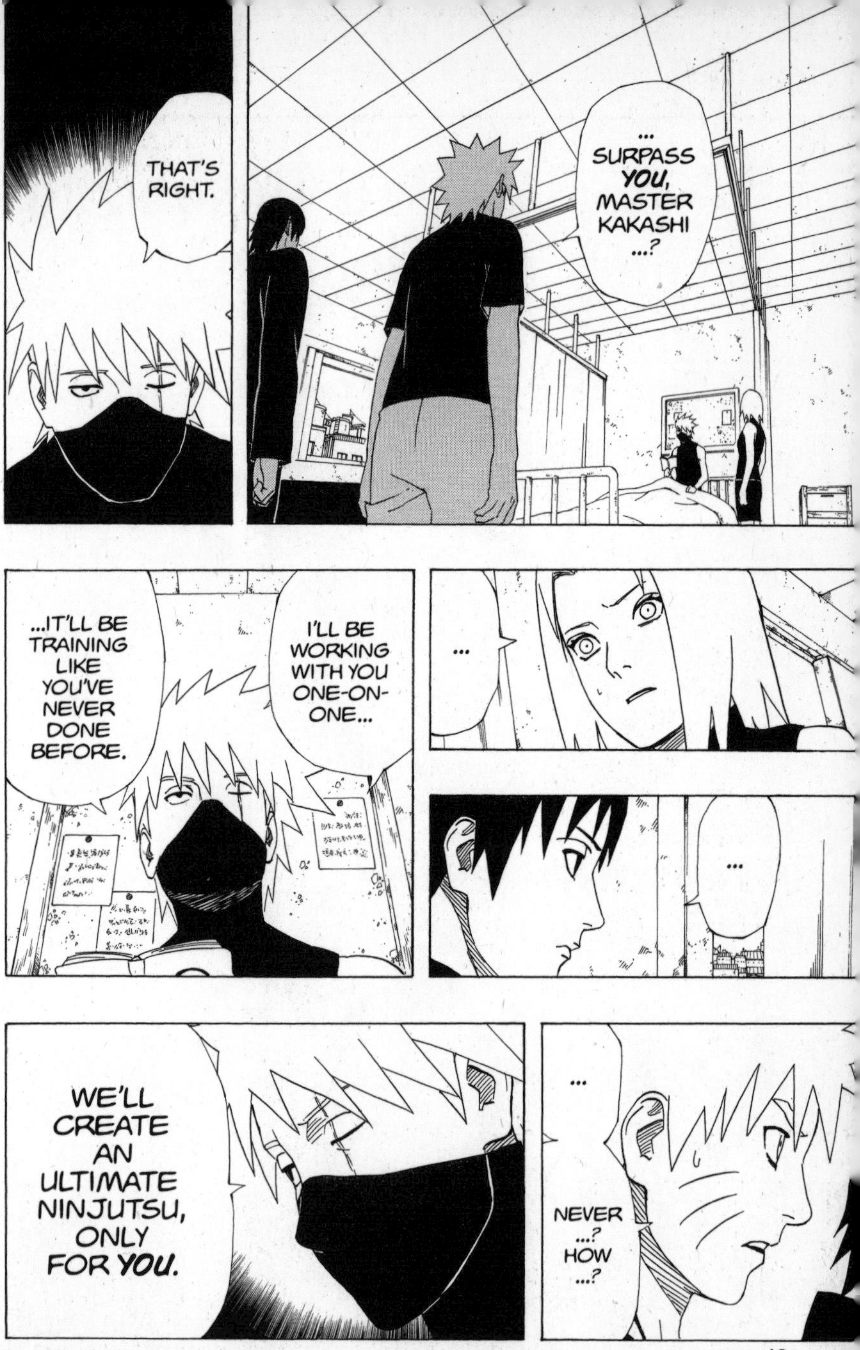
...SURPASS YOU, MASTER KAKASHI ...?
THAT'S RIGHT.
...
...
I'LL BE WORKING WITH YOU ONE-ON-ONE...
...IT'LL BE TRAINING LIKE YOU'VE NEVER DONE BEFORE.
...
NEVER ...? HOW ...?
WE'LL CREATE AN ULTIMATE NINJUTSU, ONLY FOR YOU.

READ THIS WAY

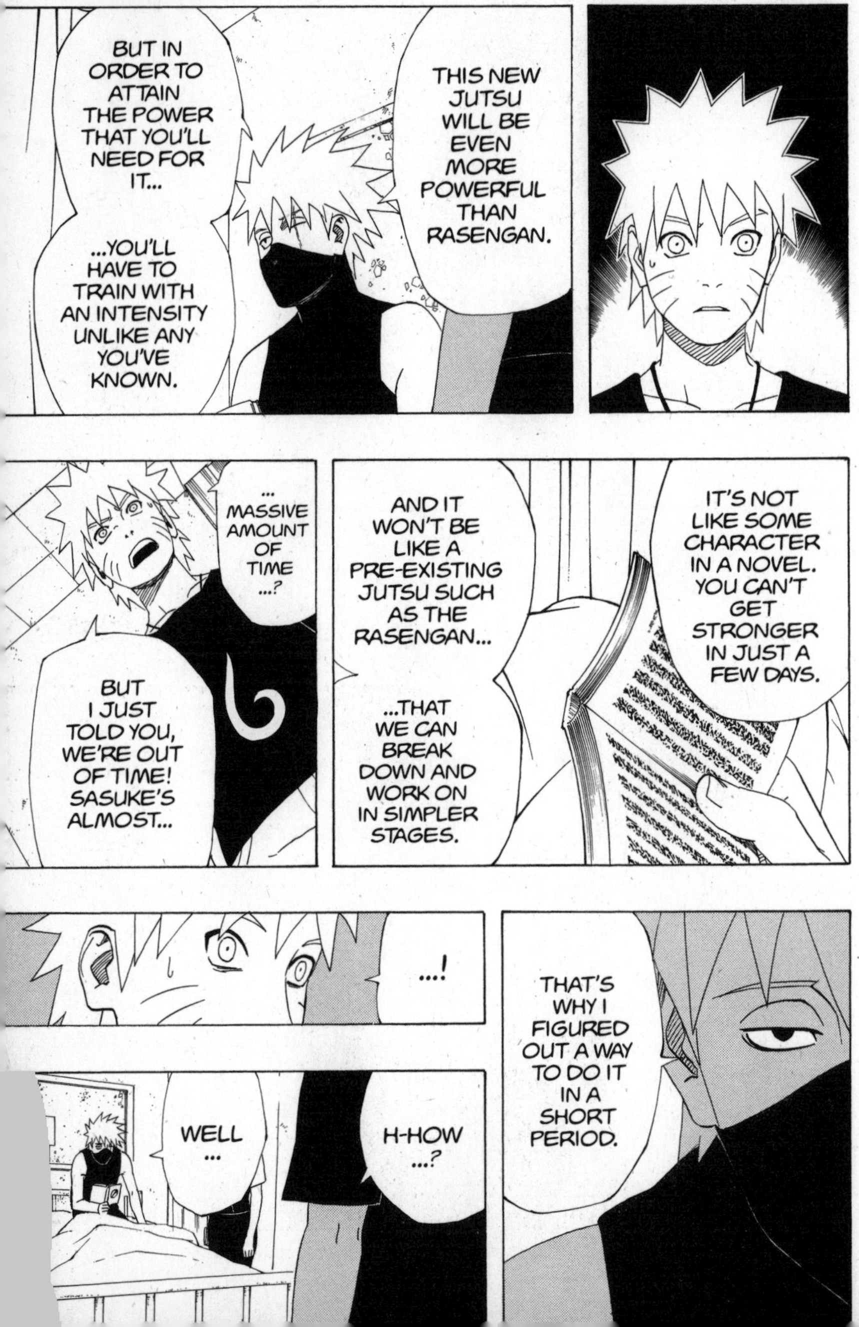

THIS NEW JUTSU WILL BE EVEN MORE POWERFUL THAN RASENGAN.
BUT IN ORDER TO ATTAIN THE POWER THAT YOU'LL NEED FOR IT...
...YOU'LL HAVE TO TRAIN WITH AN INTENSITY UNLIKE ANY YOU'VE KNOWN.
IT'S NOT LIKE SOME CHARACTER IN A NOVEL. YOU CAN'T GET STRONGER IN JUST A FEW DAYS.
AND IT WON'T BE LIKE A PRE-EXISTING JUTSU SUCH AS THE RASENGAN...
...THAT WE CAN BREAK DOWN AND WORK ON IN SIMPLER STAGES.
... MASSIVE AMOUNT OF TIME ...?
BUT I JUST TOLD YOU, WE'RE OUT OF TIME! SASUKE'S ALMOST...
THAT'S WHY I FIGURED OUT A WAY TO DO IT IN A SHORT PERIOD.
...!
H-HOW ...?
WELL ...

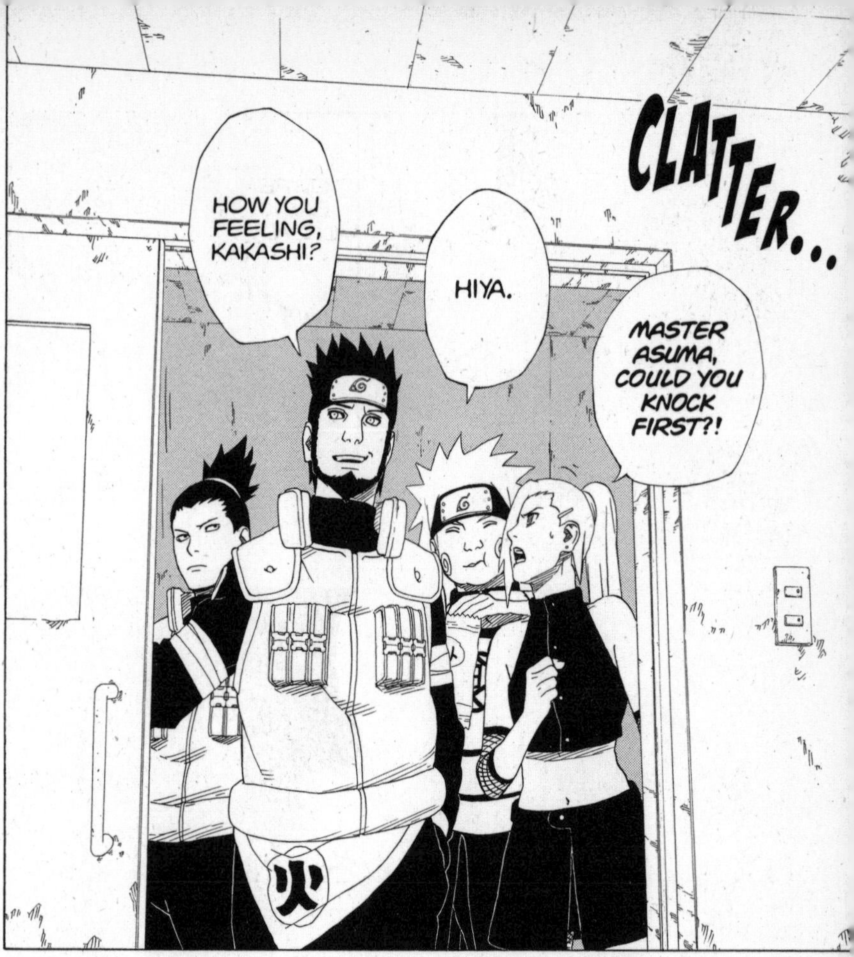
CLATTER...
MASTER ASUMA, COULD YOU KNOCK FIRST?!
HIYA.
HOW YOU FEELING, KAKASHI?

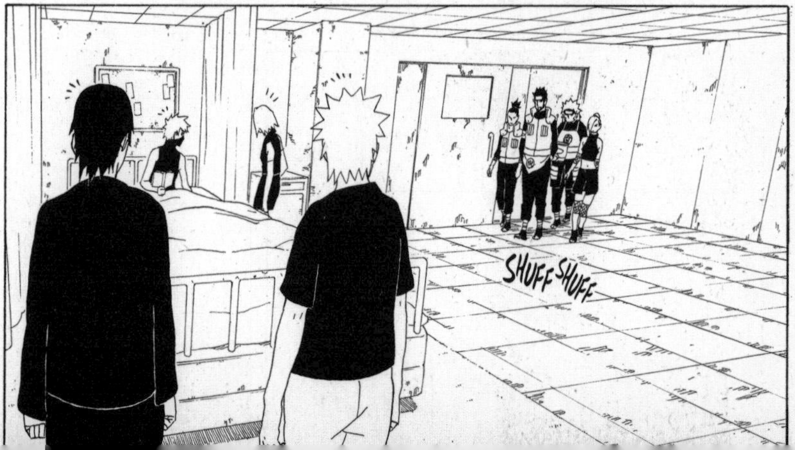
SHUFF SHUFF

!

YOU'RE BACK ALREADY ...

HEY, IF IT ISN'T NARUTO AND SAKURA.

OH!

!

YOU'RE THAT KID FROM...

HI.

?

I'LL BE HEADING OUT, THEN.

THANK YOU... FOR YOUR REPORT.

WHICH MEANS IT'S ONLY A MATTER OF TIME BEFORE THEIR NEXT FORAY INTO KONOHA TERRITORY.

IT SEEMS THE AKATSUKI IS STARTING TO REALLY MAKE THEIR MOVE.

FWSH

WE'VE GOT NO TIME LEFT TO LOSE.

IT'S DANGEROUS ...BUT ALSO THE BEST OPPORTUNITY TO SMASH THEM.

READ THIS WAY

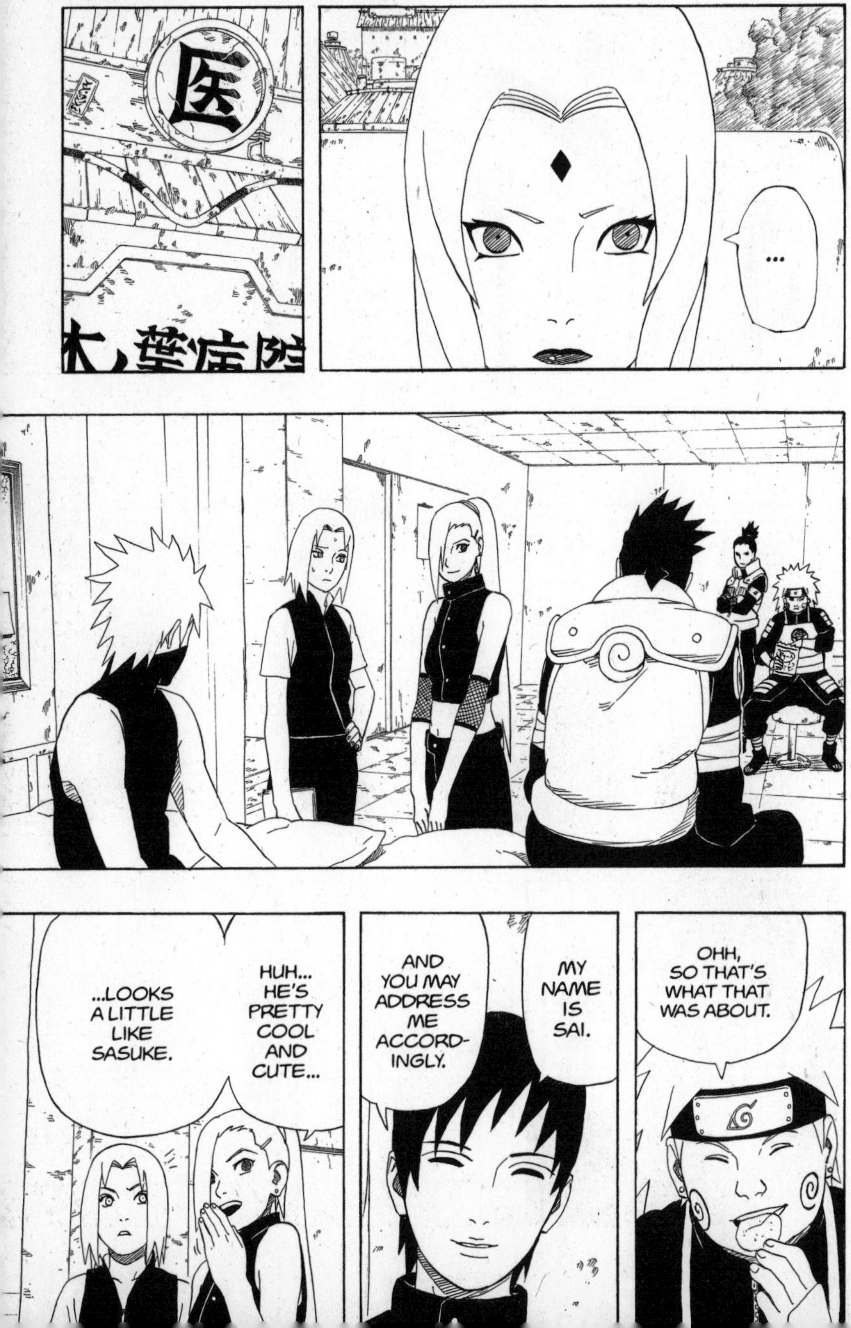
...
医
OHH, SO THAT'S WHAT THAT WAS ABOUT.
MY NAME IS SAI.
AND YOU MAY ADDRESS ME ACCORD-INGLY.
HUH... HE'S PRETTY COOL AND CUTE...
...LOOKS A LITTLE LIKE SASUKE.

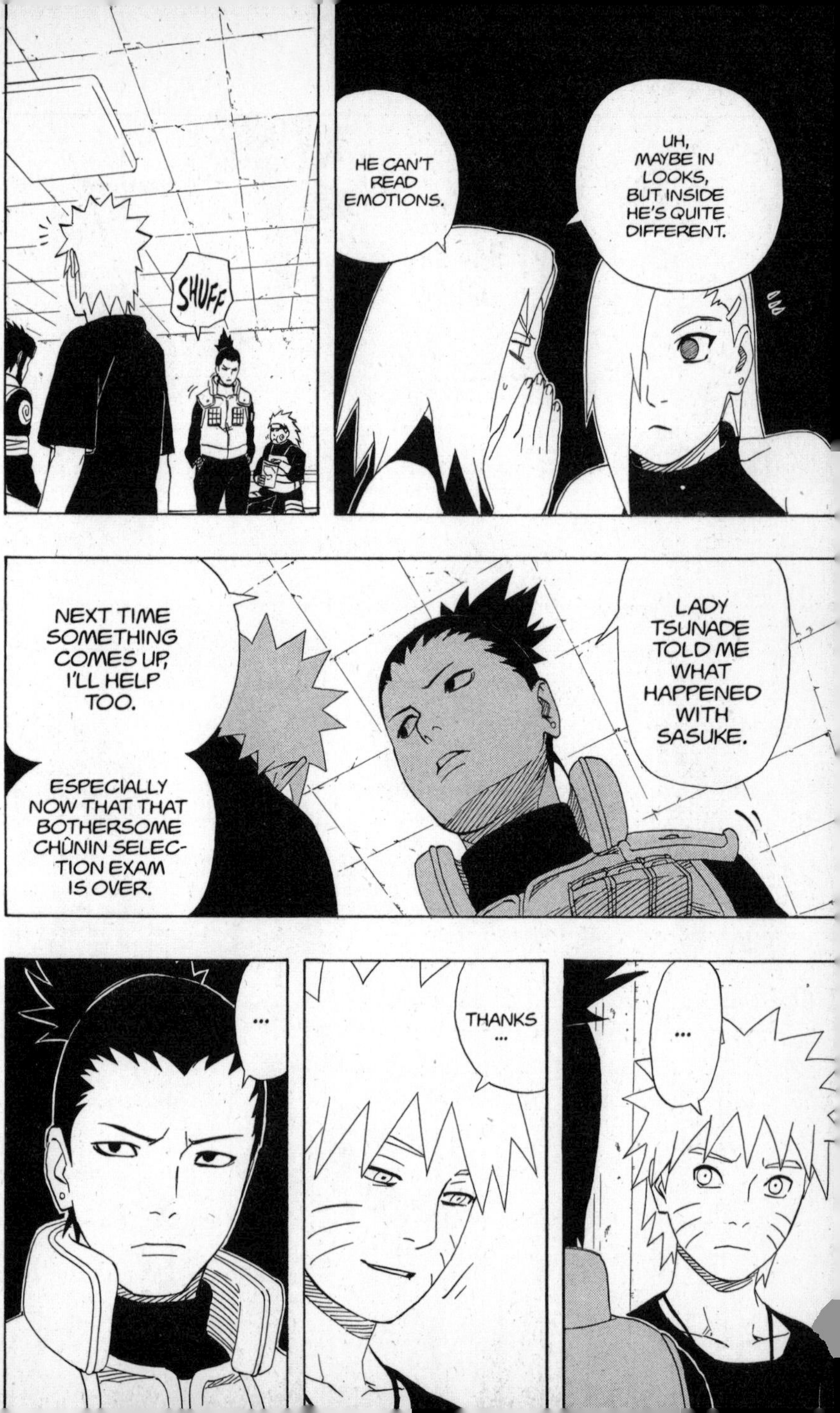
UH, MAYBE IN LOOKS, BUT INSIDE HE'S QUITE DIFFERENT.
HE CAN'T READ EMOTIONS.
SHUFF
LADY TSUNADE TOLD ME WHAT HAPPENED WITH SASUKE.
NEXT TIME SOMETHING COMES UP, I'LL HELP TOO.
ESPECIALLY NOW THAT THAT BOTHERSOME CHÛNIN SELECTION EXAM IS OVER.
...
THANKS ...
...

READ THIS WAY

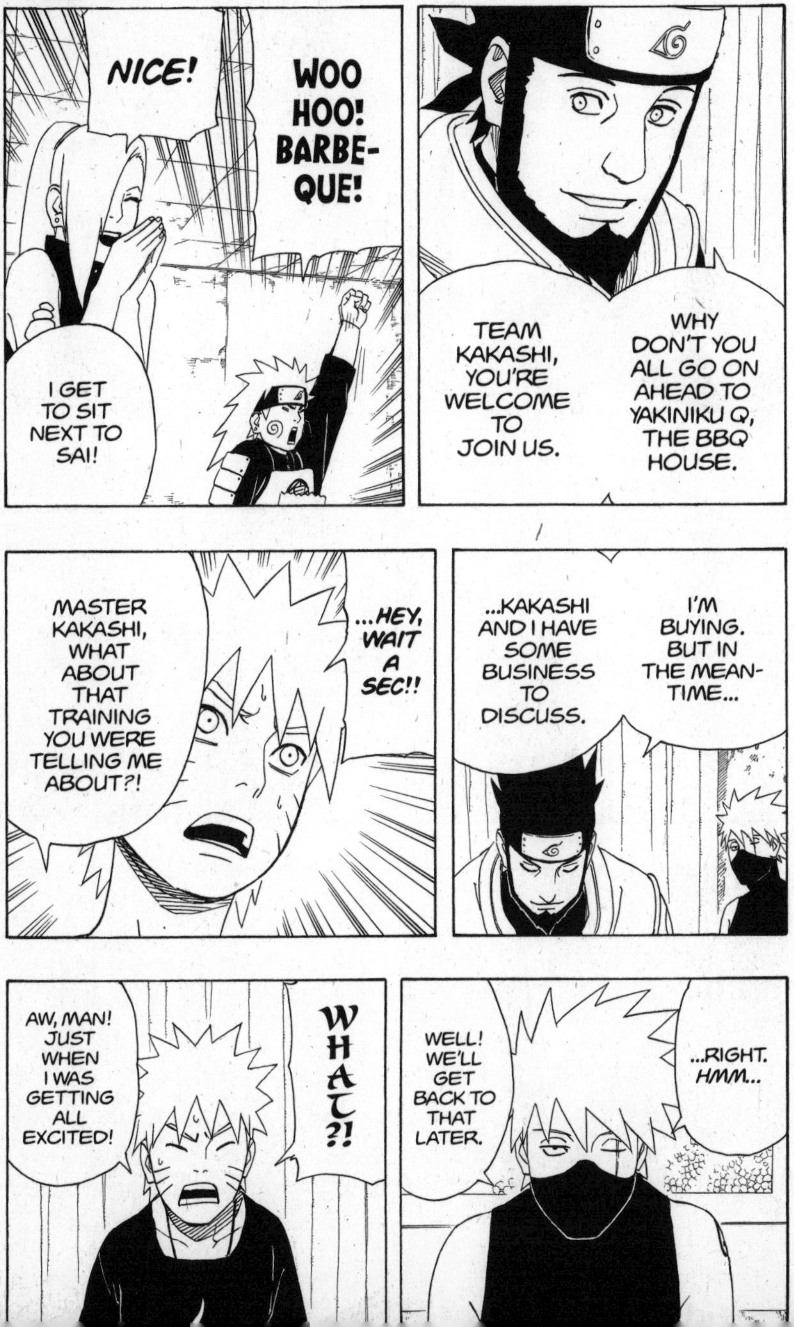
WHY DON'T YOU ALL GO ON AHEAD TO YAKINIKU Q, THE BBQ HOUSE.
TEAM KAKASHI, YOU'RE WELCOME TO JOIN US.
WOO HOO! BARBE-QUE!
NICE!
I GET TO SIT NEXT TO SAI!
I'M BUYING. BUT IN THE MEAN-TIME...
...KAKASHI AND I HAVE SOME BUSINESS TO DISCUSS.
...HEY, WAIT A SEC!!
MASTER KAKASHI, WHAT ABOUT THAT TRAINING YOU WERE TELLING ME ABOUT?!
...RIGHT. HMM...
WELL! WE'LL GET BACK TO THAT LATER.
WHAT?!
AW, MAN! JUST WHEN I WAS GETTING ALL EXCITED!

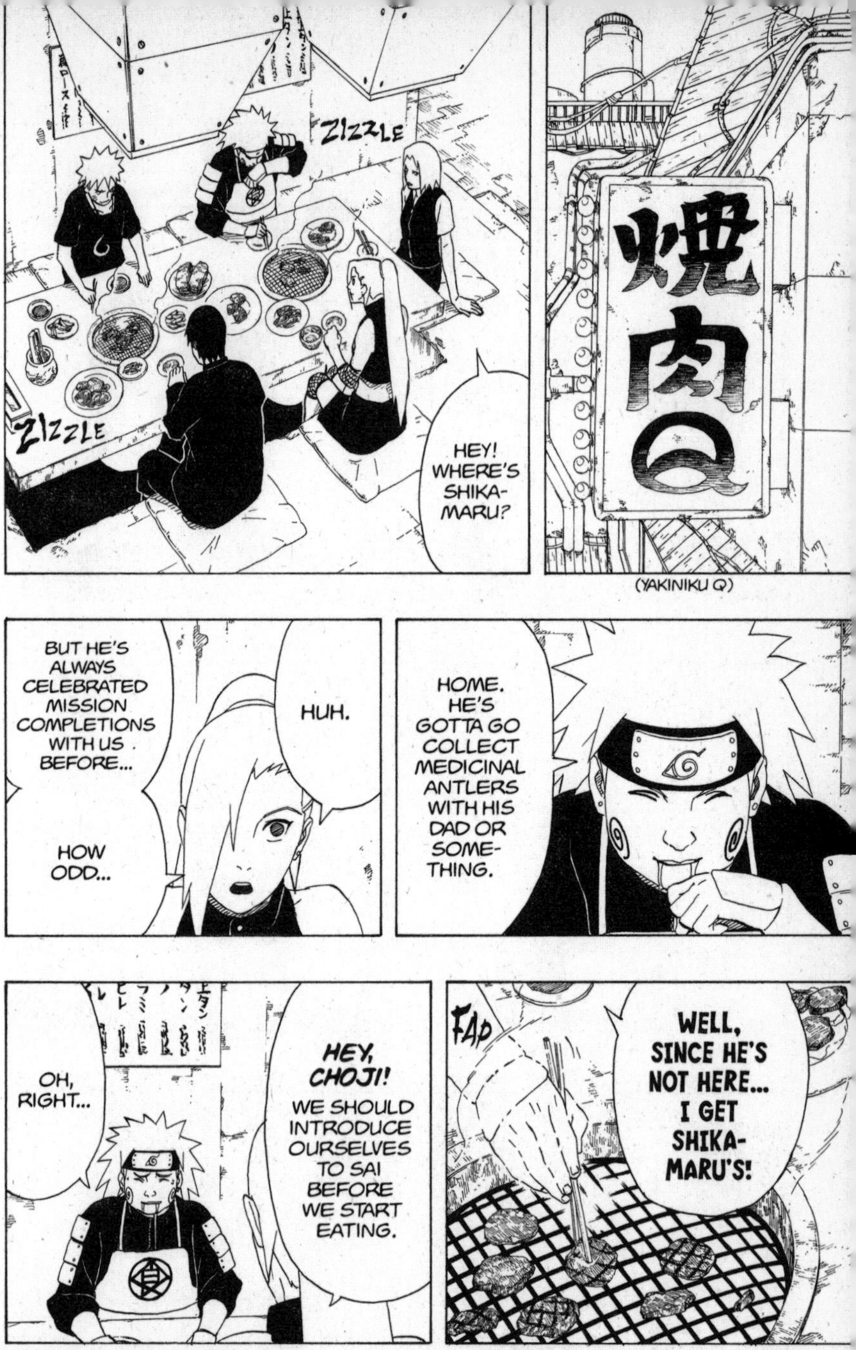
焼肉Q
(YAKINIKU Q)
ZIZZLE
HEY! WHERE'S SHIKA-MARU?
ZIZZLE
HOME. HE'S GOTTA GO COLLECT MEDICINAL ANTLERS WITH HIS DAD OR SOME-THING.
HUH.
BUT HE'S ALWAYS CELEBRATED MISSION COMPLETIONS WITH US BEFORE...
HOW ODD...
FAP
WELL, SINCE HE'S NOT HERE... I GET SHIKA-MARU'S!
HEY, CHOJI!
WE SHOULD INTRODUCE OURSELVES TO SAI BEFORE WE START EATING.
OH, RIGHT...

READ THIS WAY

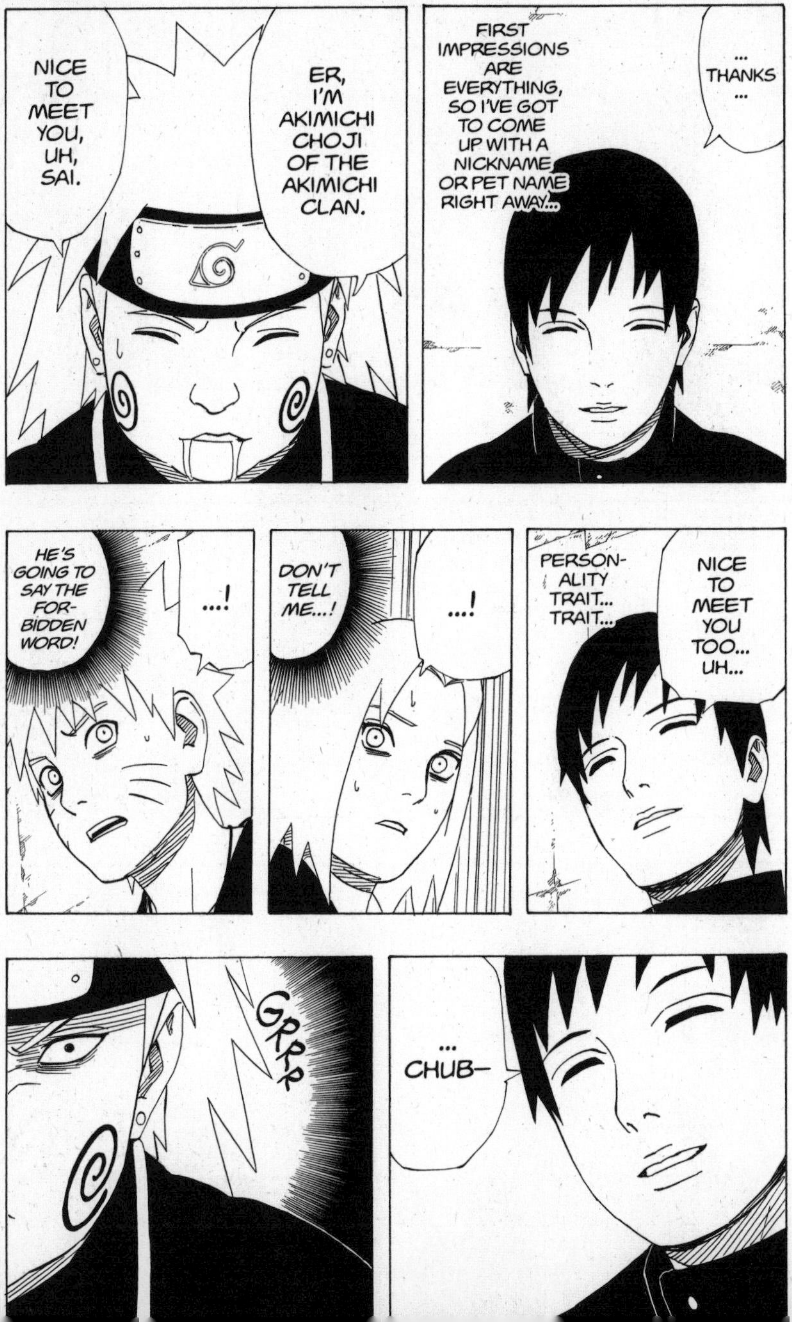
... THANKS ...
FIRST IMPRESSIONS ARE EVERYTHING, SO I'VE GOT TO COME UP WITH A NICKNAME OR PET NAME RIGHT AWAY...
ER, I'M AKIMICHI CHOJI OF THE AKIMICHI CLAN.
NICE TO MEET YOU, UH, SAI.
NICE TO MEET YOU TOO... UH...
PERSON-ALITY TRAIT... TRAIT...
...!
DON'T TELL ME...!
...!
HE'S GOING TO SAY THE FOR-BIDDEN WORD!
... CHUB–
GRRR

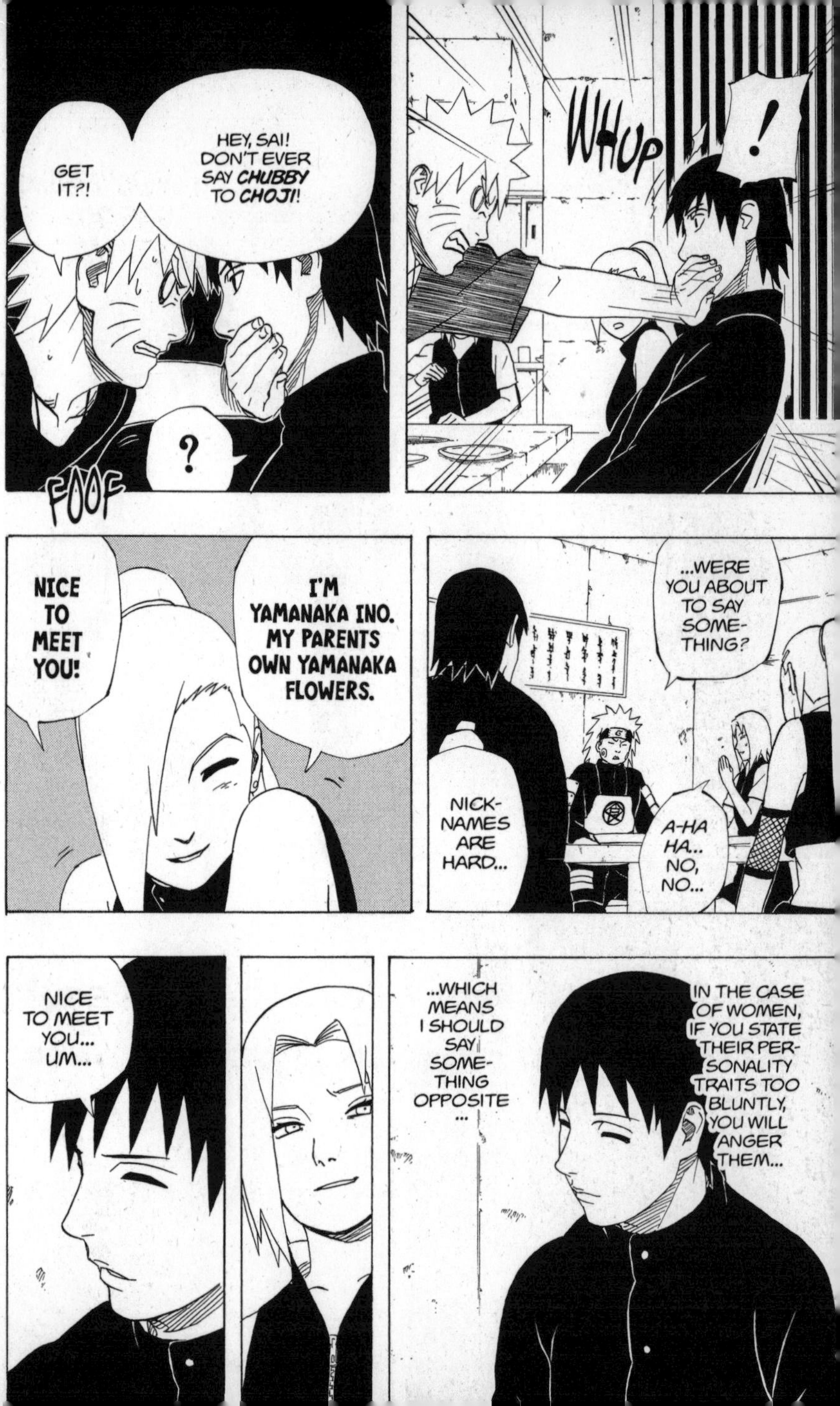
WHUP
!
HEY, SAI! DON'T EVER SAY CHUBBY TO CHOJI!
GET IT?!
?
FOOF
...WERE YOU ABOUT TO SAY SOME-THING?
A-HA HA... NO, NO...
NICK-NAMES ARE HARD...
I'M YAMANAKA INO. MY PARENTS OWN YAMANAKA FLOWERS.
NICE TO MEET YOU!
IN THE CASE OF WOMEN, IF YOU STATE THEIR PER-SONALITY TRAITS TOO BLUNTLY, YOU WILL ANGER THEM...
...WHICH MEANS I SHOULD SAY SOME-THING OPPOSITE ...
NICE TO MEET YOU... UM...

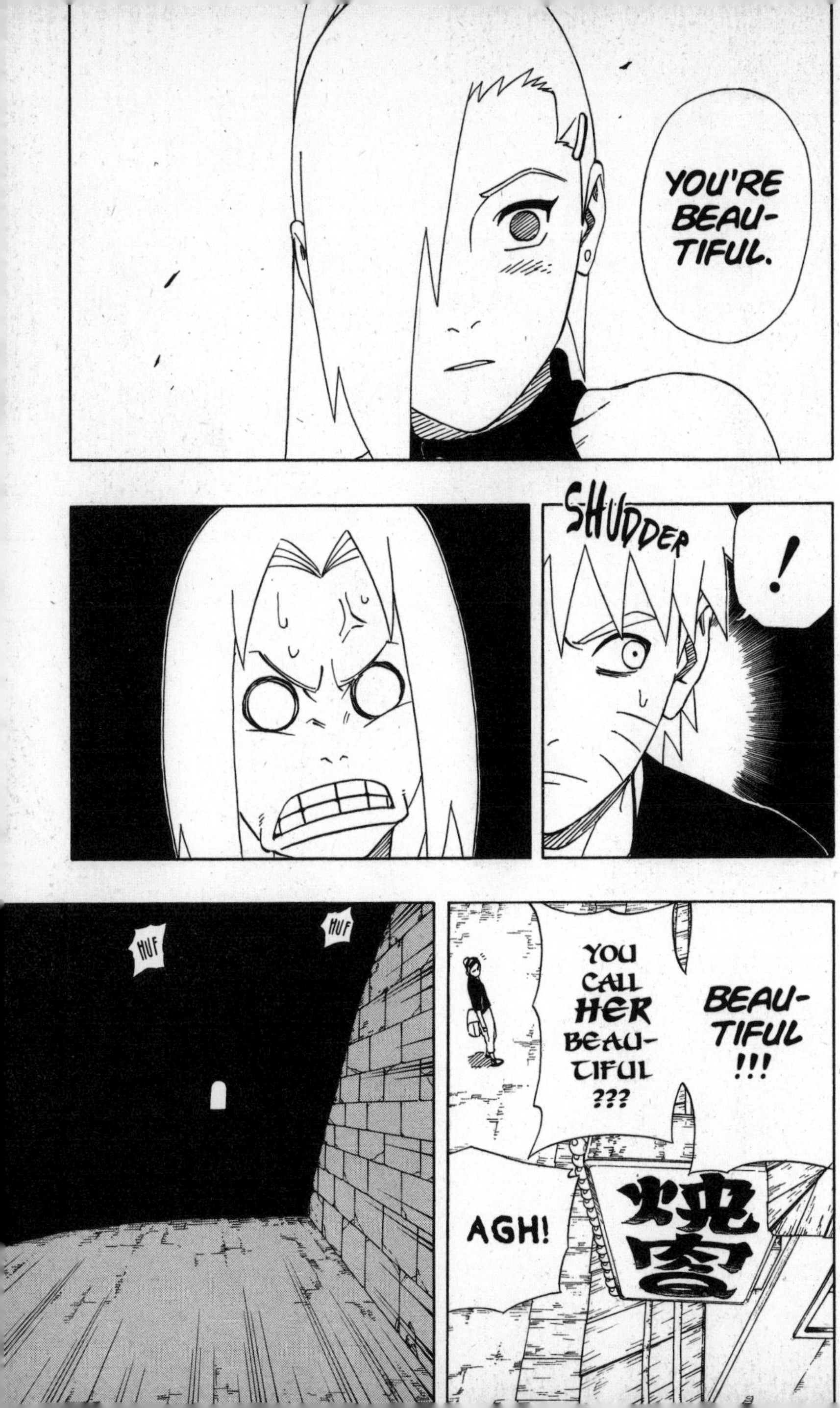
YOU'RE BEAU-TIFUL.
SHUDDER
!
YOU CALL HER BEAU-TIFUL???
BEAU-TIFUL!!!
AGH!
HUF
HUF

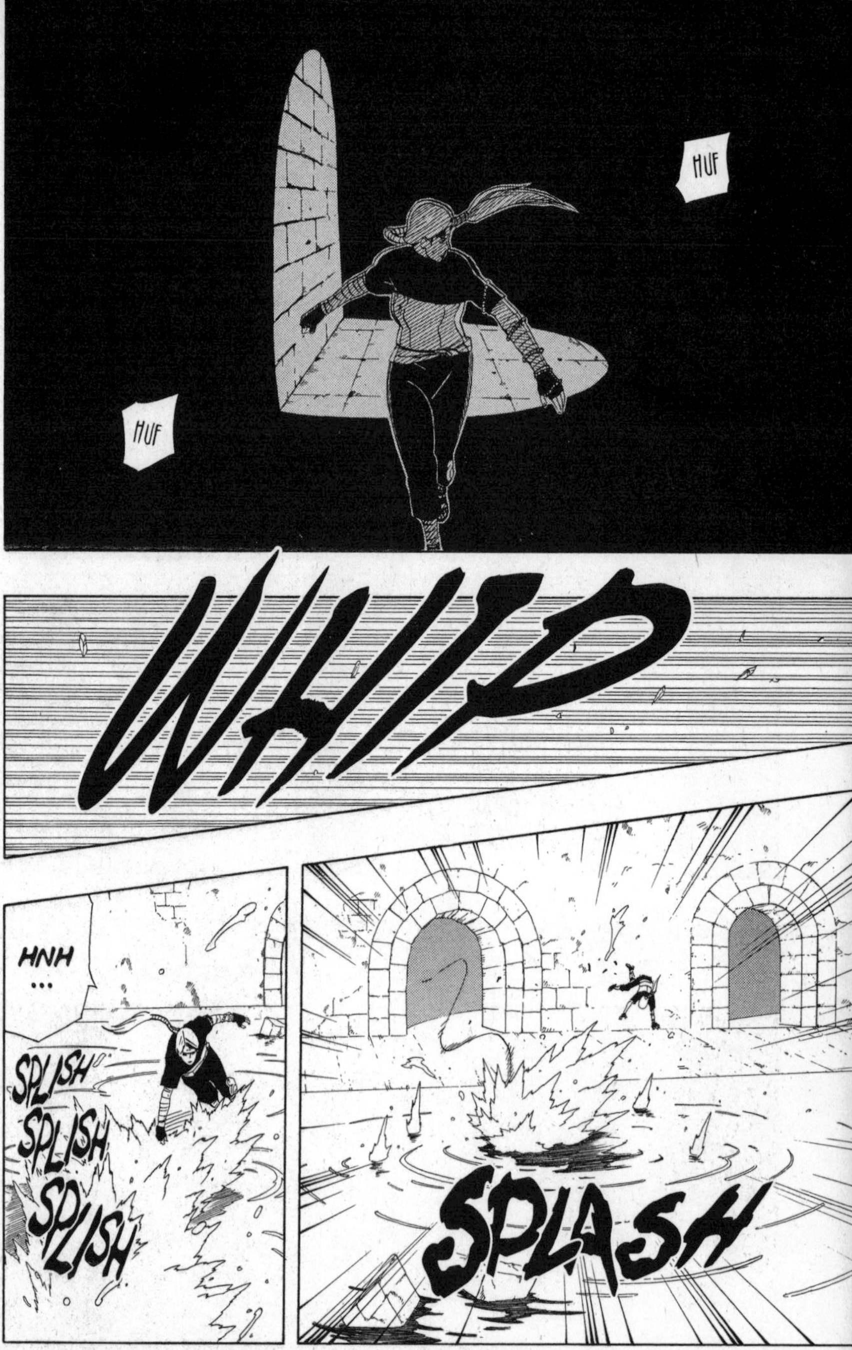
HUF
HUF
WHIP
SPLASH
HNH ...
SPLISH
SPLISH
SPLISH

READ THIS WAY

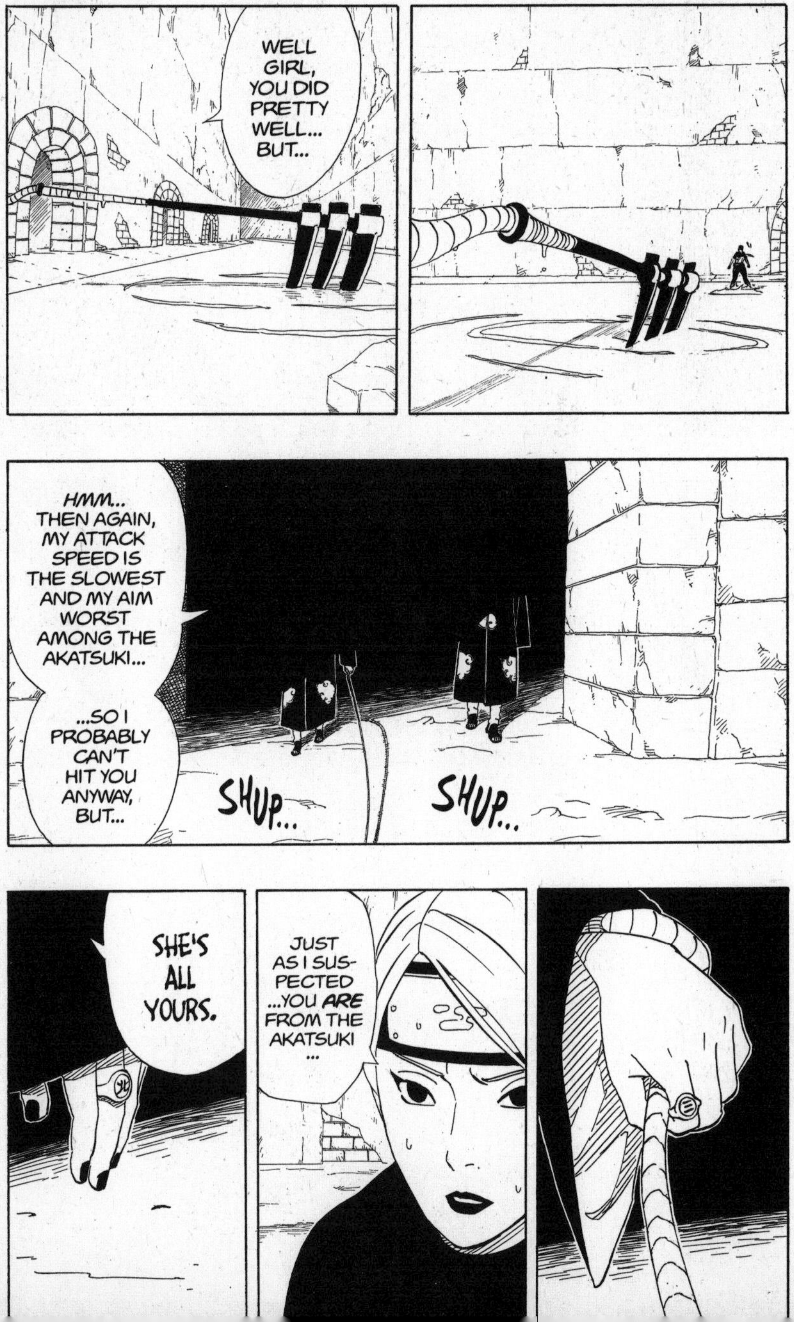
WELL GIRL, YOU DID PRETTY WELL... BUT...
HMM... THEN AGAIN, MY ATTACK SPEED IS THE SLOWEST AND MY AIM WORST AMONG THE AKATSUKI...
...SO I PROBABLY CAN'T HIT YOU ANYWAY, BUT...
SHUP...
SHUP...
JUST AS I SUS-PECTED ...YOU ARE FROM THE AKATSUKI ...
SHE'S ALL YOURS.

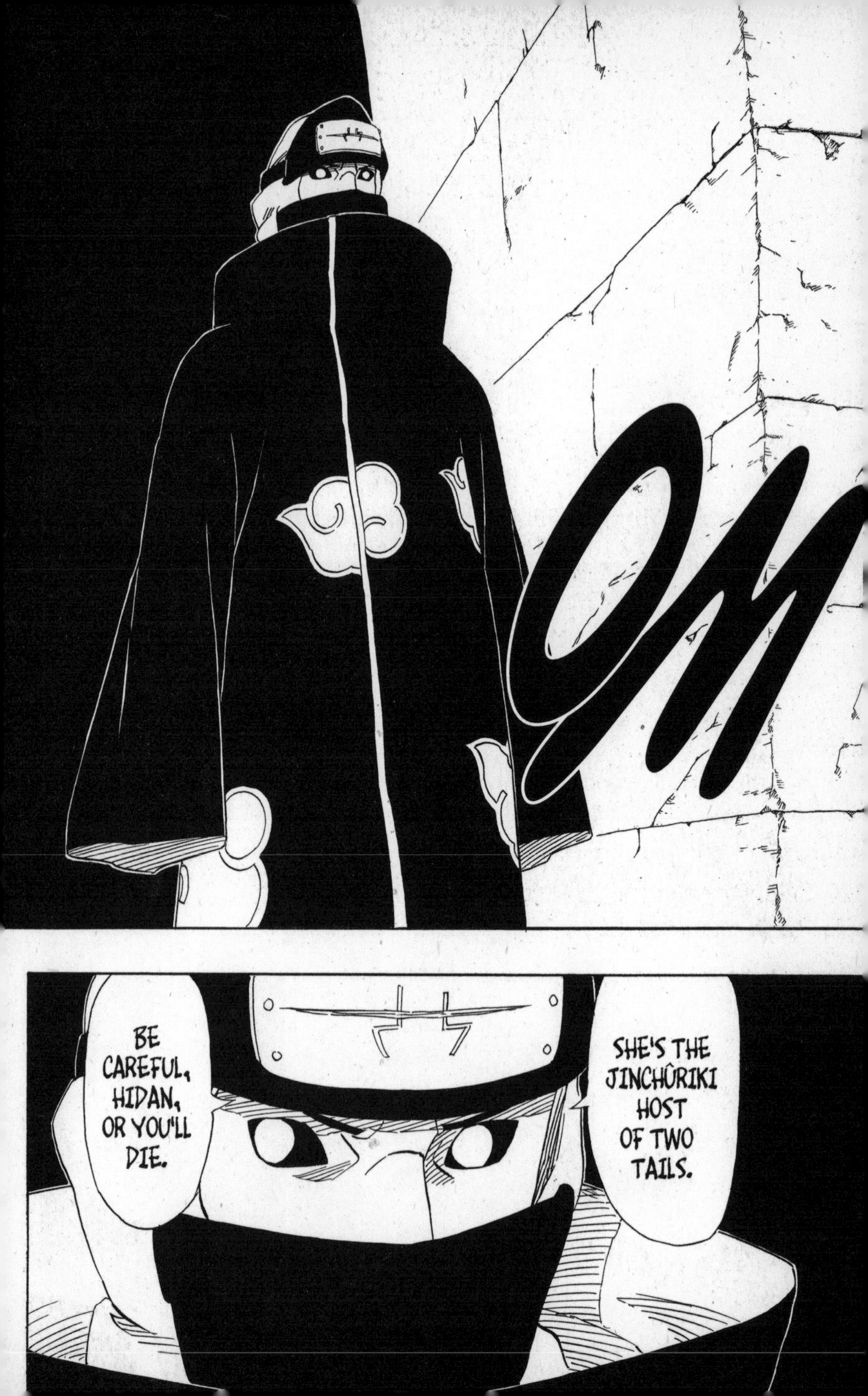
SHE'S THE JINCHÛRIKI HOST OF TWO TAILS.
BE CAREFUL, HIDAN, OR YOU'LL DIE.

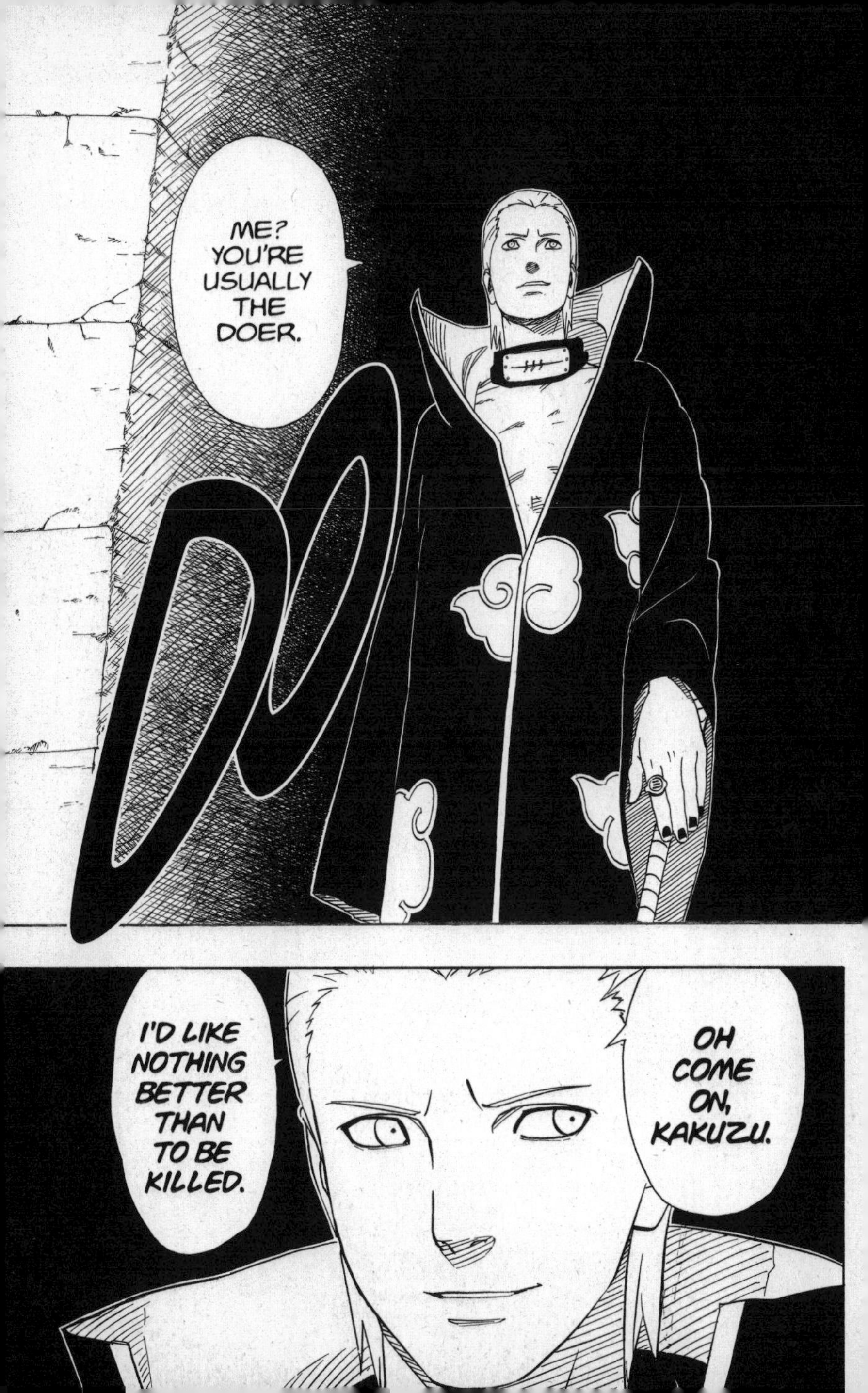
ME? YOU'RE USUALLY THE DOER.
OH COME ON, KAKUZU.
I'D LIKE NOTHING BETTER THAN TO BE KILLED.

NARUTO

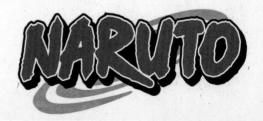

Number 313: The New-Two!!

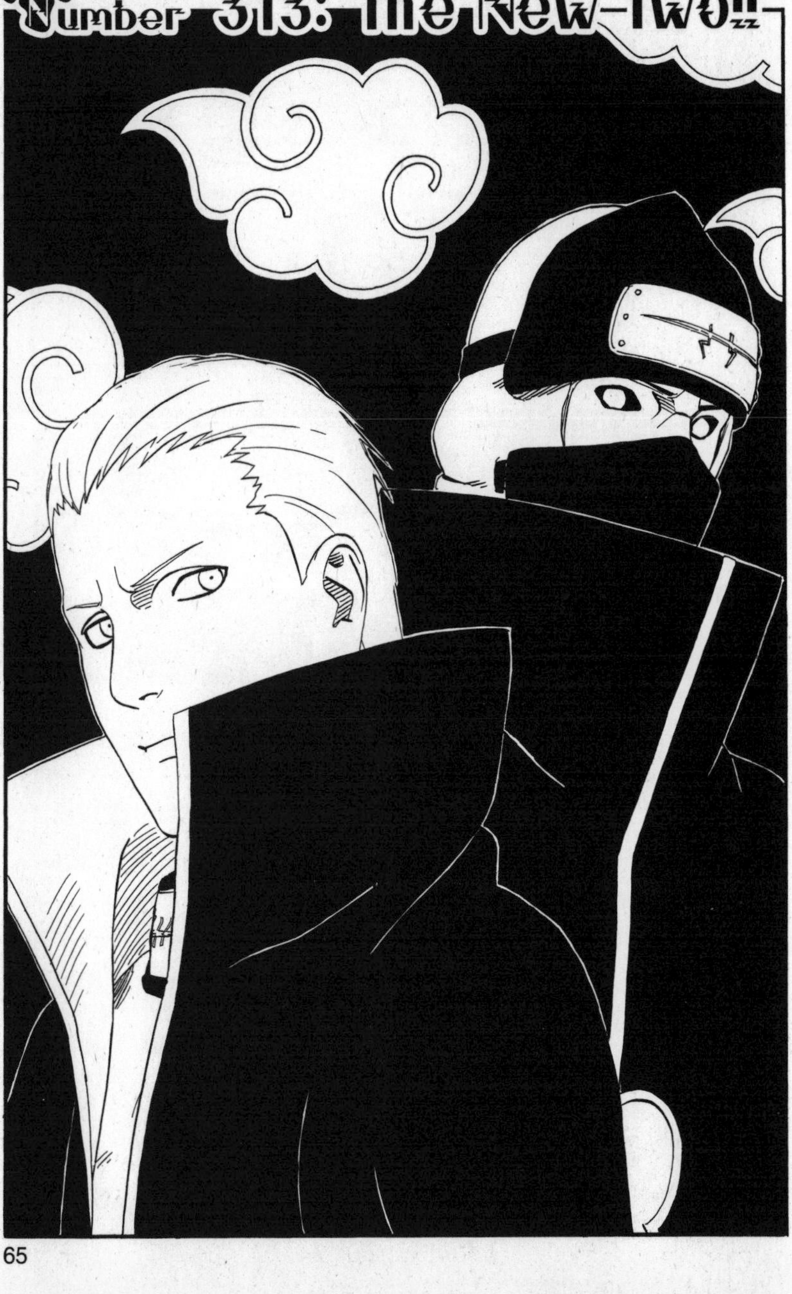

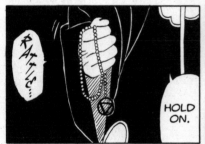

RATTLE...

HOLD ON.

LET'S DO IT.

...

BEFORE I DO ANY-THING...

...I MUST CONFER WITH MY KAMI.

YOU AND YOUR DEITY. ALWAYS SUCH A BOTHER.

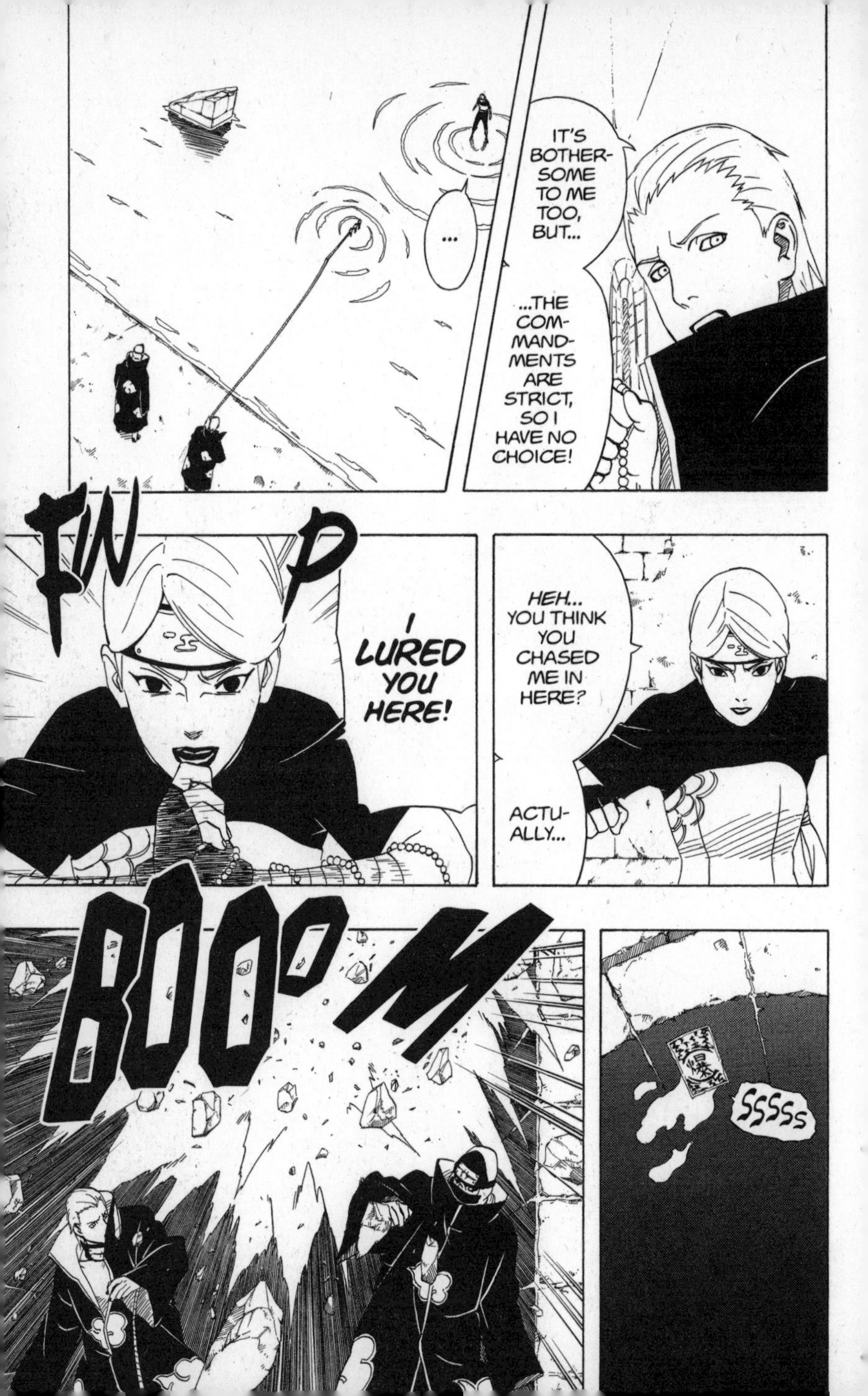
IT'S BOTHER-SOME TO ME TOO, BUT...
...THE COM-MAND-MENTS ARE STRICT, SO I HAVE NO CHOICE!
...
HEH... YOU THINK YOU CHASED ME IN HERE?
ACTU-ALLY...
I LURED YOU HERE!
FWP
SSSSs
BOOOM

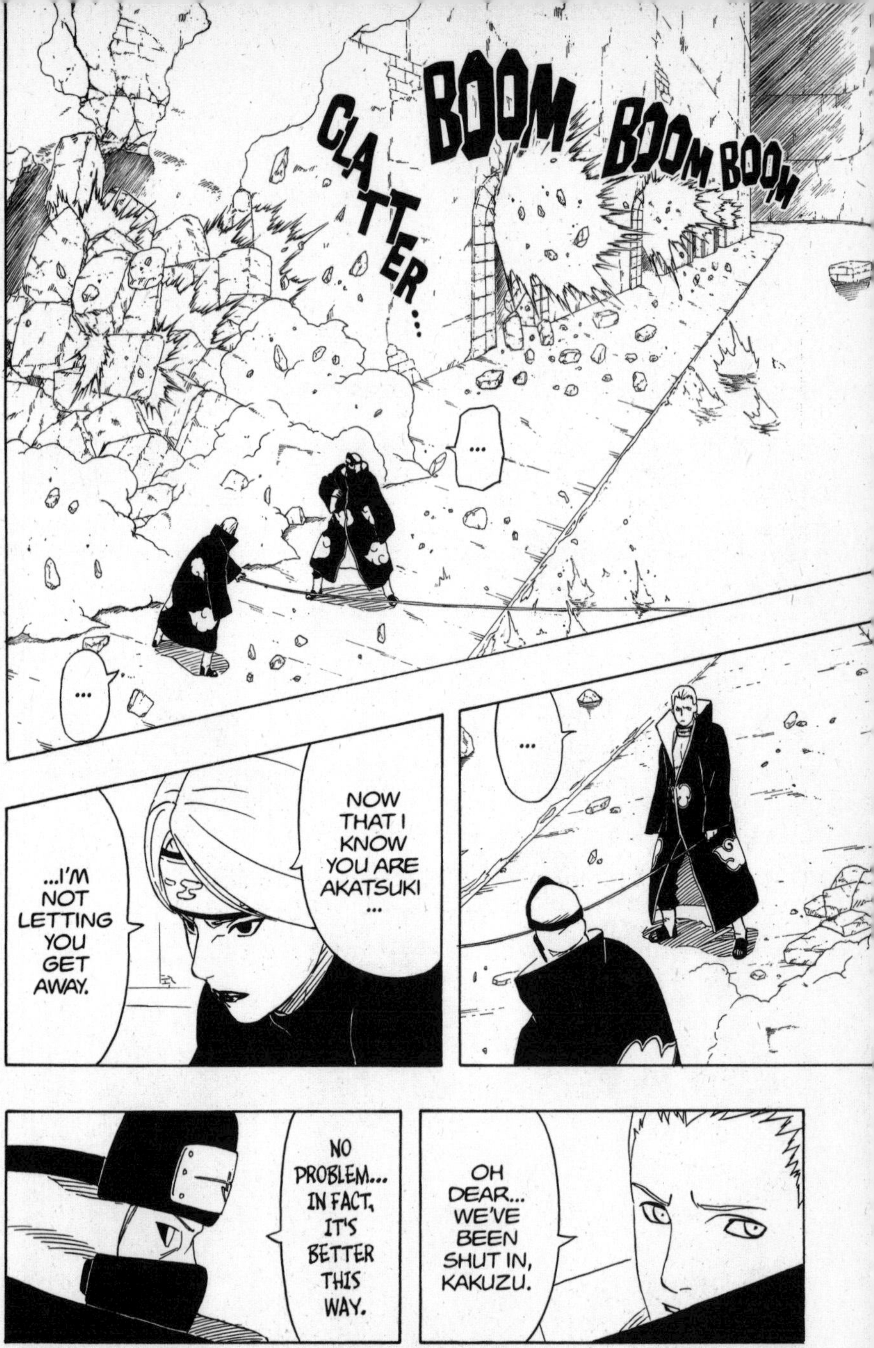
BOOM BOOM
BOOM
CLATTER...
...
...
...
NOW THAT I KNOW YOU ARE AKATSUKI...
...I'M NOT LETTING YOU GET AWAY.
OH DEAR... WE'VE BEEN SHUT IN, KAKUZU.
NO PROBLEM... IN FACT, IT'S BETTER THIS WAY.

READ THIS WAY

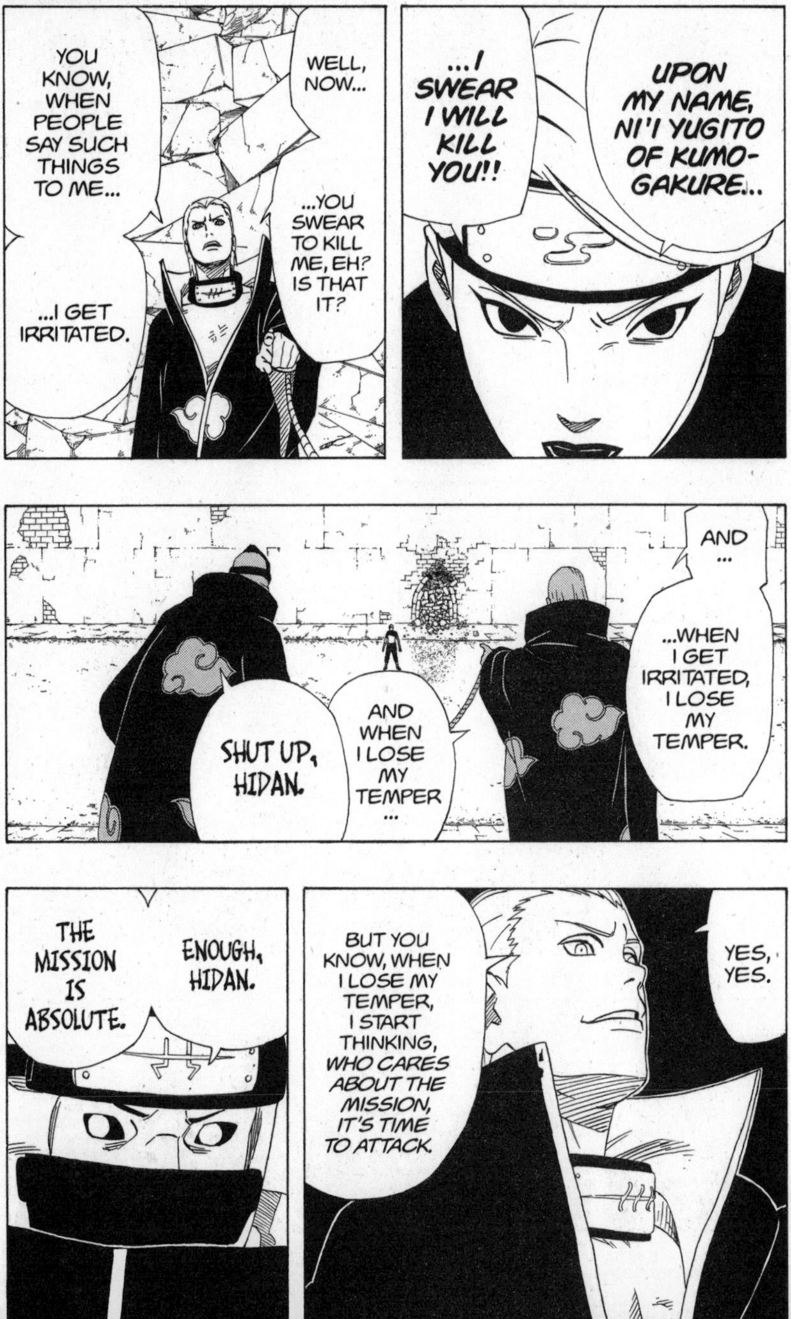
UPON MY NAME, NI'I YUGITO OF KUMO-GAKURE...
...I SWEAR I WILL KILL YOU!!
WELL, NOW...
...YOU SWEAR TO KILL ME, EH? IS THAT IT?
YOU KNOW, WHEN PEOPLE SAY SUCH THINGS TO ME...
...I GET IRRITATED.
AND ...
...WHEN I GET IRRITATED, I LOSE MY TEMPER.
AND WHEN I LOSE MY TEMPER ...
SHUT UP, HIDAN.
YES, YES.
BUT YOU KNOW, WHEN I LOSE MY TEMPER, I START THINKING, WHO CARES ABOUT THE MISSION, IT'S TIME TO ATTACK.
ENOUGH, HIDAN.
THE MISSION IS ABSOLUTE.

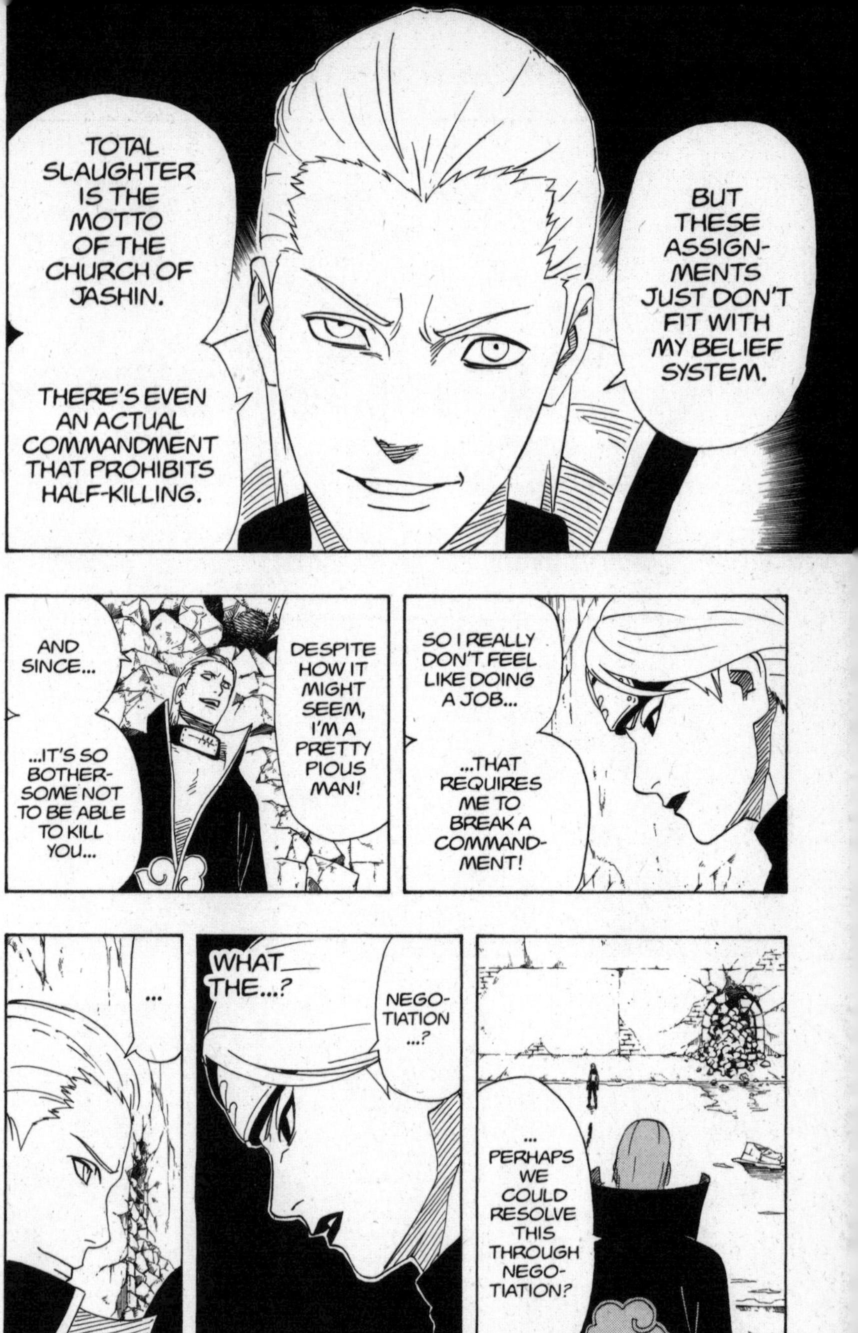
BUT THESE ASSIGNMENTS JUST DON'T FIT WITH MY BELIEF SYSTEM.
TOTAL SLAUGHTER IS THE MOTTO OF THE CHURCH OF JASHIN.
THERE'S EVEN AN ACTUAL COMMANDMENT THAT PROHIBITS HALF-KILLING.
SO I REALLY DON'T FEEL LIKE DOING A JOB...
...THAT REQUIRES ME TO BREAK A COMMANDMENT!
DESPITE HOW IT MIGHT SEEM, I'M A PRETTY PIOUS MAN!
AND SINCE...
...IT'S SO BOTHERSOME NOT TO BE ABLE TO KILL YOU...
... PERHAPS WE COULD RESOLVE THIS THROUGH NEGOTIATION?
WHAT THE...?
NEGOTIATION...?
...

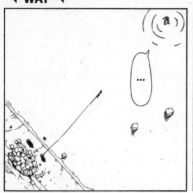

...

OH, COME ON. JUST SURRENDER, WHY DON'T YOU?

YOU MUST BE JOKING!!

VWOOOSH

VWOOO

I'LL TAKE THAT AS A *NO*, THEN...

ARE YOU AN IDIOT, HIDAN?

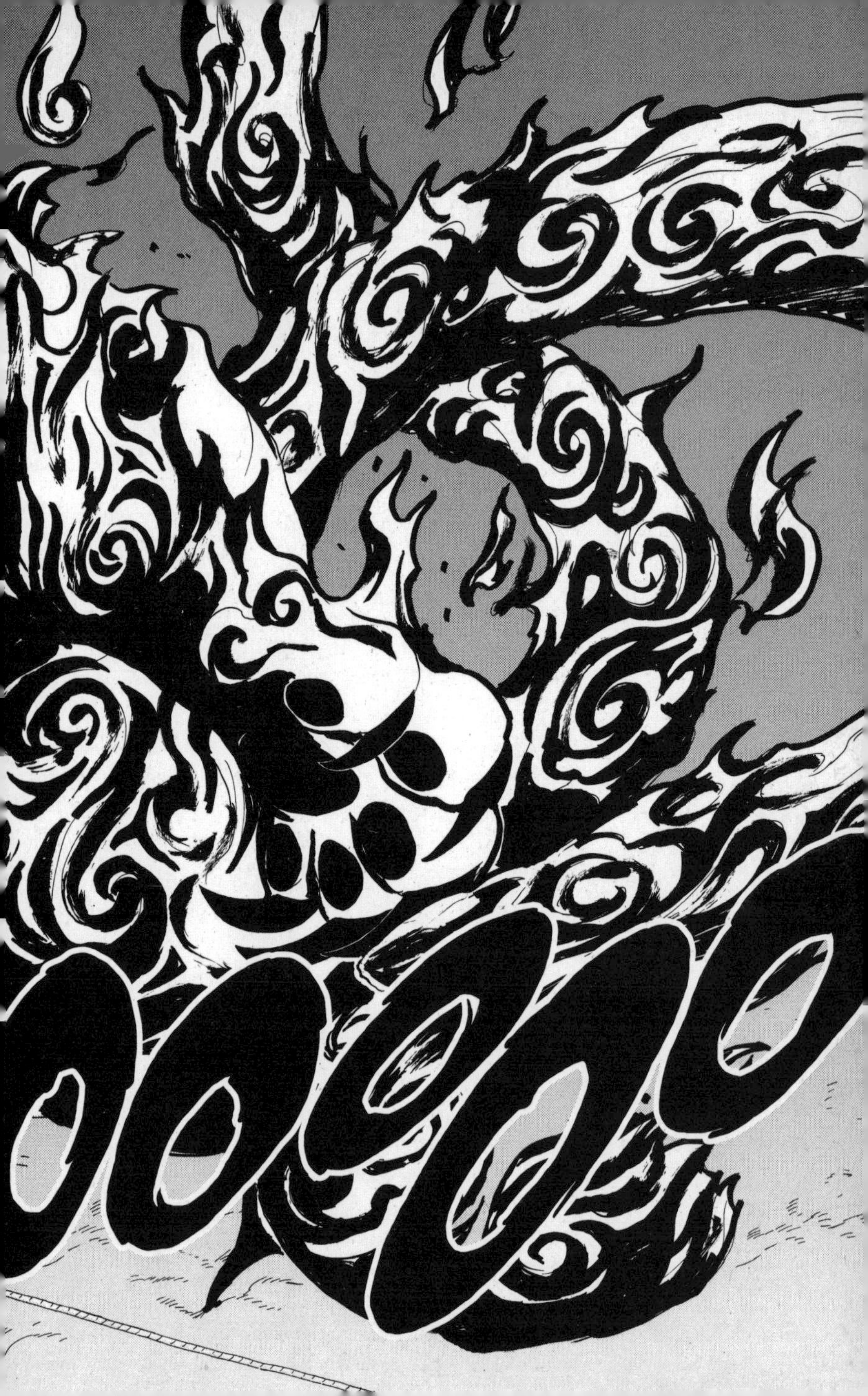

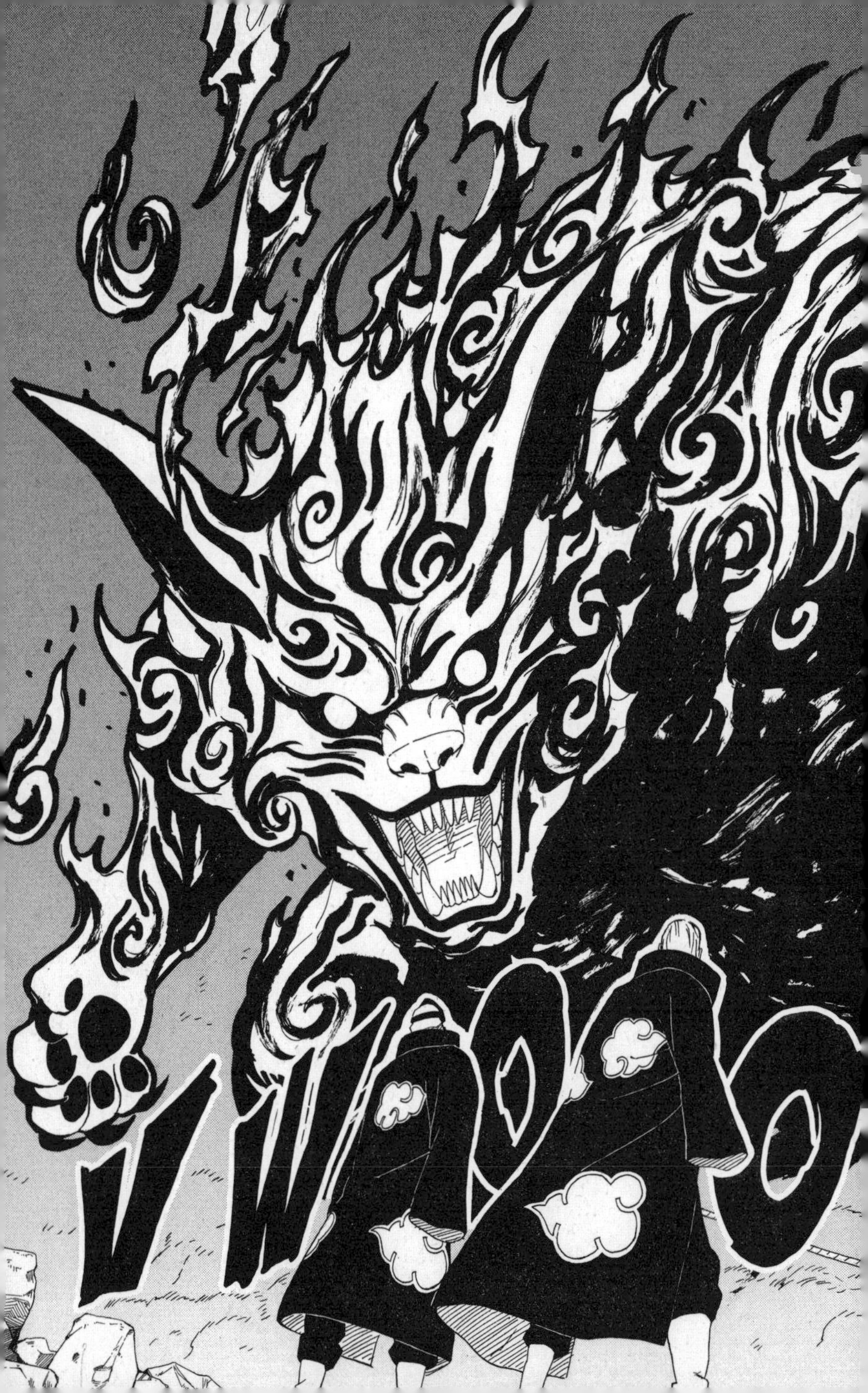
VWOOOO

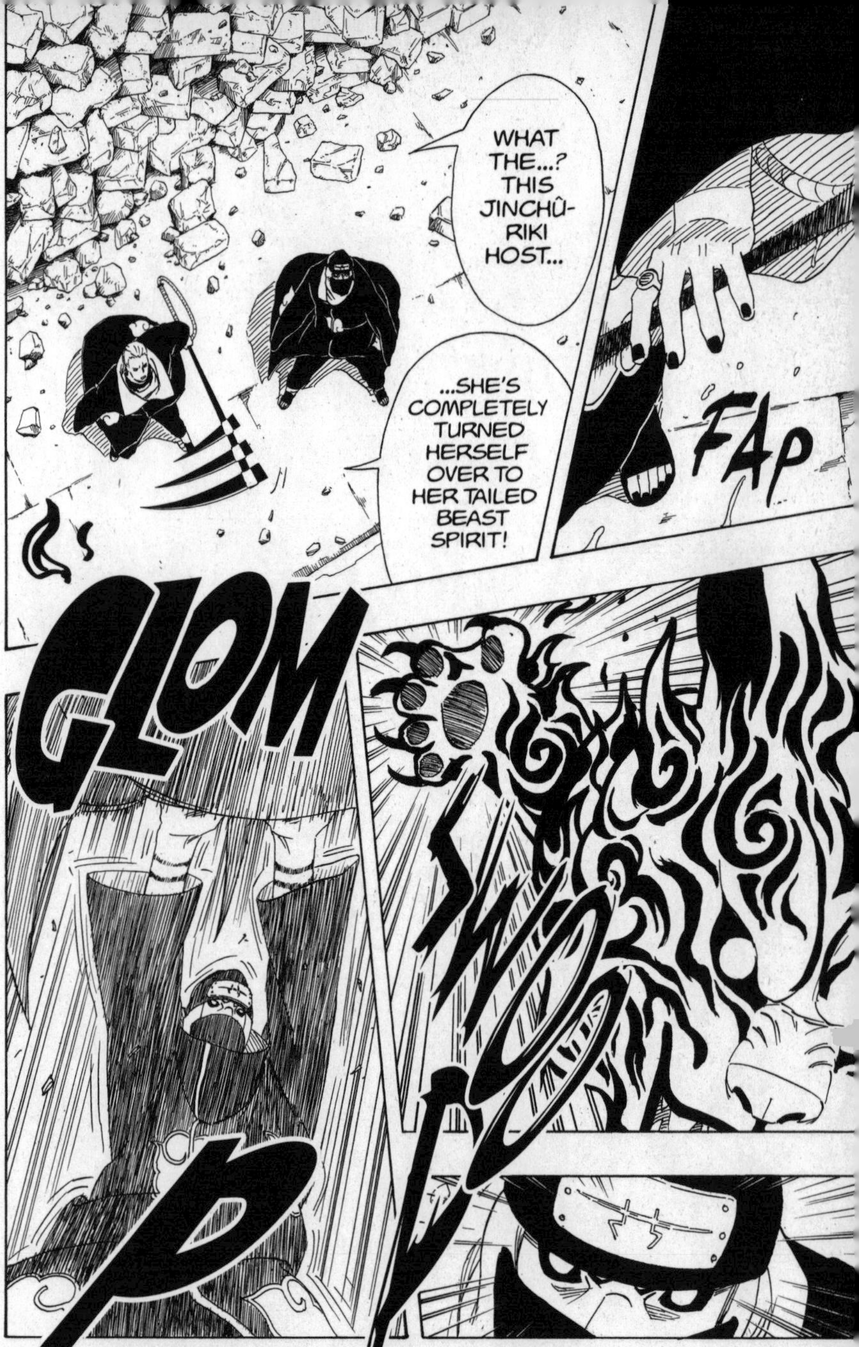
FAP
WHAT THE...? THIS JINCHÛ-RIKI HOST...
...SHE'S COMPLETELY TURNED HERSELF OVER TO HER TAILED BEAST SPIRIT!
GLOM

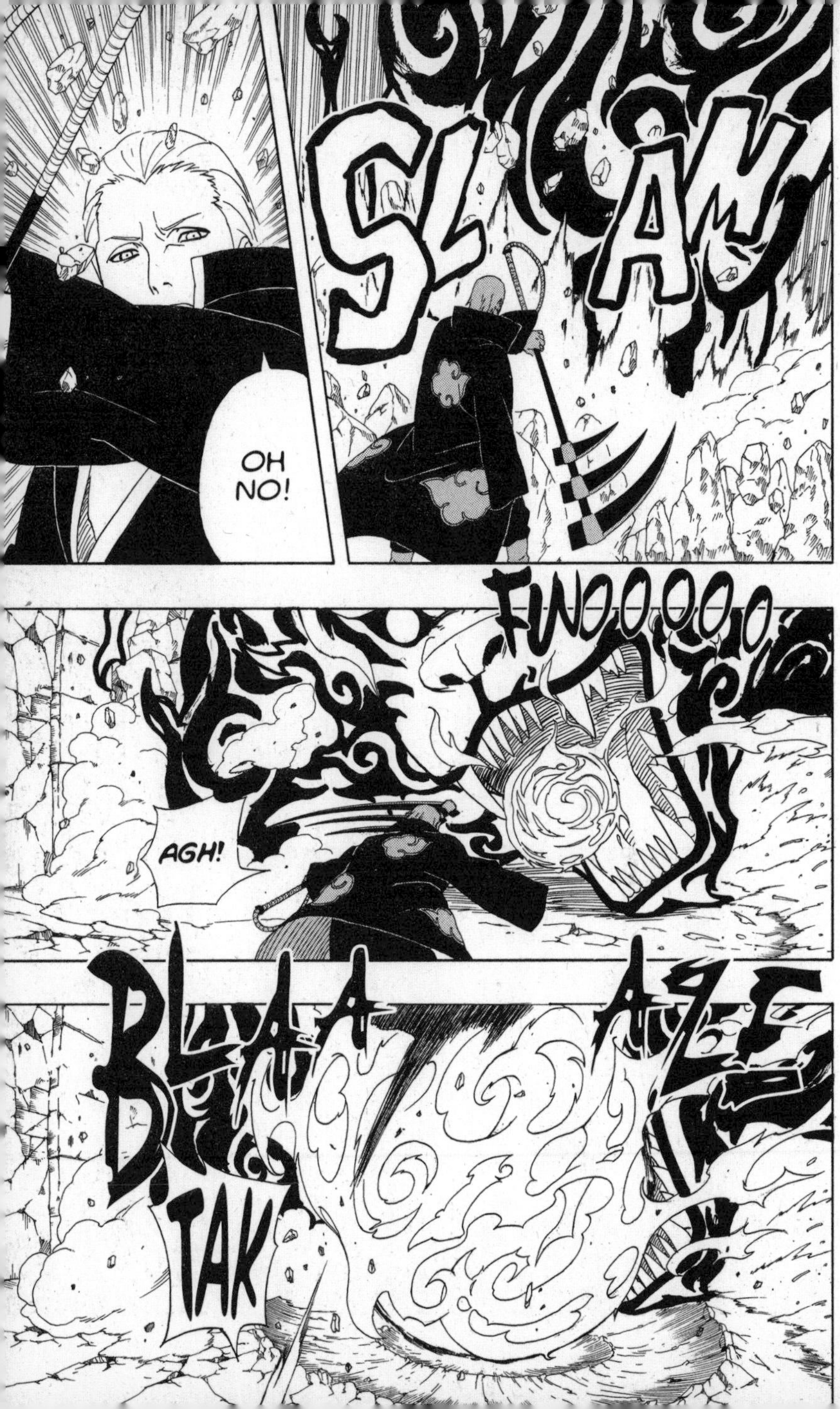
SLAM
OH NO!
FWOOOOO
AGH!
BLAAAZE
TAK

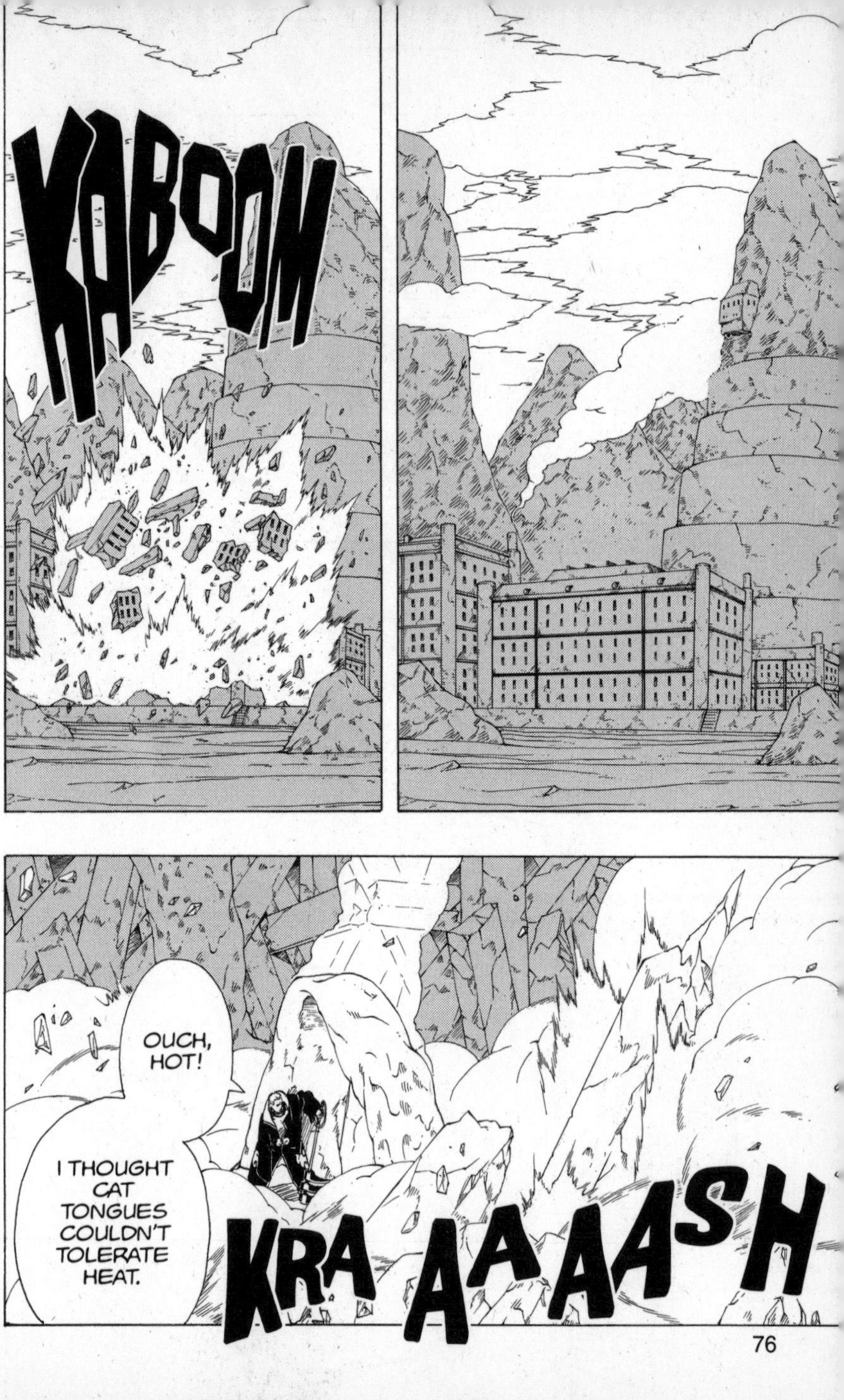
KABOOM
OUCH, HOT!
I THOUGHT CAT TONGUES COULDN'T TOLERATE HEAT.
KRAAAASH

READ THIS WAY

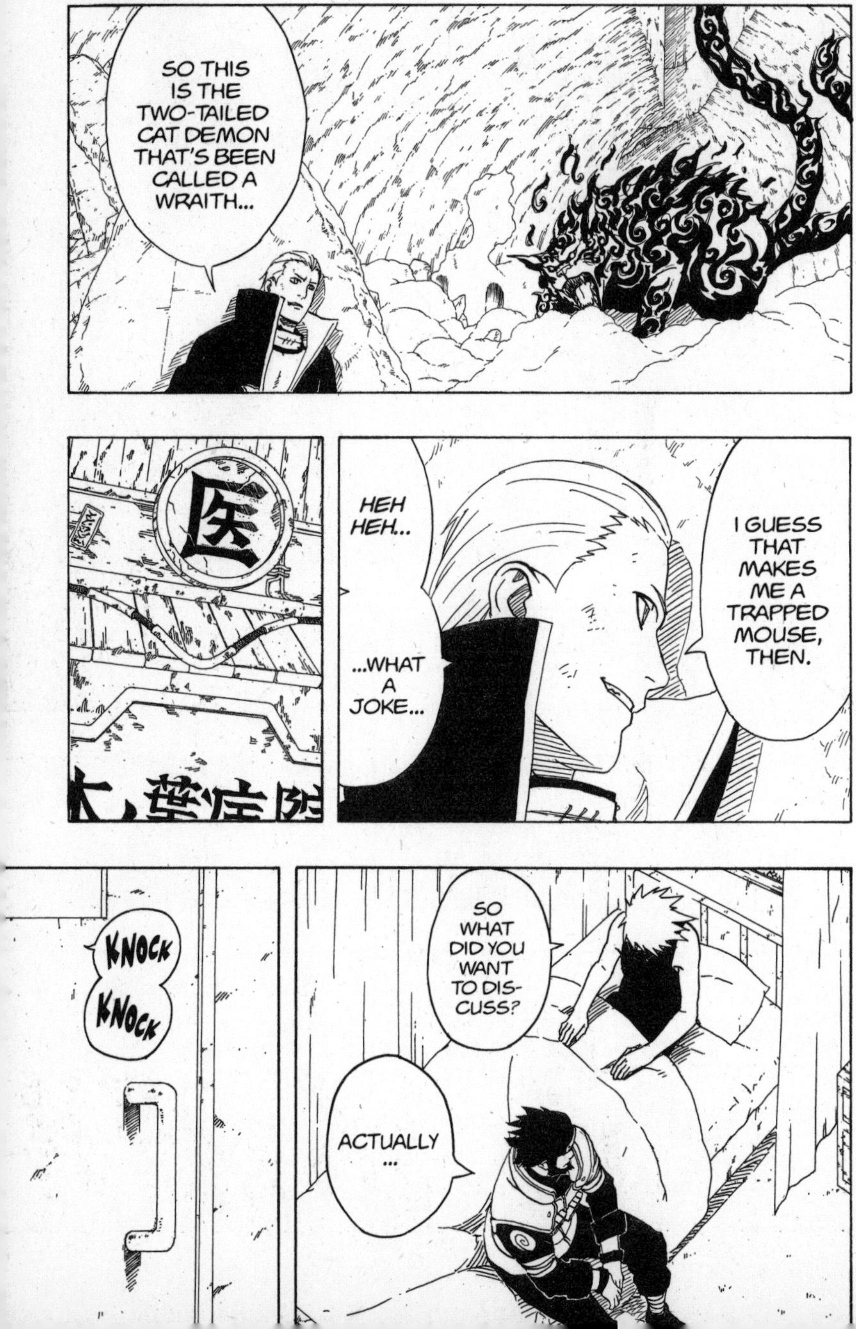

SO THIS IS THE TWO-TAILED CAT DEMON THAT'S BEEN CALLED A WRAITH...
I GUESS THAT MAKES ME A TRAPPED MOUSE, THEN.
HEH HEH...
...WHAT A JOKE...
医
SO WHAT DID YOU WANT TO DISCUSS?
ACTUALLY ...
KNOCK
KNOCK

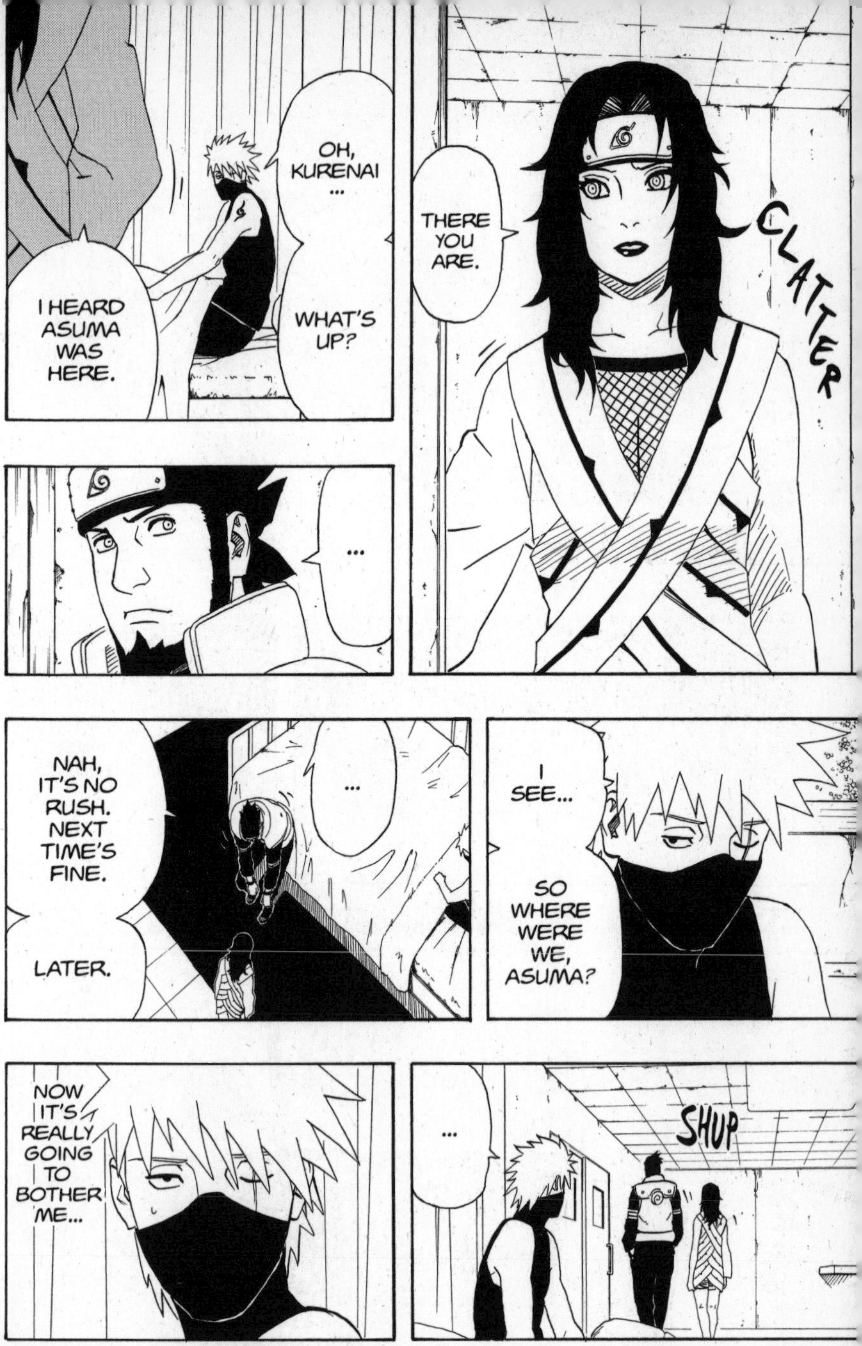
CLATTER
THERE YOU ARE.
OH, KURENAI ...
WHAT'S UP?
I HEARD ASUMA WAS HERE.
...
I SEE...
SO WHERE WERE WE, ASUMA?
...
NAH, IT'S NO RUSH. NEXT TIME'S FINE.
LATER.
SHUP
...
NOW IT'S REALLY GOING TO BOTHER ME...

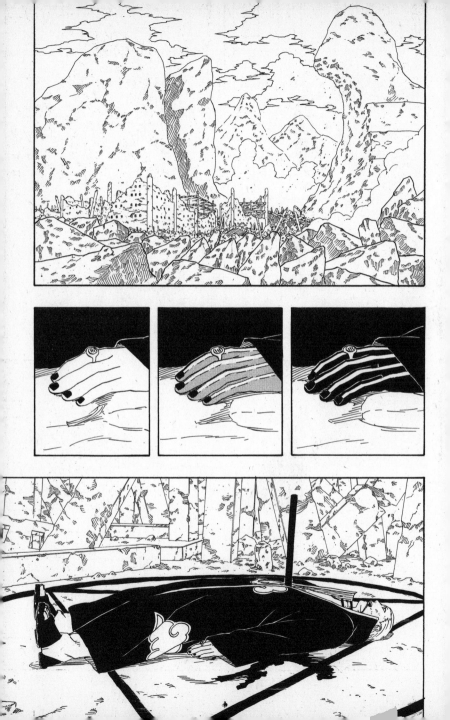

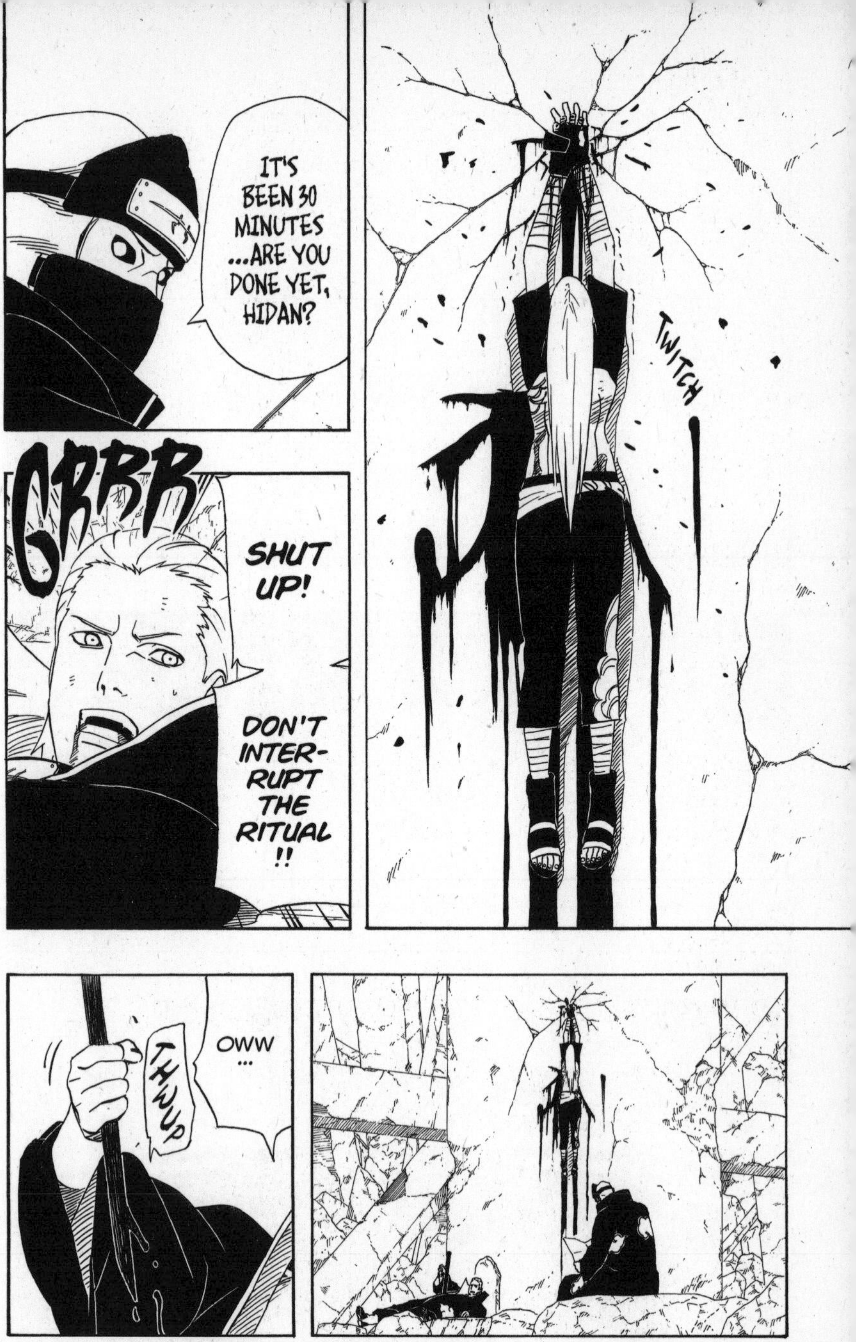
TWITCH
IT'S BEEN 30 MINUTES ...ARE YOU DONE YET, HIDAN?
GRRR
SHUT UP!
DON'T INTER-RUPT THE RITUAL!!
OWW ...
THWUP

READ THIS WAY

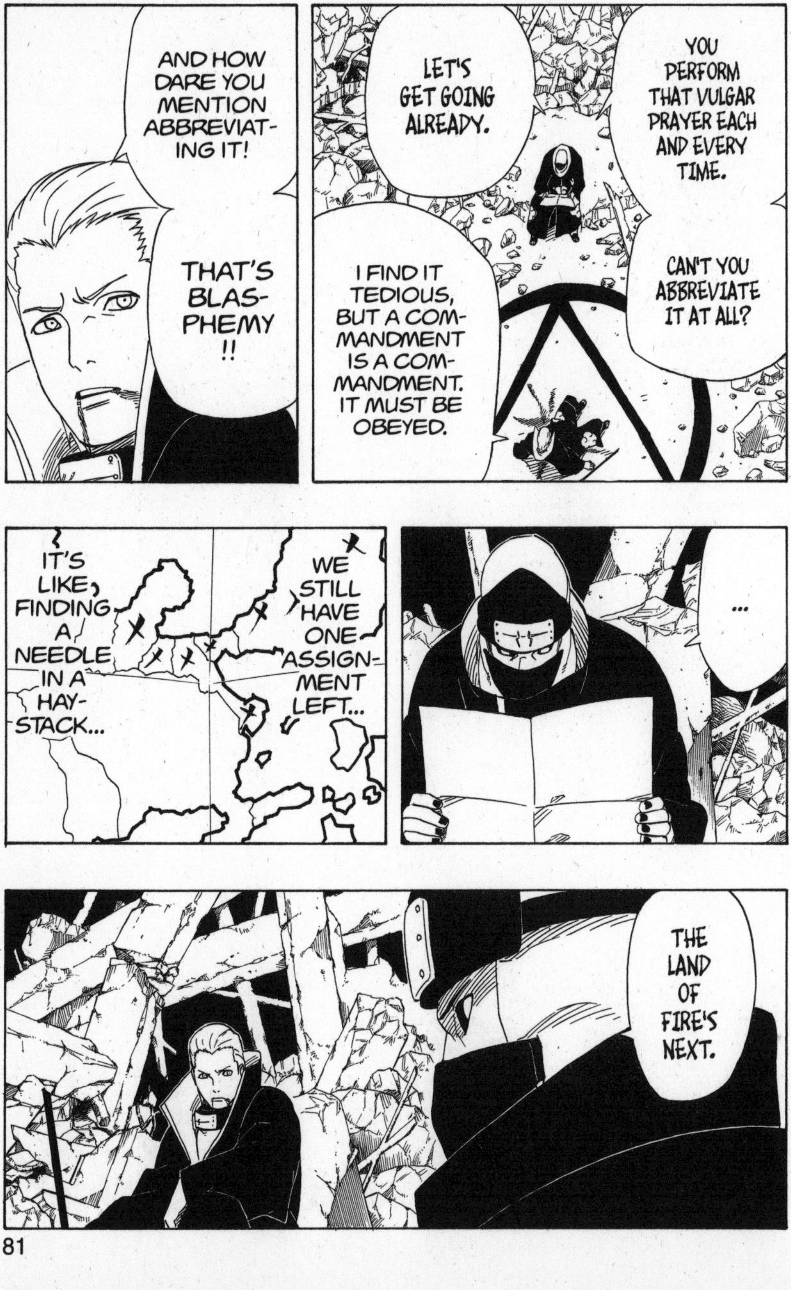

YOU PERFORM THAT VULGAR PRAYER EACH AND EVERY TIME.
LET'S GET GOING ALREADY.
CAN'T YOU ABBREVIATE IT AT ALL?
I FIND IT TEDIOUS, BUT A COMMANDMENT IS A COMMANDMENT. IT MUST BE OBEYED.
AND HOW DARE YOU MENTION ABBREVIATING IT!
THAT'S BLASPHEMY!!
...
WE STILL HAVE ONE ASSIGNMENT LEFT...
IT'S LIKE, FINDING A NEEDLE IN A HAYSTACK...
THE LAND OF FIRE'S NEXT.

NARUTO

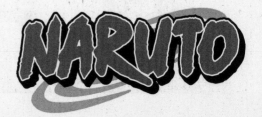

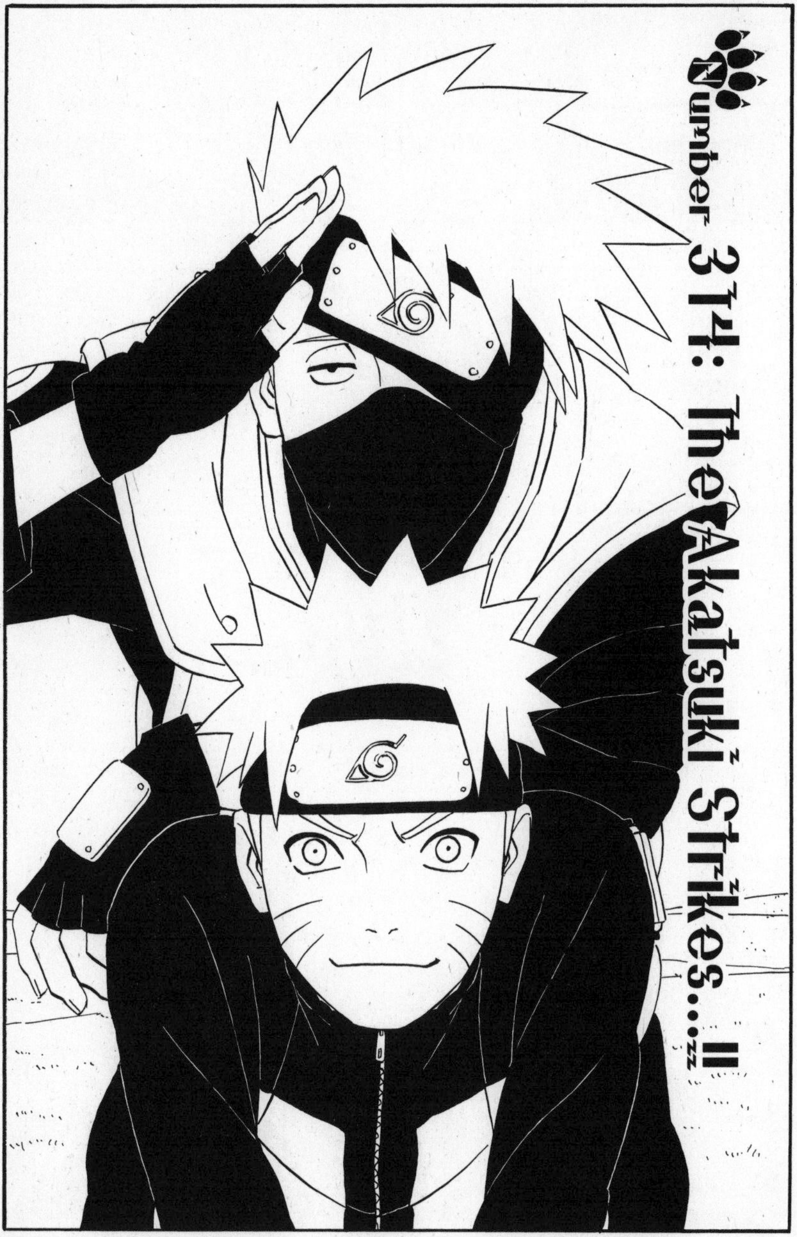
Number 314: The Akatsuki Strikes...!!

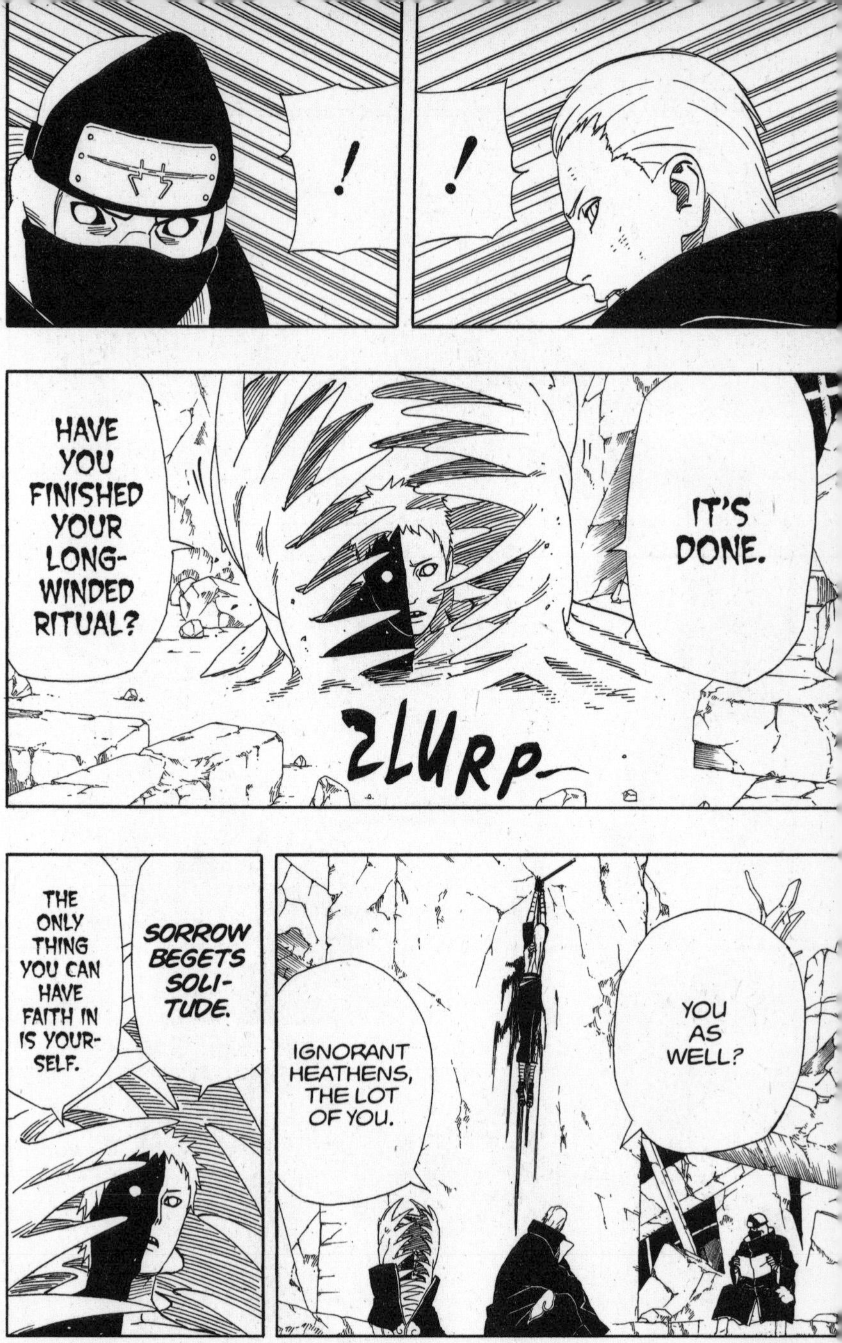
!
!
IT'S DONE.
HAVE YOU FINISHED YOUR LONG-WINDED RITUAL?
ZLURP
YOU AS WELL?
IGNORANT HEATHENS, THE LOT OF YOU.
SORROW BEGETS SOLI-TUDE.
THE ONLY THING YOU CAN HAVE FAITH IN IS YOUR-SELF.

READ THIS WAY

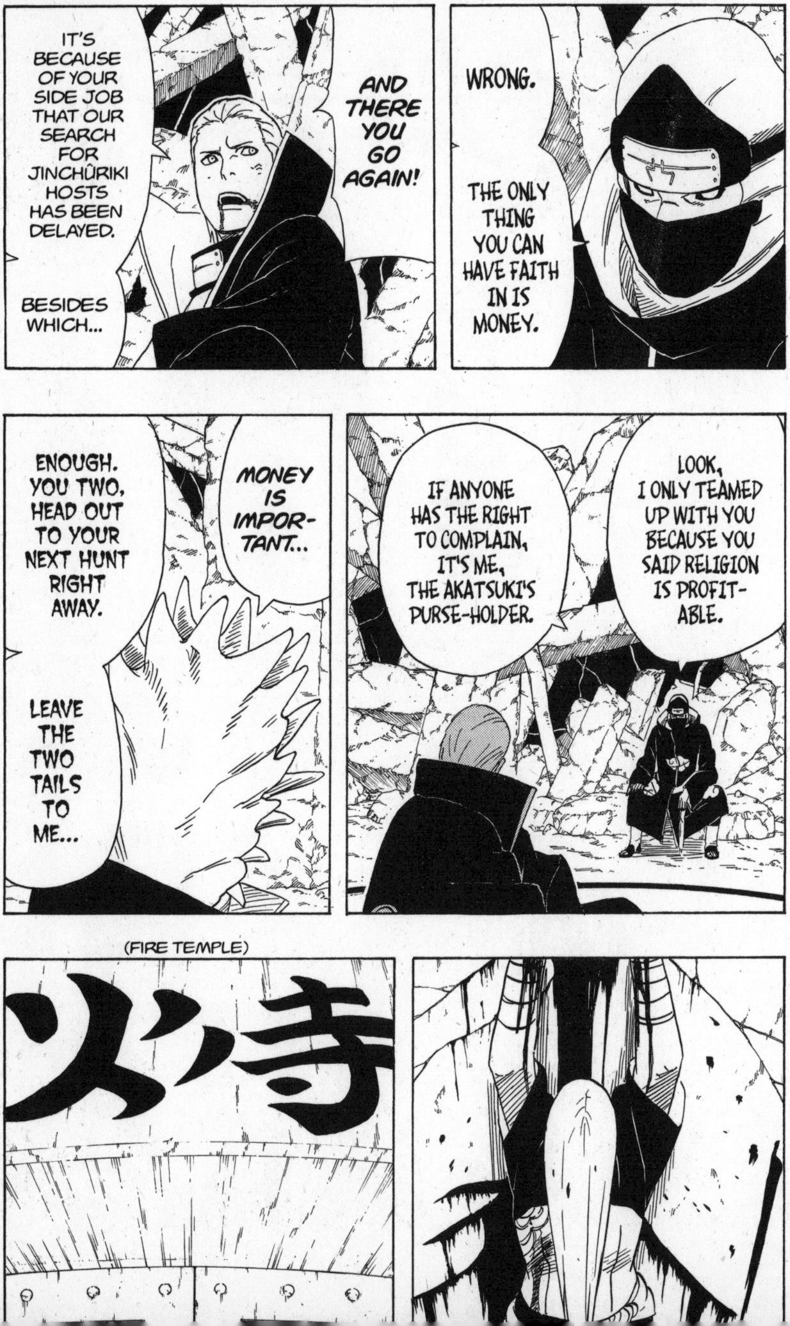

WRONG.
THE ONLY THING YOU CAN HAVE FAITH IN IS MONEY.
AND THERE YOU GO AGAIN!
IT'S BECAUSE OF YOUR SIDE JOB THAT OUR SEARCH FOR JINCHÛRIKI HOSTS HAS BEEN DELAYED.
BESIDES WHICH...
LOOK, I ONLY TEAMED UP WITH YOU BECAUSE YOU SAID RELIGION IS PROFIT-ABLE.
IF ANYONE HAS THE RIGHT TO COMPLAIN, IT'S ME, THE AKATSUKI'S PURSE-HOLDER.
MONEY IS IMPOR-TANT...
ENOUGH. YOU TWO, HEAD OUT TO YOUR NEXT HUNT RIGHT AWAY.
LEAVE THE TWO TAILS TO ME...
(FIRE TEMPLE)
火ノ寺

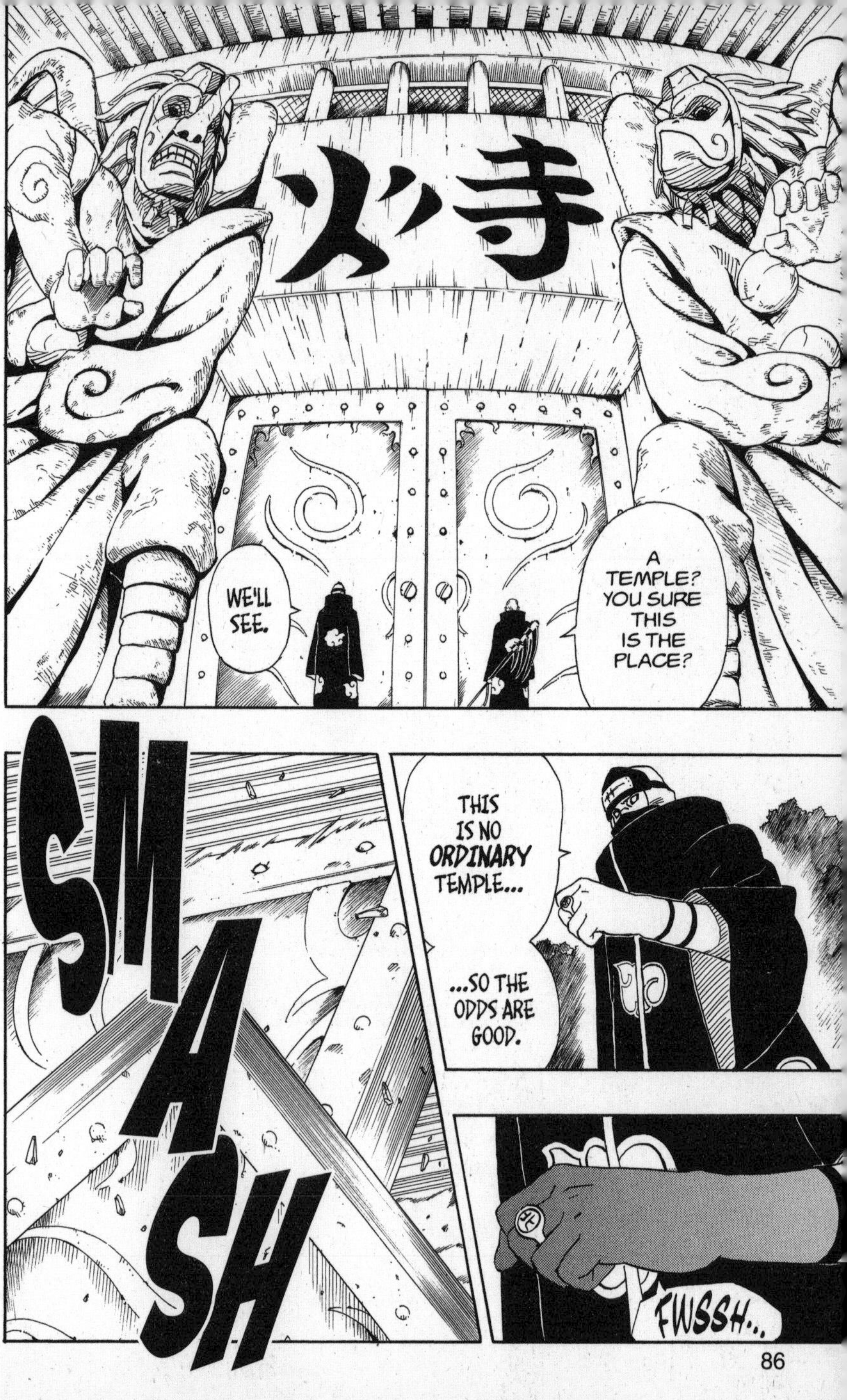
A TEMPLE? YOU SURE THIS IS THE PLACE?
WE'LL SEE.
THIS IS NO ORDINARY TEMPLE...
...SO THE ODDS ARE GOOD.
FWSSH...
SMASH

READ THIS WAY

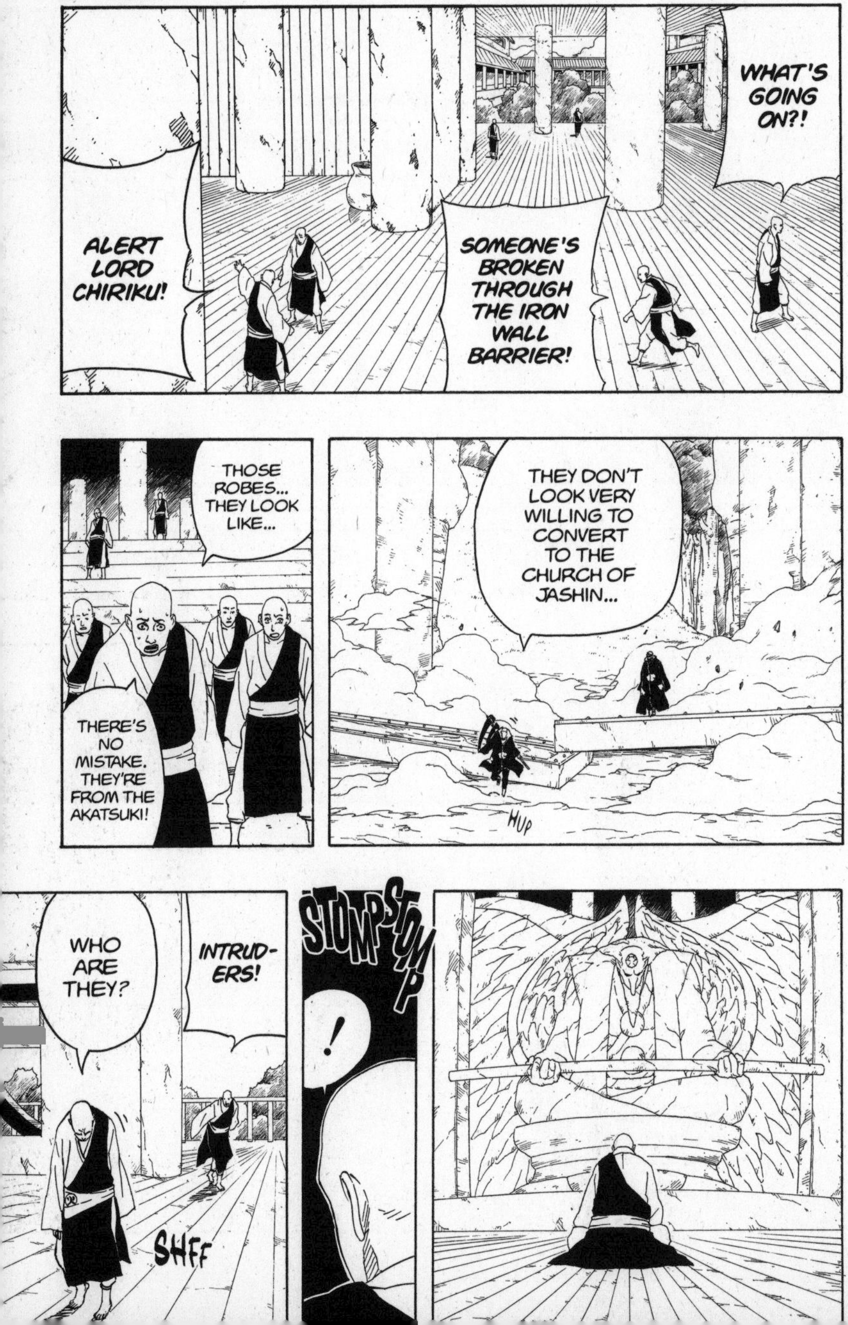
WHAT'S GOING ON?!
SOMEONE'S BROKEN THROUGH THE IRON WALL BARRIER!
ALERT LORD CHIRIKU!
THEY DON'T LOOK VERY WILLING TO CONVERT TO THE CHURCH OF JASHIN...
HUP
THOSE ROBES... THEY LOOK LIKE...
THERE'S NO MISTAKE. THEY'RE FROM THE AKATSUKI!
STOMP STOMP
!
INTRUD-ERS!
WHO ARE THEY?
SHFF

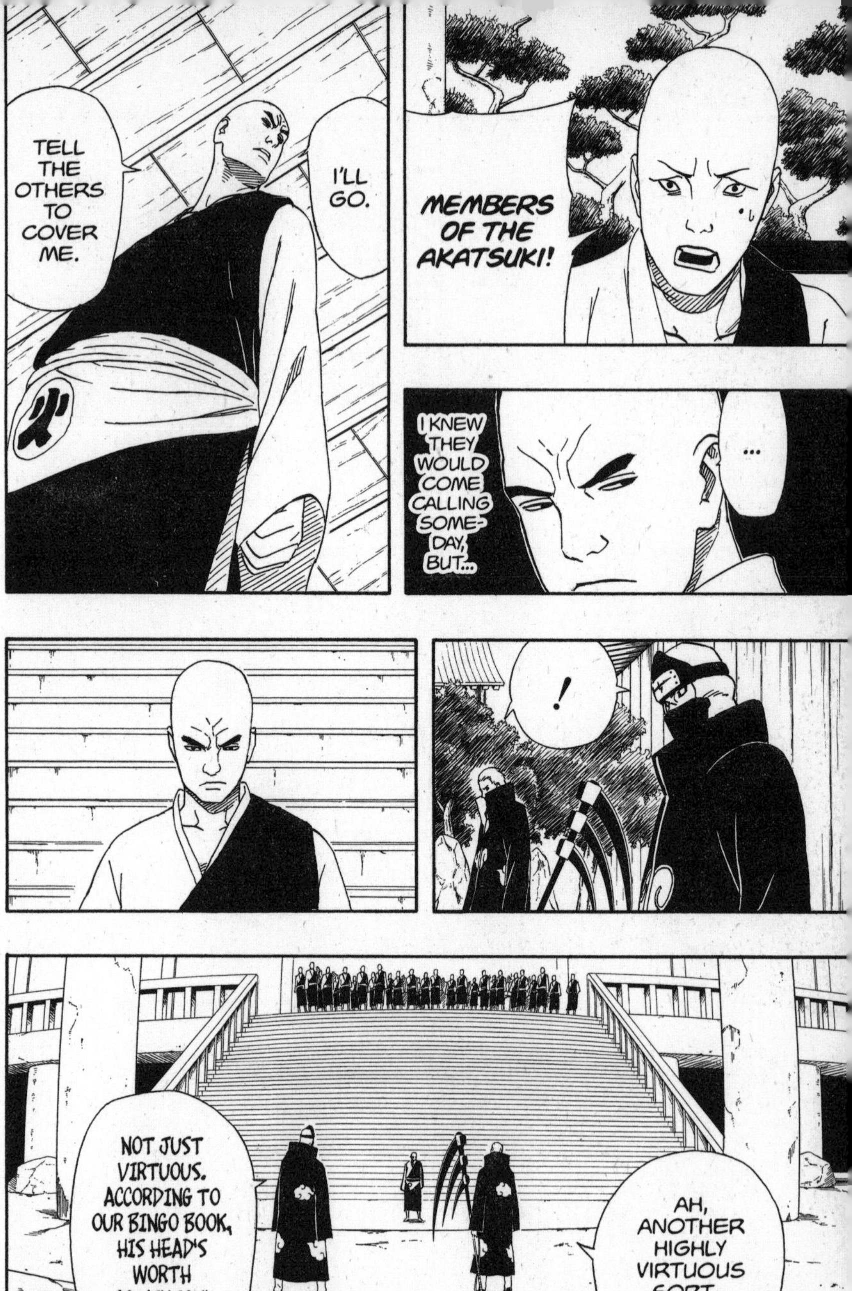
MEMBERS OF THE AKATSUKI!
...
I KNEW THEY WOULD COME CALLING SOME-DAY, BUT...
I'LL GO.
TELL THE OTHERS TO COVER ME.
!
AH, ANOTHER HIGHLY VIRTUOUS SORT...
NOT JUST VIRTUOUS. ACCORDING TO OUR BINGO BOOK, HIS HEAD'S WORTH 30 MILLION!

READ THIS WAY

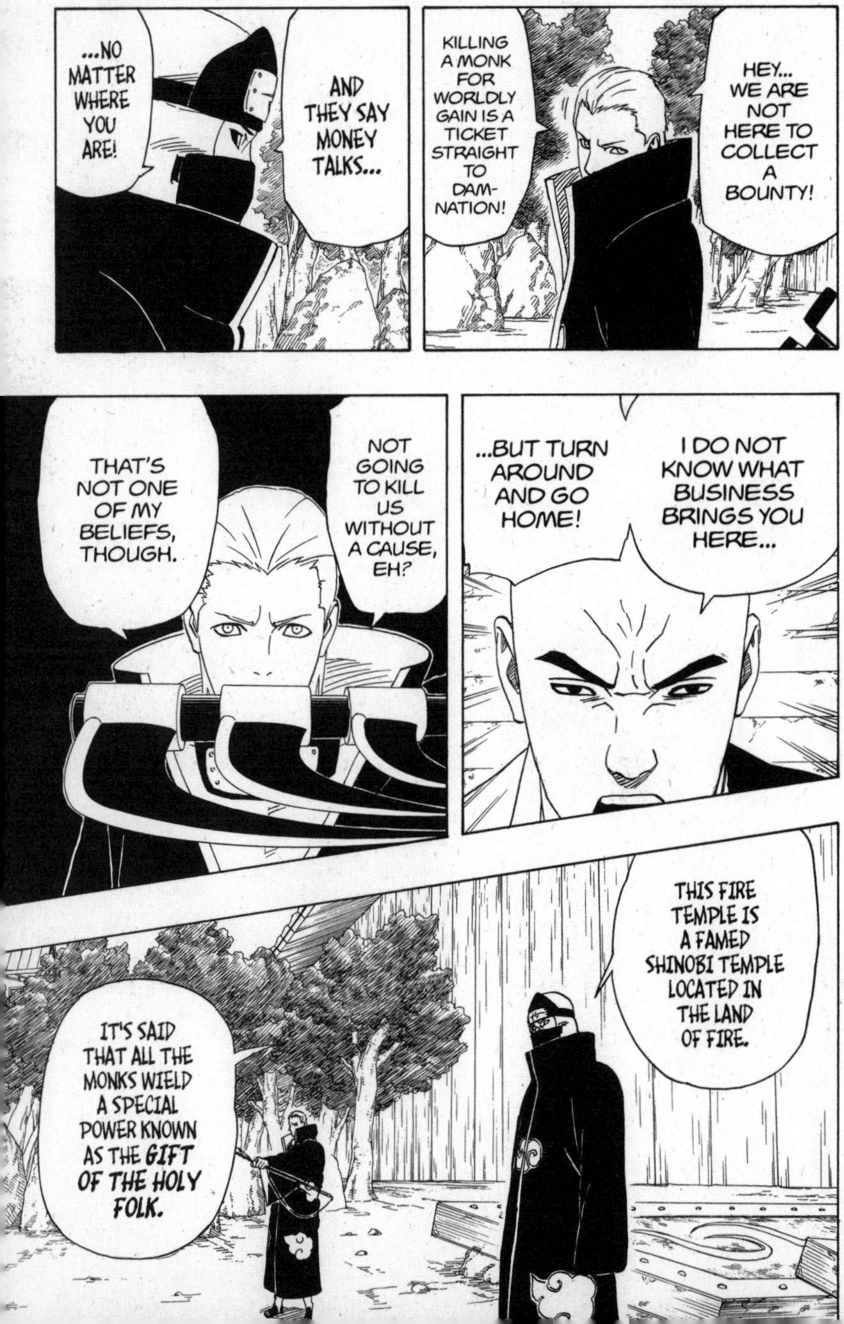

HEY... WE ARE NOT HERE TO COLLECT A BOUNTY!
KILLING A MONK FOR WORLDLY GAIN IS A TICKET STRAIGHT TO DAM-NATION!
AND THEY SAY MONEY TALKS...
...NO MATTER WHERE YOU ARE!
I DO NOT KNOW WHAT BUSINESS BRINGS YOU HERE...
...BUT TURN AROUND AND GO HOME!
NOT GOING TO KILL US WITHOUT A CAUSE, EH?
THAT'S NOT ONE OF MY BELIEFS, THOUGH.
THIS FIRE TEMPLE IS A FAMED SHINOBI TEMPLE LOCATED IN THE LAND OF FIRE.
IT'S SAID THAT ALL THE MONKS WIELD A SPECIAL POWER KNOWN AS THE GIFT OF THE HOLY FOLK.

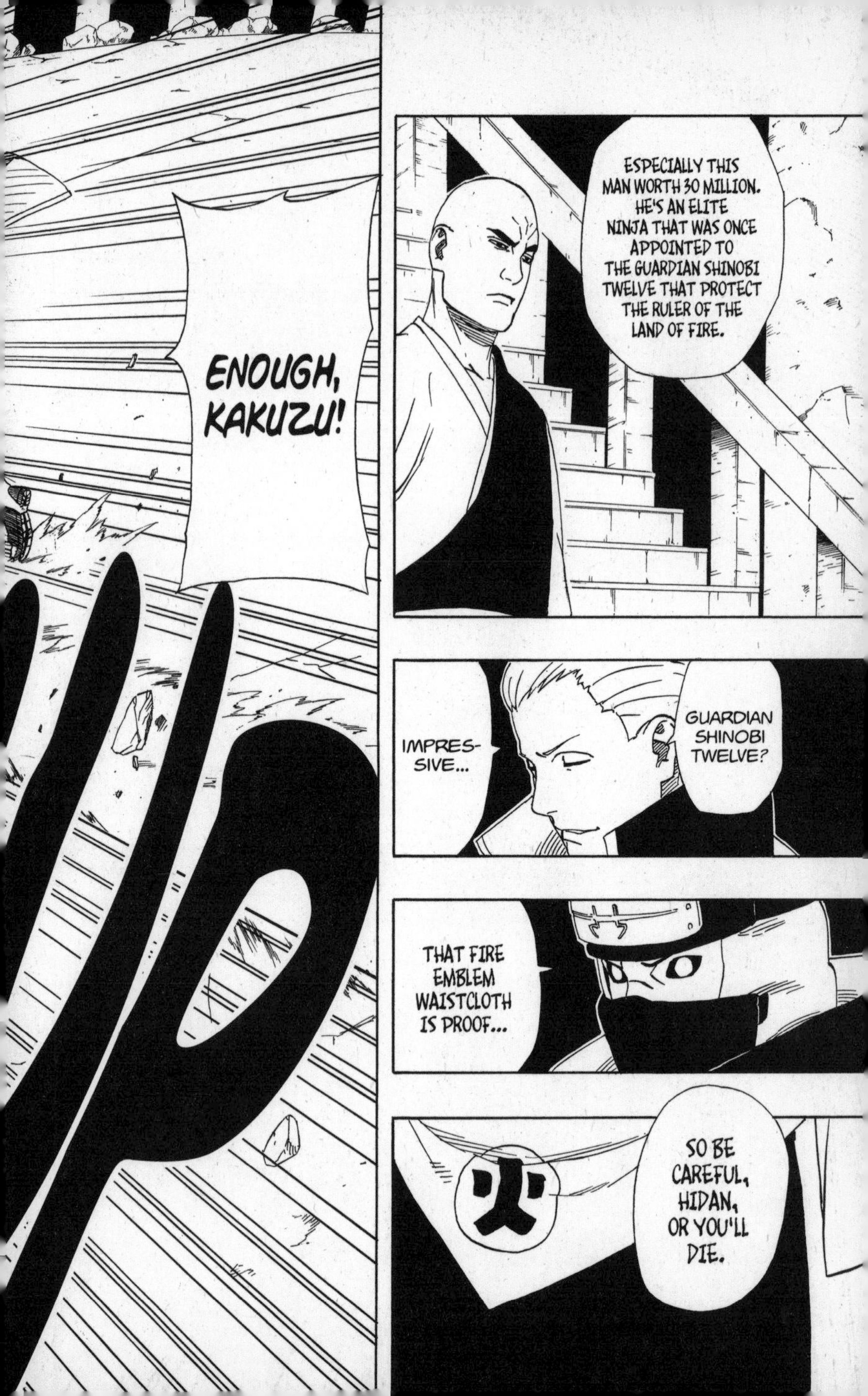
ESPECIALLY THIS MAN WORTH 30 MILLION. HE'S AN ELITE NINJA THAT WAS ONCE APPOINTED TO THE GUARDIAN SHINOBI TWELVE THAT PROTECT THE RULER OF THE LAND OF FIRE.
GUARDIAN SHINOBI TWELVE?
IMPRES-SIVE...
THAT FIRE EMBLEM WAISTCLOTH IS PROOF...
SO BE CAREFUL, HIDAN, OR YOU'LL DIE.
ENOUGH, KAKUZU!

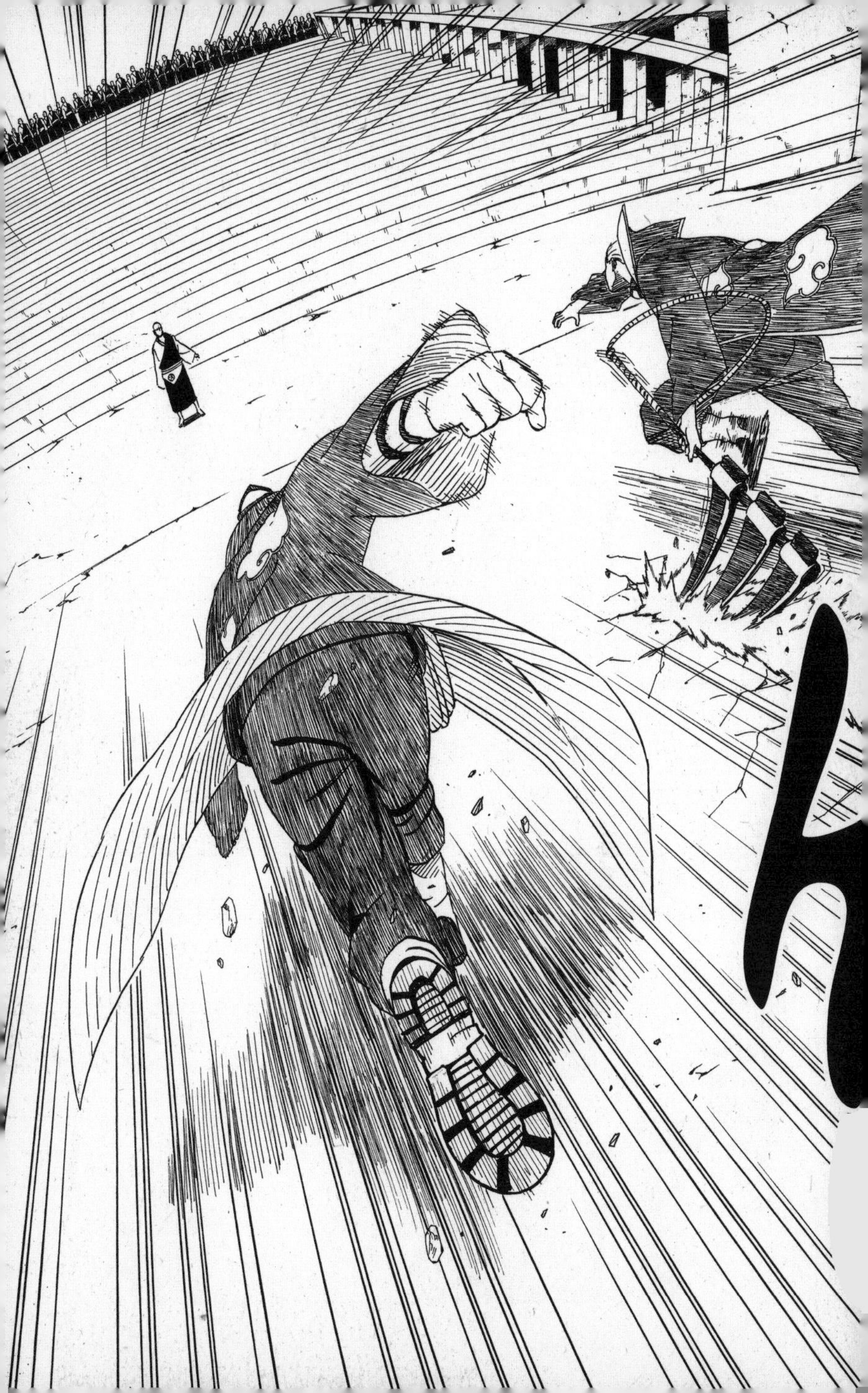

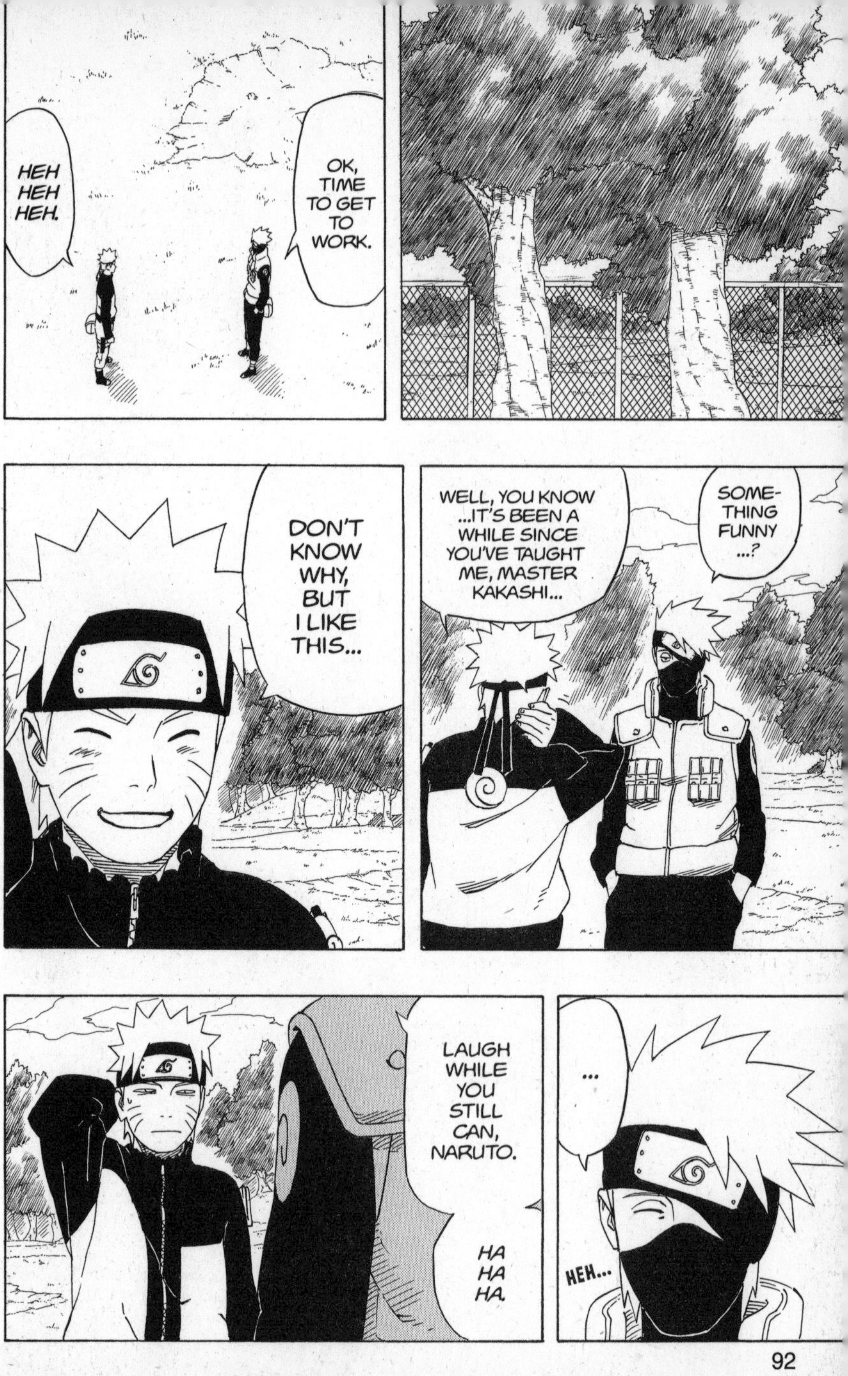
OK, TIME TO GET TO WORK.
HEH HEH HEH.
SOME-THING FUNNY ...?
WELL, YOU KNOW ...IT'S BEEN A WHILE SINCE YOU'VE TAUGHT ME, MASTER KAKASHI...
DON'T KNOW WHY, BUT I LIKE THIS...
...
HEH...
LAUGH WHILE YOU STILL CAN, NARUTO.
HA HA HA.

READ THIS WAY

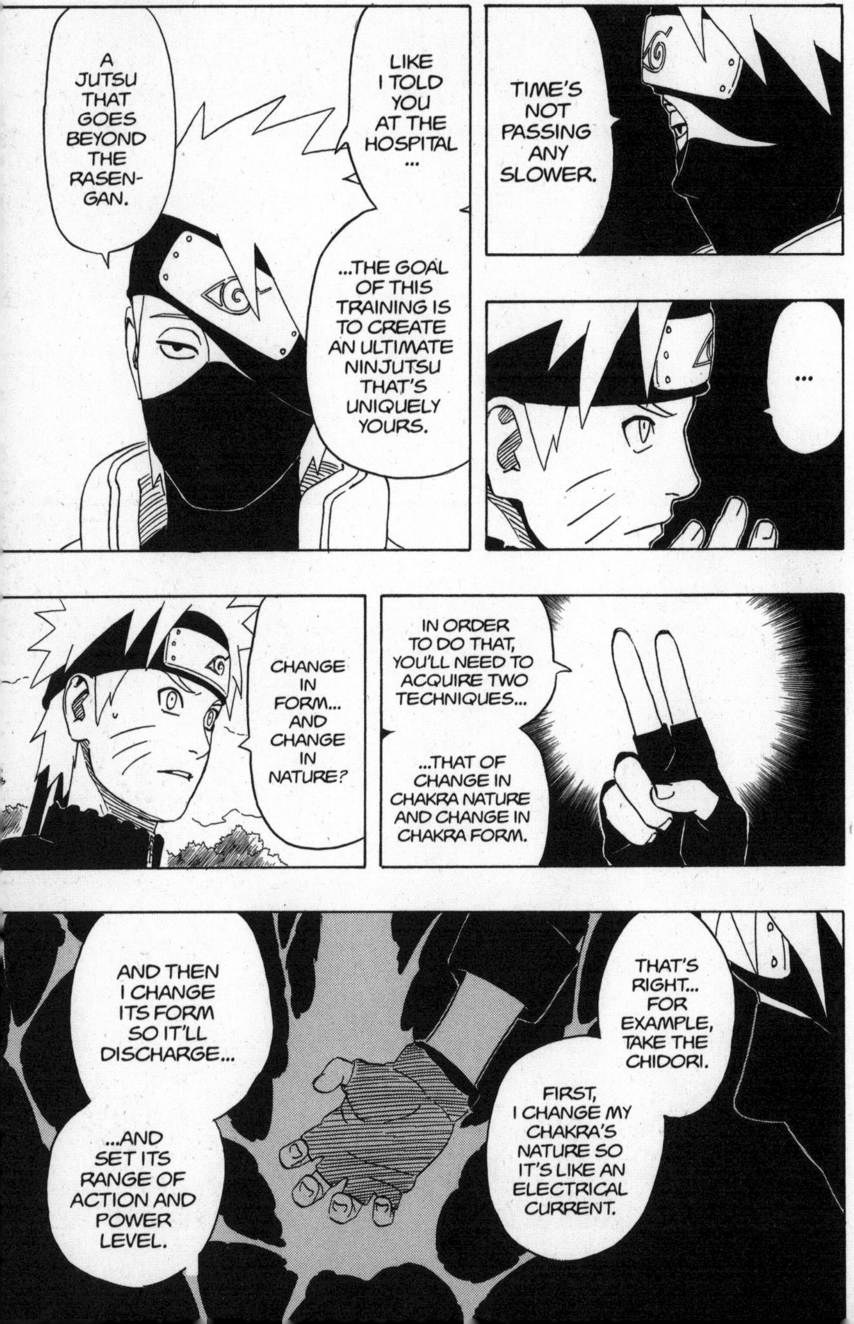
TIME'S NOT PASSING ANY SLOWER.
...
LIKE I TOLD YOU AT THE HOSPITAL ...
...THE GOAL OF THIS TRAINING IS TO CREATE AN ULTIMATE NINJUTSU THAT'S UNIQUELY YOURS.
A JUTSU THAT GOES BEYOND THE RASEN-GAN.
IN ORDER TO DO THAT, YOU'LL NEED TO ACQUIRE TWO TECHNIQUES...
...THAT OF CHANGE IN CHAKRA NATURE AND CHANGE IN CHAKRA FORM.
CHANGE IN FORM... AND CHANGE IN NATURE?
THAT'S RIGHT... FOR EXAMPLE, TAKE THE CHIDORI.
FIRST, I CHANGE MY CHAKRA'S NATURE SO IT'S LIKE AN ELECTRICAL CURRENT.
AND THEN I CHANGE ITS FORM SO IT'LL DISCHARGE...
...AND SET ITS RANGE OF ACTION AND POWER LEVEL.

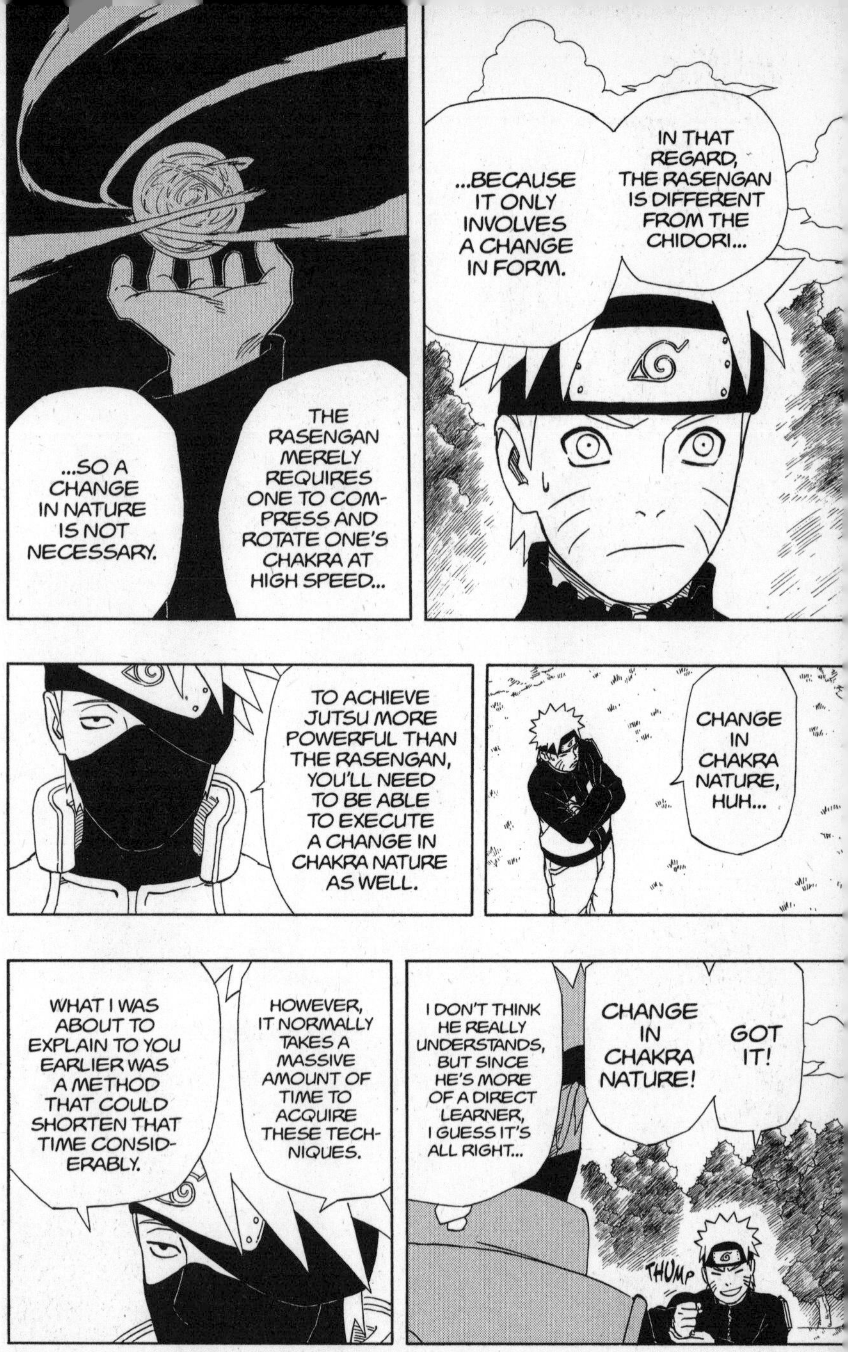

IN THAT REGARD, THE RASENGAN IS DIFFERENT FROM THE CHIDORI...
...BECAUSE IT ONLY INVOLVES A CHANGE IN FORM.
THE RASENGAN MERELY REQUIRES ONE TO COMPRESS AND ROTATE ONE'S CHAKRA AT HIGH SPEED...
...SO A CHANGE IN NATURE IS NOT NECESSARY.
CHANGE IN CHAKRA NATURE, HUH...
TO ACHIEVE JUTSU MORE POWERFUL THAN THE RASENGAN, YOU'LL NEED TO BE ABLE TO EXECUTE A CHANGE IN CHAKRA NATURE AS WELL.
GOT IT!
CHANGE IN CHAKRA NATURE!
THUMP
I DON'T THINK HE REALLY UNDERSTANDS, BUT SINCE HE'S MORE OF A DIRECT LEARNER, I GUESS IT'S ALL RIGHT...
HOWEVER, IT NORMALLY TAKES A MASSIVE AMOUNT OF TIME TO ACQUIRE THESE TECHNIQUES.
WHAT I WAS ABOUT TO EXPLAIN TO YOU EARLIER WAS A METHOD THAT COULD SHORTEN THAT TIME CONSIDERABLY.

READ THIS WAY

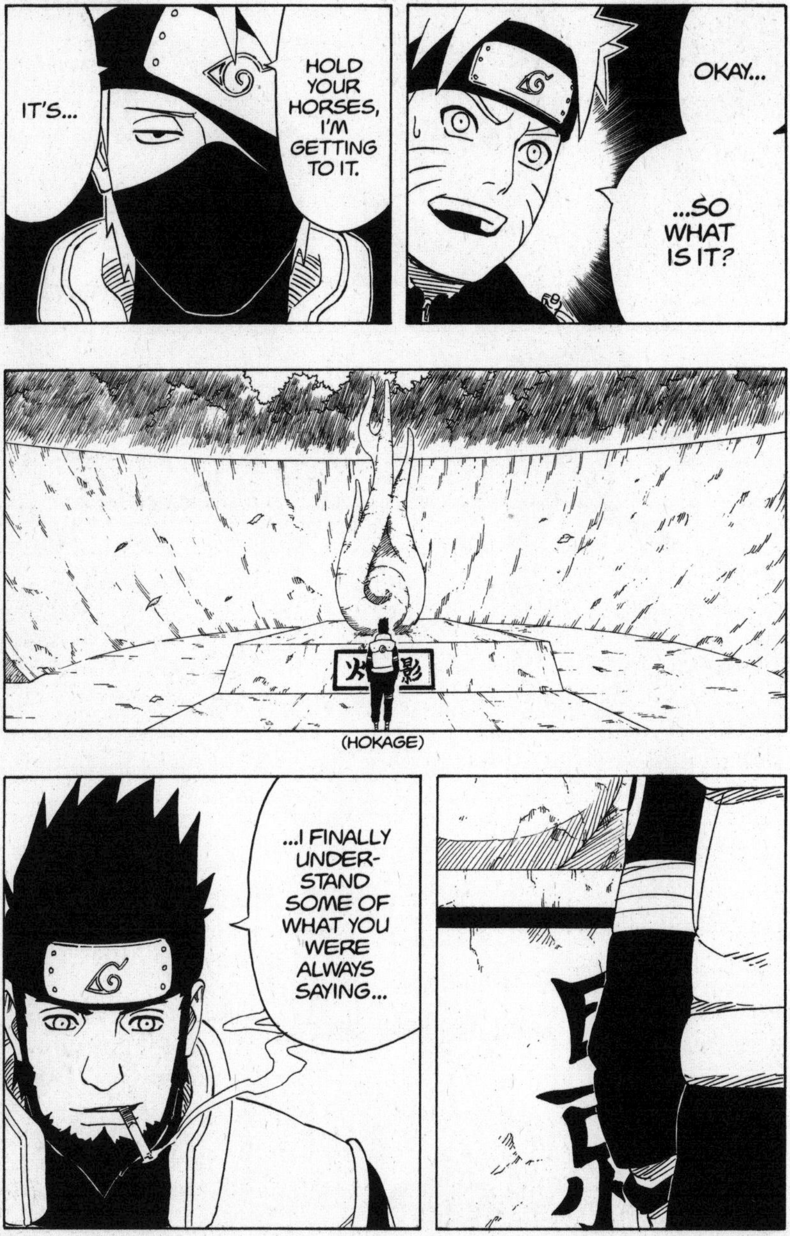
OKAY...
...SO WHAT IS IT?
HOLD YOUR HORSES, I'M GETTING TO IT.
IT'S...
火影
(HOKAGE)
...I FINALLY UNDER-STAND SOME OF WHAT YOU WERE ALWAYS SAYING...

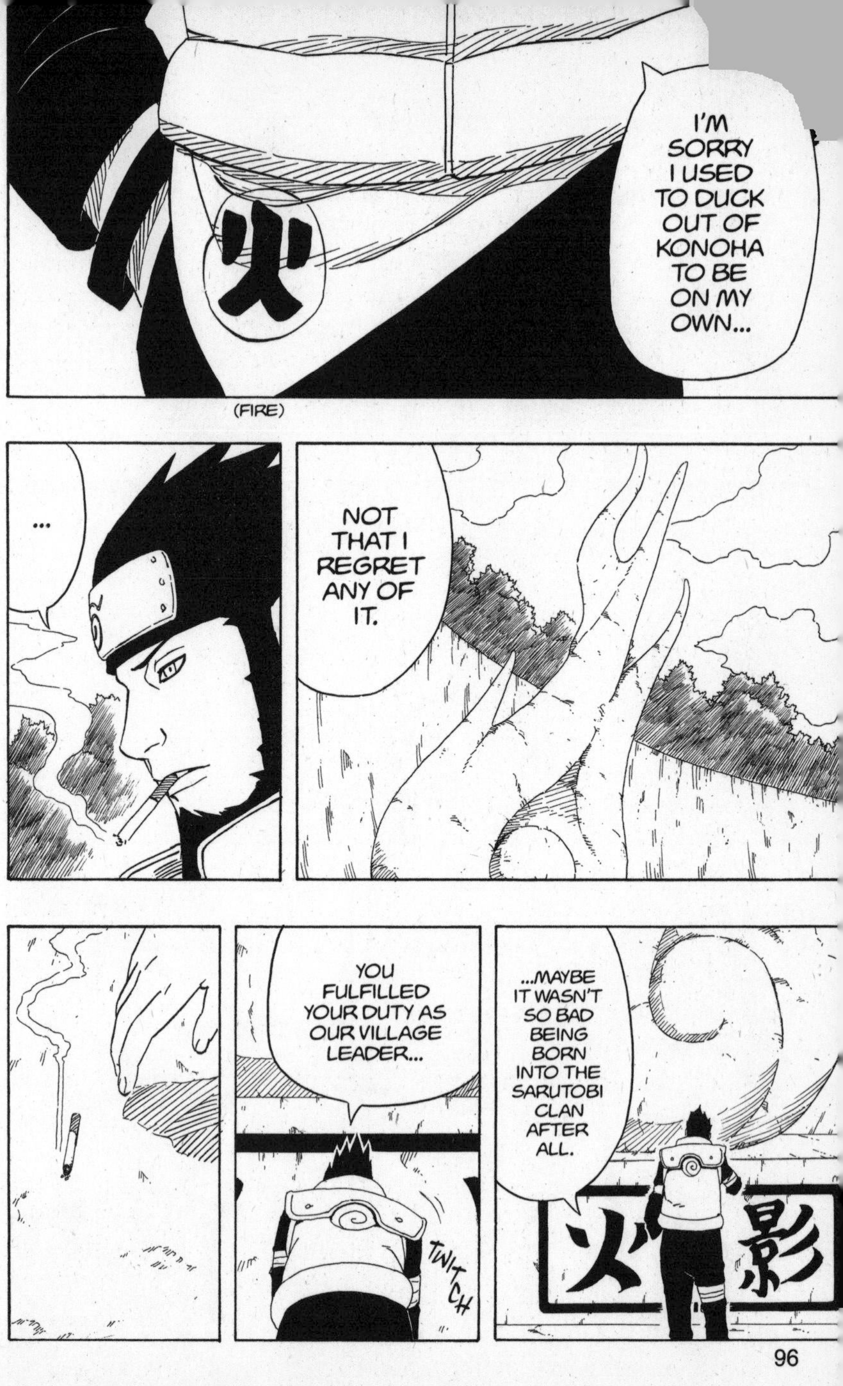
I'M SORRY I USED TO DUCK OUT OF KONOHA TO BE ON MY OWN...
(FIRE)
NOT THAT I REGRET ANY OF IT.
...
...MAYBE IT WASN'T SO BAD BEING BORN INTO THE SARUTOBI CLAN AFTER ALL.
YOU FULFILLED YOUR DUTY AS OUR VILLAGE LEADER...
TWITCH

...AND YOU REALLY WERE A COOL DAD...

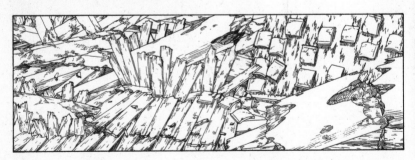

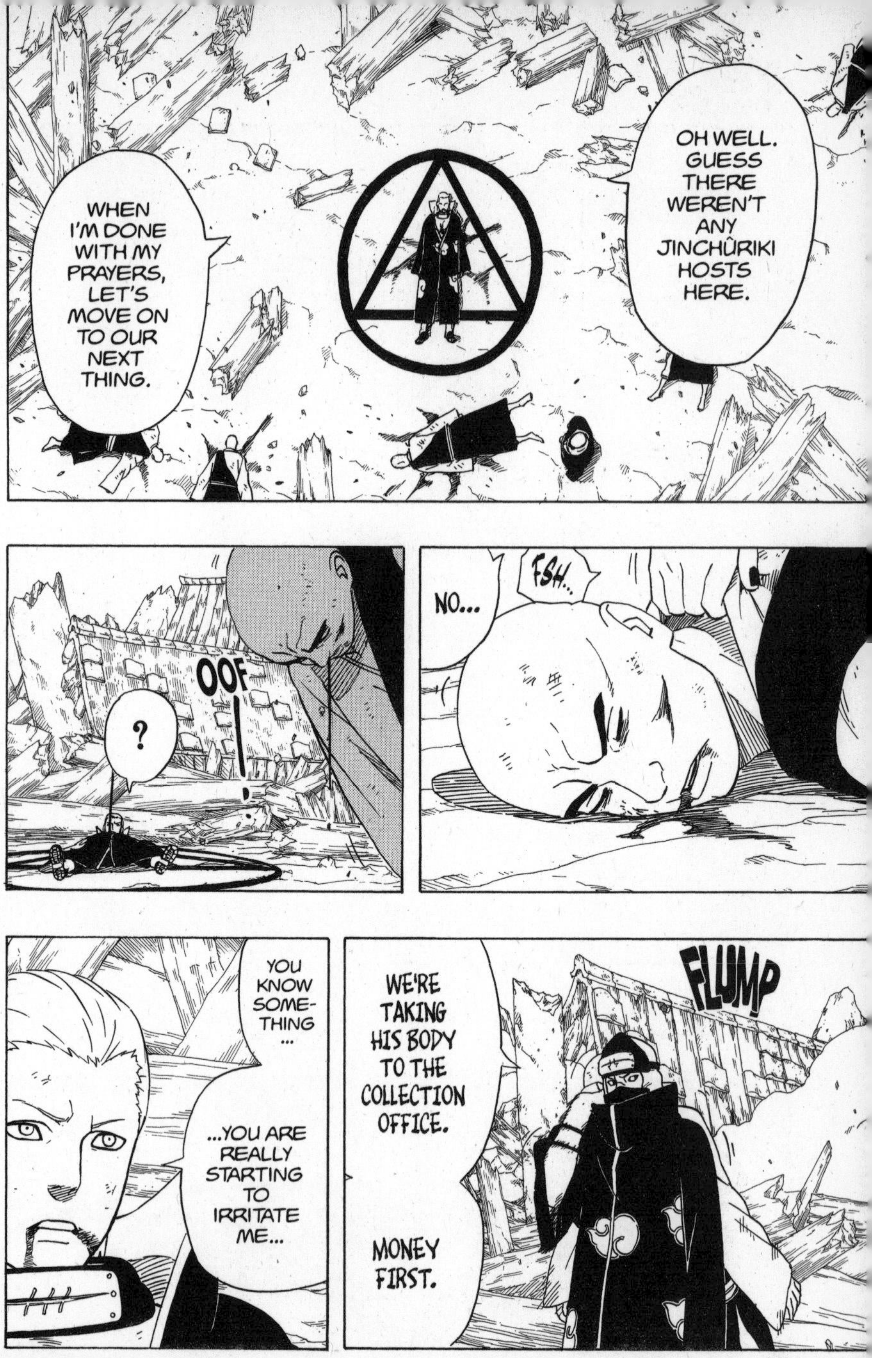
OH WELL. GUESS THERE WEREN'T ANY JINCHÛRIKI HOSTS HERE.
WHEN I'M DONE WITH MY PRAYERS, LET'S MOVE ON TO OUR NEXT THING.
FSH...
NO...
OOF
?
FLUMP
WE'RE TAKING HIS BODY TO THE COLLECTION OFFICE.
MONEY FIRST.
YOU KNOW SOME-THING...
...YOU ARE REALLY STARTING TO IRRITATE ME...

READ THIS WAY

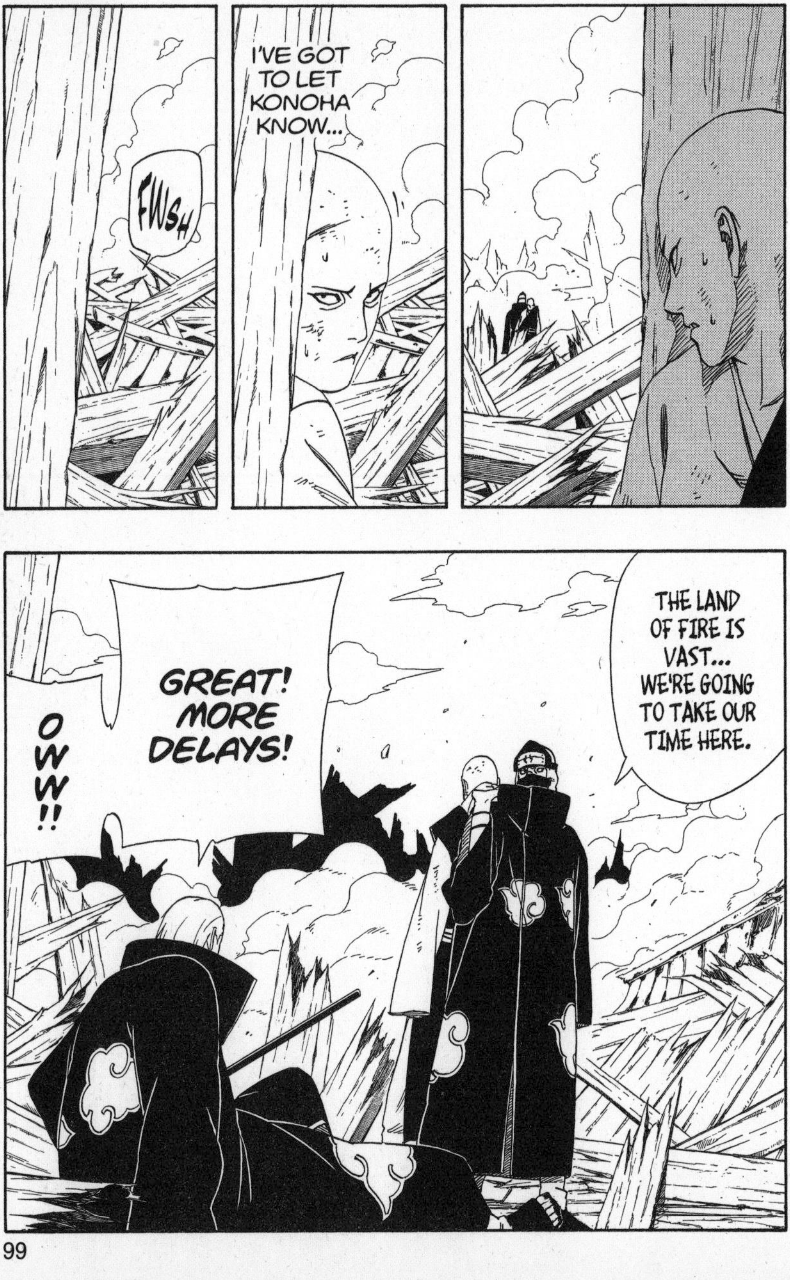
I'VE GOT TO LET KONOHA KNOW...
FWSH
THE LAND OF FIRE IS VAST... WE'RE GOING TO TAKE OUR TIME HERE.
GREAT! MORE DELAYS!
OWW!!

NARUTO

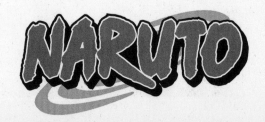

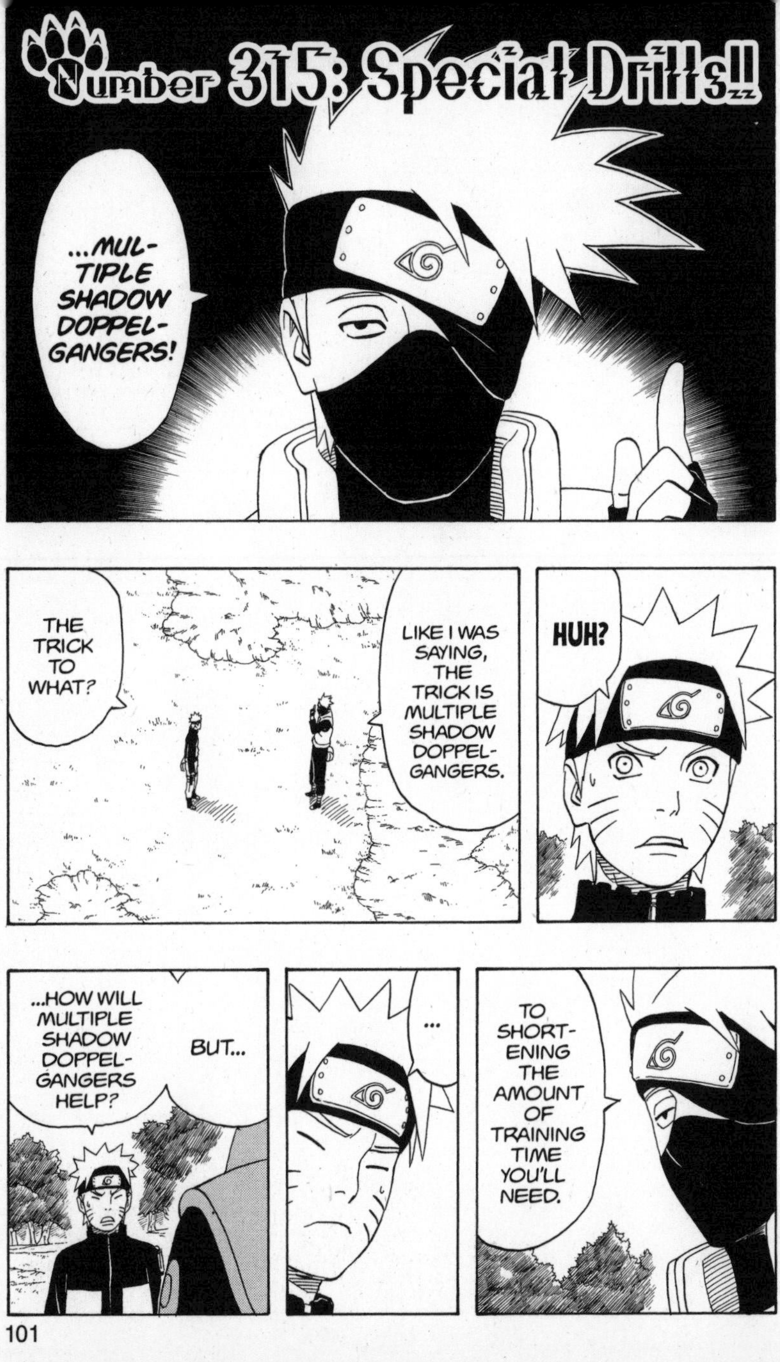
Number 315: Special Drills!!
...MULTIPLE SHADOW DOPPELGANGERS!
HUH?
LIKE I WAS SAYING, THE TRICK IS MULTIPLE SHADOW DOPPELGANGERS.
THE TRICK TO WHAT?
TO SHORTENING THE AMOUNT OF TRAINING TIME YOU'LL NEED.
...
BUT...
...HOW WILL MULTIPLE SHADOW DOPPELGANGERS HELP?

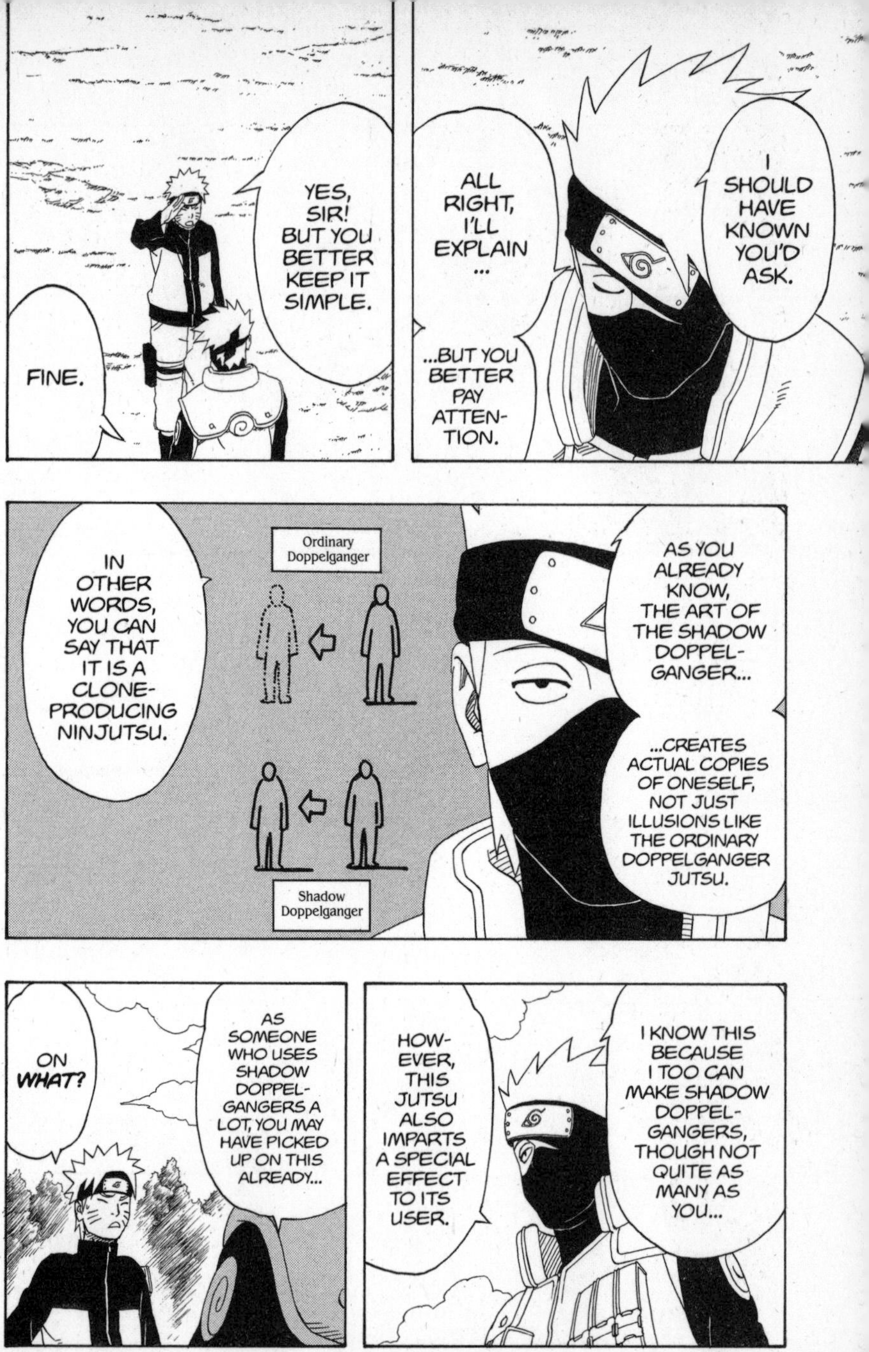
I SHOULD HAVE KNOWN YOU'D ASK.
ALL RIGHT, I'LL EXPLAIN ...
...BUT YOU BETTER PAY ATTEN-TION.
YES, SIR! BUT YOU BETTER KEEP IT SIMPLE.
FINE.
AS YOU ALREADY KNOW, THE ART OF THE SHADOW DOPPEL-GANGER...
...CREATES ACTUAL COPIES OF ONESELF, NOT JUST ILLUSIONS LIKE THE ORDINARY DOPPELGANGER JUTSU.
Ordinary Doppelganger
Shadow Doppelganger
IN OTHER WORDS, YOU CAN SAY THAT IT IS A CLONE-PRODUCING NINJUTSU.
I KNOW THIS BECAUSE I TOO CAN MAKE SHADOW DOPPEL-GANGERS, THOUGH NOT QUITE AS MANY AS YOU...
HOW-EVER, THIS JUTSU ALSO IMPARTS A SPECIAL EFFECT TO ITS USER.
AS SOMEONE WHO USES SHADOW DOPPEL-GANGERS A LOT, YOU MAY HAVE PICKED UP ON THIS ALREADY...
ON *WHAT?*

READ THIS WAY

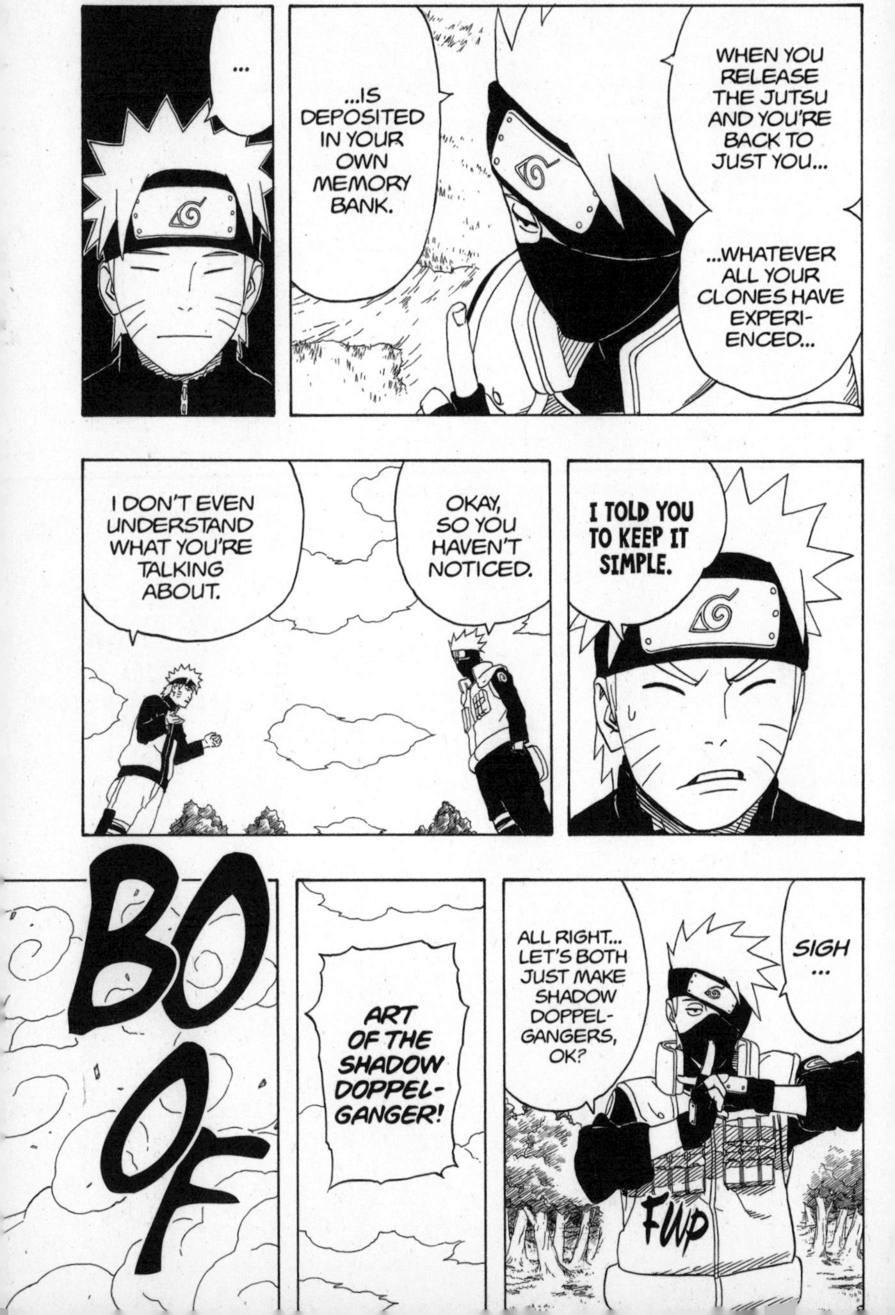
WHEN YOU RELEASE THE JUTSU AND YOU'RE BACK TO JUST YOU...
...WHATEVER ALL YOUR CLONES HAVE EXPERIENCED...
...IS DEPOSITED IN YOUR OWN MEMORY BANK.
...
I TOLD YOU TO KEEP IT SIMPLE.
OKAY, SO YOU HAVEN'T NOTICED.
I DON'T EVEN UNDERSTAND WHAT YOU'RE TALKING ABOUT.
SIGH ...
ALL RIGHT... LET'S BOTH JUST MAKE SHADOW DOPPELGANGERS, OK?
FWP
ART OF THE SHADOW DOPPELGANGER!
BOOF

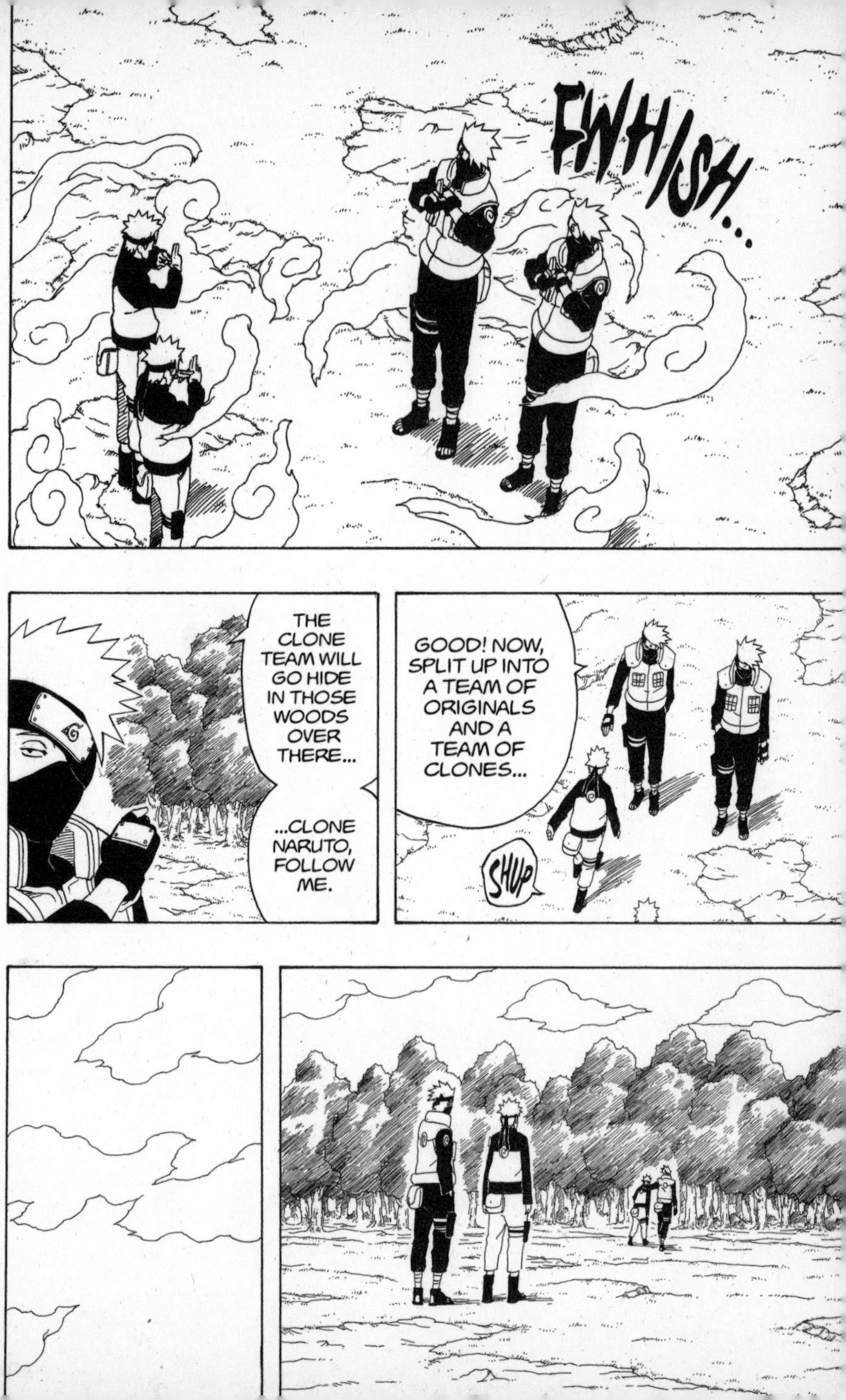
FWHISH...
GOOD! NOW, SPLIT UP INTO A TEAM OF ORIGINALS AND A TEAM OF CLONES...
SHUP
THE CLONE TEAM WILL GO HIDE IN THOSE WOODS OVER THERE...
...CLONE NARUTO, FOLLOW ME.

READ THIS WAY

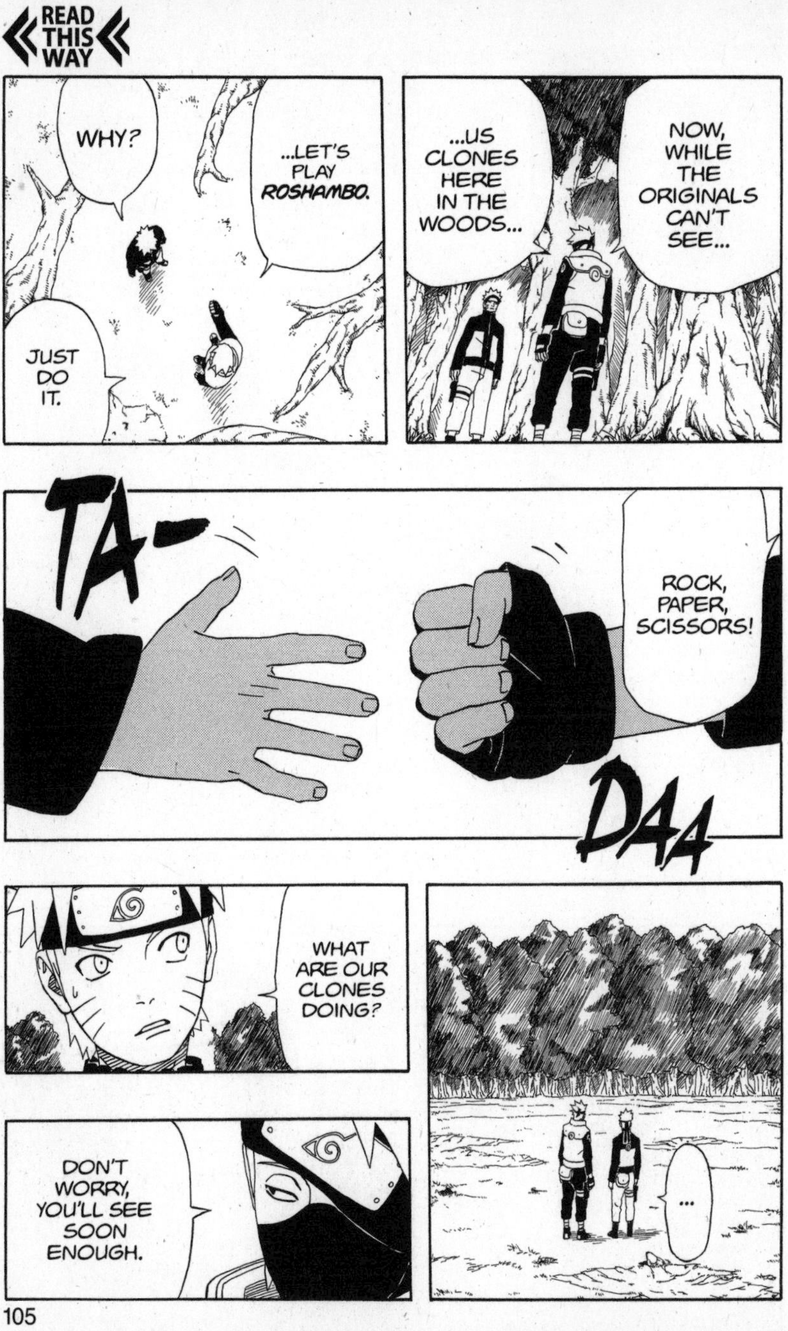

NOW, WHILE THE ORIGINALS CAN'T SEE...
...US CLONES HERE IN THE WOODS...
...LET'S PLAY ROSHAMBO.
WHY?
JUST DO IT.
ROCK, PAPER, SCISSORS!
TA-
DAA
...
WHAT ARE OUR CLONES DOING?
DON'T WORRY, YOU'LL SEE SOON ENOUGH.

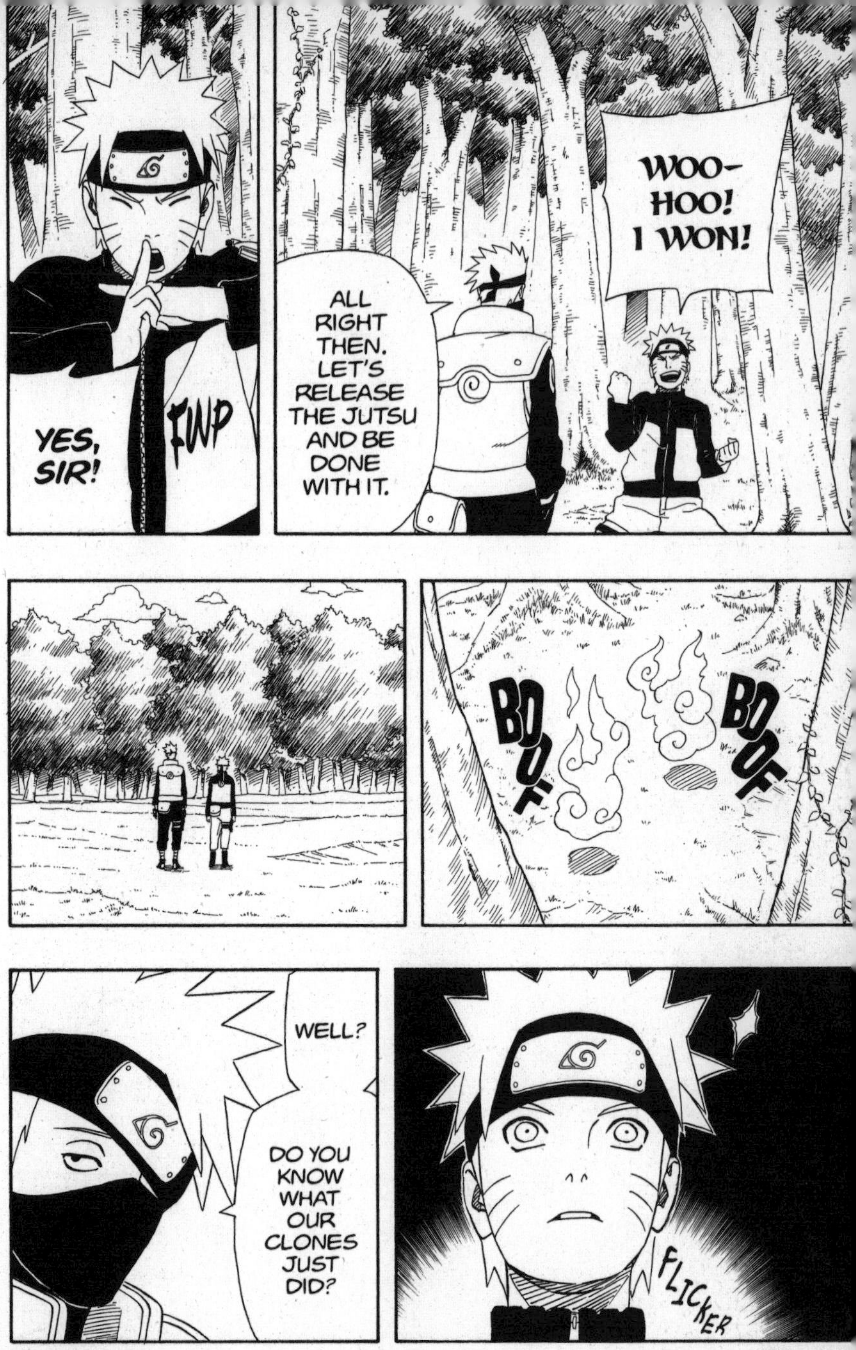
WOO-HOO! I WON!
ALL RIGHT THEN. LET'S RELEASE THE JUTSU AND BE DONE WITH IT.
FWP
YES, SIR!
BOOF
BOOF
FLICKER
WELL?
DO YOU KNOW WHAT OUR CLONES JUST DID?

READ THIS WAY

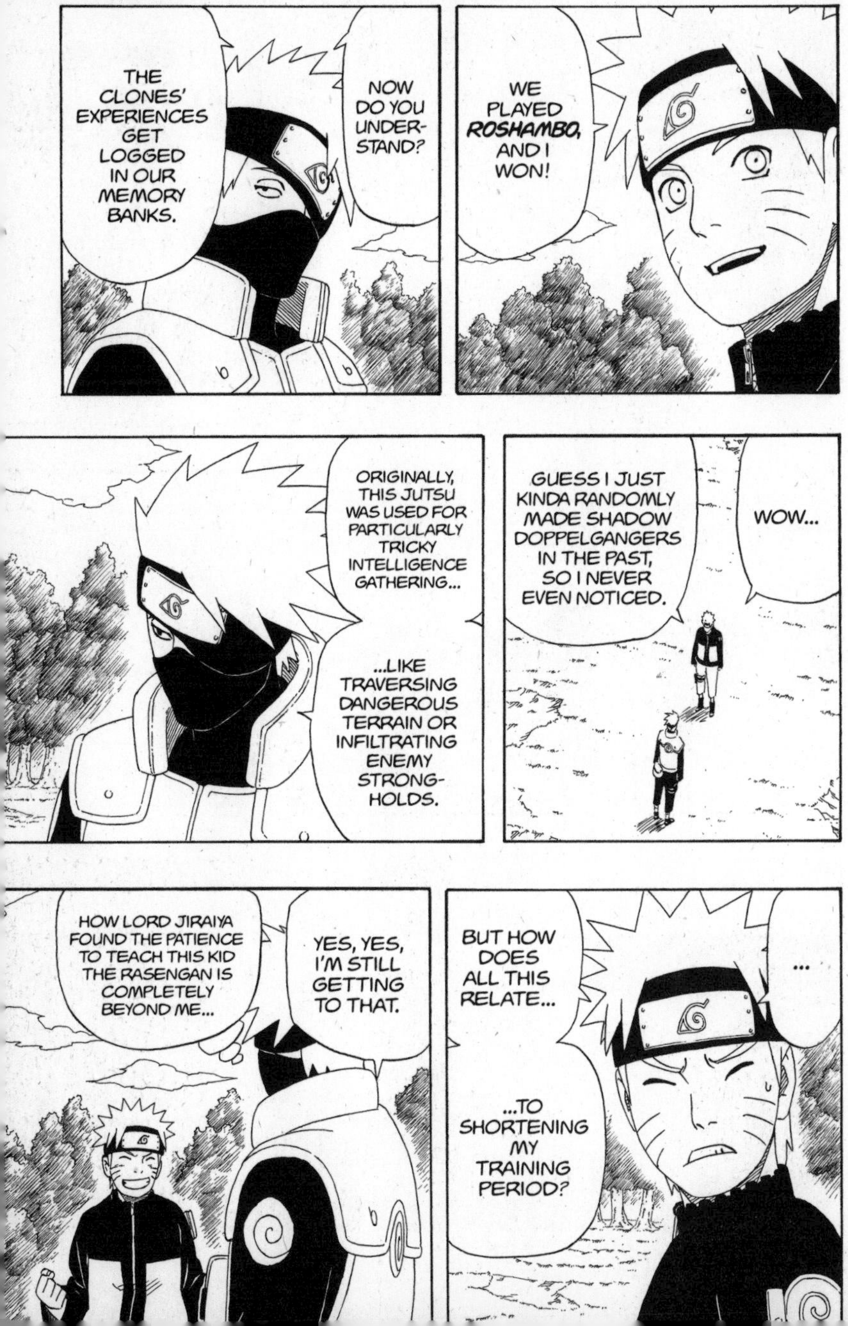
WE PLAYED ROSHAMBO, AND I WON!
NOW DO YOU UNDERSTAND?
THE CLONES' EXPERIENCES GET LOGGED IN OUR MEMORY BANKS.
WOW...
GUESS I JUST KINDA RANDOMLY MADE SHADOW DOPPELGANGERS IN THE PAST, SO I NEVER EVEN NOTICED.
ORIGINALLY, THIS JUTSU WAS USED FOR PARTICULARLY TRICKY INTELLIGENCE GATHERING...
...LIKE TRAVERSING DANGEROUS TERRAIN OR INFILTRATING ENEMY STRONG-HOLDS.
...
BUT HOW DOES ALL THIS RELATE...
...TO SHORTENING MY TRAINING PERIOD?
YES, YES, I'M STILL GETTING TO THAT.
HOW LORD JIRAIYA FOUND THE PATIENCE TO TEACH THIS KID THE RASENGAN IS COMPLETELY BEYOND ME...

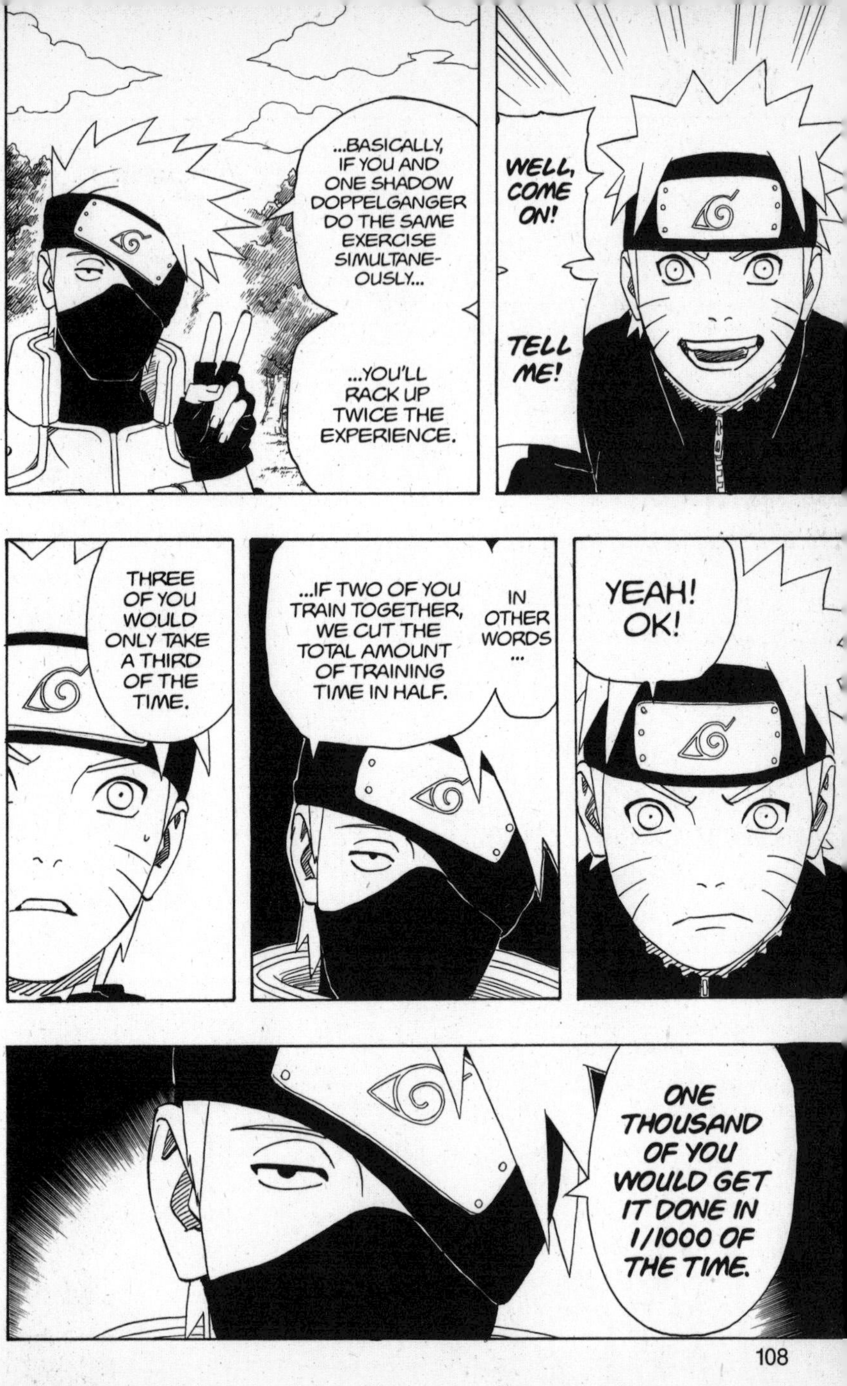
WELL, COME ON!
TELL ME!
...BASICALLY, IF YOU AND ONE SHADOW DOPPELGANGER DO THE SAME EXERCISE SIMULTANE-OUSLY...
...YOU'LL RACK UP TWICE THE EXPERIENCE.
YEAH! OK!
IN OTHER WORDS...
...IF TWO OF YOU TRAIN TOGETHER, WE CUT THE TOTAL AMOUNT OF TRAINING TIME IN HALF.
THREE OF YOU WOULD ONLY TAKE A THIRD OF THE TIME.
ONE THOUSAND OF YOU WOULD GET IT DONE IN 1/1000 OF THE TIME.

READ THIS WAY

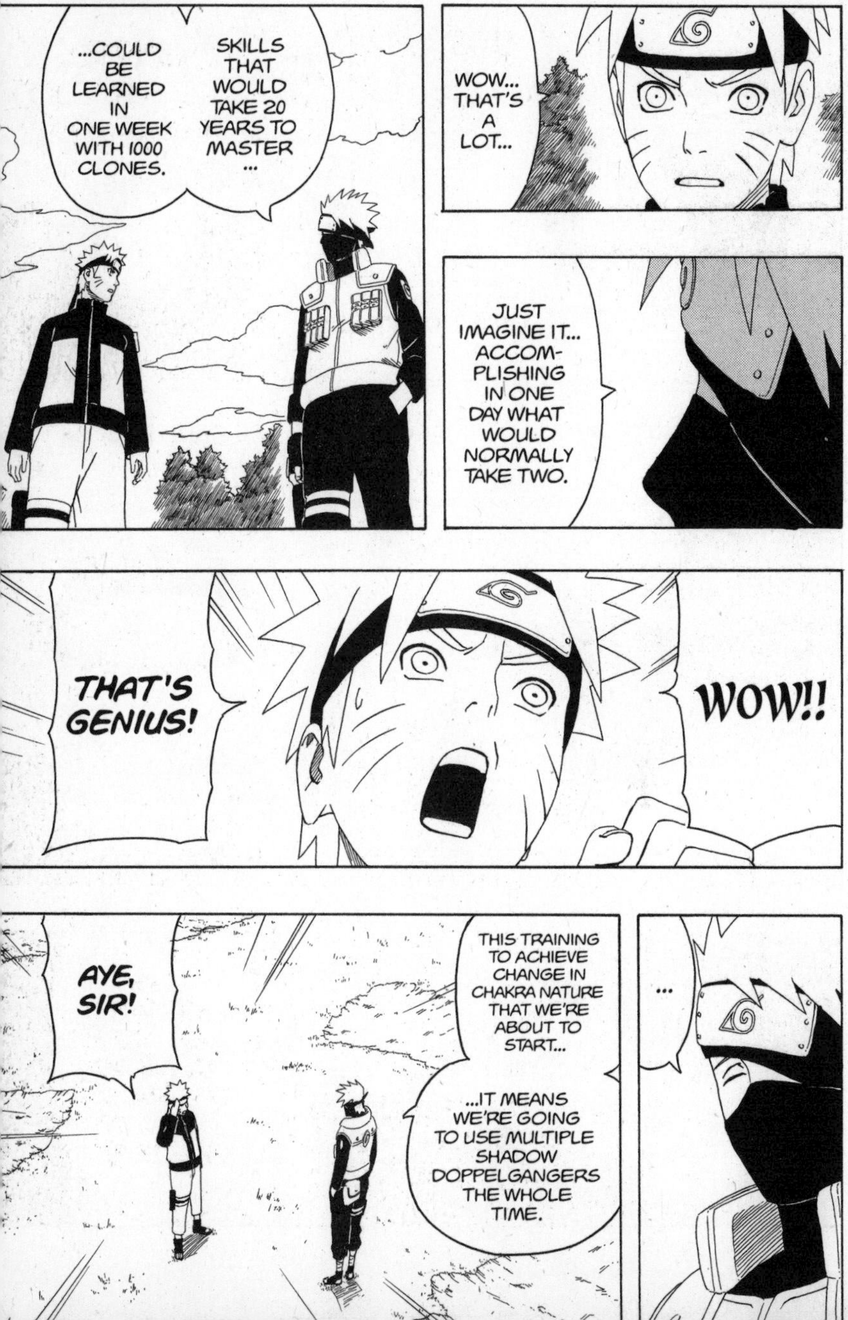

WOW... THAT'S A LOT...
JUST IMAGINE IT... ACCOM-PLISHING IN ONE DAY WHAT WOULD NORMALLY TAKE TWO.
SKILLS THAT WOULD TAKE 20 YEARS TO MASTER...
...COULD BE LEARNED IN ONE WEEK WITH 1000 CLONES.
WOW!!
THAT'S GENIUS!
...
THIS TRAINING TO ACHIEVE CHANGE IN CHAKRA NATURE THAT WE'RE ABOUT TO START...
...IT MEANS WE'RE GOING TO USE MULTIPLE SHADOW DOPPELGANGERS THE WHOLE TIME.
AYE, SIR!

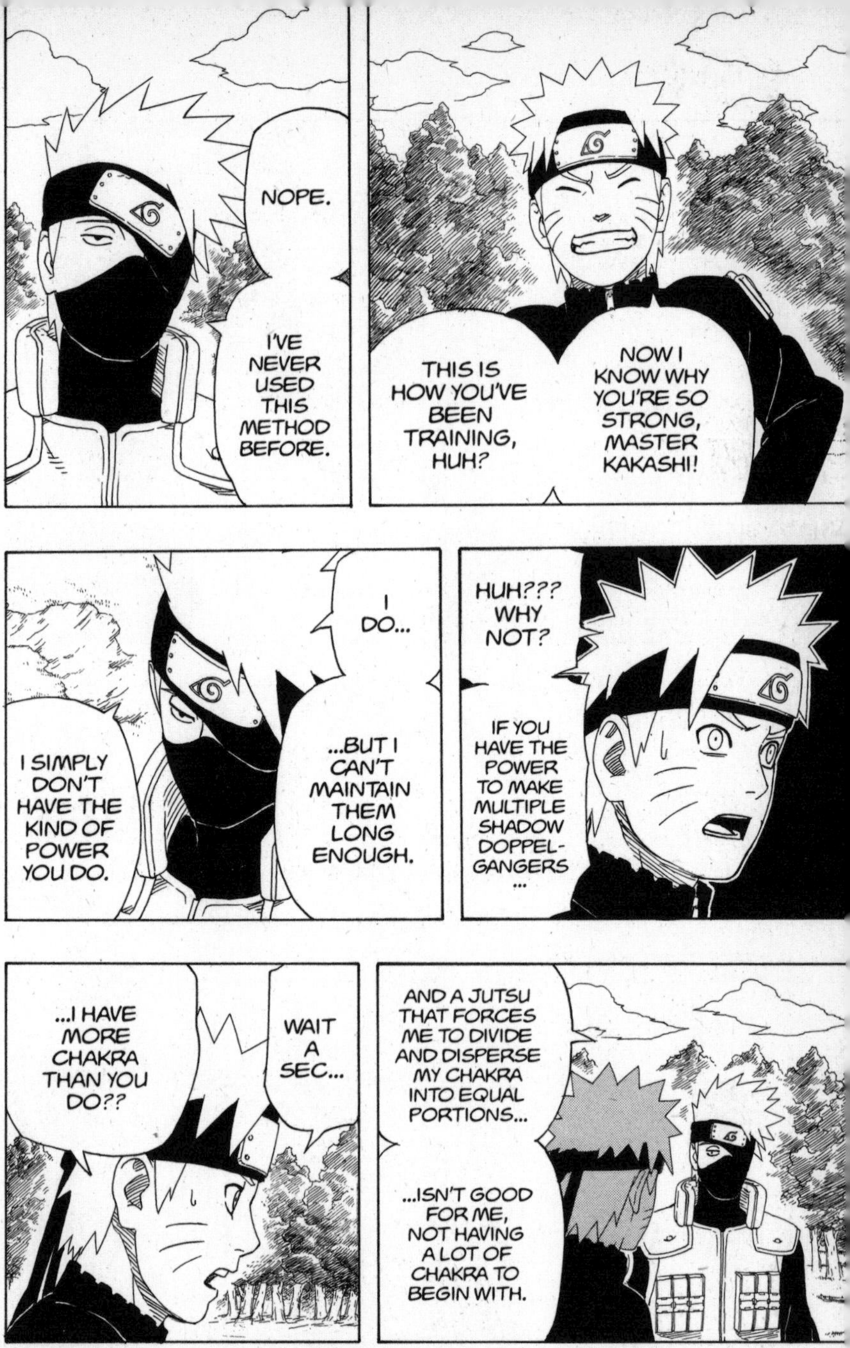
NOW I KNOW WHY YOU'RE SO STRONG, MASTER KAKASHI!
THIS IS HOW YOU'VE BEEN TRAINING, HUH?
NOPE.
I'VE NEVER USED THIS METHOD BEFORE.
HUH??? WHY NOT?
IF YOU HAVE THE POWER TO MAKE MULTIPLE SHADOW DOPPEL-GANGERS...
I DO...
...BUT I CAN'T MAINTAIN THEM LONG ENOUGH.
I SIMPLY DON'T HAVE THE KIND OF POWER YOU DO.
AND A JUTSU THAT FORCES ME TO DIVIDE AND DISPERSE MY CHAKRA INTO EQUAL PORTIONS...
...ISN'T GOOD FOR ME, NOT HAVING A LOT OF CHAKRA TO BEGIN WITH.
WAIT A SEC...
...I HAVE MORE CHAKRA THAN YOU DO??

READ THIS WAY

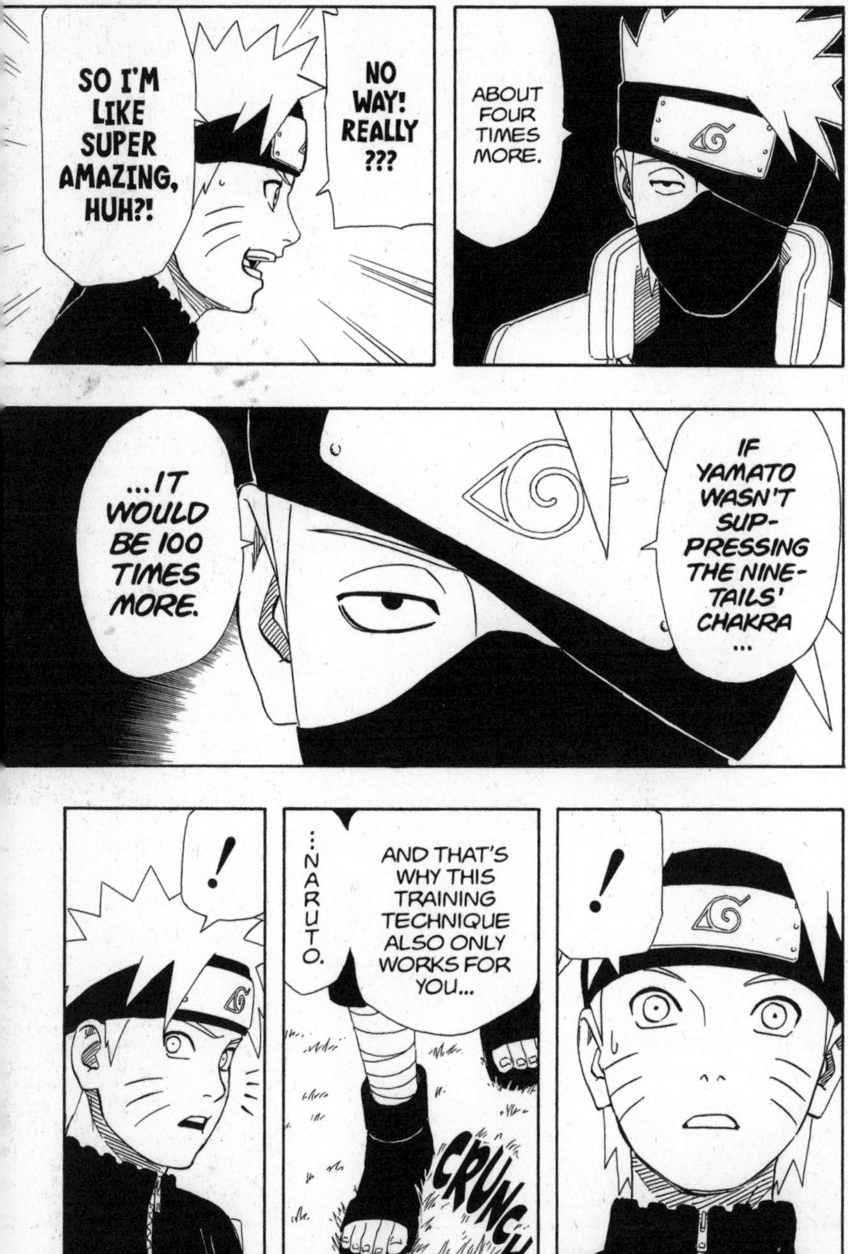
ABOUT FOUR TIMES MORE.
NO WAY! REALLY ???
SO I'M LIKE SUPER AMAZING, HUH?!
IF YAMATO WASN'T SUP-PRESSING THE NINE-TAILS' CHAKRA ...
...IT WOULD BE 100 TIMES MORE.
!
AND THAT'S WHY THIS TRAINING TECHNIQUE ALSO ONLY WORKS FOR YOU...
...NARUTO.
CRUNCH
!

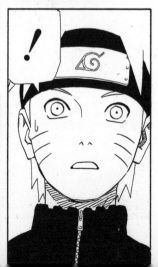

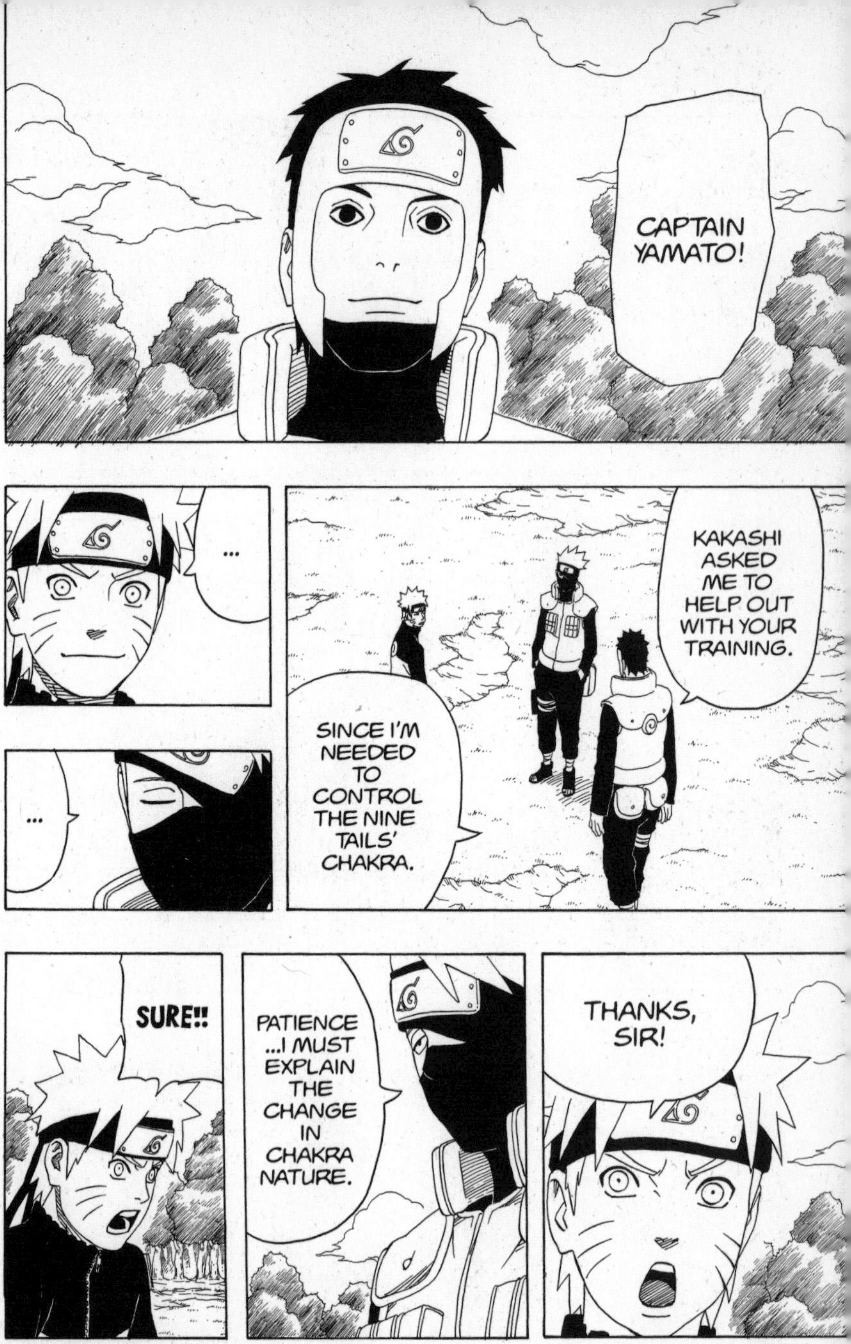
CAPTAIN YAMATO!
KAKASHI ASKED ME TO HELP OUT WITH YOUR TRAINING.
SINCE I'M NEEDED TO CONTROL THE NINE TAILS' CHAKRA.
...
...
THANKS, SIR!
PATIENCE ...I MUST EXPLAIN THE CHANGE IN CHAKRA NATURE.
SURE!!

READ THIS WAY

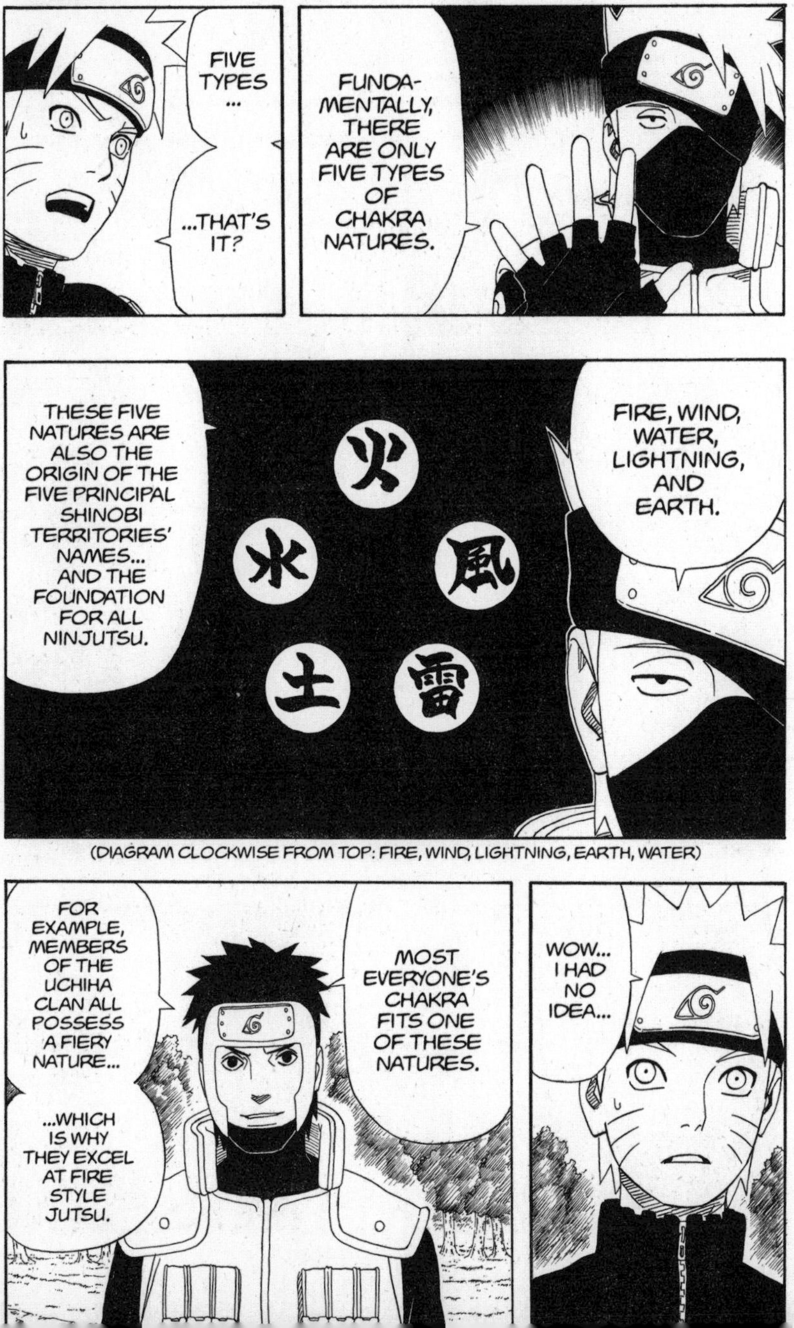
FUNDAMENTALLY, THERE ARE ONLY FIVE TYPES OF CHAKRA NATURES.
FIVE TYPES...
...THAT'S IT?
FIRE, WIND, WATER, LIGHTNING, AND EARTH.
火
風
雷
土
水
THESE FIVE NATURES ARE ALSO THE ORIGIN OF THE FIVE PRINCIPAL SHINOBI TERRITORIES' NAMES... AND THE FOUNDATION FOR ALL NINJUTSU.
(DIAGRAM CLOCKWISE FROM TOP: FIRE, WIND, LIGHTNING, EARTH, WATER)
WOW... I HAD NO IDEA...
MOST EVERYONE'S CHAKRA FITS ONE OF THESE NATURES.
FOR EXAMPLE, MEMBERS OF THE UCHIHA CLAN ALL POSSESS A FIERY NATURE...
...WHICH IS WHY THEY EXCEL AT FIRE STYLE JUTSU.

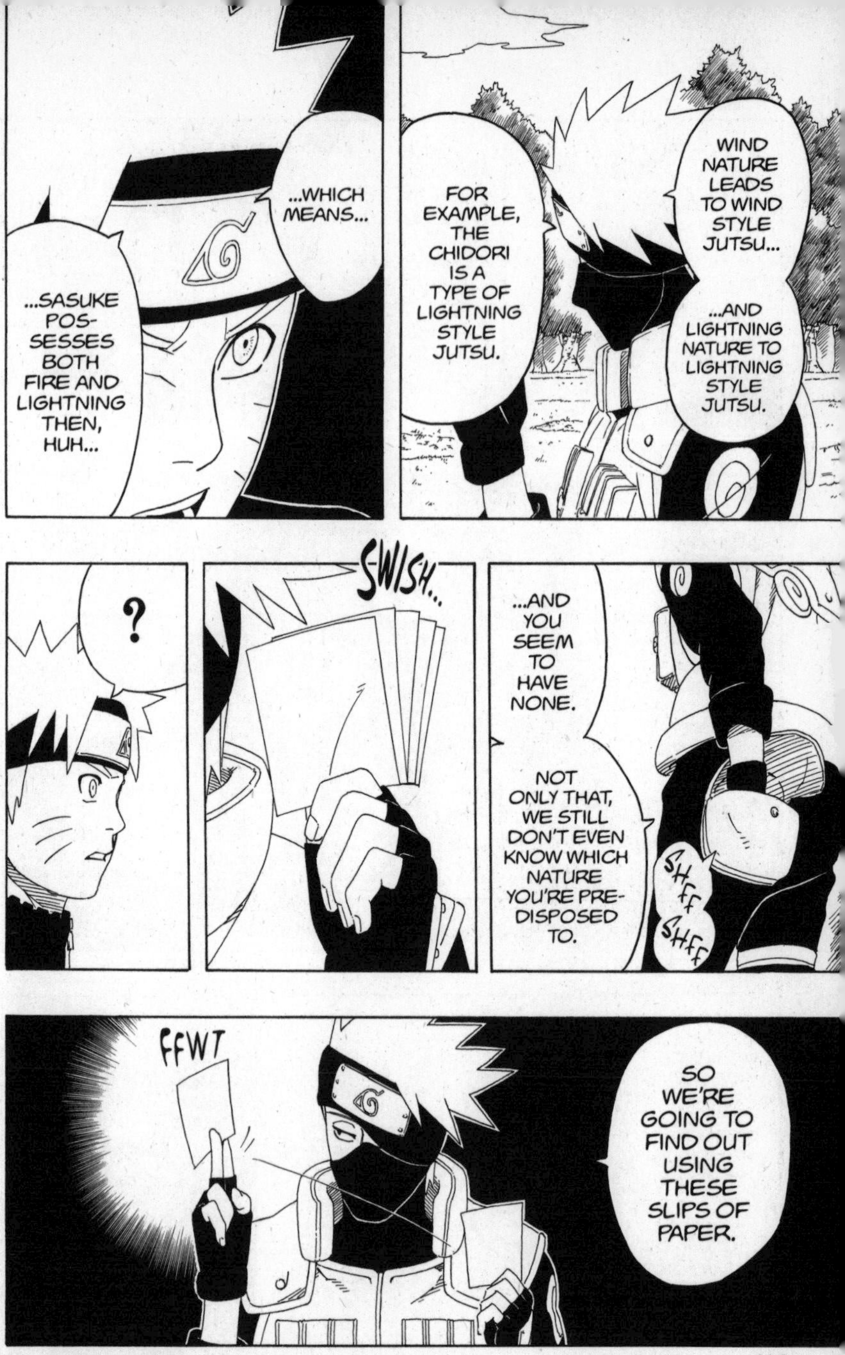
WIND NATURE LEADS TO WIND STYLE JUTSU...
...AND LIGHTNING NATURE TO LIGHTNING STYLE JUTSU.
FOR EXAMPLE, THE CHIDORI IS A TYPE OF LIGHTNING STYLE JUTSU.
...WHICH MEANS...
...SASUKE POSSESSES BOTH FIRE AND LIGHTNING THEN, HUH...
...AND YOU SEEM TO HAVE NONE.
NOT ONLY THAT, WE STILL DON'T EVEN KNOW WHICH NATURE YOU'RE PREDISPOSED TO.
SHFF SHFF
SWISH...
?
SO WE'RE GOING TO FIND OUT USING THESE SLIPS OF PAPER.
FFWT

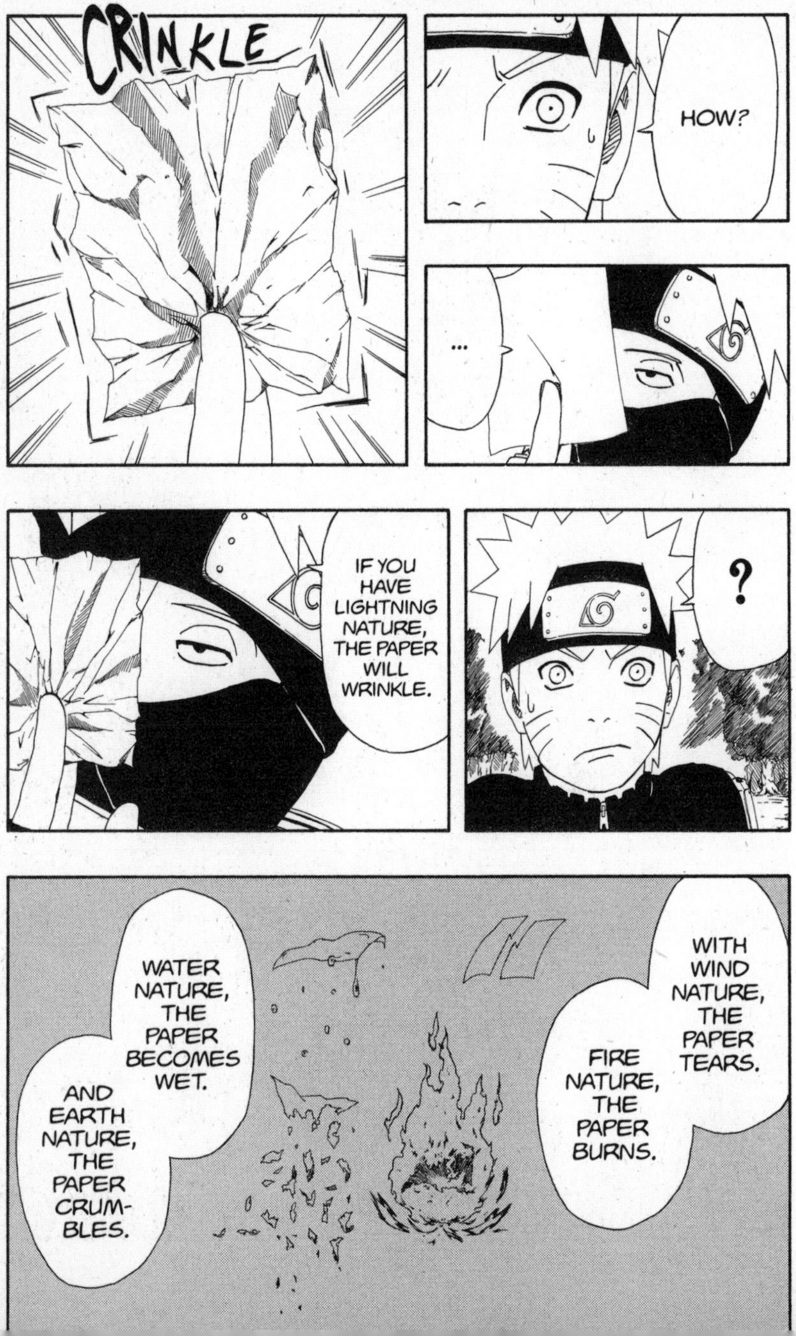
HOW?
...
CRINKLE
?
IF YOU HAVE LIGHTNING NATURE, THE PAPER WILL WRINKLE.
WITH WIND NATURE, THE PAPER TEARS.
FIRE NATURE, THE PAPER BURNS.
WATER NATURE, THE PAPER BECOMES WET.
AND EARTH NATURE, THE PAPER CRUM-BLES.

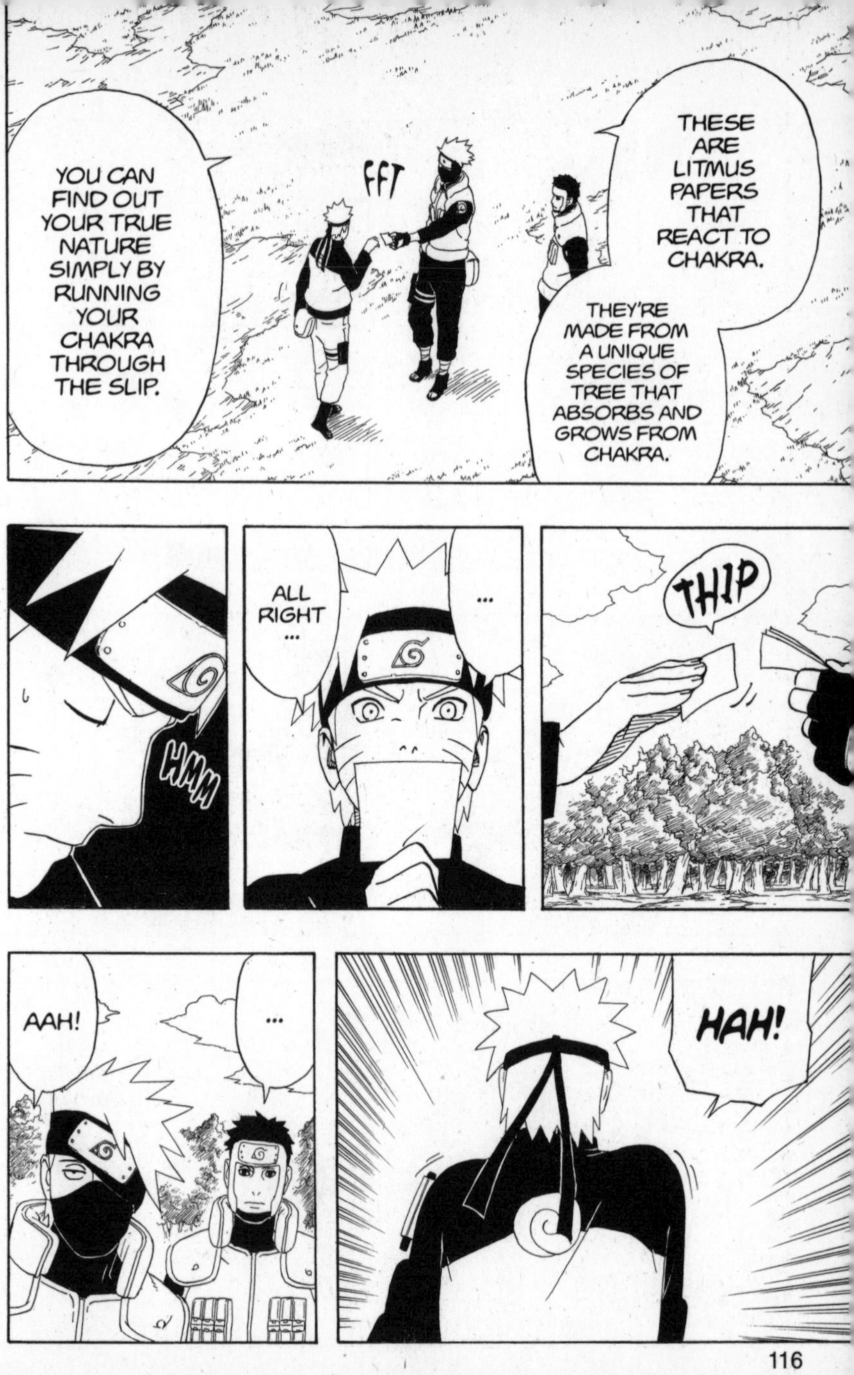
THESE ARE LITMUS PAPERS THAT REACT TO CHAKRA.
THEY'RE MADE FROM A UNIQUE SPECIES OF TREE THAT ABSORBS AND GROWS FROM CHAKRA.
FFT
YOU CAN FIND OUT YOUR TRUE NATURE SIMPLY BY RUNNING YOUR CHAKRA THROUGH THE SLIP.
THIP
...
ALL RIGHT ...
HMM
HAH!
...
AAH!

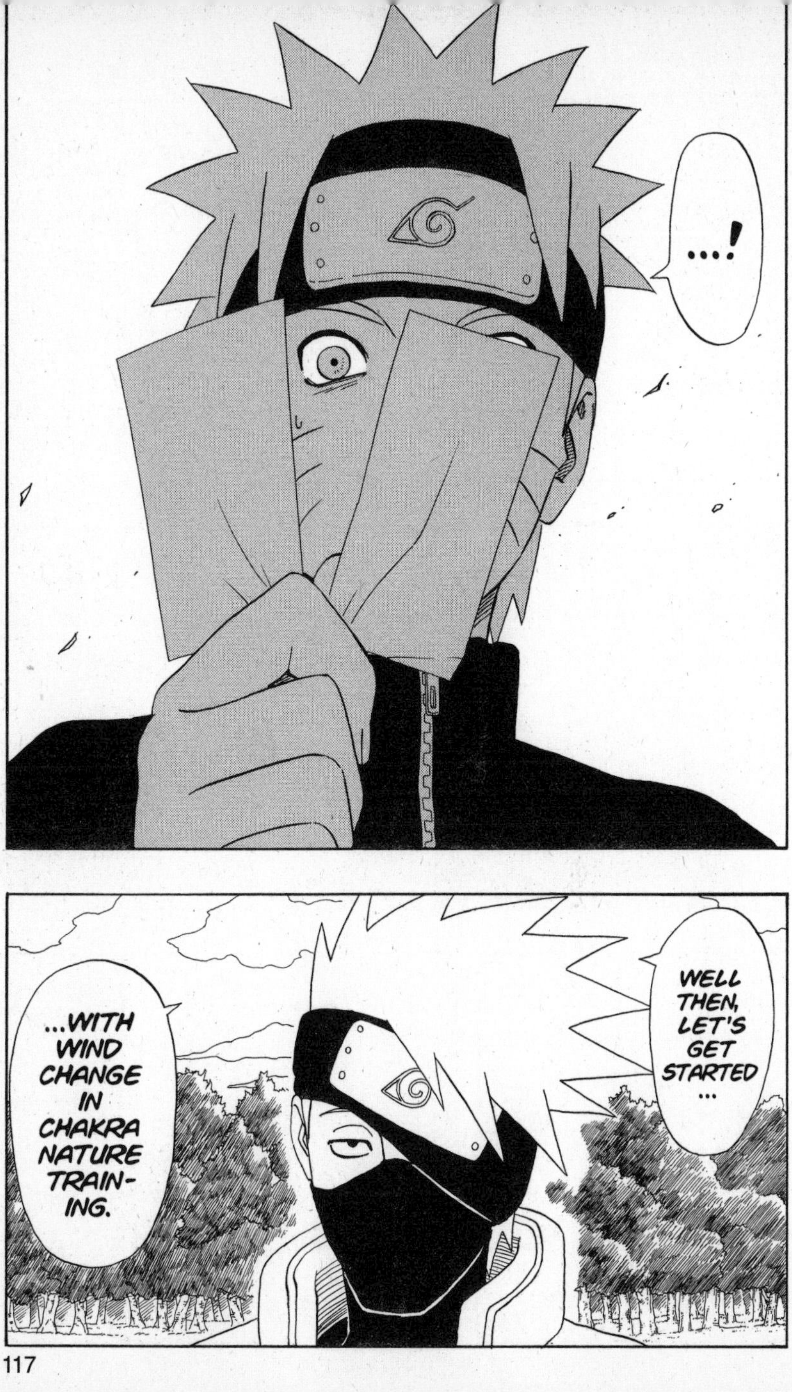
...!
WELL THEN, LET'S GET STARTED...
...WITH WIND CHANGE IN CHAKRA NATURE TRAIN-ING.

NARUTO

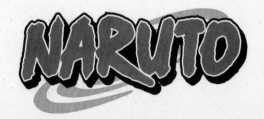

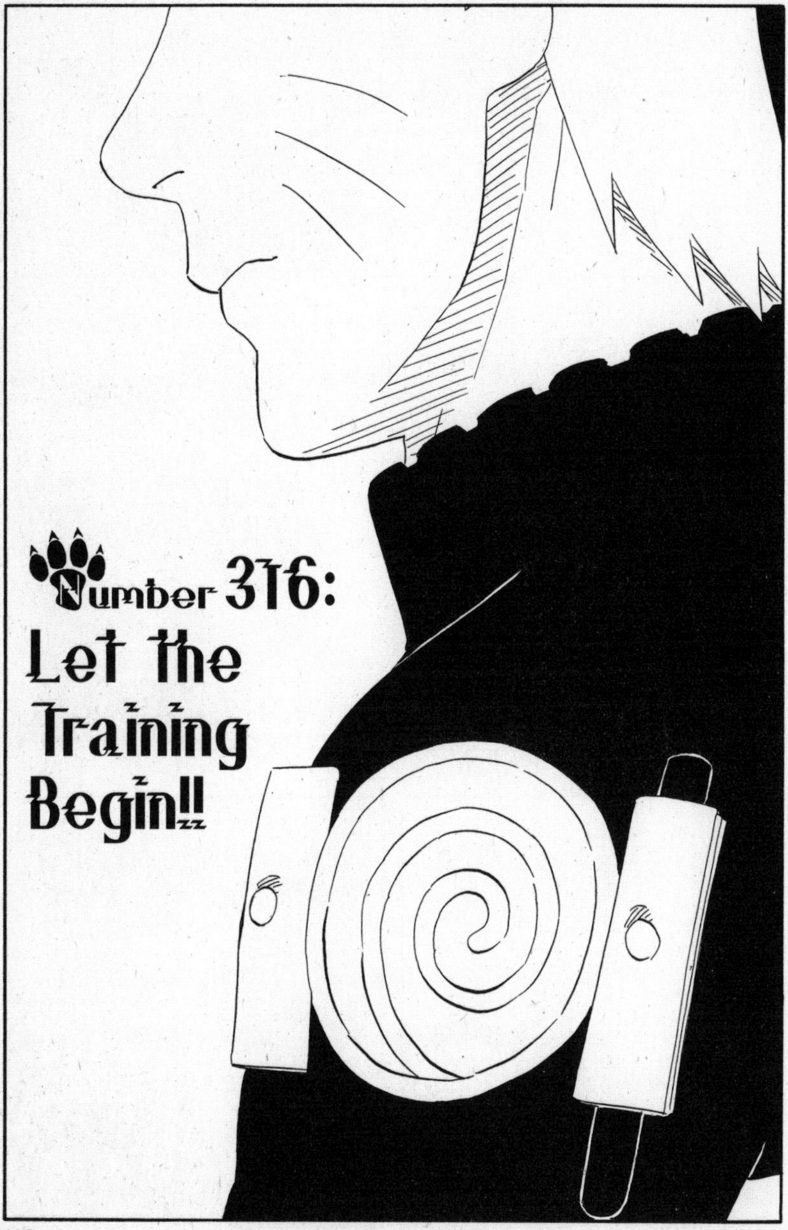
Number 316:
Let the Training Begin!!

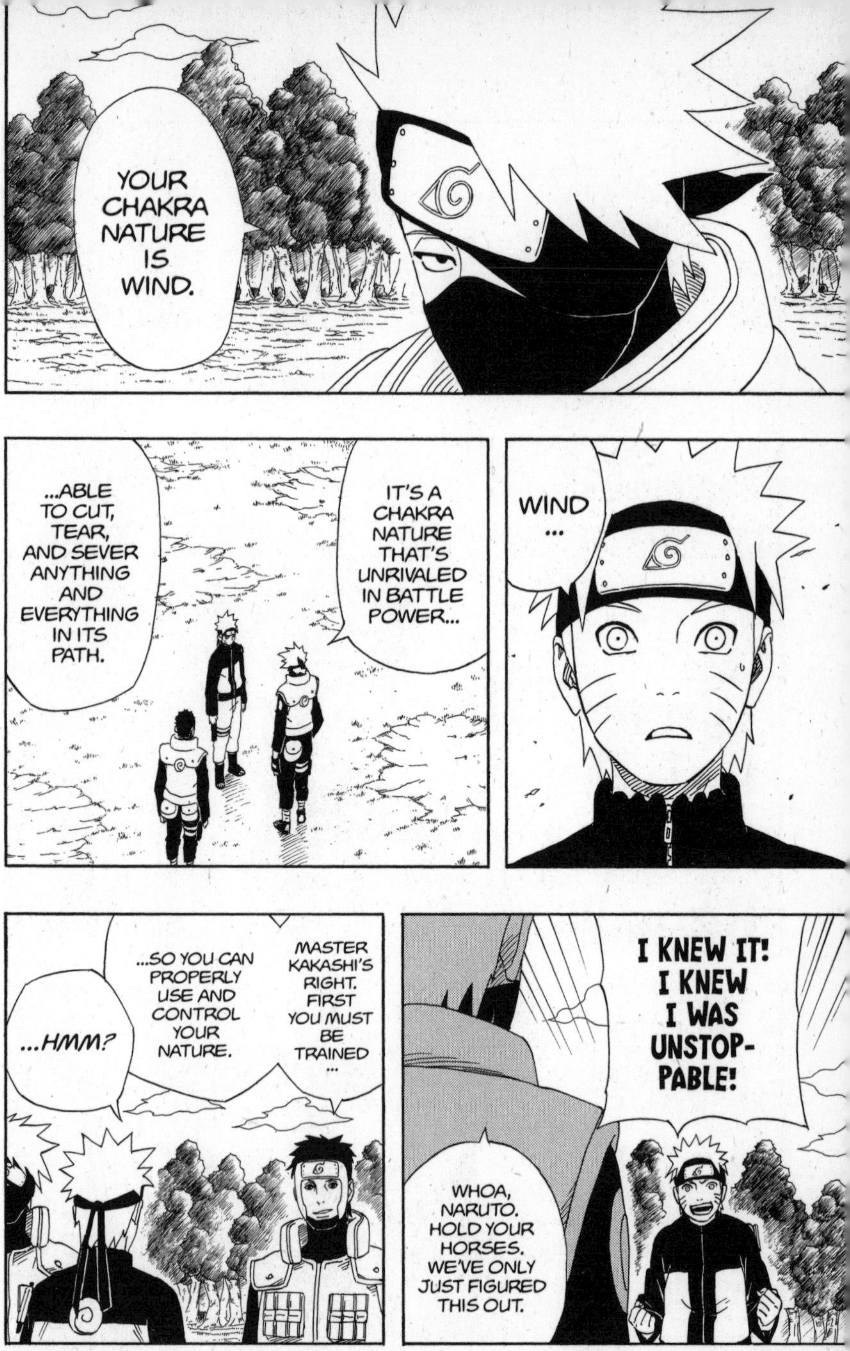
YOUR CHAKRA NATURE IS WIND.
WIND ...
IT'S A CHAKRA NATURE THAT'S UNRIVALED IN BATTLE POWER...
...ABLE TO CUT, TEAR, AND SEVER ANYTHING AND EVERYTHING IN ITS PATH.
I KNEW IT! I KNEW I WAS UNSTOP-PABLE!
WHOA, NARUTO. HOLD YOUR HORSES. WE'VE ONLY JUST FIGURED THIS OUT.
MASTER KAKASHI'S RIGHT. FIRST YOU MUST BE TRAINED ...
...SO YOU CAN PROPERLY USE AND CONTROL YOUR NATURE.
...HMM?

READ THIS WAY

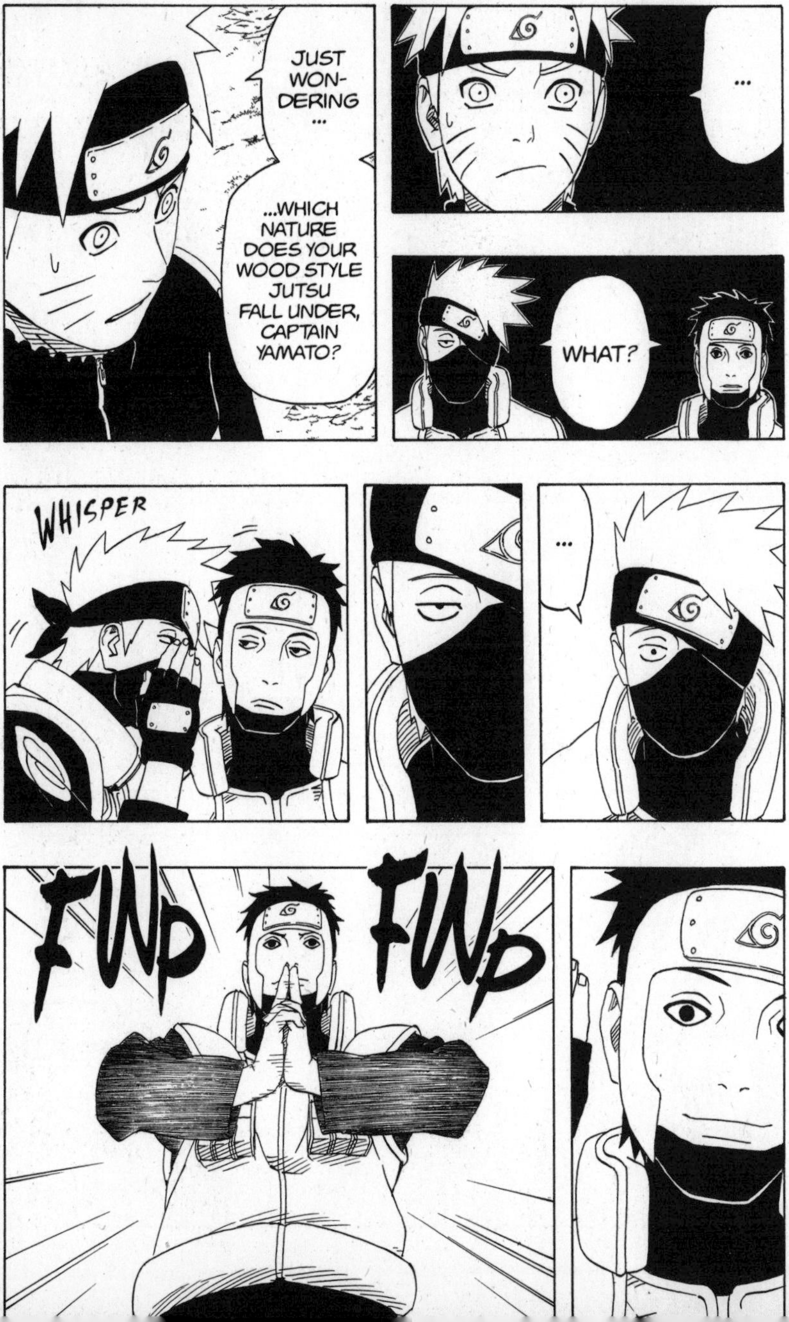
...
WHAT?
JUST WON-DERING ...
...WHICH NATURE DOES YOUR WOOD STYLE JUTSU FALL UNDER, CAPTAIN YAMATO?
...
WHISPER
FWP
FWP

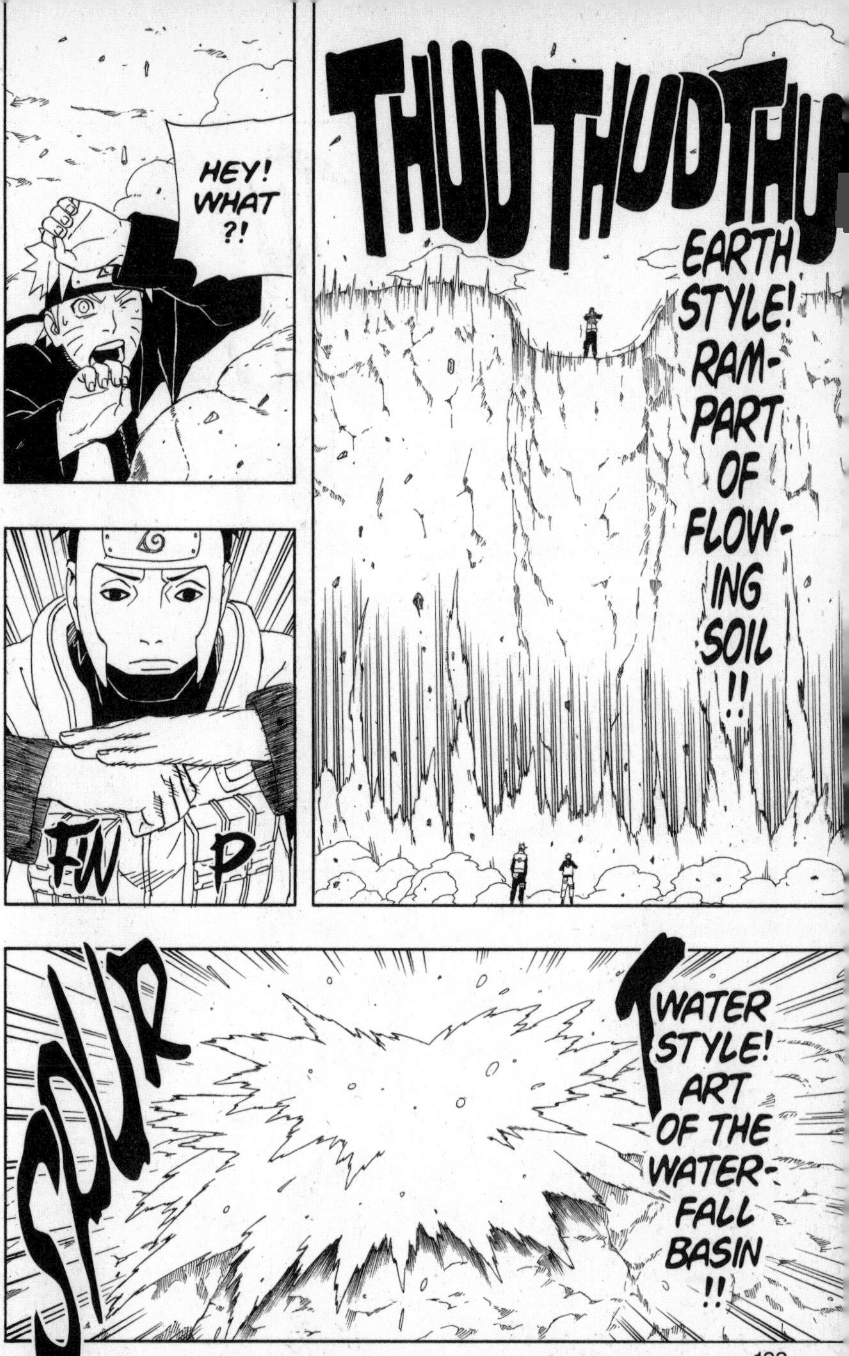
THUD THUD THU
EARTH STYLE! RAMPART OF FLOWING SOIL!!
HEY! WHAT?!
FWP
WATER STYLE! ART OF THE WATERFALL BASIN!!
SPLUR

READ THIS WAY

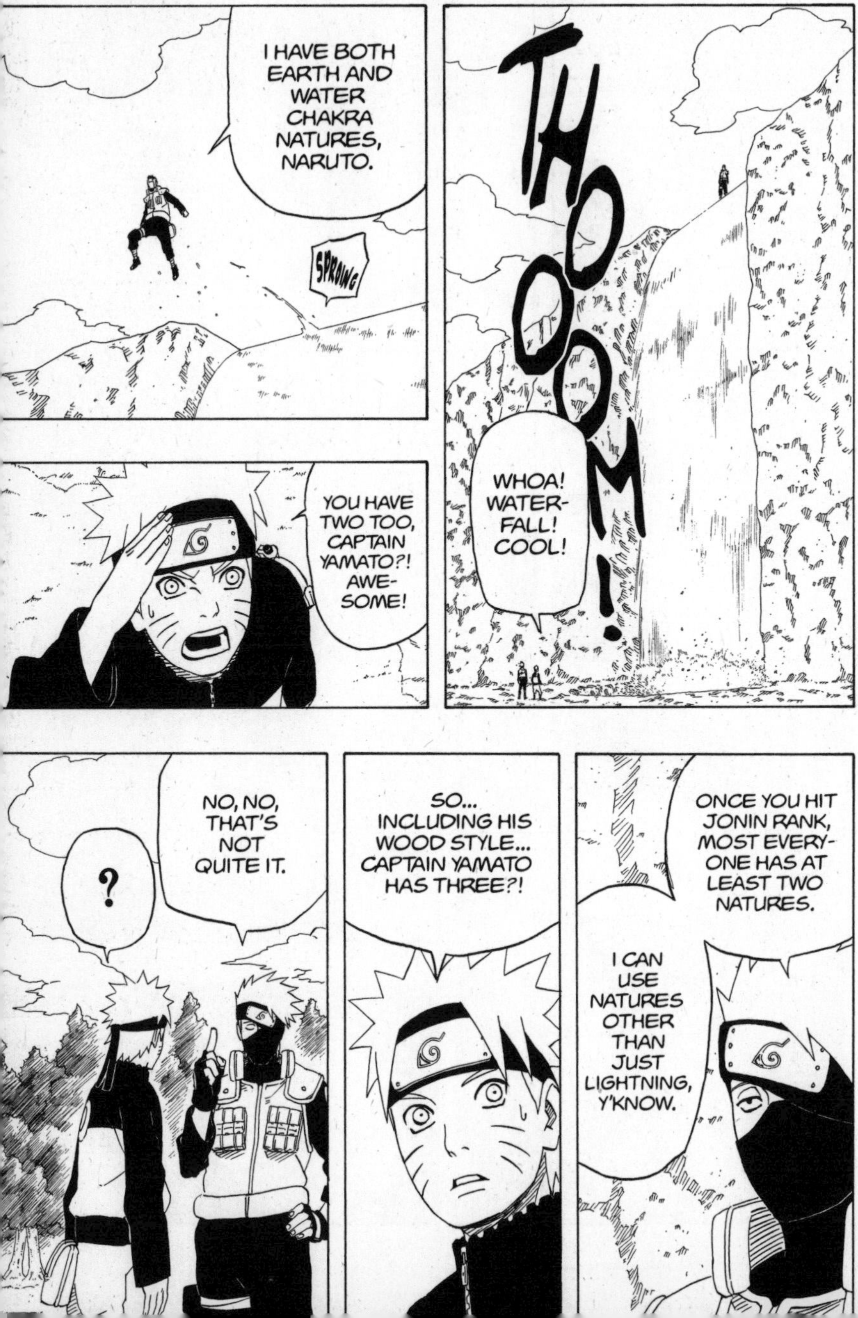
THOOOM!
WHOA! WATER-FALL! COOL!
I HAVE BOTH EARTH AND WATER CHAKRA NATURES, NARUTO.
SPROING
YOU HAVE TWO TOO, CAPTAIN YAMATO?! AWE-SOME!
ONCE YOU HIT JONIN RANK, MOST EVERY-ONE HAS AT LEAST TWO NATURES.
I CAN USE NATURES OTHER THAN JUST LIGHTNING, Y'KNOW.
SO... INCLUDING HIS WOOD STYLE... CAPTAIN YAMATO HAS THREE?!
NO, NO, THAT'S NOT QUITE IT.
?

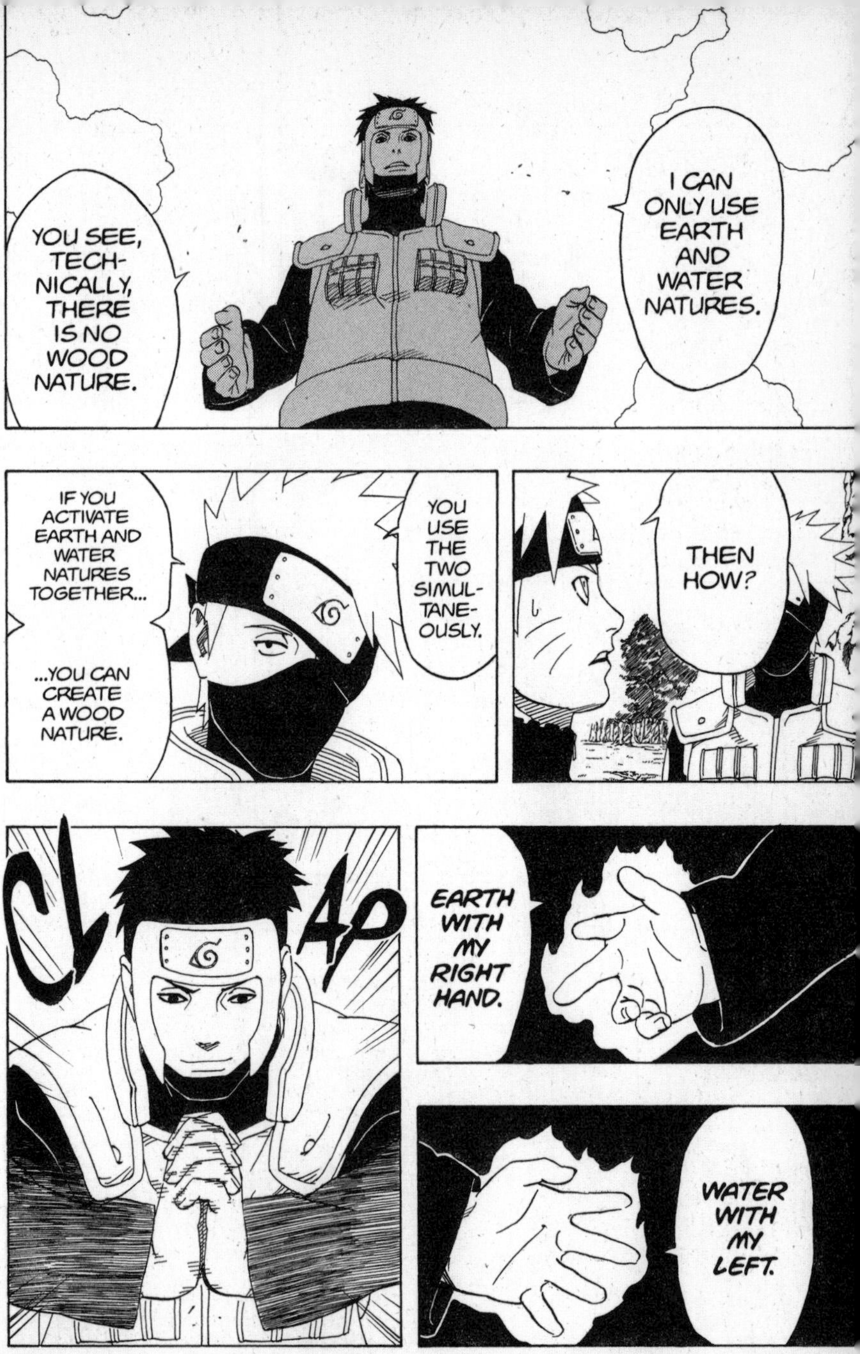
I CAN ONLY USE EARTH AND WATER NATURES.
YOU SEE, TECHNICALLY, THERE IS NO WOOD NATURE.
THEN HOW?
YOU USE THE TWO SIMULTANEOUSLY.
IF YOU ACTIVATE EARTH AND WATER NATURES TOGETHER...
...YOU CAN CREATE A WOOD NATURE.
EARTH WITH MY RIGHT HAND.
WATER WITH MY LEFT.
CLAP

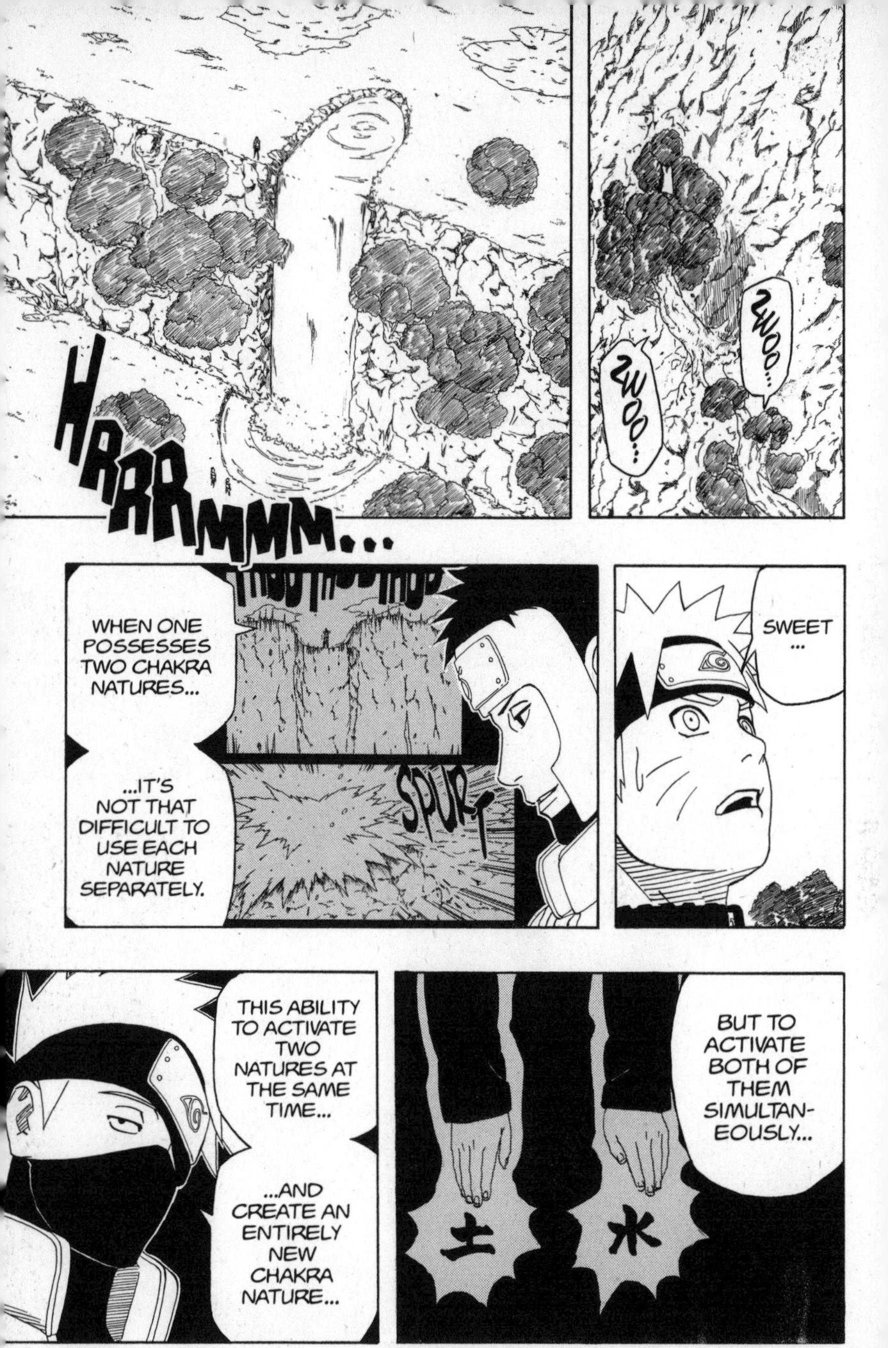
ZWOO...
ZWOO...
HRRRMMMM...
SWEET...
WHEN ONE POSSESSES TWO CHAKRA NATURES...
...IT'S NOT THAT DIFFICULT TO USE EACH NATURE SEPARATELY.
SPURT
BUT TO ACTIVATE BOTH OF THEM SIMULTANEOUSLY...
土
水
THIS ABILITY TO ACTIVATE TWO NATURES AT THE SAME TIME...
...AND CREATE AN ENTIRELY NEW CHAKRA NATURE...

(EARTH) (WATER)

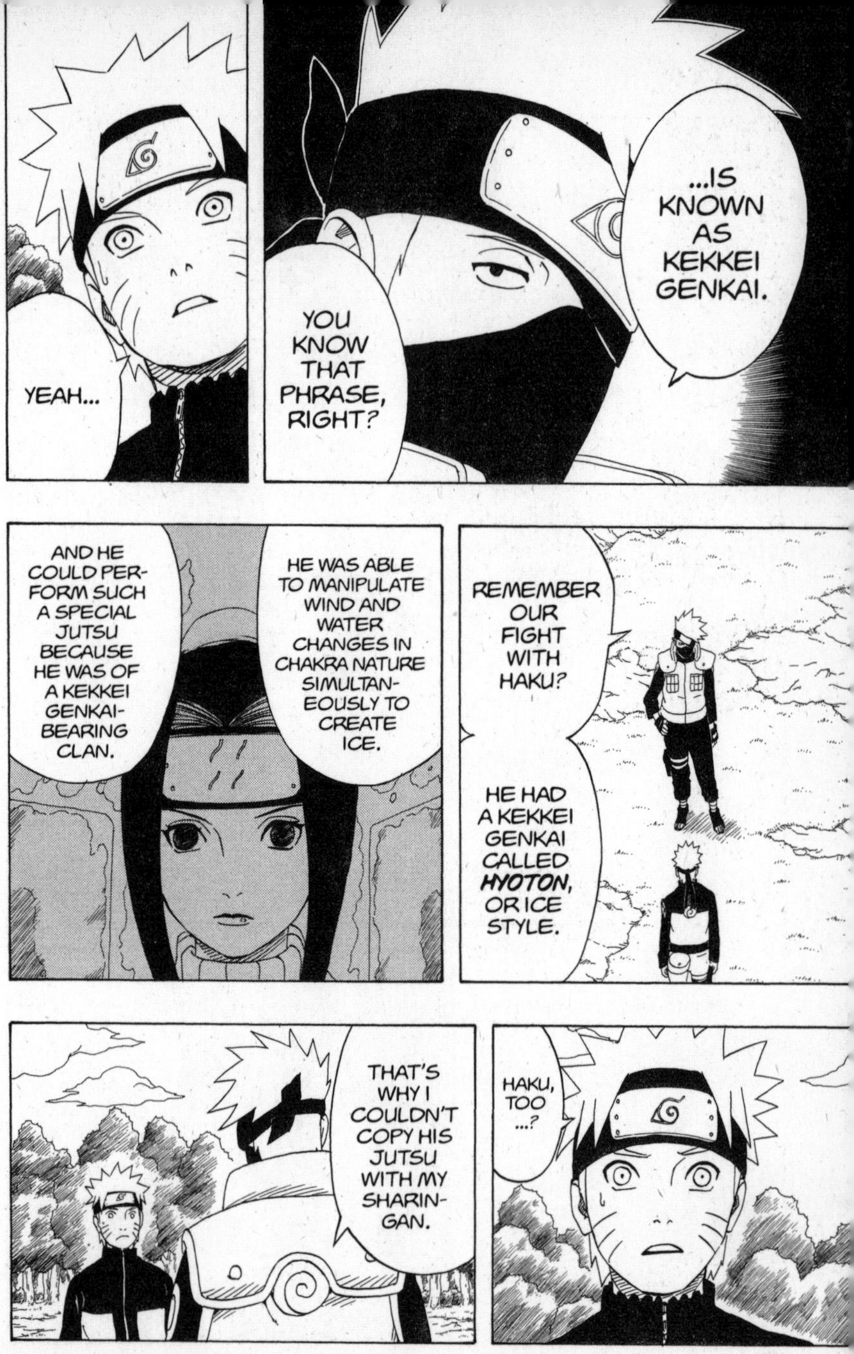
...IS KNOWN AS KEKKEI GENKAI.
YOU KNOW THAT PHRASE, RIGHT?
YEAH...
REMEMBER OUR FIGHT WITH HAKU?
HE HAD A KEKKEI GENKAI CALLED *HYOTON*, OR ICE STYLE.
HE WAS ABLE TO MANIPULATE WIND AND WATER CHANGES IN CHAKRA NATURE SIMULTANEOUSLY TO CREATE ICE.
AND HE COULD PERFORM SUCH A SPECIAL JUTSU BECAUSE HE WAS OF A KEKKEI GENKAI-BEARING CLAN.
HAKU, TOO ...?
THAT'S WHY I COULDN'T COPY HIS JUTSU WITH MY SHARINGAN.

READ THIS WAY

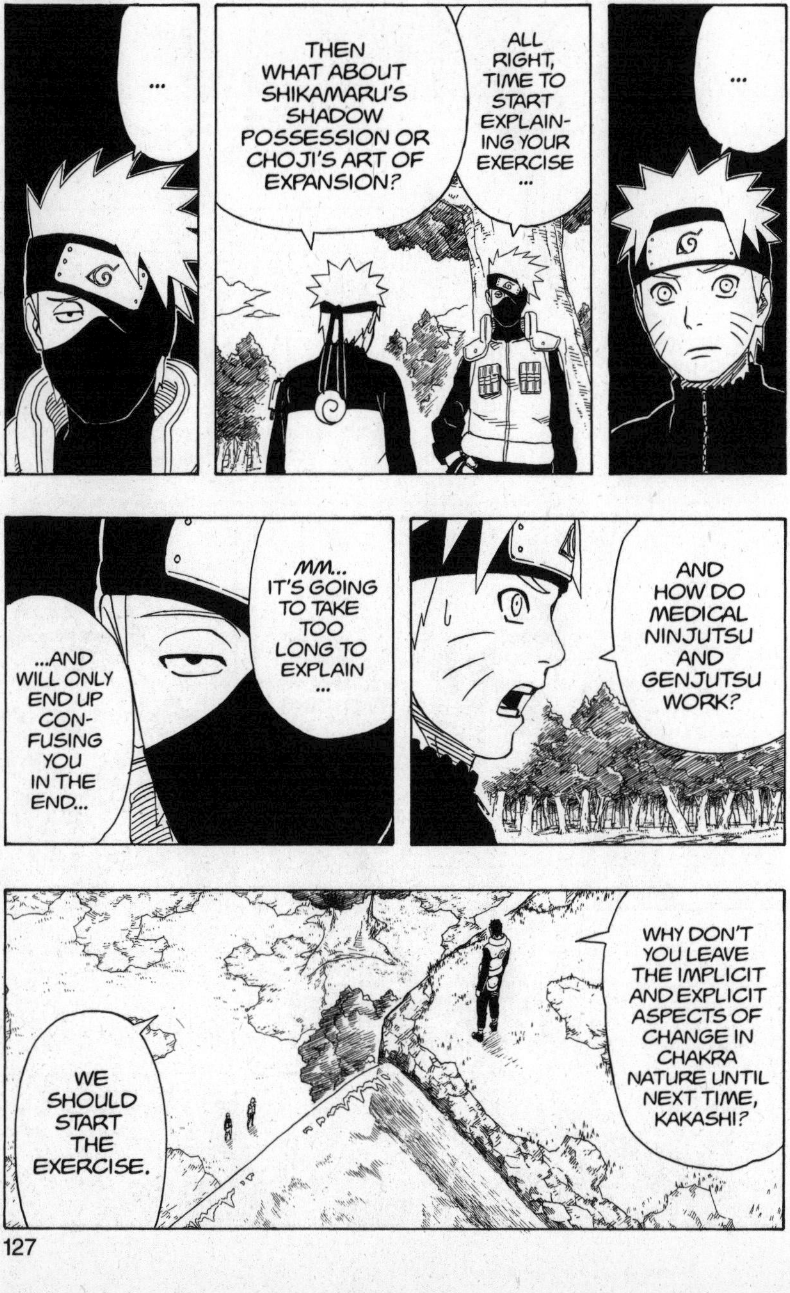
...
ALL RIGHT, TIME TO START EXPLAINING YOUR EXERCISE...
THEN WHAT ABOUT SHIKAMARU'S SHADOW POSSESSION OR CHOJI'S ART OF EXPANSION?
...
AND HOW DO MEDICAL NINJUTSU AND GENJUTSU WORK?
MM... IT'S GOING TO TAKE TOO LONG TO EXPLAIN...
...AND WILL ONLY END UP CONFUSING YOU IN THE END...
WHY DON'T YOU LEAVE THE IMPLICIT AND EXPLICIT ASPECTS OF CHANGE IN CHAKRA NATURE UNTIL NEXT TIME, KAKASHI?
WE SHOULD START THE EXERCISE.

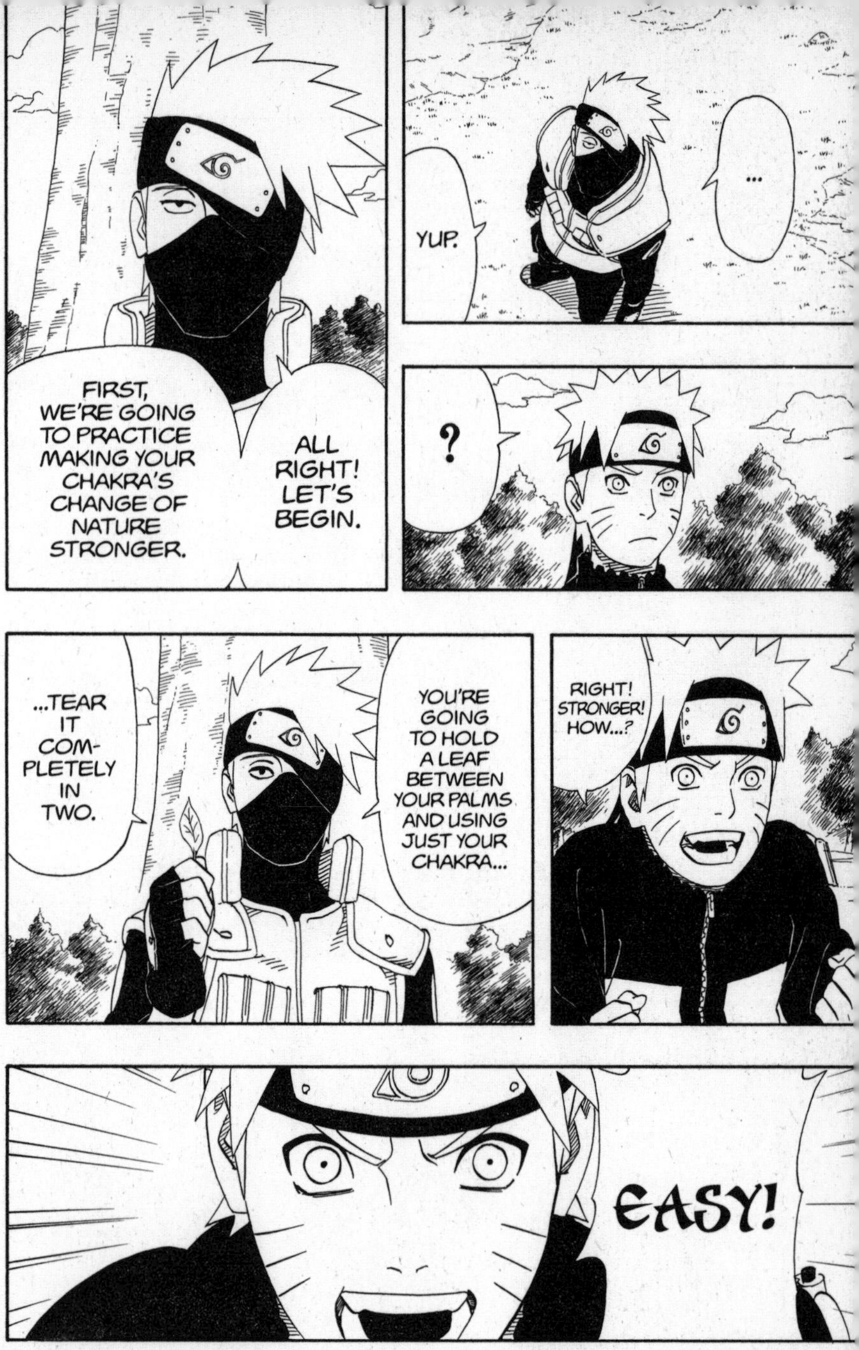
...
YUP.
?
ALL RIGHT! LET'S BEGIN.
FIRST, WE'RE GOING TO PRACTICE MAKING YOUR CHAKRA'S CHANGE OF NATURE STRONGER.
RIGHT! STRONGER! HOW...?
YOU'RE GOING TO HOLD A LEAF BETWEEN YOUR PALMS AND USING JUST YOUR CHAKRA...
...TEAR IT COM- PLETELY IN TWO.
EASY!

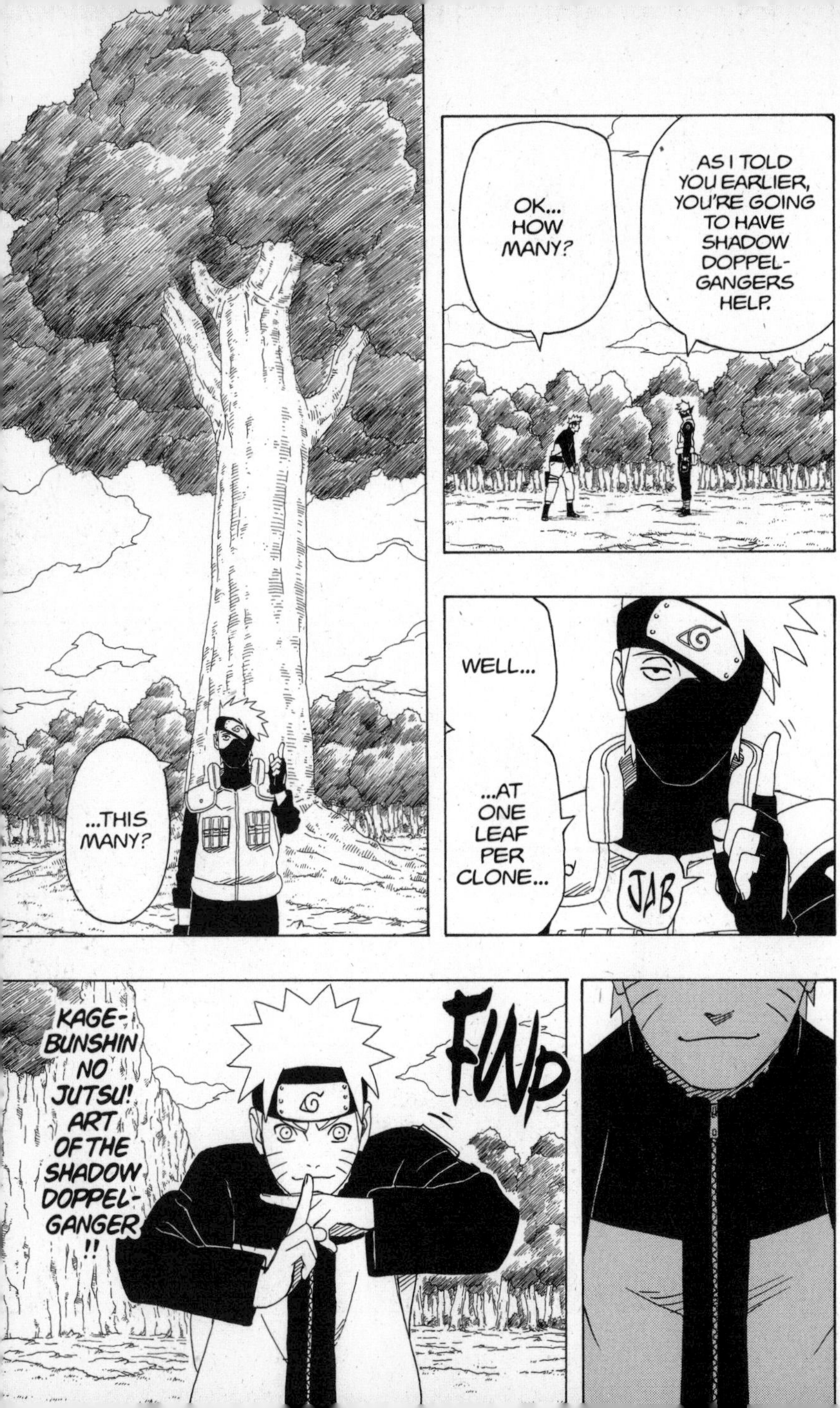
AS I TOLD YOU EARLIER, YOU'RE GOING TO HAVE SHADOW DOPPEL-GANGERS HELP.
OK... HOW MANY?
WELL...
...AT ONE LEAF PER CLONE...
JAB
...THIS MANY?
FWP
KAGE-BUNSHIN NO JUTSU! ART OF THE SHADOW DOPPEL-GANGER!!

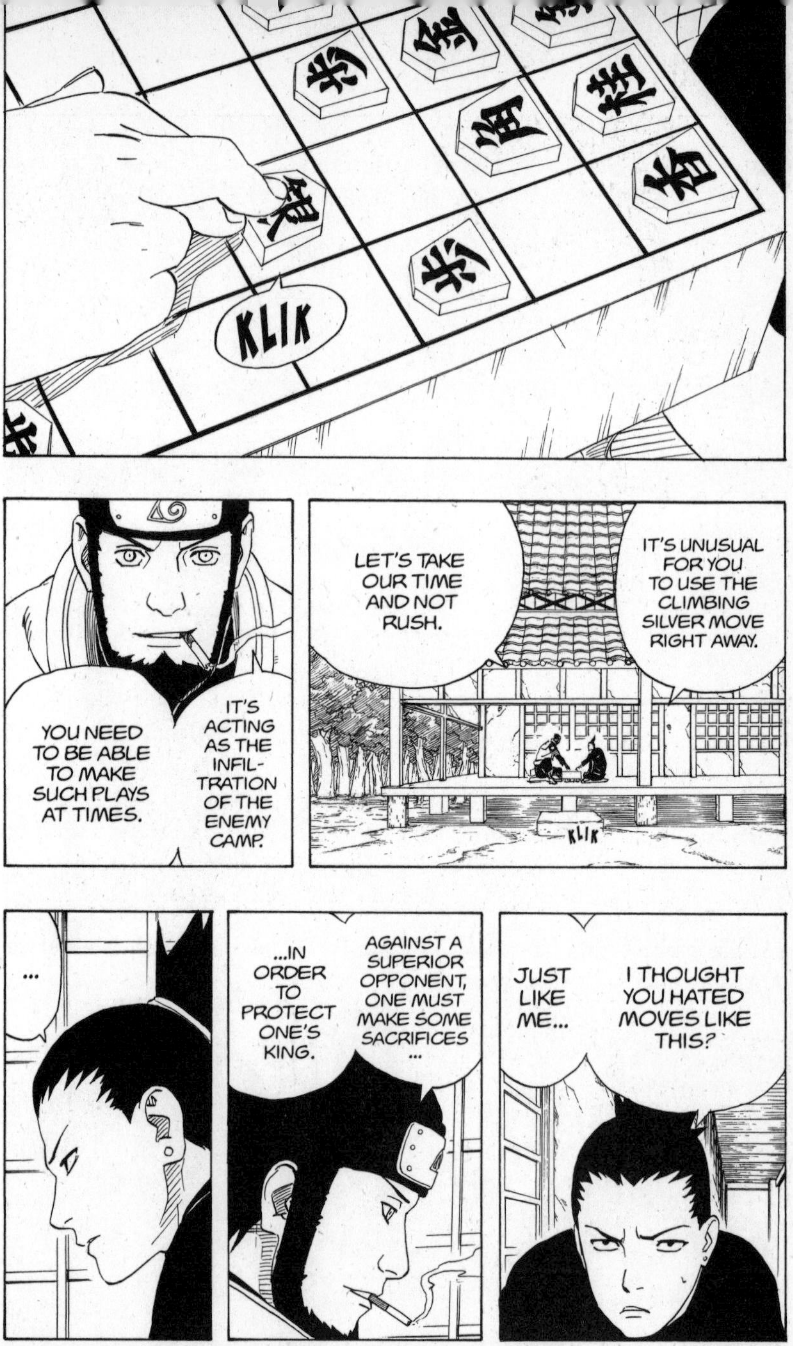
KLIK
IT'S UNUSUAL FOR YOU TO USE THE CLIMBING SILVER MOVE RIGHT AWAY.
LET'S TAKE OUR TIME AND NOT RUSH.
KLIK
IT'S ACTING AS THE INFIL-TRATION OF THE ENEMY CAMP.
YOU NEED TO BE ABLE TO MAKE SUCH PLAYS AT TIMES.
I THOUGHT YOU HATED MOVES LIKE THIS?
JUST LIKE ME...
AGAINST A SUPERIOR OPPONENT, ONE MUST MAKE SOME SACRIFICES...
...IN ORDER TO PROTECT ONE'S KING.
...

READ THIS WAY

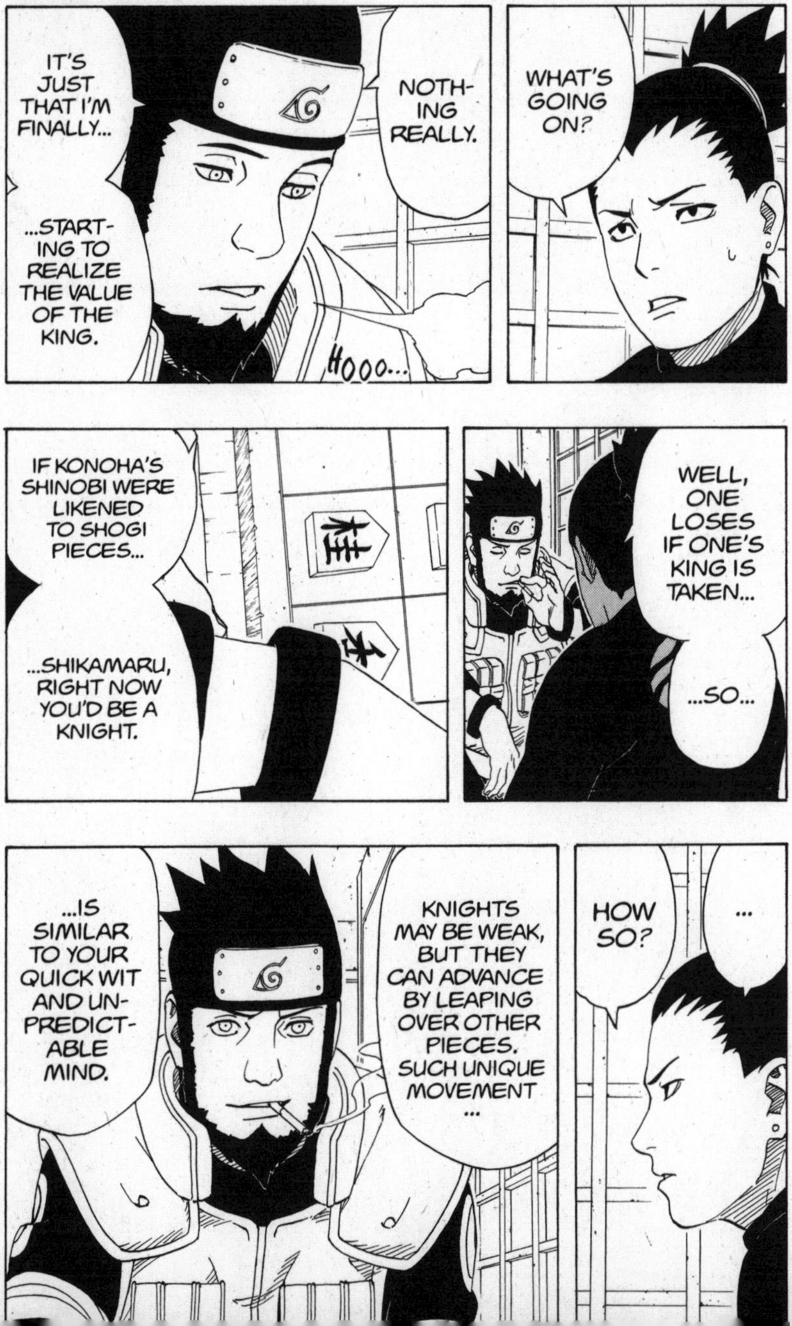
WHAT'S GOING ON?
NOTHING REALLY.
IT'S JUST THAT I'M FINALLY...
...STARTING TO REALIZE THE VALUE OF THE KING.
HOOO...
WELL, ONE LOSES IF ONE'S KING IS TAKEN...
...SO...
IF KONOHA'S SHINOBI WERE LIKENED TO SHOGI PIECES...
...SHIKAMARU, RIGHT NOW YOU'D BE A KNIGHT.
...
HOW SO?
KNIGHTS MAY BE WEAK, BUT THEY CAN ADVANCE BY LEAPING OVER OTHER PIECES. SUCH UNIQUE MOVEMENT...
...IS SIMILAR TO YOUR QUICK WIT AND UNPREDICTABLE MIND.

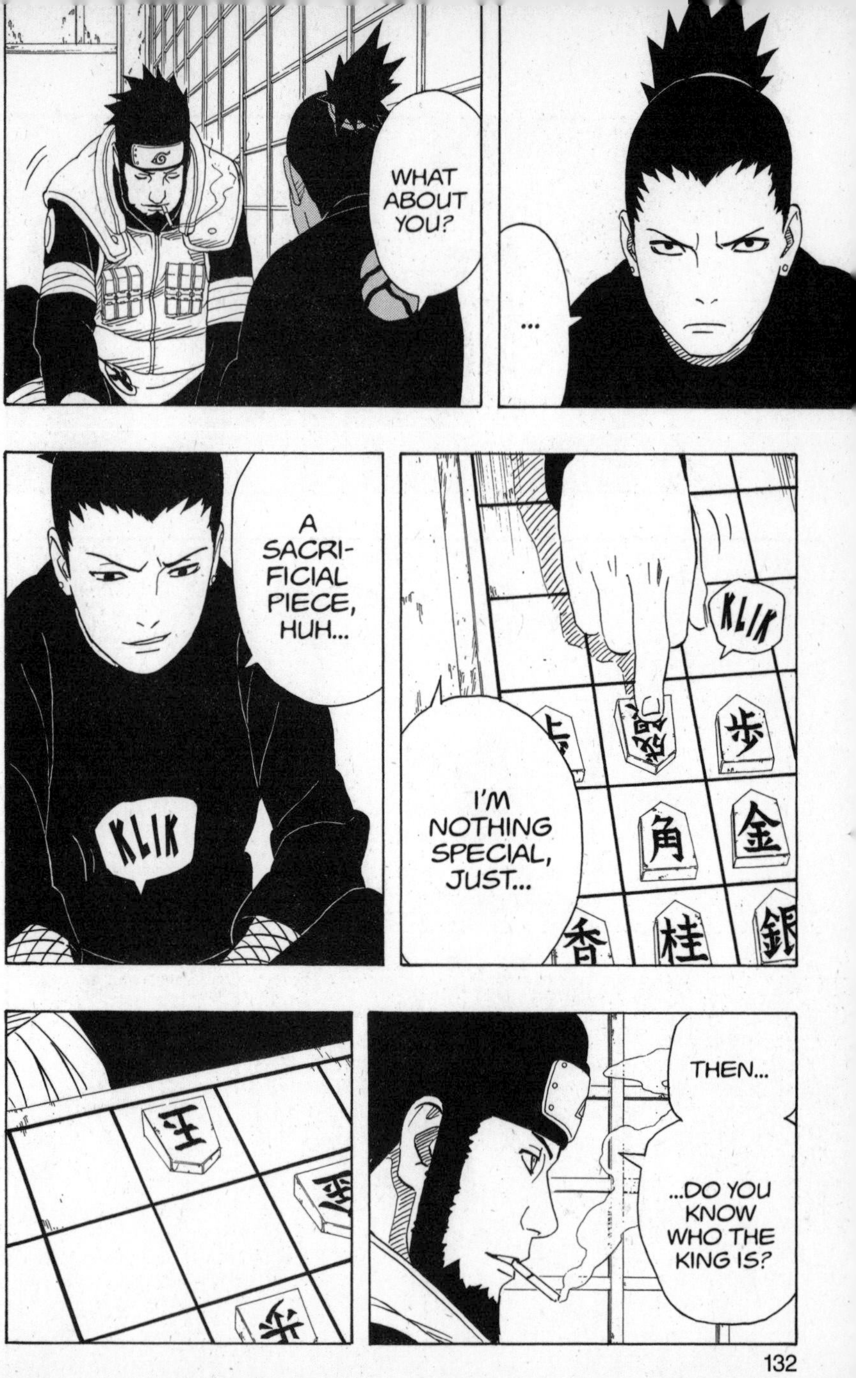
...
WHAT ABOUT YOU?
KLIK
I'M NOTHING SPECIAL, JUST...
歩
角
金
香
桂
銀
A SACRIFICIAL PIECE, HUH...
KLIK
THEN...
...DO YOU KNOW WHO THE KING IS?

READ THIS WAY

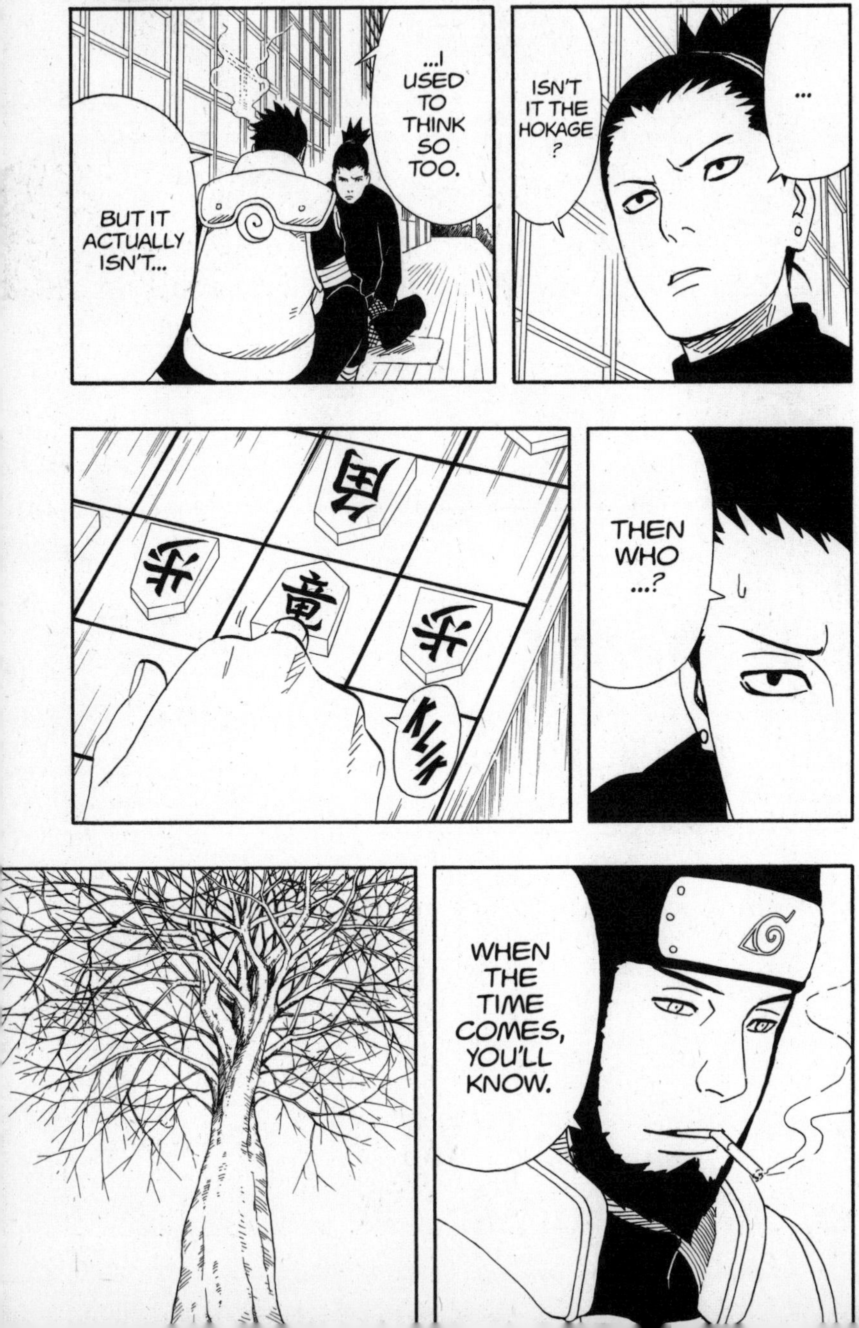
...
ISN'T IT THE HOKAGE?
...I USED TO THINK SO TOO.
BUT IT ACTUALLY ISN'T...
THEN WHO ...?
KLIK
WHEN THE TIME COMES, YOU'LL KNOW.

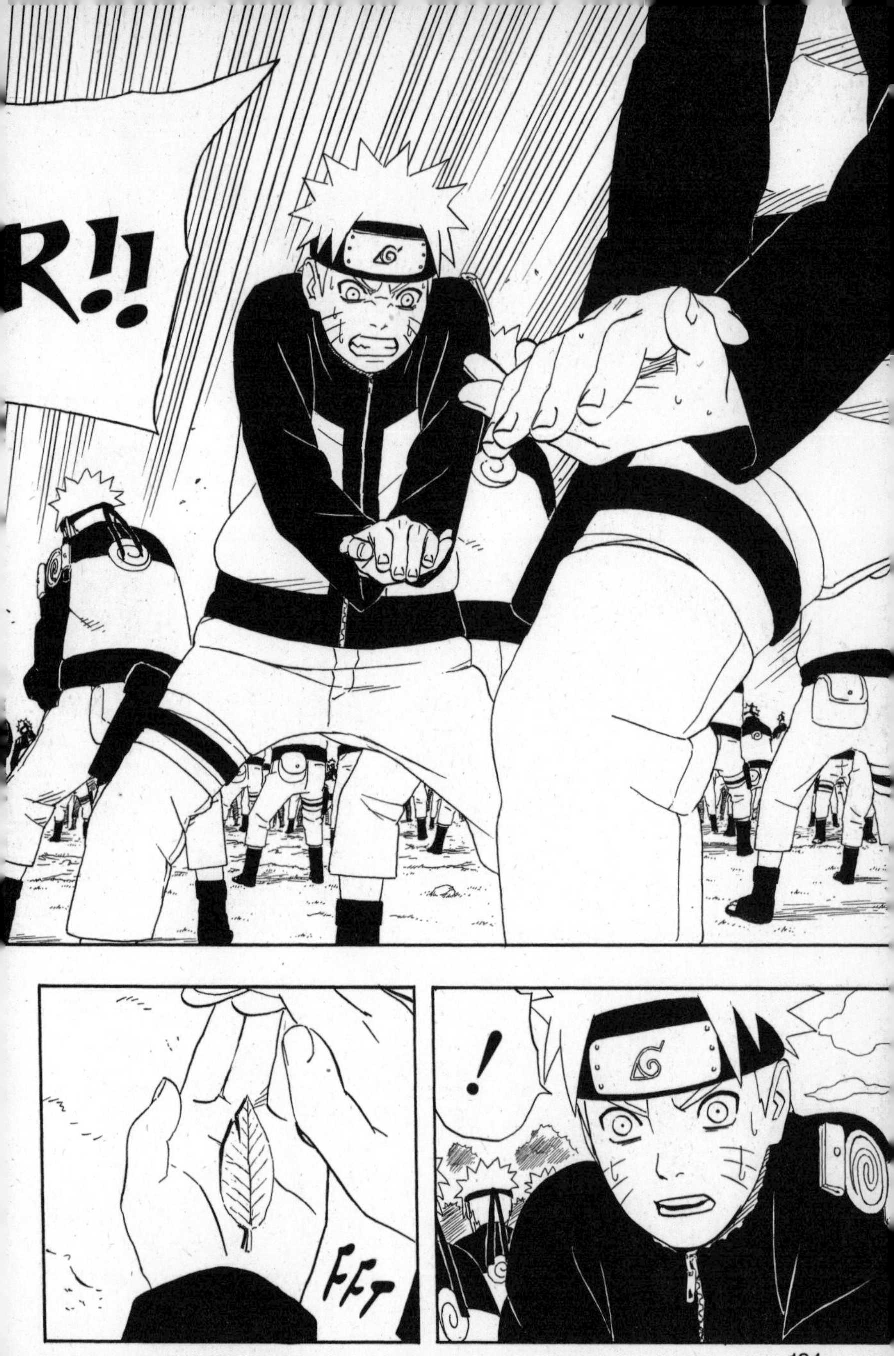
R!!
!
FFT

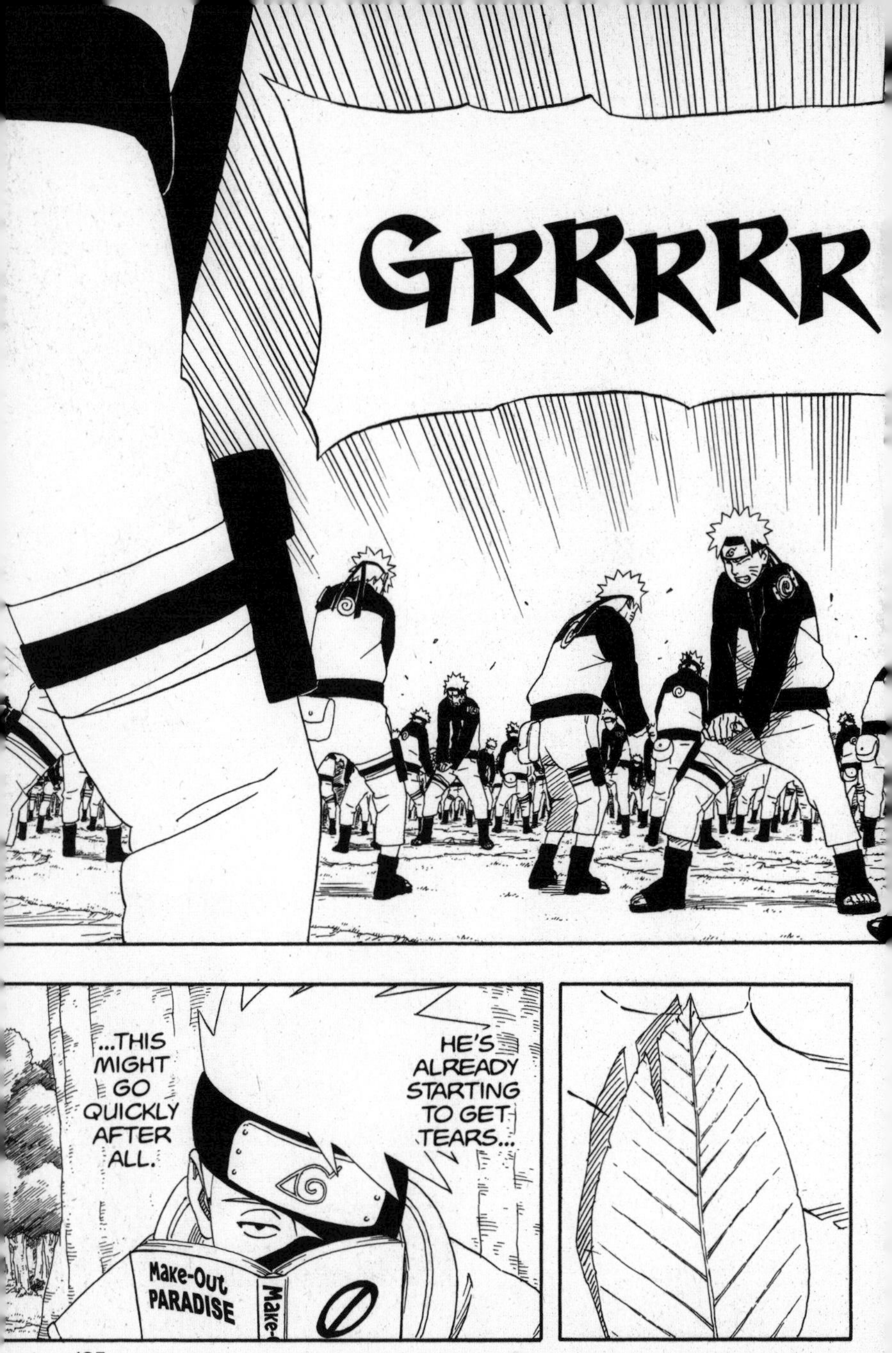
GRRRRR
HE'S ALREADY STARTING TO GET TEARS...
...THIS MIGHT GO QUICKLY AFTER ALL.
Make-Out PARADISE
Make-

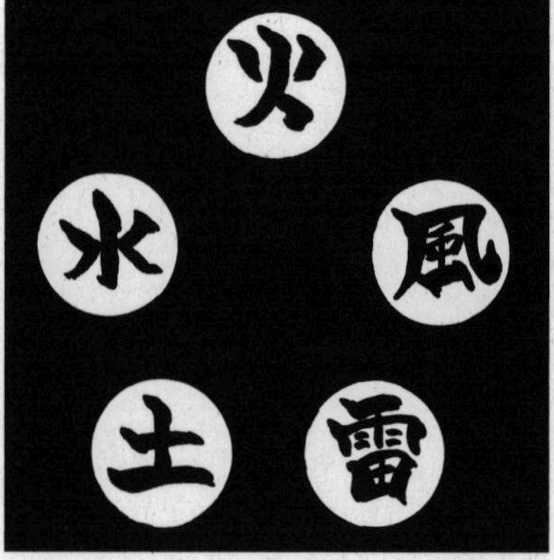
火
風
雷
土
水

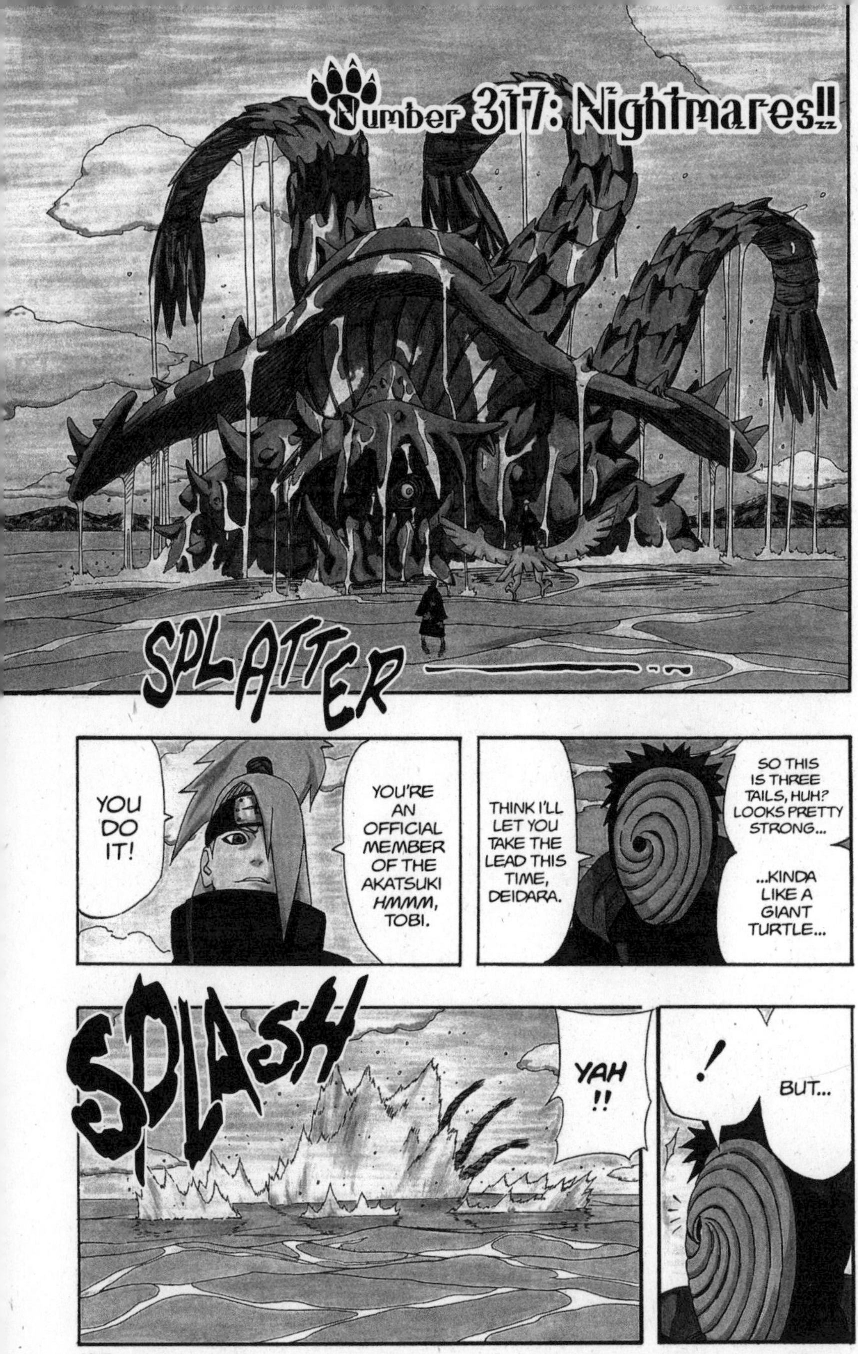
Number 317: Nightmares!!
SPLATTER
SO THIS IS THREE TAILS, HUH? LOOKS PRETTY STRONG...
...KINDA LIKE A GIANT TURTLE...
THINK I'LL LET YOU TAKE THE LEAD THIS TIME, DEIDARA.
YOU'RE AN OFFICIAL MEMBER OF THE AKATSUKI HMMM, TOBI.
YOU DO IT!
!
BUT...
YAH!!
SPLASH

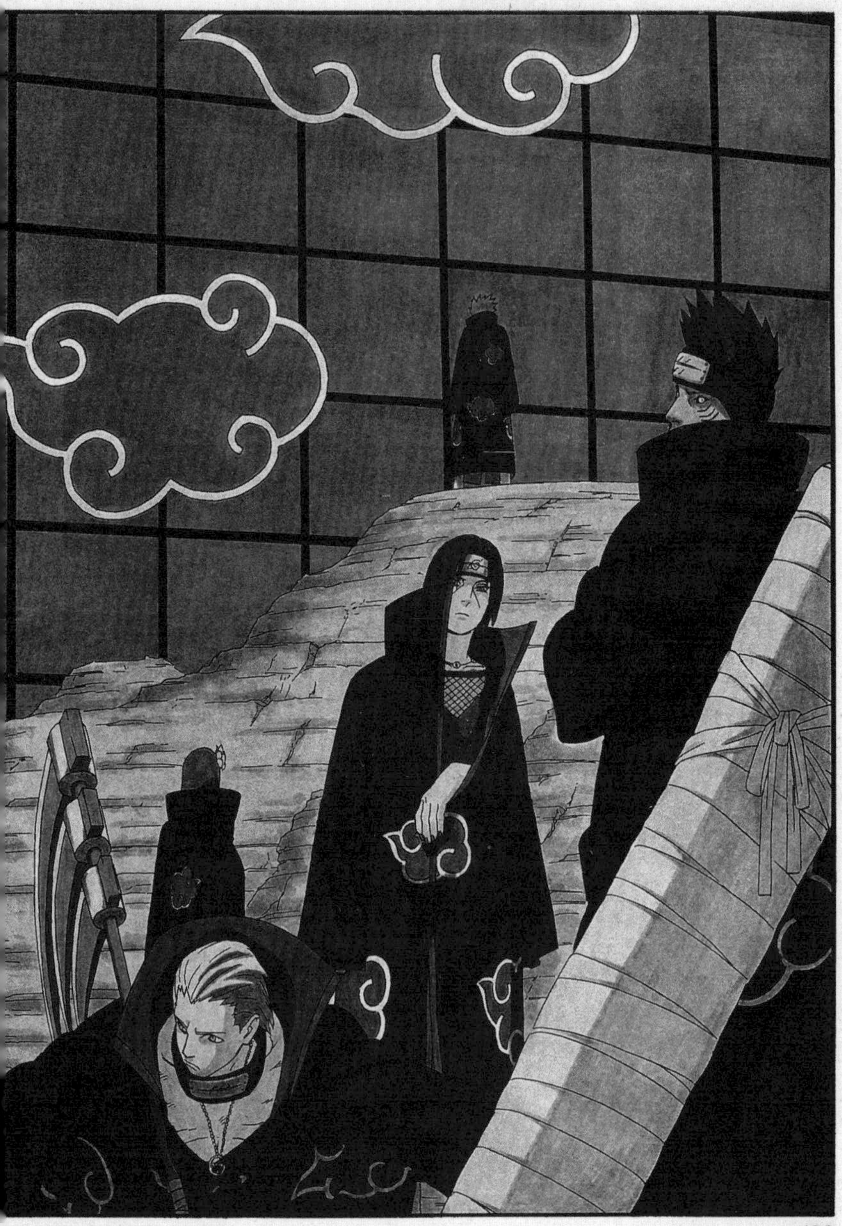

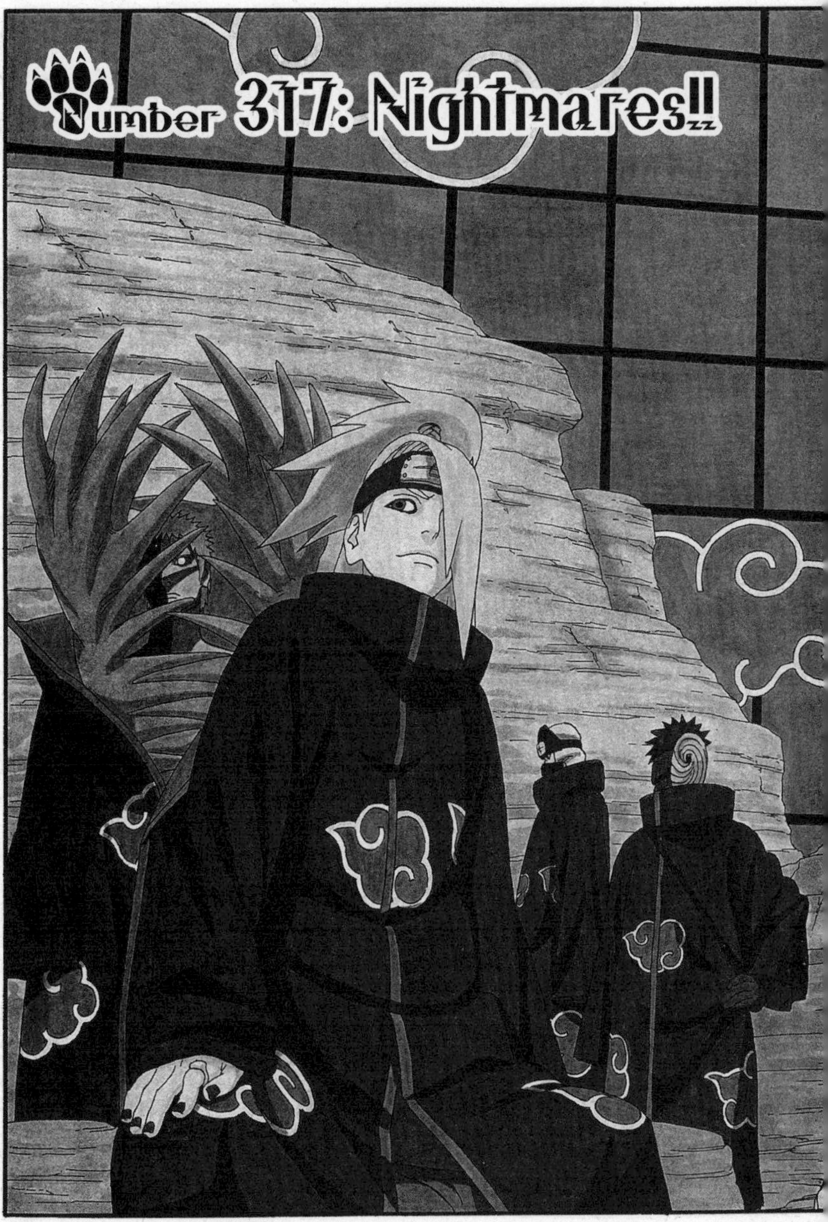
Number 317: Nightmares!!

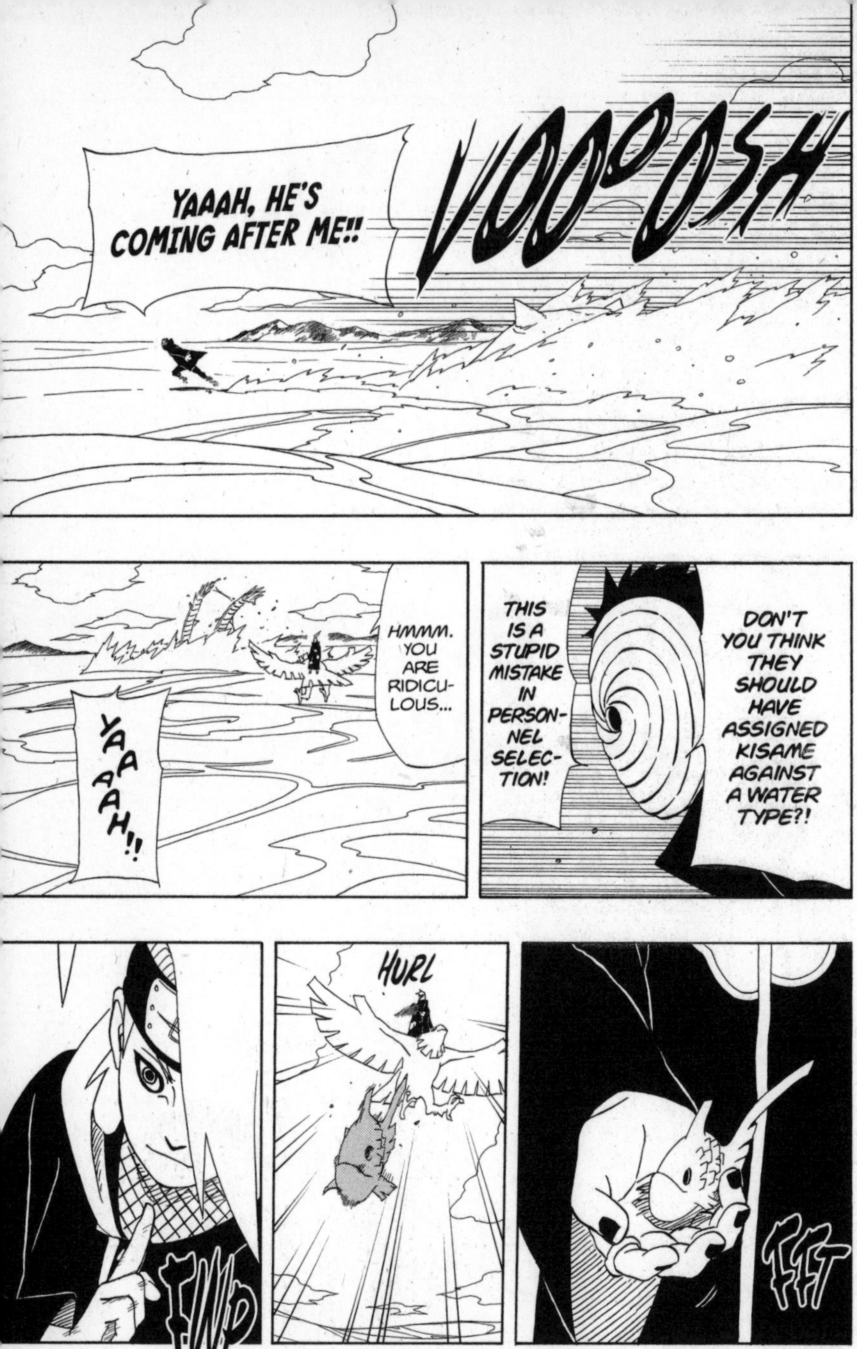
VOOOOSH
YAAAH, HE'S COMING AFTER ME!!
DON'T YOU THINK THEY SHOULD HAVE ASSIGNED KISAME AGAINST A WATER TYPE?!
THIS IS A STUPID MISTAKE IN PERSONNEL SELECTION!
HMMM. YOU ARE RIDICULOUS...
YAAAAH!!
FFT
HURL
FWD

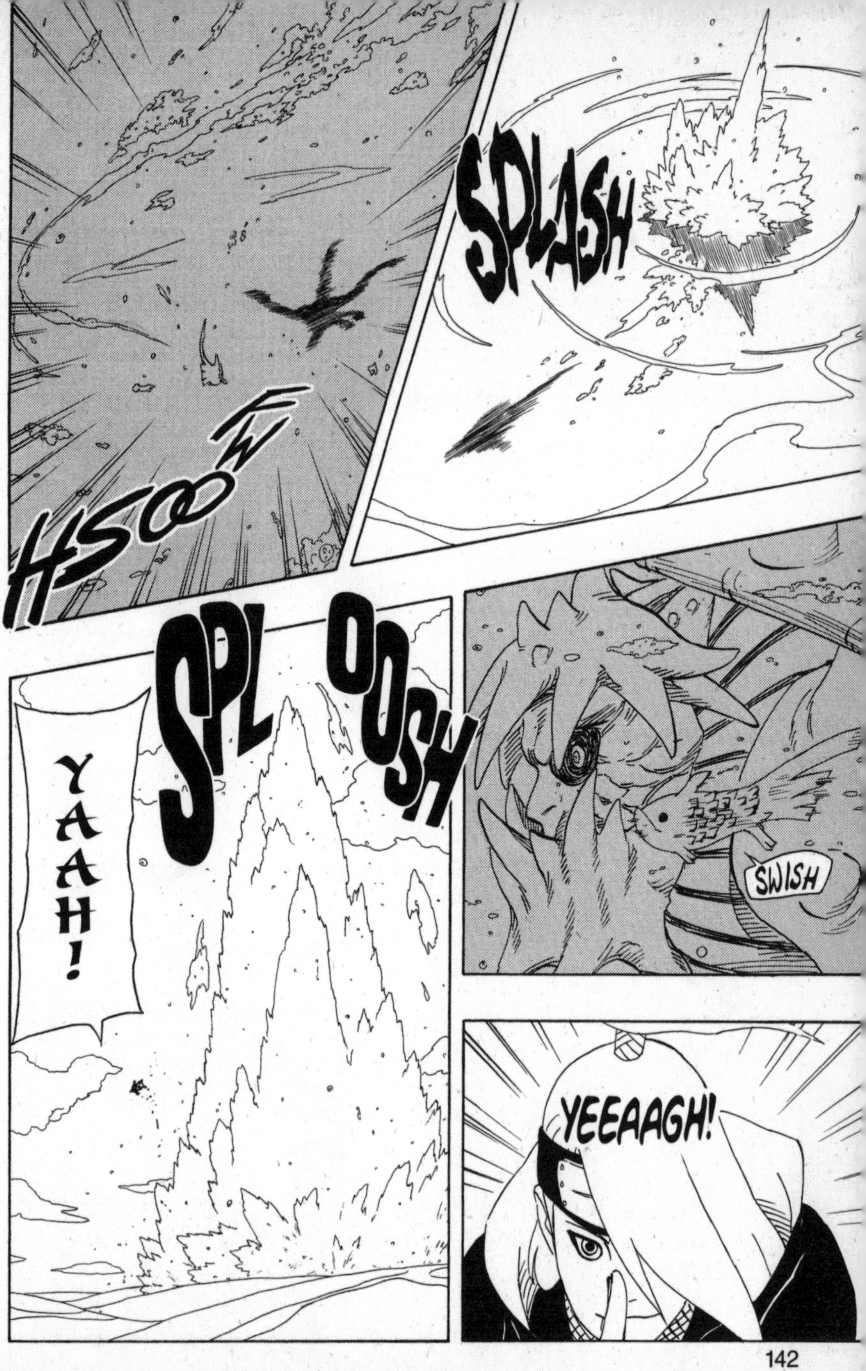

SPLASH
H-SOOW
SWISH
YEEAAGH!
SPLOOSH
YAAH!

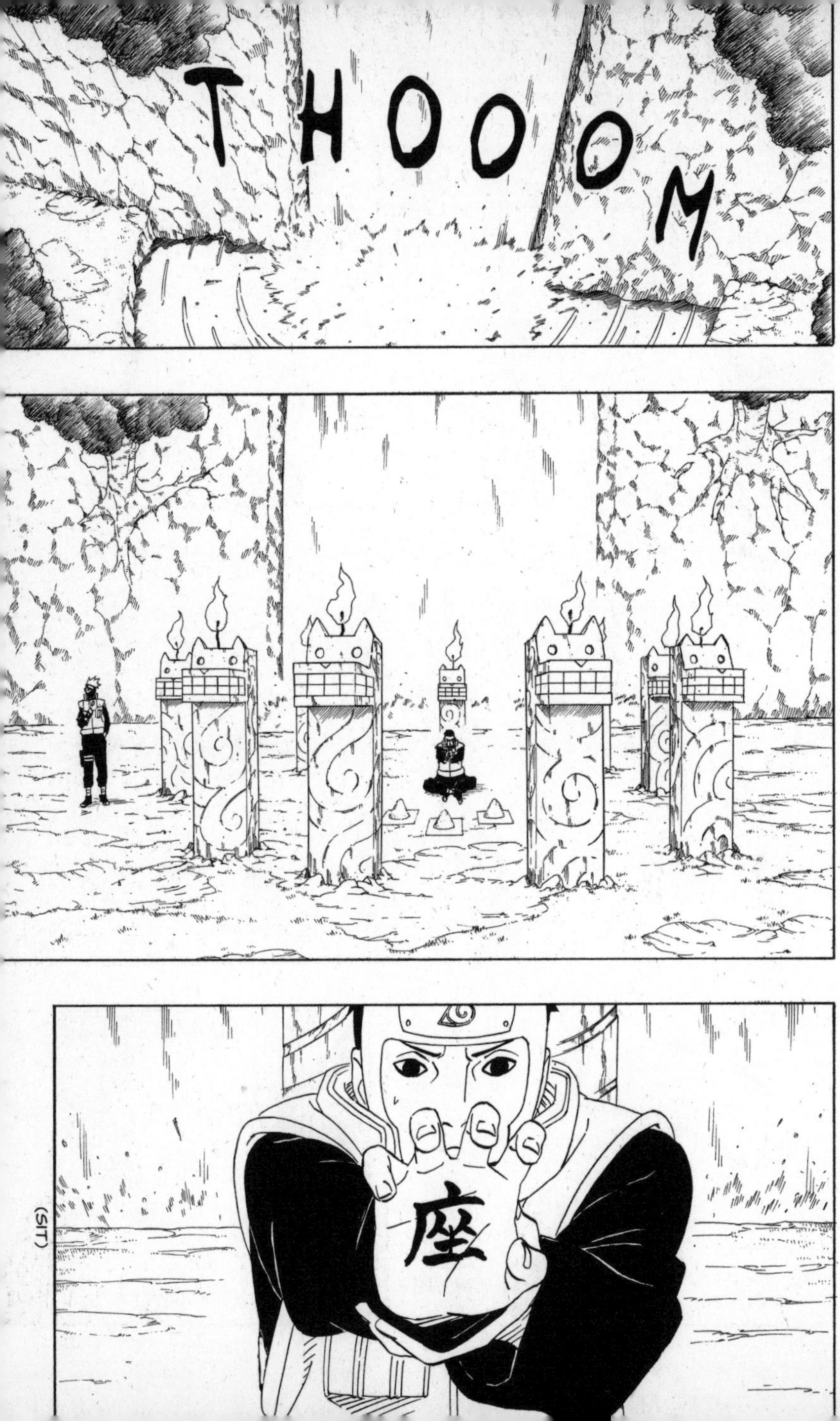
THOOOM
座
(SIT)

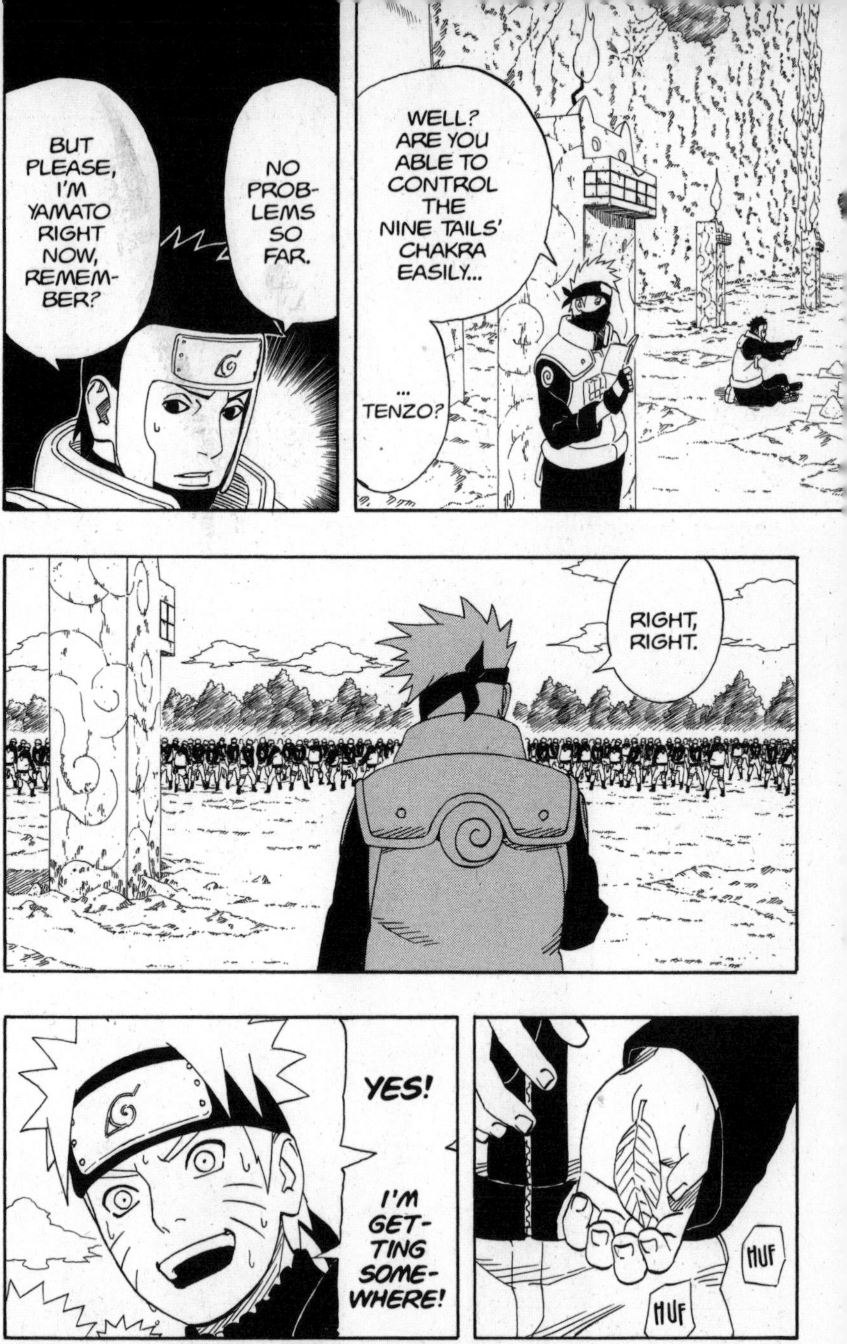
WELL? ARE YOU ABLE TO CONTROL THE NINE TAILS' CHAKRA EASILY...
... TENZO?
NO PROBLEMS SO FAR.
BUT PLEASE, I'M YAMATO RIGHT NOW, REMEMBER?
RIGHT, RIGHT.
HUF
HUF
YES!
I'M GETTING SOMEWHERE!

READ THIS WAY

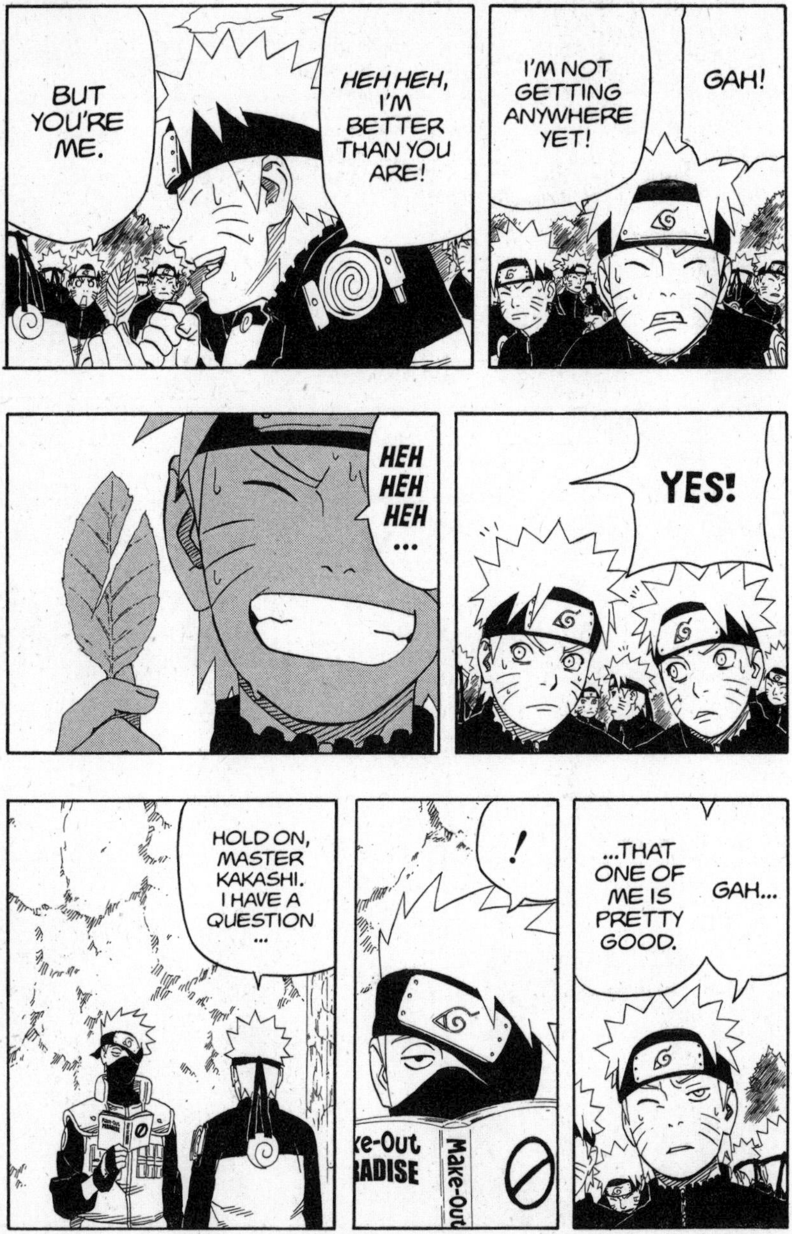
GAH!
I'M NOT GETTING ANYWHERE YET!
HEH HEH, I'M BETTER THAN YOU ARE!
BUT YOU'RE ME.
YES!
HEH HEH HEH...
GAH...
...THAT ONE OF ME IS PRETTY GOOD.
!
Make-Out
HOLD ON, MASTER KAKASHI. I HAVE A QUESTION...

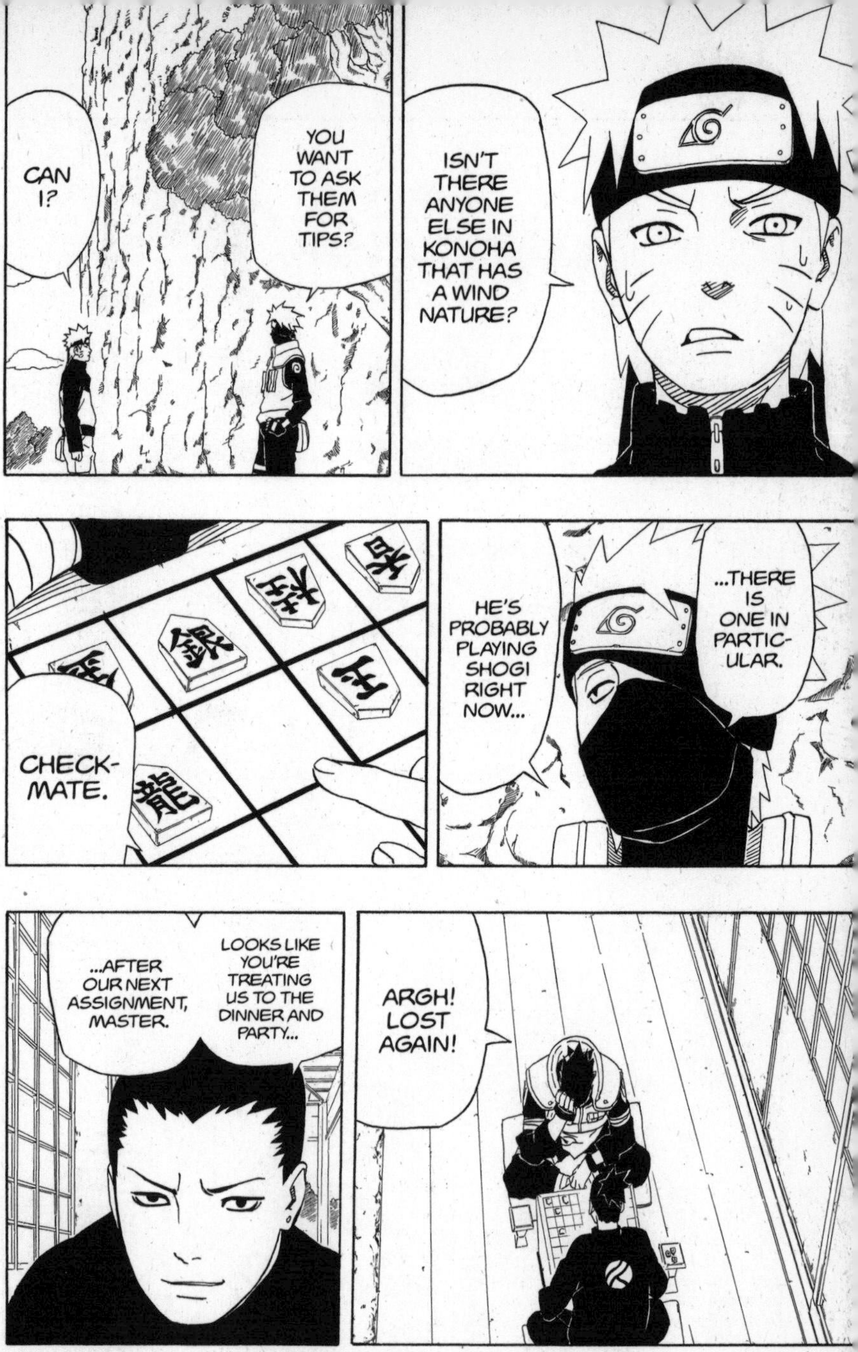
ISN'T THERE ANYONE ELSE IN KONOHA THAT HAS A WIND NATURE?
YOU WANT TO ASK THEM FOR TIPS?
CAN I?
...THERE IS ONE IN PARTICULAR.
HE'S PROBABLY PLAYING SHOGI RIGHT NOW...
CHECKMATE.
ARGH! LOST AGAIN!
LOOKS LIKE YOU'RE TREATING US TO THE DINNER AND PARTY...
...AFTER OUR NEXT ASSIGNMENT, MASTER.

READ THIS WAY

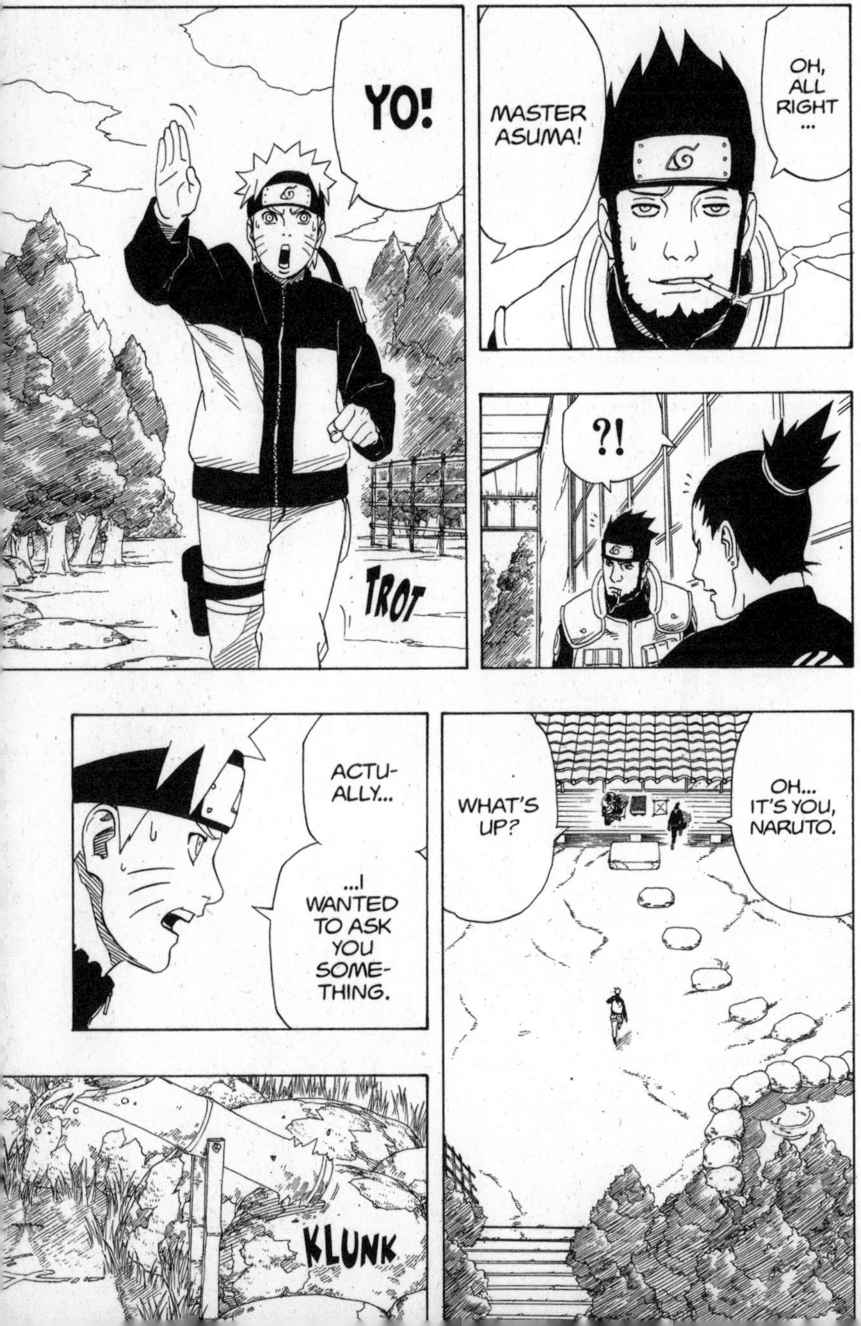

OH, ALL RIGHT ...
MASTER ASUMA!
?!
YO!
TROT
OH... IT'S YOU, NARUTO.
WHAT'S UP?
ACTU-ALLY...
...I WANTED TO ASK YOU SOME-THING.
KLUNK

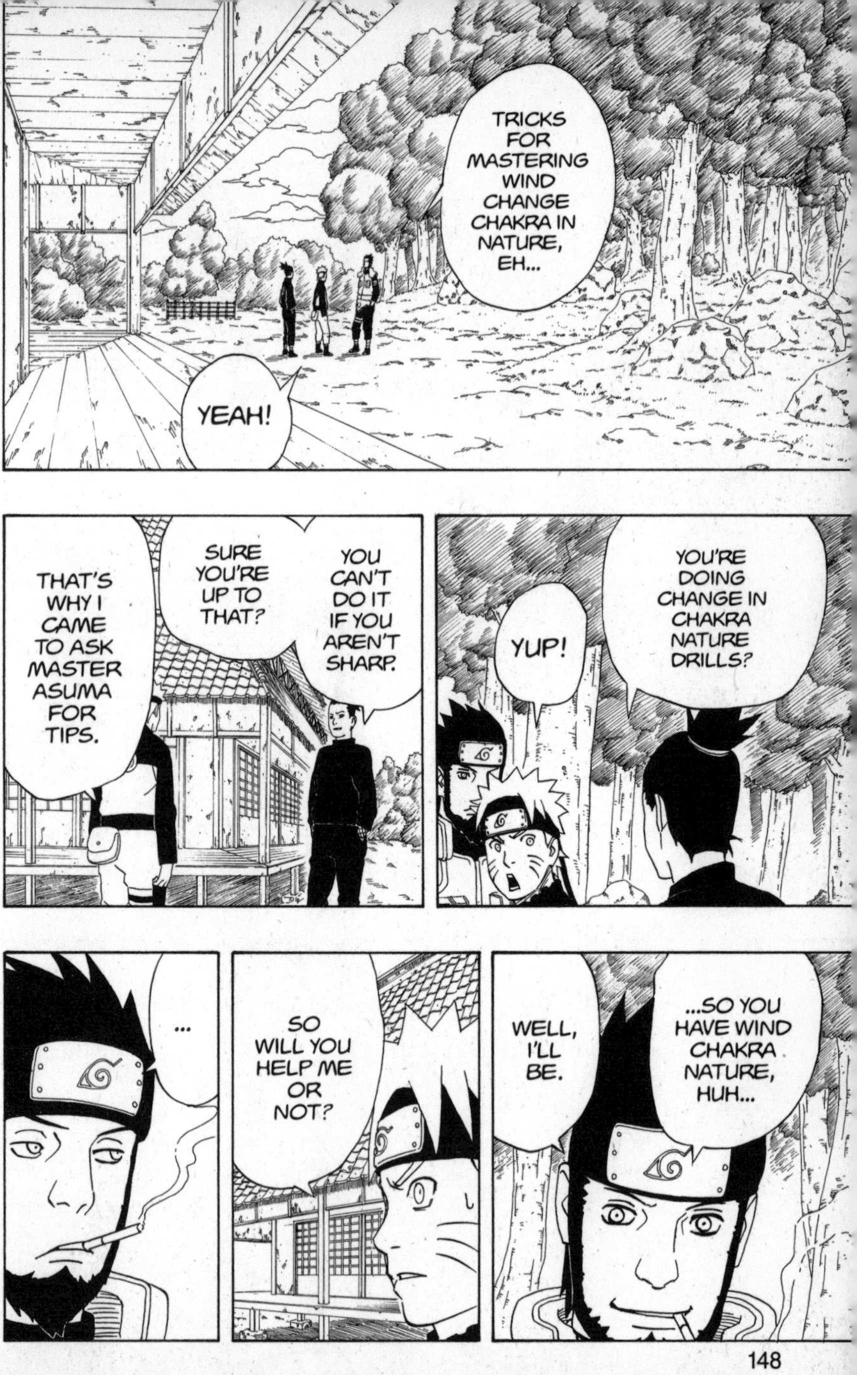
TRICKS FOR MASTERING WIND CHANGE CHAKRA IN NATURE, EH...
YEAH!
YOU'RE DOING CHANGE IN CHAKRA NATURE DRILLS?
YUP!
YOU CAN'T DO IT IF YOU AREN'T SHARP.
SURE YOU'RE UP TO THAT?
THAT'S WHY I CAME TO ASK MASTER ASUMA FOR TIPS.
...SO YOU HAVE WIND CHAKRA NATURE, HUH...
WELL, I'LL BE.
SO WILL YOU HELP ME OR NOT?
...

READ THIS WAY

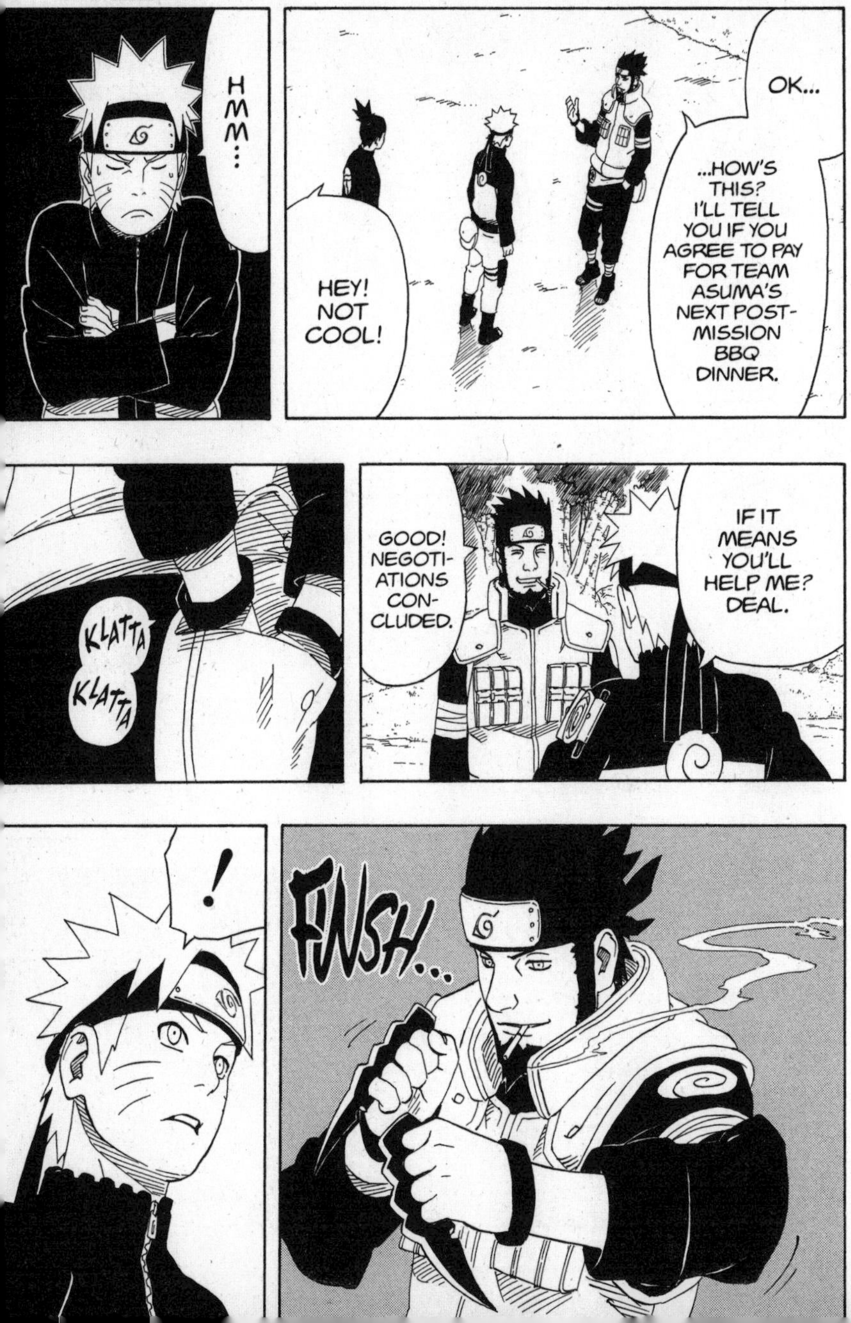
OK...
...HOW'S THIS? I'LL TELL YOU IF YOU AGREE TO PAY FOR TEAM ASUMA'S NEXT POST-MISSION BBQ DINNER.
HEY! NOT COOL!
HMM...
IF IT MEANS YOU'LL HELP ME? DEAL.
GOOD! NEGOTIATIONS CONCLUDED.
KLATTA
KLATTA
FWSH...
!

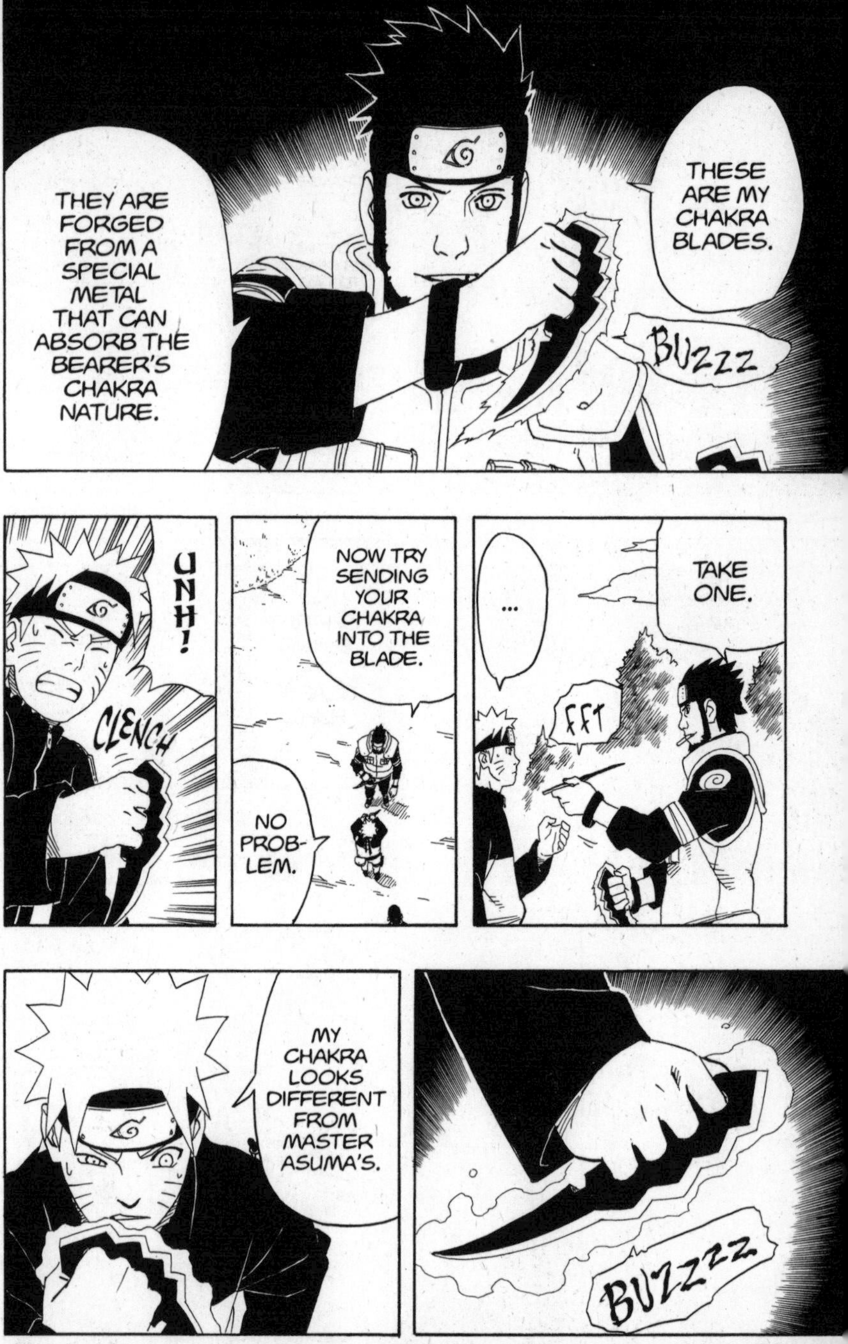
THESE ARE MY CHAKRA BLADES.
BUZZZ
THEY ARE FORGED FROM A SPECIAL METAL THAT CAN ABSORB THE BEARER'S CHAKRA NATURE.
TAKE ONE.
FFT
...
NOW TRY SENDING YOUR CHAKRA INTO THE BLADE.
NO PROB-LEM.
UNH!
CLENCH
BUZZZZ
MY CHAKRA LOOKS DIFFERENT FROM MASTER ASUMA'S.

READ THIS WAY

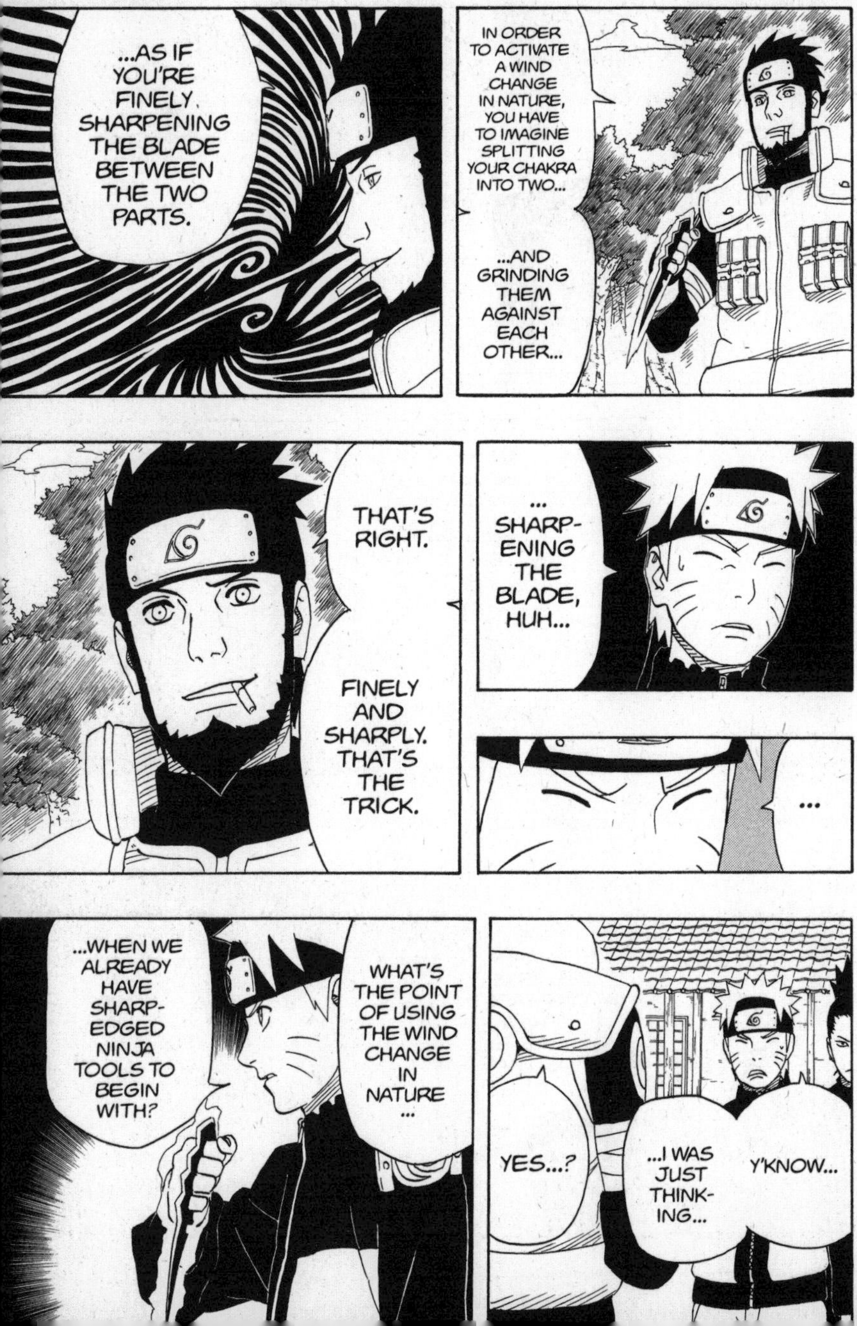

IN ORDER TO ACTIVATE A WIND CHANGE IN NATURE, YOU HAVE TO IMAGINE SPLITTING YOUR CHAKRA INTO TWO...
...AND GRINDING THEM AGAINST EACH OTHER...
...AS IF YOU'RE FINELY SHARPENING THE BLADE BETWEEN THE TWO PARTS.
... SHARPENING THE BLADE, HUH...
...
THAT'S RIGHT.
FINELY AND SHARPLY. THAT'S THE TRICK.
Y'KNOW...
...I WAS JUST THINKING...
YES...?
WHAT'S THE POINT OF USING THE WIND CHANGE IN NATURE ...
...WHEN WE ALREADY HAVE SHARP-EDGED NINJA TOOLS TO BEGIN WITH?

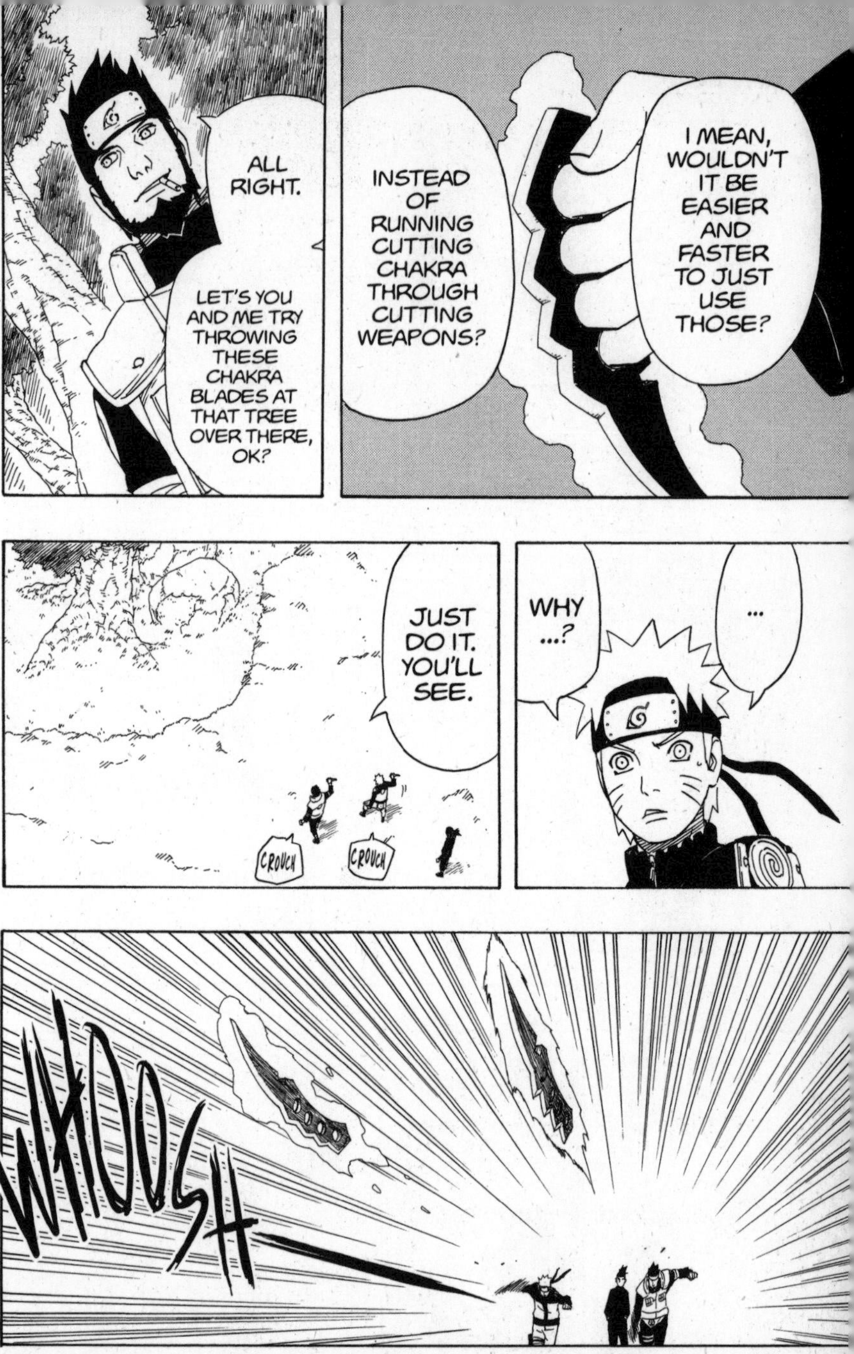
I MEAN, WOULDN'T IT BE EASIER AND FASTER TO JUST USE THOSE?
INSTEAD OF RUNNING CUTTING CHAKRA THROUGH CUTTING WEAPONS?
ALL RIGHT.
LET'S YOU AND ME TRY THROWING THESE CHAKRA BLADES AT THAT TREE OVER THERE, OK?
...
WHY ...?
JUST DO IT. YOU'LL SEE.
CROUCH
CROUCH
WHOOSH

READ THIS WAY

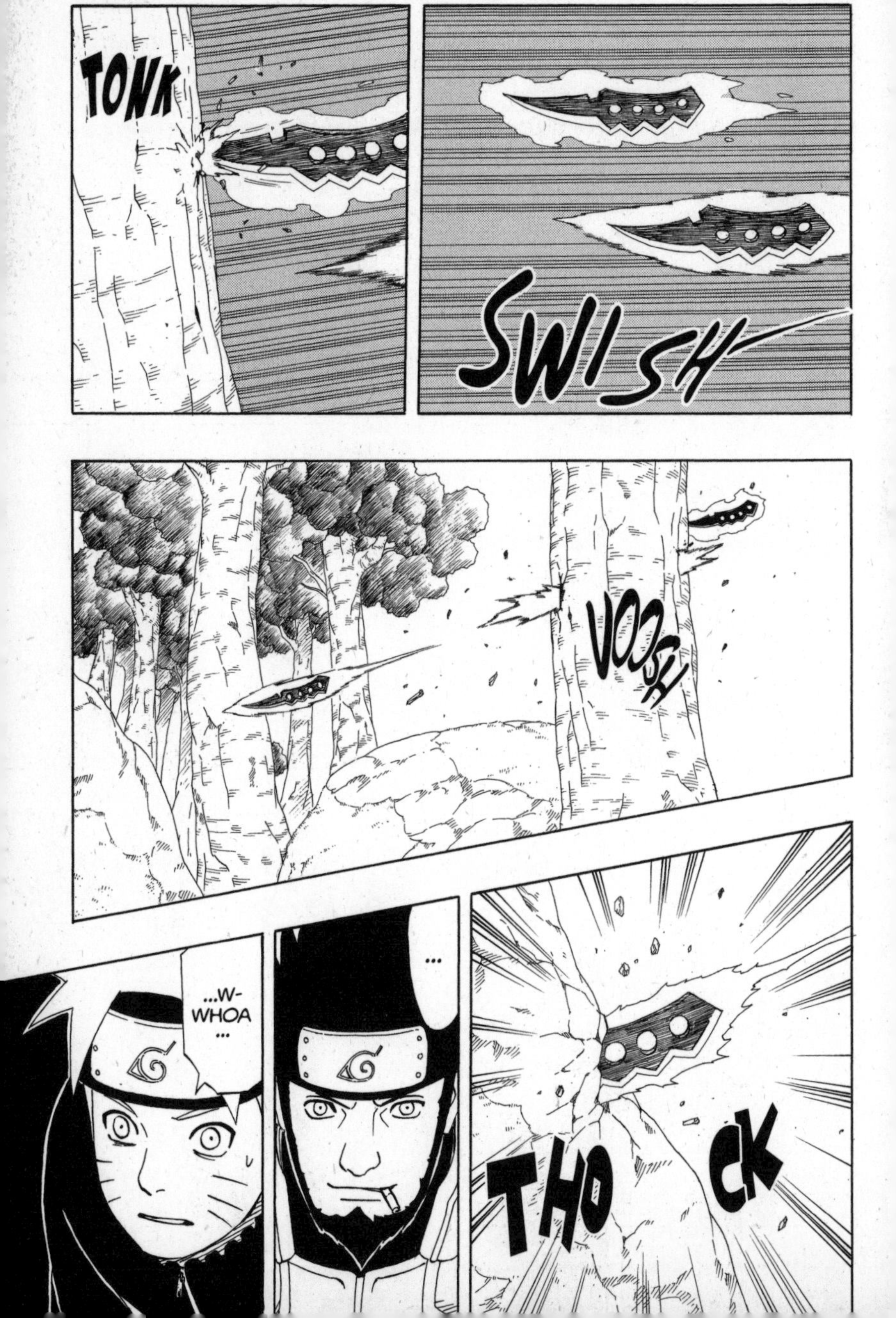
SWISH
TONK
VOOSH
THO CK
...
...W-WHOA ...

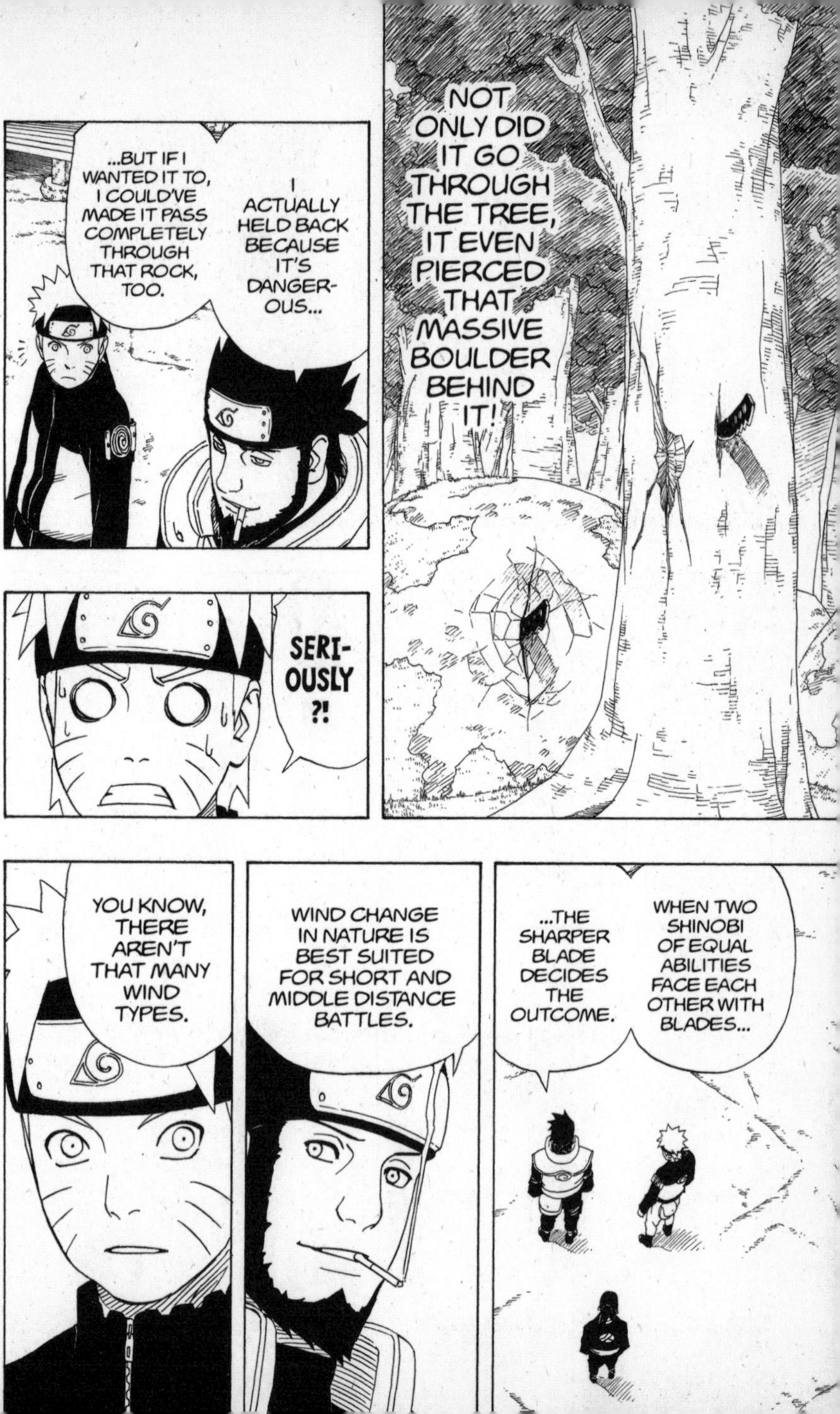
NOT ONLY DID IT GO THROUGH THE TREE, IT EVEN PIERCED THAT MASSIVE BOULDER BEHIND IT!
I ACTUALLY HELD BACK BECAUSE IT'S DANGER-OUS...
...BUT IF I WANTED IT TO, I COULD'VE MADE IT PASS COMPLETELY THROUGH THAT ROCK, TOO.
SERI-OUSLY ?!
WHEN TWO SHINOBI OF EQUAL ABILITIES FACE EACH OTHER WITH BLADES...
...THE SHARPER BLADE DECIDES THE OUTCOME.
WIND CHANGE IN NATURE IS BEST SUITED FOR SHORT AND MIDDLE DISTANCE BATTLES.
YOU KNOW, THERE AREN'T THAT MANY WIND TYPES.

WILL DO!

THANKS!

FEEL FREE TO DROP BY ANYTIME WITH QUESTIONS.

AS LONG AS YOU'RE WILLING TO PAY.

FWP

WHAT THE? THAT WAS A CLONE?

BO OF

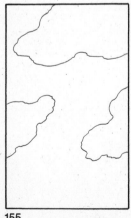

I THINK NARUTO FORGOT WE HAVE CHOJI ON OUR TEAM.

YOU'RE CRUEL...

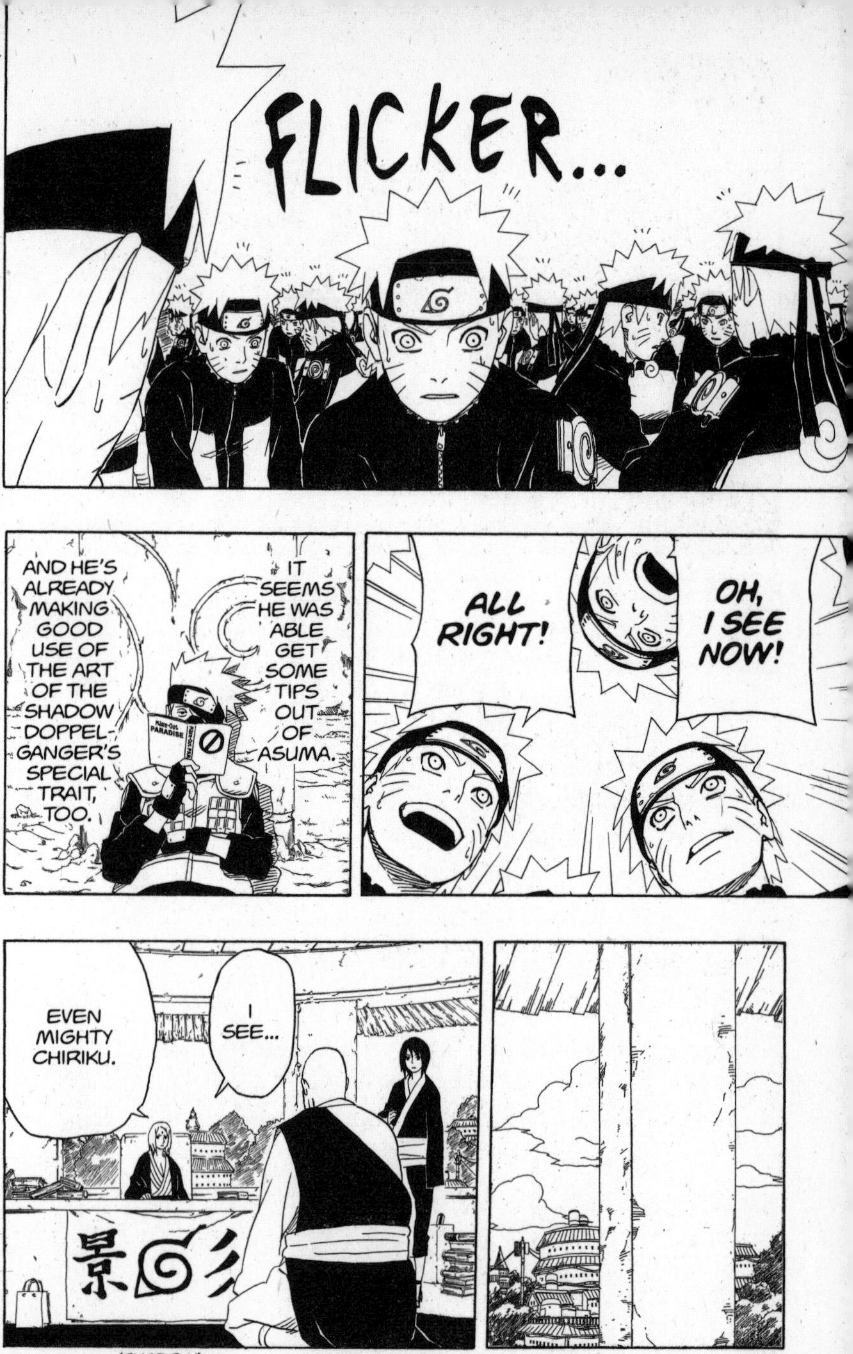

FLICKER...
OH, I SEE NOW!
ALL RIGHT!
IT SEEMS HE WAS ABLE GET SOME TIPS OUT OF ASUMA.
AND HE'S ALREADY MAKING GOOD USE OF THE ART OF THE SHADOW DOPPELGANGER'S SPECIAL TRAIT, TOO.
I SEE...
EVEN MIGHTY CHIRIKU.

(SHADOW)

READ THIS WAY

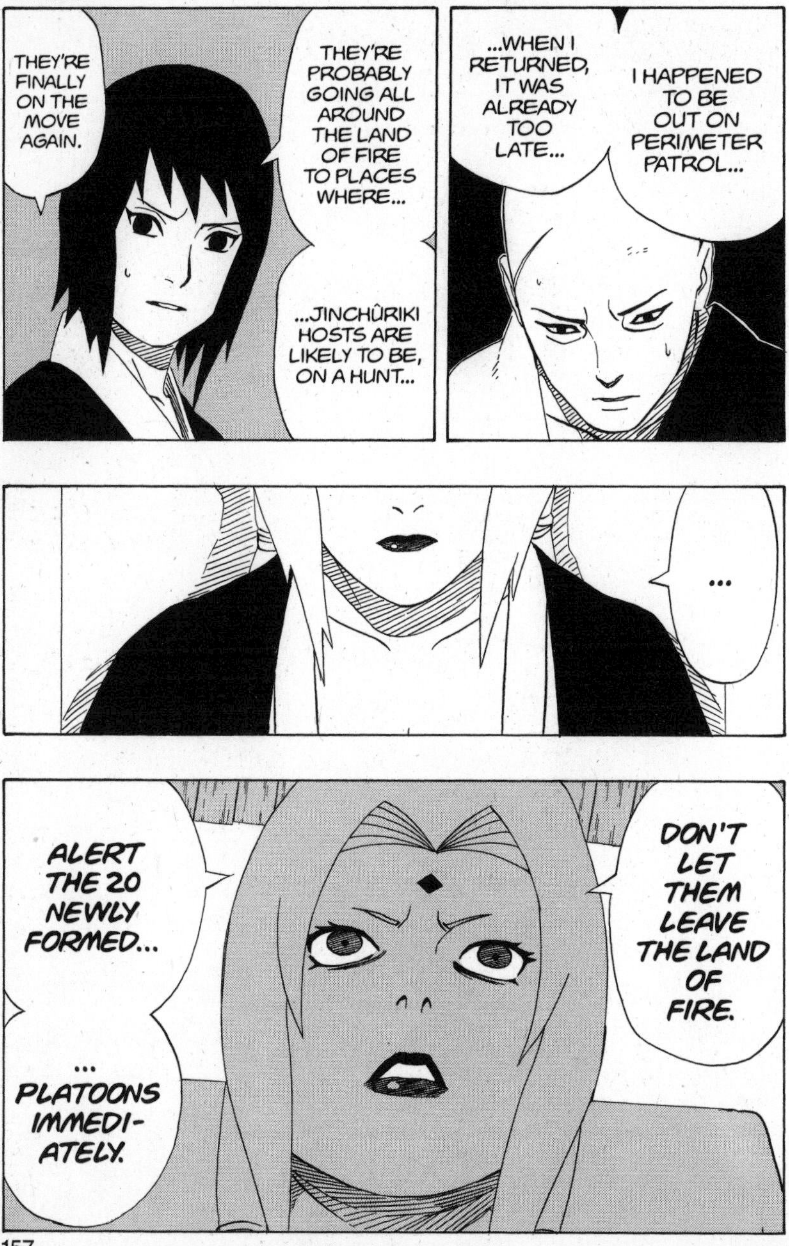
I HAPPENED TO BE OUT ON PERIMETER PATROL...
...WHEN I RETURNED, IT WAS ALREADY TOO LATE...
THEY'RE PROBABLY GOING ALL AROUND THE LAND OF FIRE TO PLACES WHERE...
...JINCHÛRIKI HOSTS ARE LIKELY TO BE, ON A HUNT...
THEY'RE FINALLY ON THE MOVE AGAIN.
...
DON'T LET THEM LEAVE THE LAND OF FIRE.
ALERT THE 20 NEWLY FORMED...
...PLATOONS IMMEDI-ATELY.

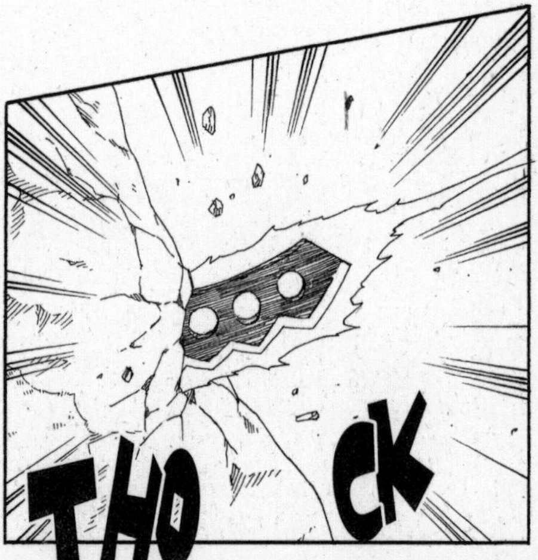
THO CK

Number 318: Smooth Training

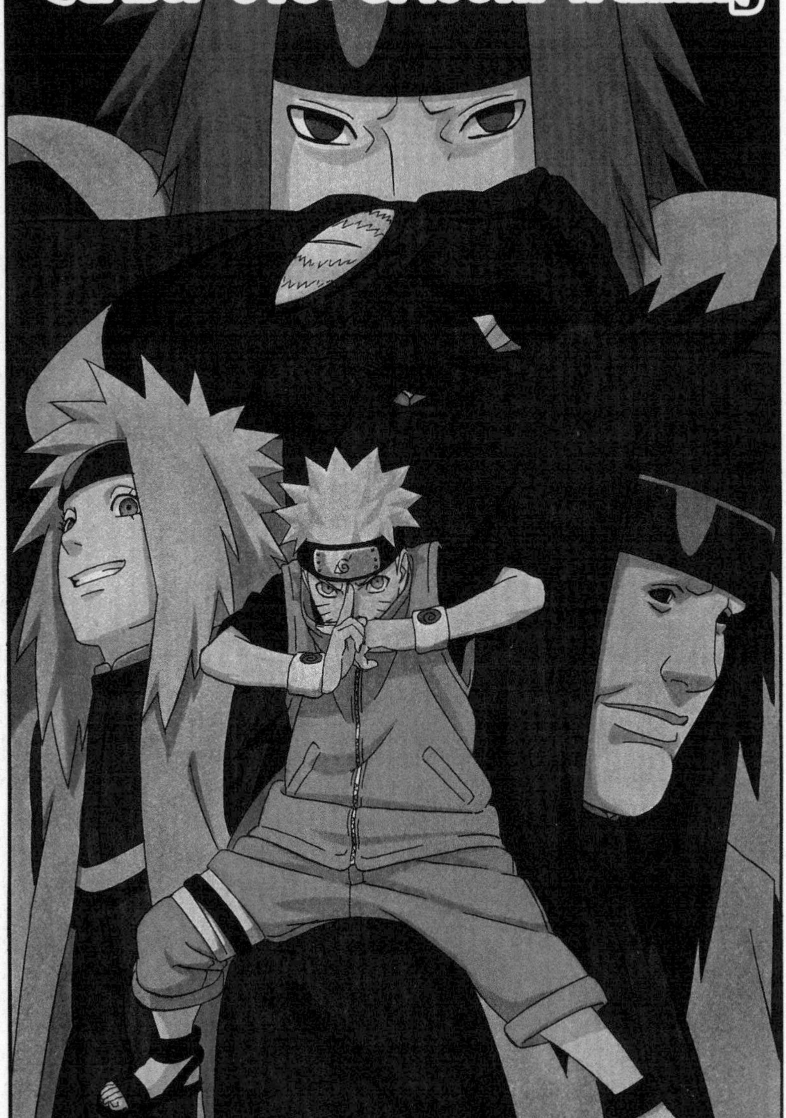

READ THIS WAY

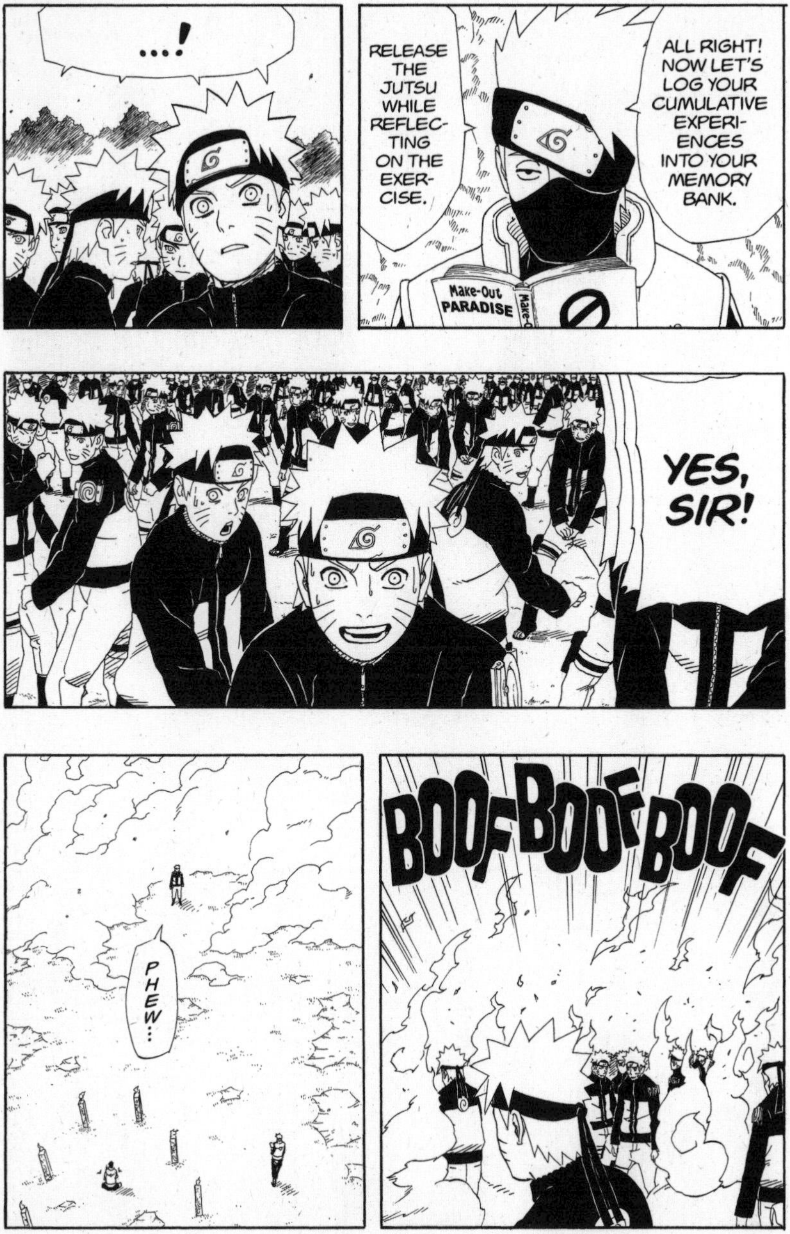
ALL RIGHT! NOW LET'S LOG YOUR CUMULATIVE EXPERIENCES INTO YOUR MEMORY BANK.
RELEASE THE JUTSU WHILE REFLECTING ON THE EXERCISE.
Make-Out PARADISE
...!
YES, SIR!
BOOF BOOF BOOF
PHEW...

READ THIS WAY

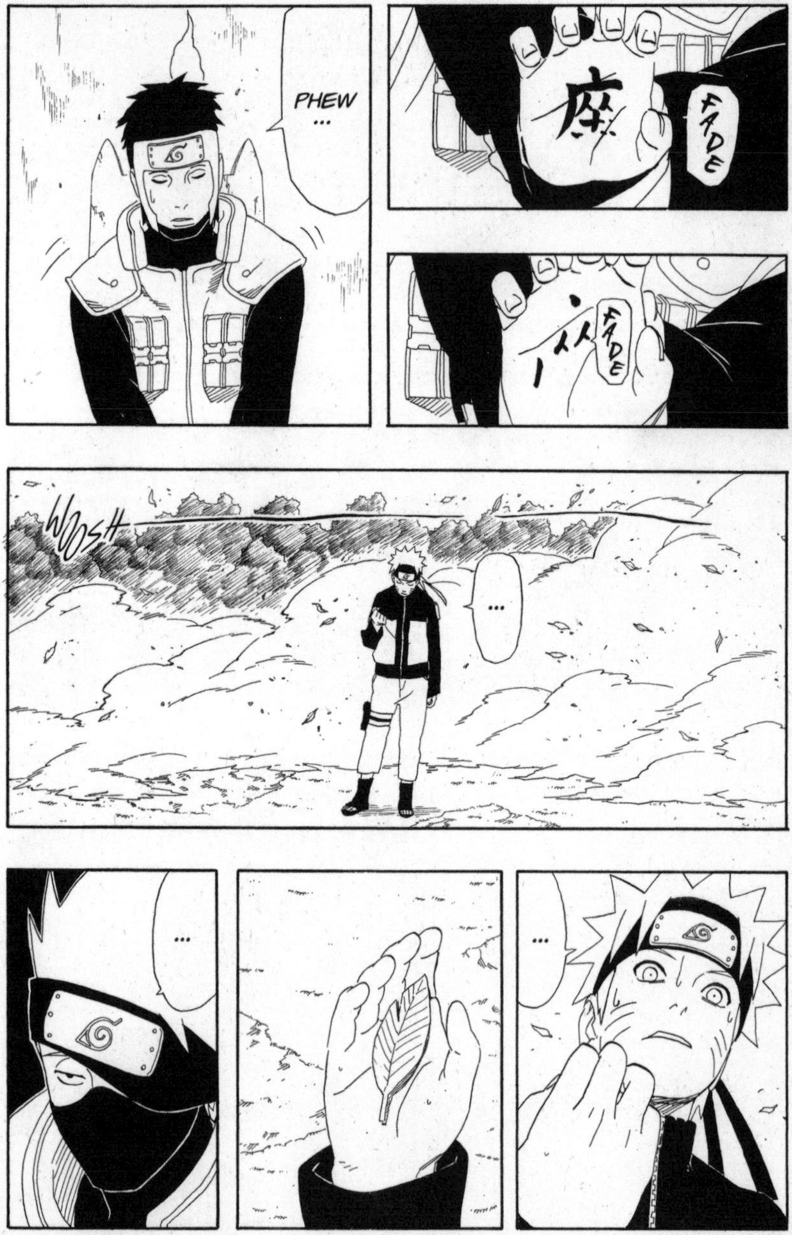
FADE
FADE
PHEW ...
WOOSH
...
...
...

READ THIS WAY

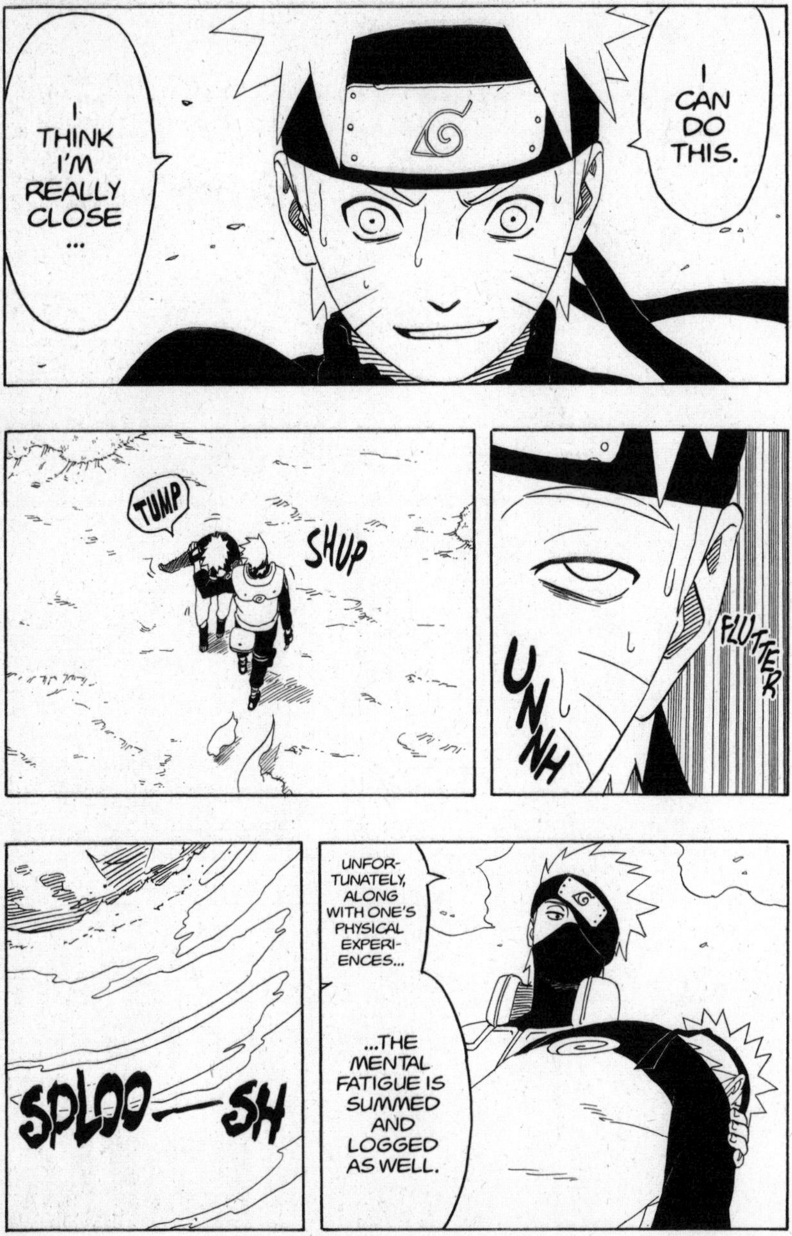

I CAN DO THIS.
I THINK I'M REALLY CLOSE ...
UNNH
FLUTTER
TUMP
SHUP
UNFOR-TUNATELY, ALONG WITH ONE'S PHYSICAL EXPERI-ENCES...
...THE MENTAL FATIGUE IS SUMMED AND LOGGED AS WELL.
SPLOO—SH

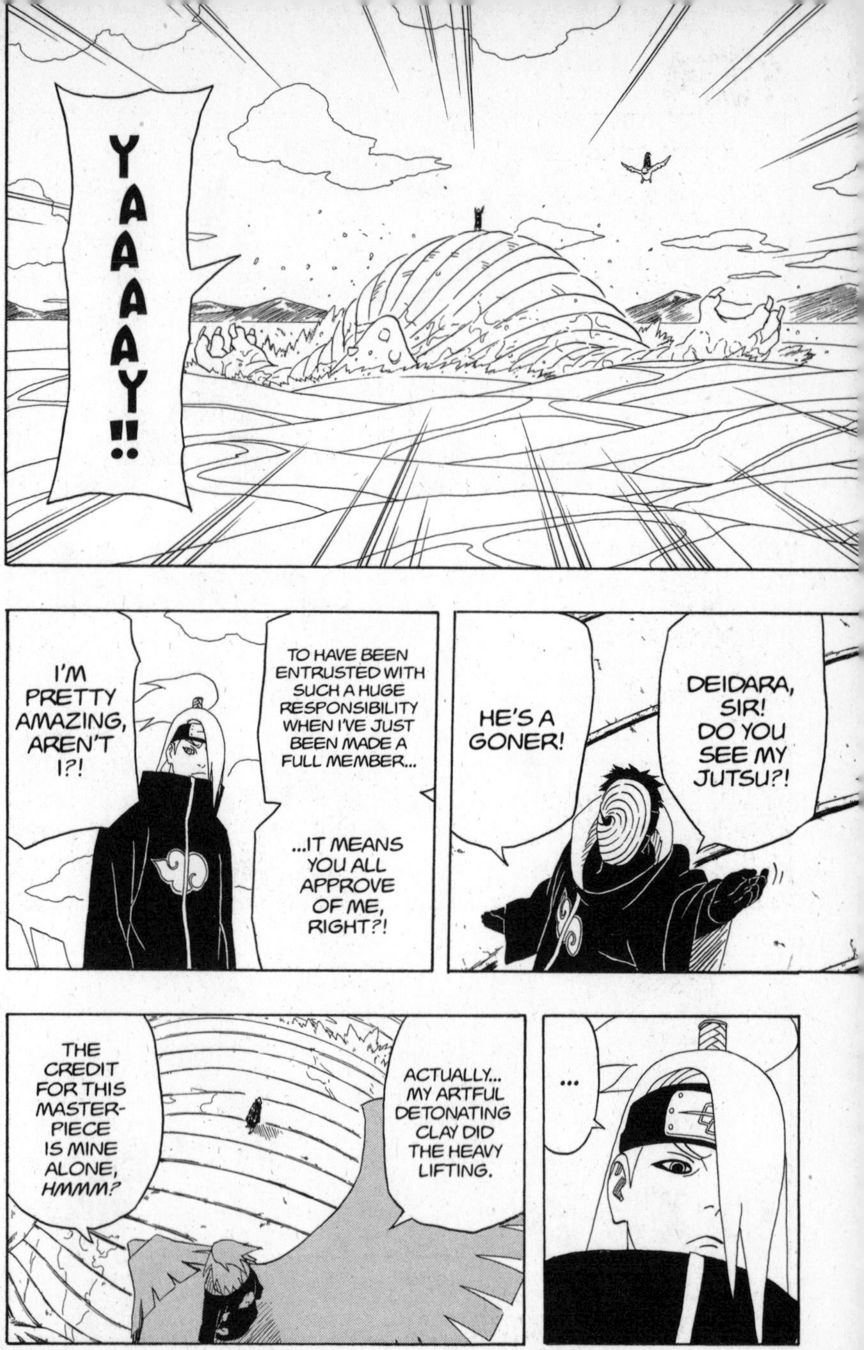
YAAAAY!!
DEIDARA, SIR! DO YOU SEE MY JUTSU?!
HE'S A GONER!
TO HAVE BEEN ENTRUSTED WITH SUCH A HUGE RESPONSIBILITY WHEN I'VE JUST BEEN MADE A FULL MEMBER...
...IT MEANS YOU ALL APPROVE OF ME, RIGHT?!
I'M PRETTY AMAZING, AREN'T I?!
...
ACTUALLY... MY ARTFUL DETONATING CLAY DID THE HEAVY LIFTING.
THE CREDIT FOR THIS MASTER-PIECE IS MINE ALONE, HMMM?

READ THIS WAY

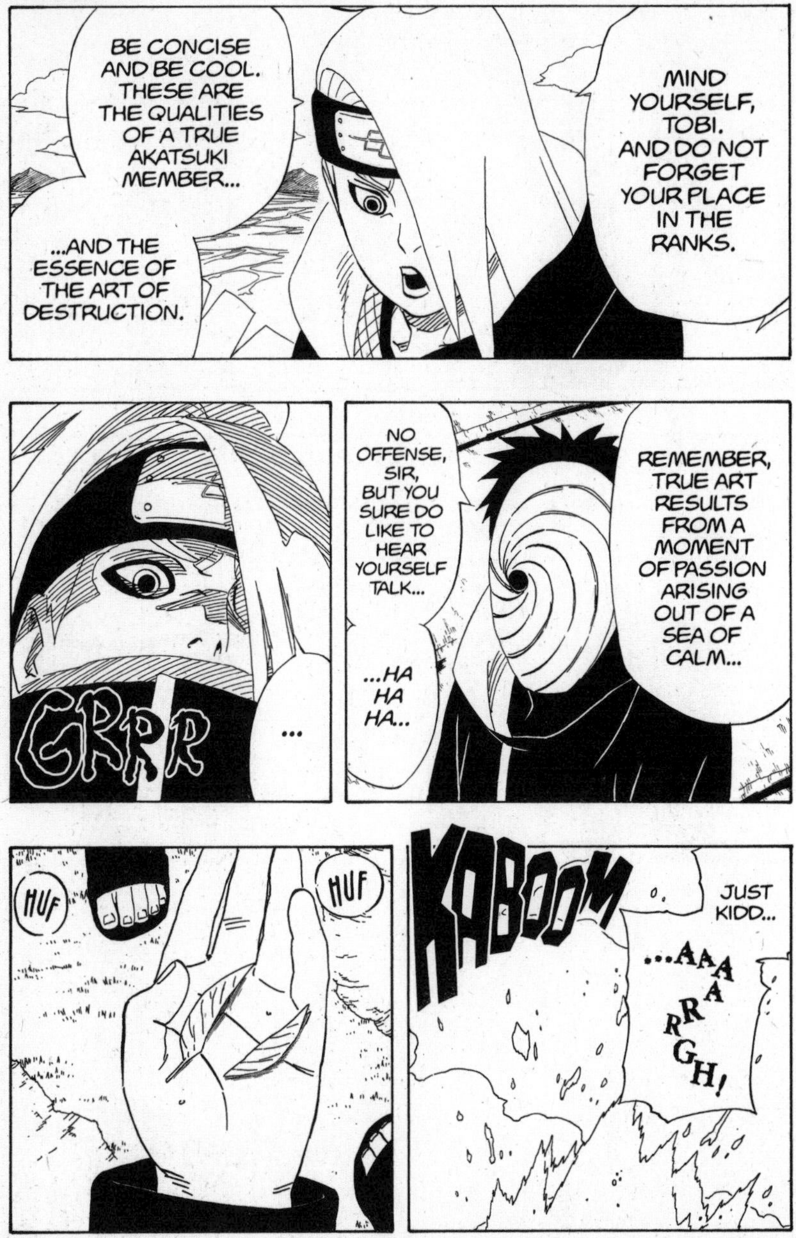
MIND YOURSELF, TOBI. AND DO NOT FORGET YOUR PLACE IN THE RANKS.
BE CONCISE AND BE COOL. THESE ARE THE QUALITIES OF A TRUE AKATSUKI MEMBER...
...AND THE ESSENCE OF THE ART OF DESTRUCTION.
REMEMBER, TRUE ART RESULTS FROM A MOMENT OF PASSION ARISING OUT OF A SEA OF CALM...
NO OFFENSE, SIR, BUT YOU SURE DO LIKE TO HEAR YOURSELF TALK...
...HA HA HA...
...
GRRR
JUST KIDD...
...AAAARRRGH!
KABOOM
HUF
HUF

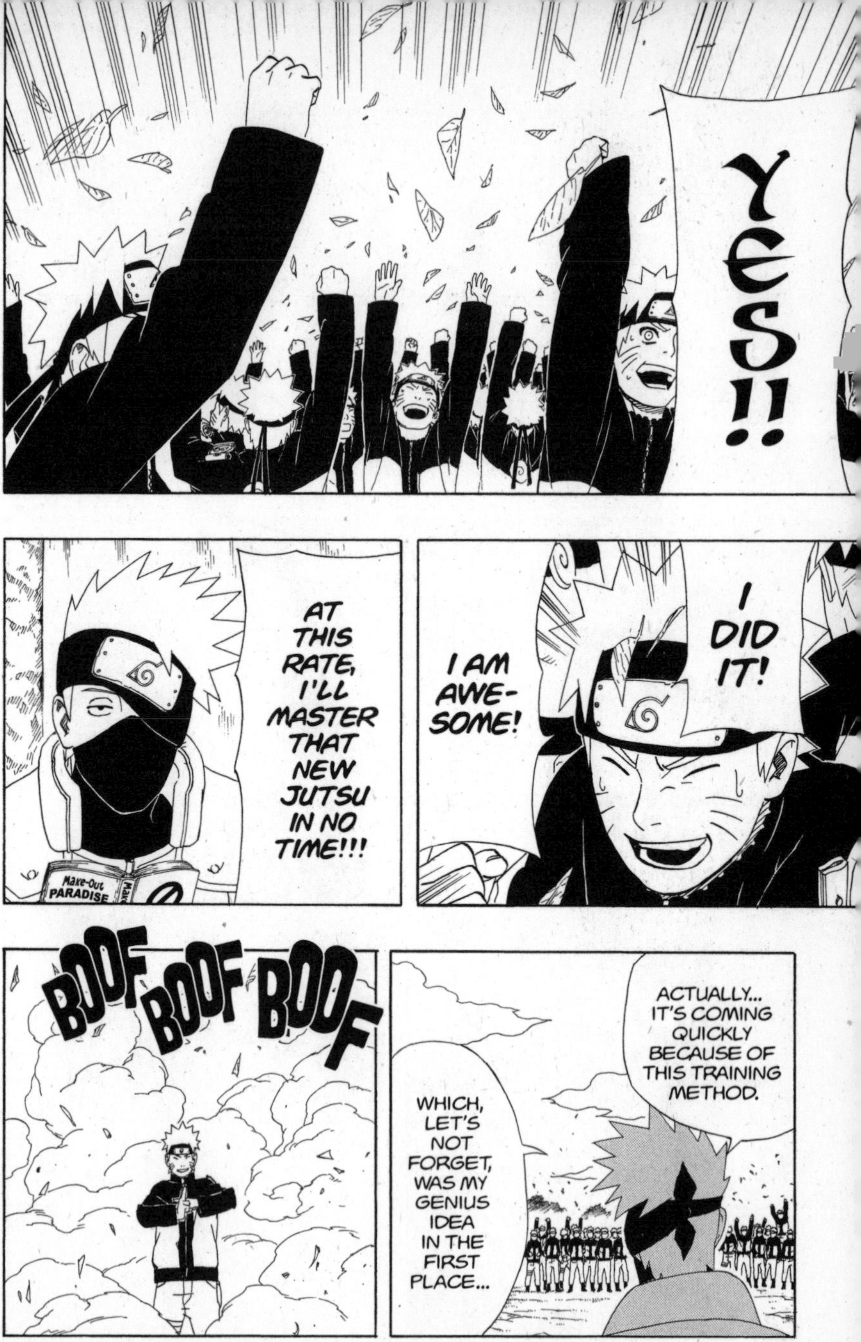
YES!!
I DID IT!
I AM AWESOME!
AT THIS RATE, I'LL MASTER THAT NEW JUTSU IN NO TIME!!!
ACTUALLY... IT'S COMING QUICKLY BECAUSE OF THIS TRAINING METHOD.
WHICH, LET'S NOT FORGET, WAS MY GENIUS IDEA IN THE FIRST PLACE...
BOOF BOOF BOOF
Make-Out PARADISE

READ THIS WAY

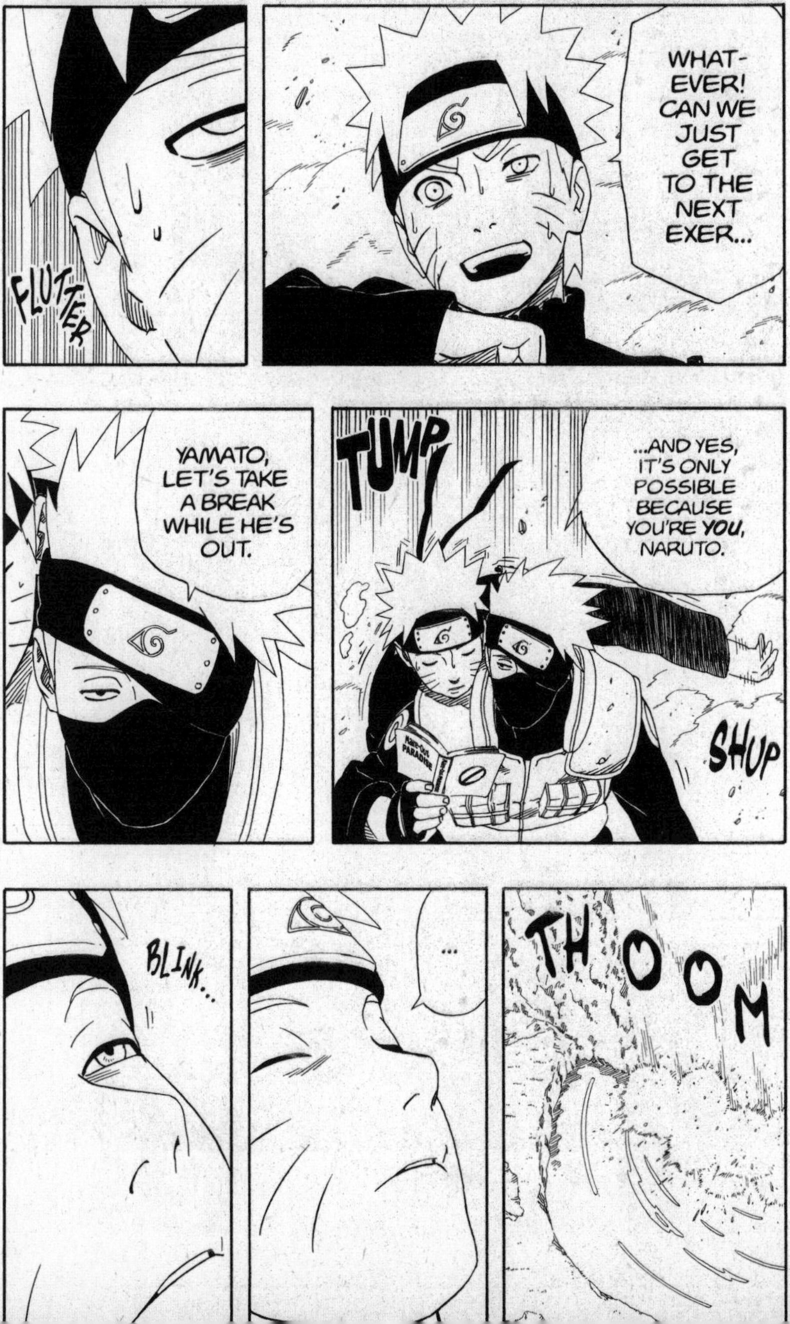
WHAT-EVER! CAN WE JUST GET TO THE NEXT EXER...
FLUTTER
...AND YES, IT'S ONLY POSSIBLE BECAUSE YOU'RE *YOU*, NARUTO.
TUMP
SHUP
YAMATO, LET'S TAKE A BREAK WHILE HE'S OUT.
THOOM
...
BLINK...

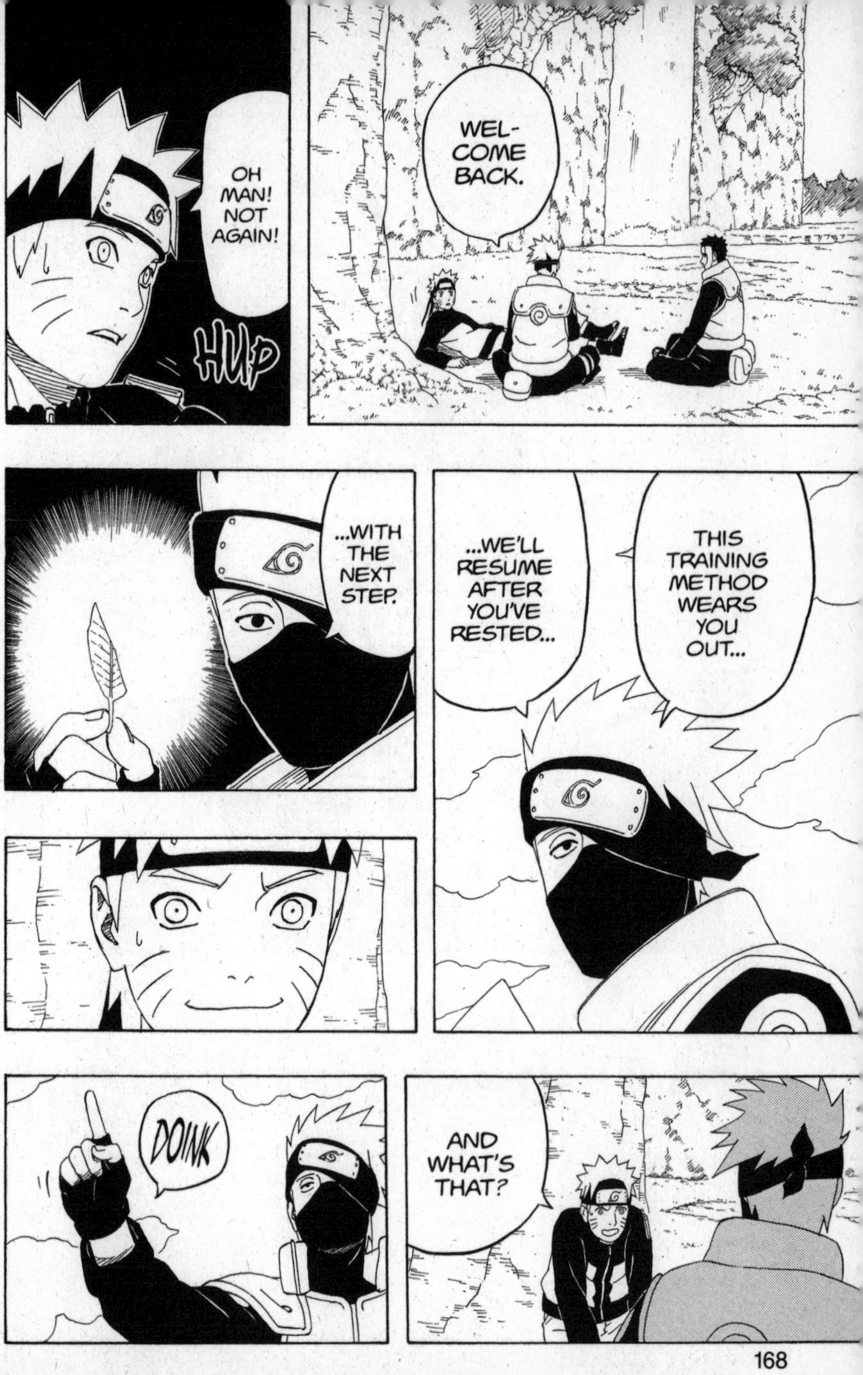
WEL-COME BACK.
OH MAN! NOT AGAIN!
HUP
THIS TRAINING METHOD WEARS YOU OUT...
...WE'LL RESUME AFTER YOU'VE RESTED...
...WITH THE NEXT STEP.
AND WHAT'S THAT?
DOINK

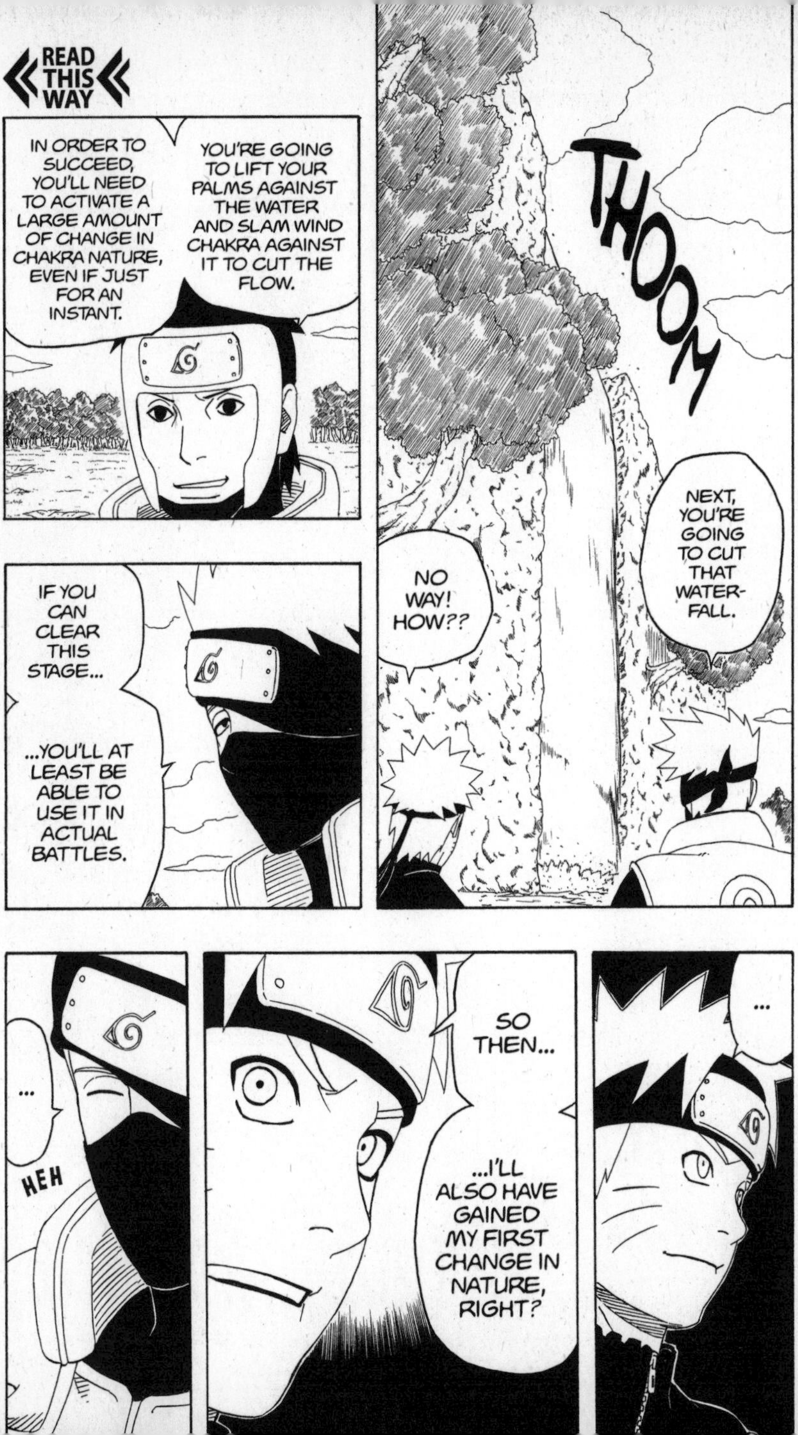
READ THIS WAY
THOOM
NEXT, YOU'RE GOING TO CUT THAT WATER-FALL.
NO WAY! HOW??
YOU'RE GOING TO LIFT YOUR PALMS AGAINST THE WATER AND SLAM WIND CHAKRA AGAINST IT TO CUT THE FLOW.
IN ORDER TO SUCCEED, YOU'LL NEED TO ACTIVATE A LARGE AMOUNT OF CHANGE IN CHAKRA NATURE, EVEN IF JUST FOR AN INSTANT.
IF YOU CAN CLEAR THIS STAGE...
...YOU'LL AT LEAST BE ABLE TO USE IT IN ACTUAL BATTLES.
...
SO THEN...
...I'LL ALSO HAVE GAINED MY FIRST CHANGE IN NATURE, RIGHT?
...
HEH

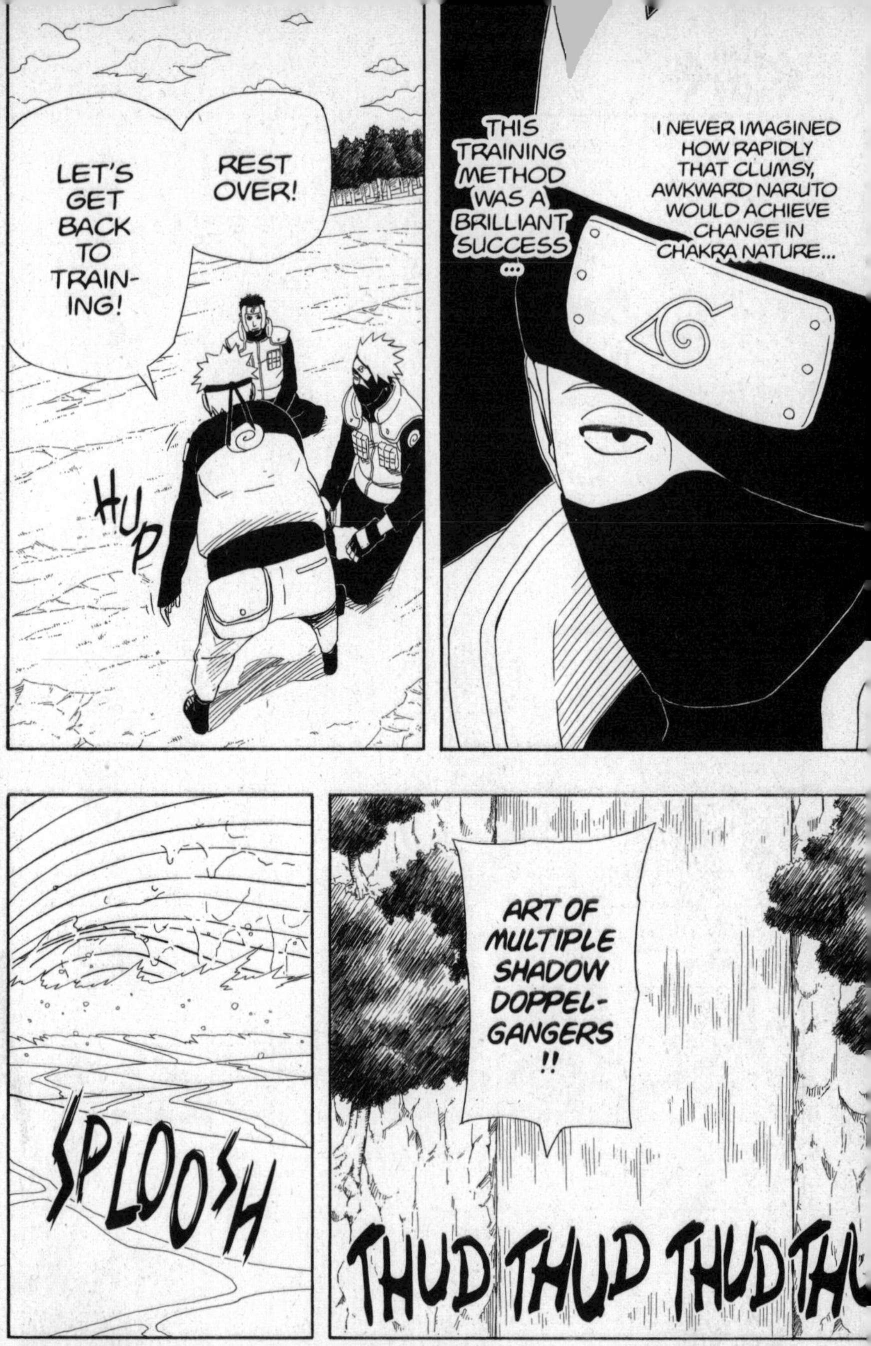
I NEVER IMAGINED HOW RAPIDLY THAT CLUMSY, AWKWARD NARUTO WOULD ACHIEVE CHANGE IN CHAKRA NATURE...
THIS TRAINING METHOD WAS A BRILLIANT SUCCESS...
REST OVER!
LET'S GET BACK TO TRAIN-ING!
HUP
ART OF MULTIPLE SHADOW DOPPEL-GANGERS!!
THUD THUD THUD THU
SPLOOSH

READ THIS WAY

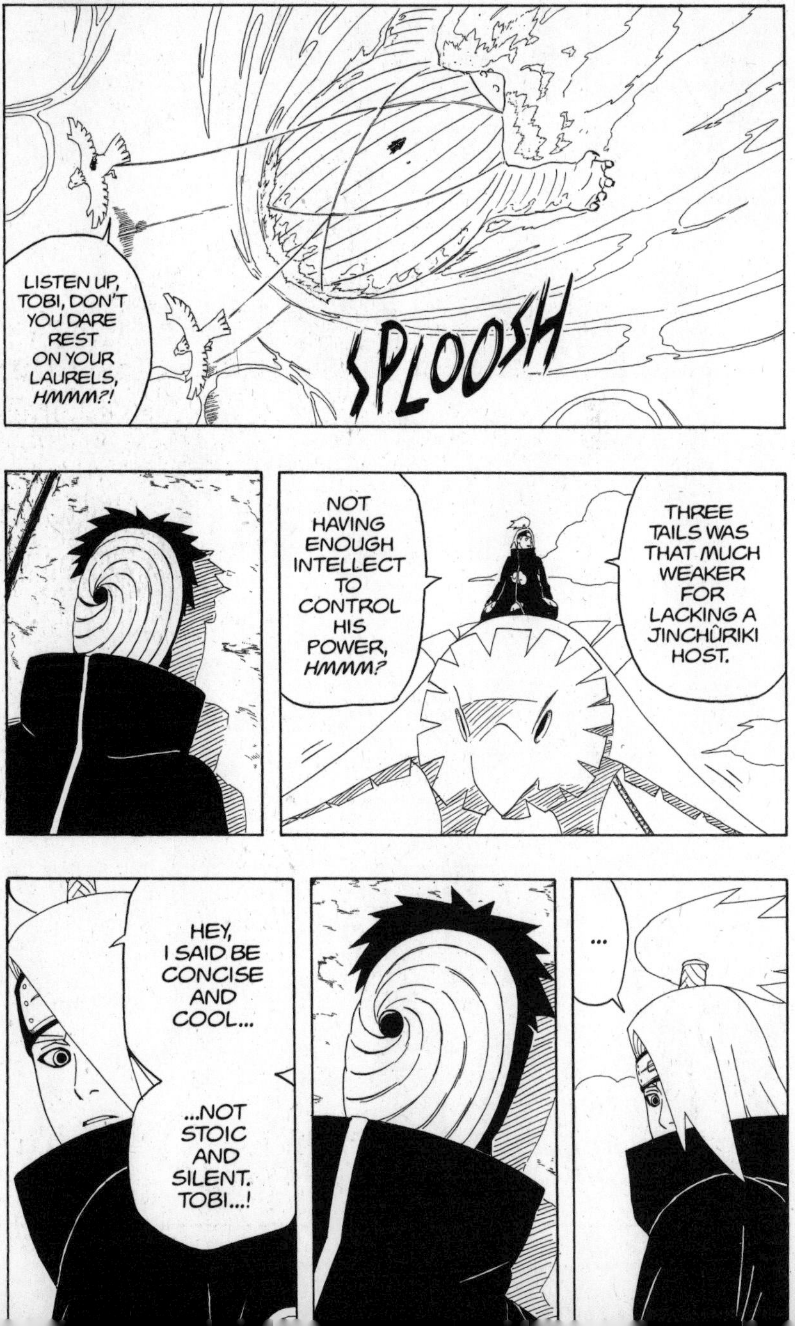
LISTEN UP, TOBI, DON'T YOU DARE REST ON YOUR LAURELS, HMMM?!
SPLOOSH
THREE TAILS WAS THAT MUCH WEAKER FOR LACKING A JINCHÛRIKI HOST.
NOT HAVING ENOUGH INTELLECT TO CONTROL HIS POWER, HMMM?
...
HEY, I SAID BE CONCISE AND COOL...
...NOT STOIC AND SILENT. TOBI...!

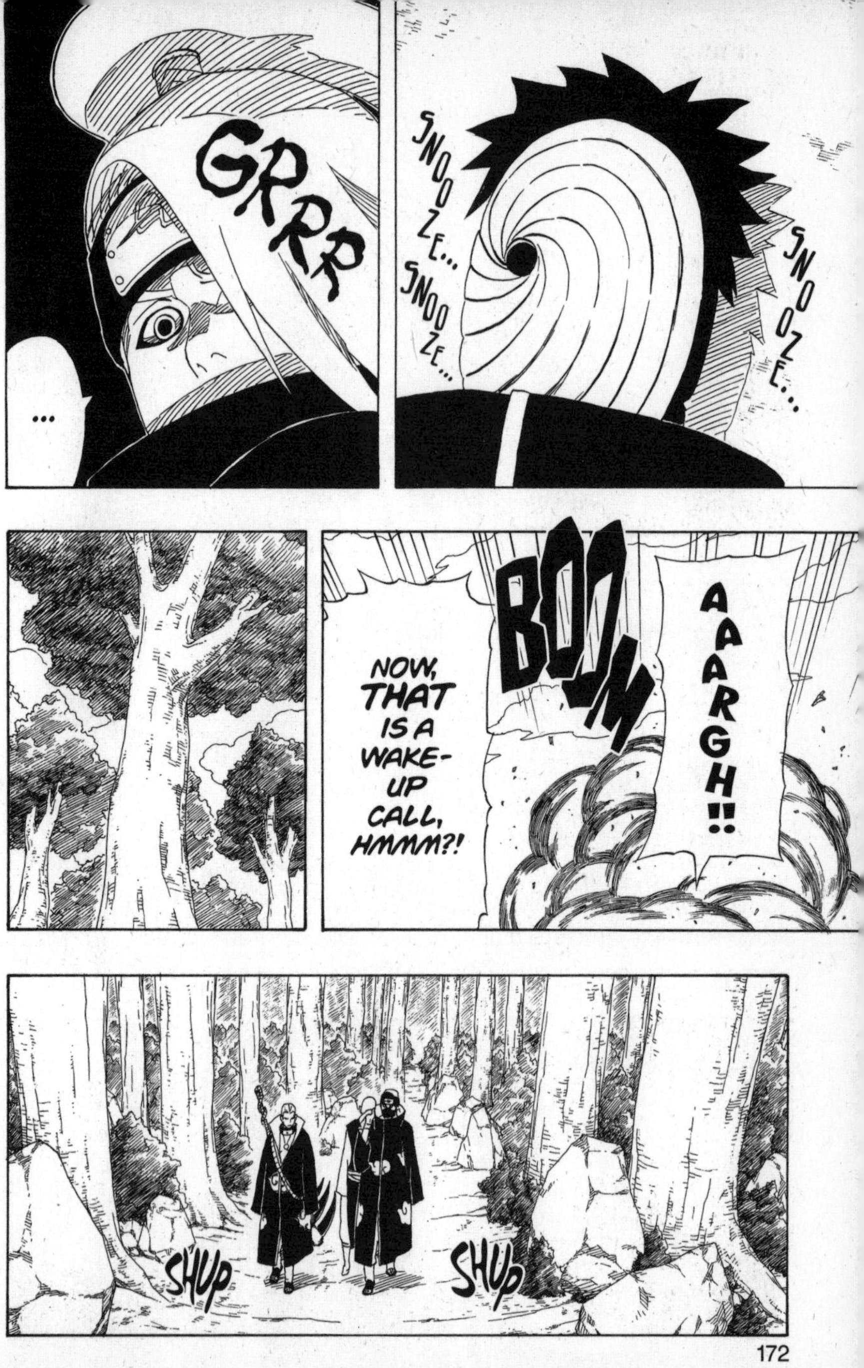
SNOOZE...
SNOOZE...
SNOOZE...
GRRR
...
AAARGH!!
BOOM
NOW, THAT IS A WAKE-UP CALL, HMMM?!
SHUP
SHUP

READ THIS WAY

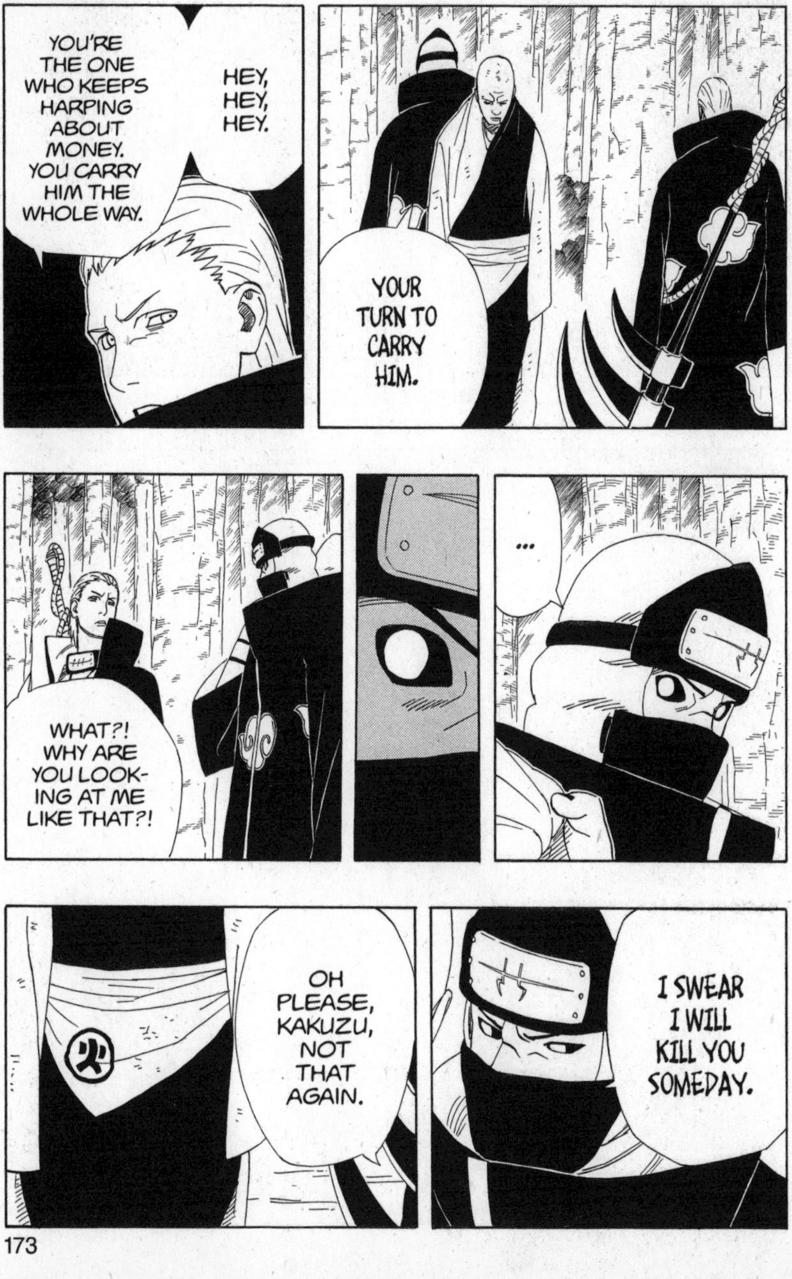
YOUR TURN TO CARRY HIM.
HEY, HEY, HEY.
YOU'RE THE ONE WHO KEEPS HARPING ABOUT MONEY. YOU CARRY HIM THE WHOLE WAY.
...
WHAT?! WHY ARE YOU LOOK-ING AT ME LIKE THAT?!
I SWEAR I WILL KILL YOU SOMEDAY.
OH PLEASE, KAKUZU, NOT THAT AGAIN.

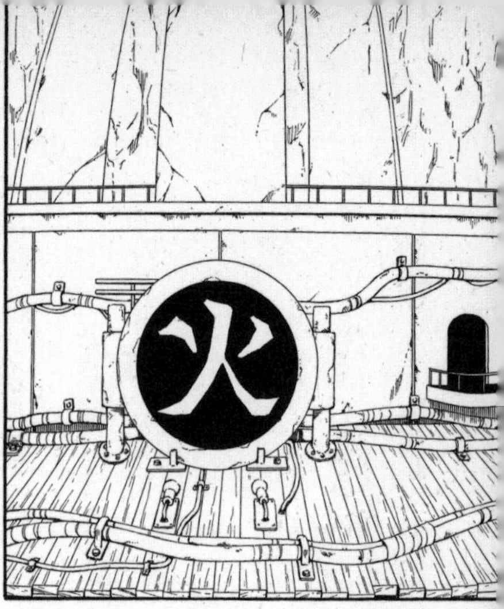
火

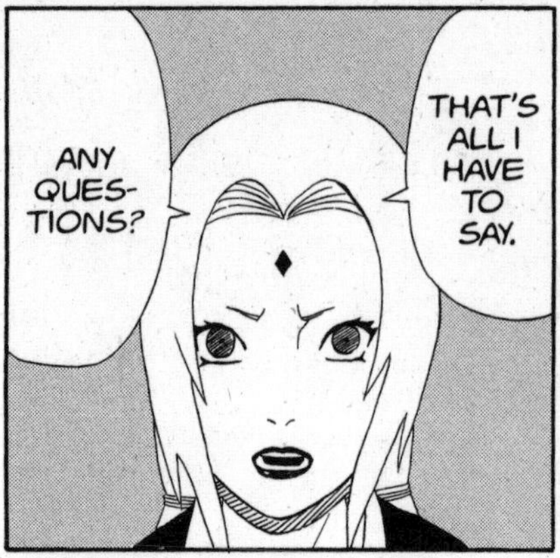
THAT'S ALL I HAVE TO SAY.
ANY QUES-TIONS?

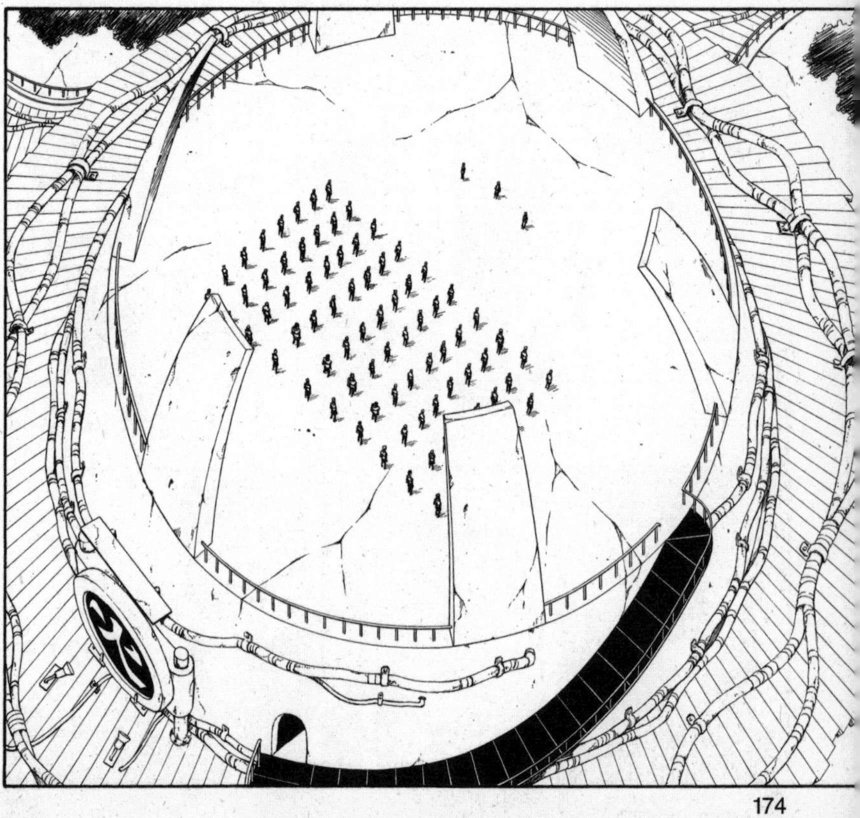

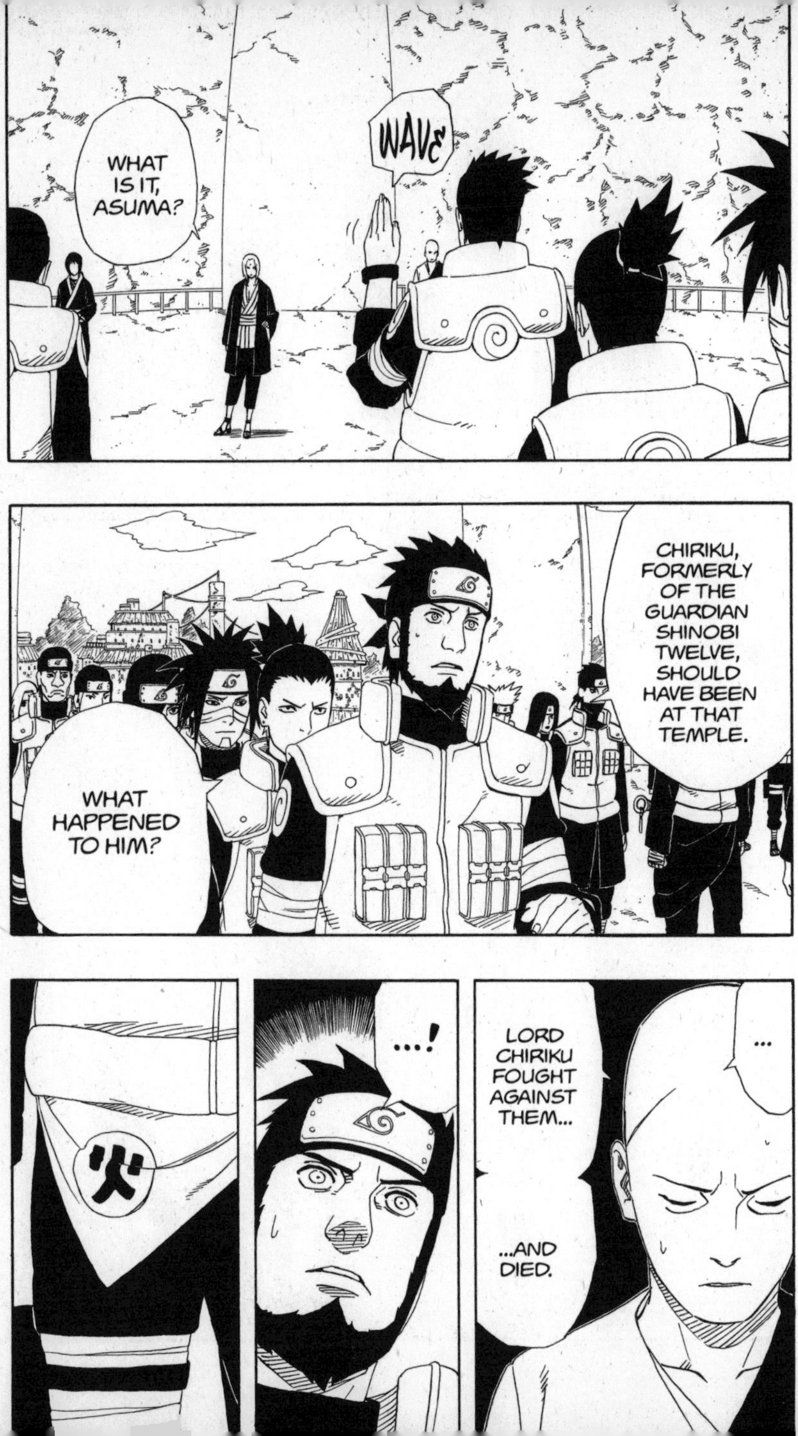
WAVE
WHAT IS IT, ASUMA?
CHIRIKU, FORMERLY OF THE GUARDIAN SHINOBI TWELVE, SHOULD HAVE BEEN AT THAT TEMPLE.
WHAT HAPPENED TO HIM?
...
LORD CHIRIKU FOUGHT AGAINST THEM...
...AND DIED.
...!

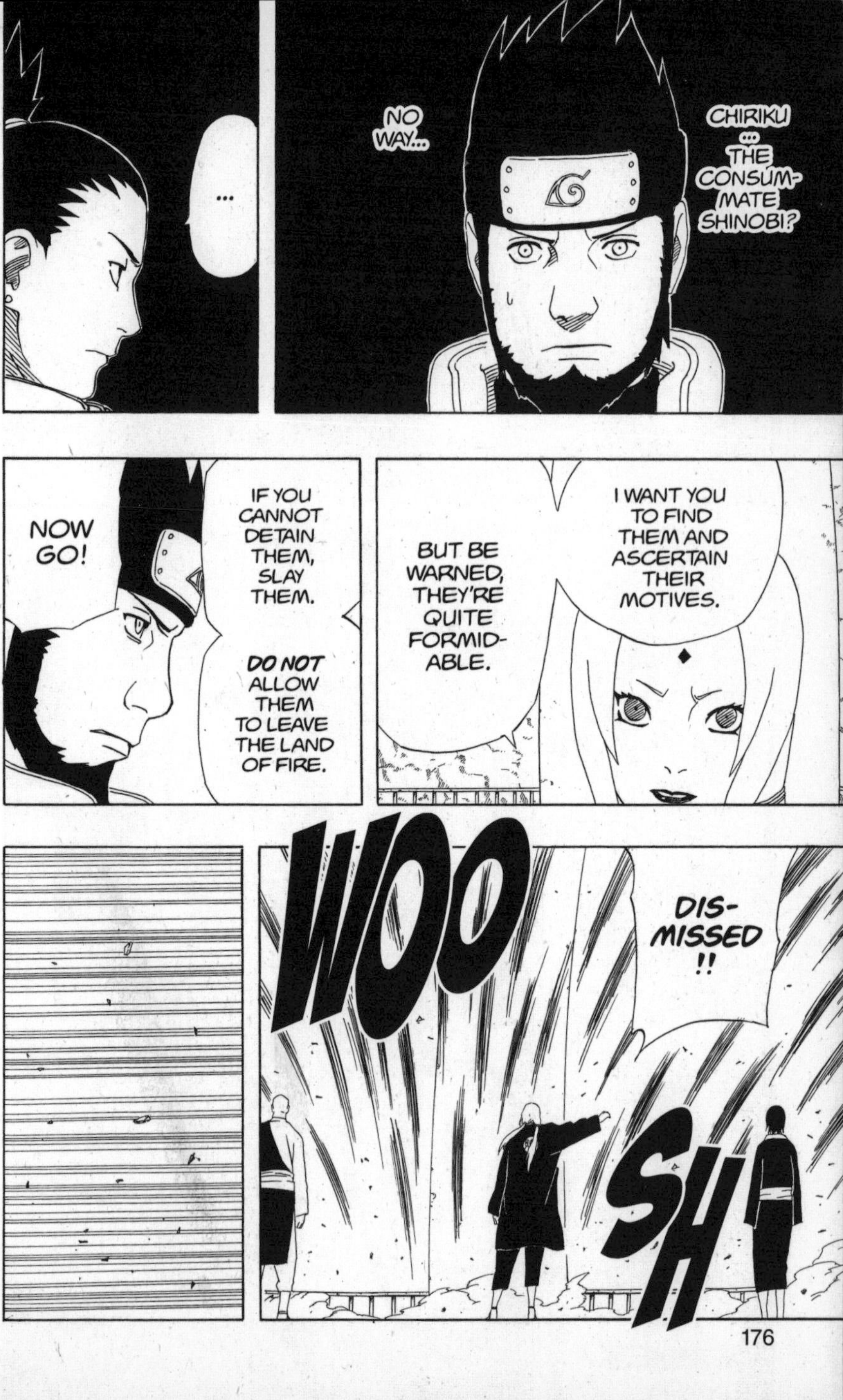
CHIRIKU... THE CONSUMMATE SHINOBI?
NO WAY...
...
I WANT YOU TO FIND THEM AND ASCERTAIN THEIR MOTIVES.
BUT BE WARNED, THEY'RE QUITE FORMIDABLE.
IF YOU CANNOT DETAIN THEM, SLAY THEM.
DO NOT ALLOW THEM TO LEAVE THE LAND OF FIRE.
NOW GO!
DISMISSED!!
WOOSH

READ THIS WAY

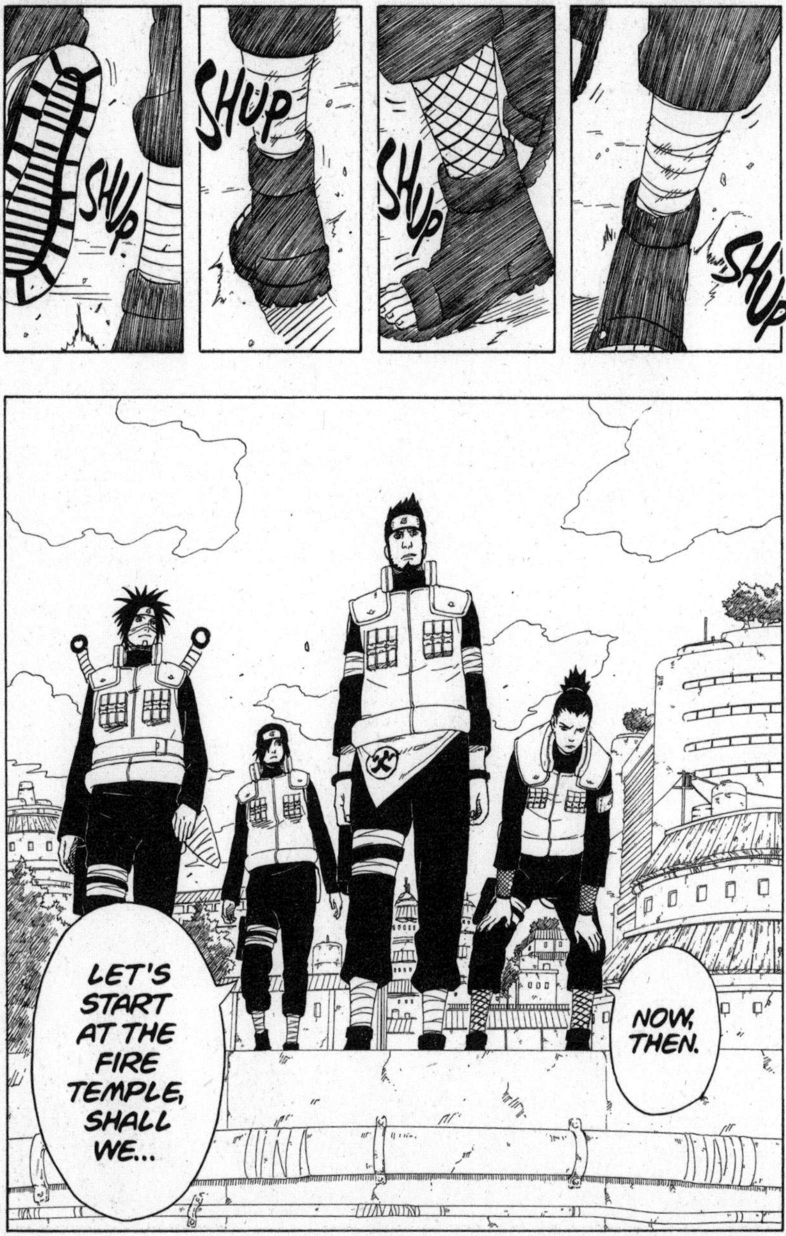
SHUP
SHUP
SHUP
SHUP
NOW, THEN.
LET'S START AT THE FIRE TEMPLE, SHALL WE...

NARUTO

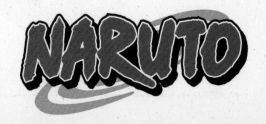

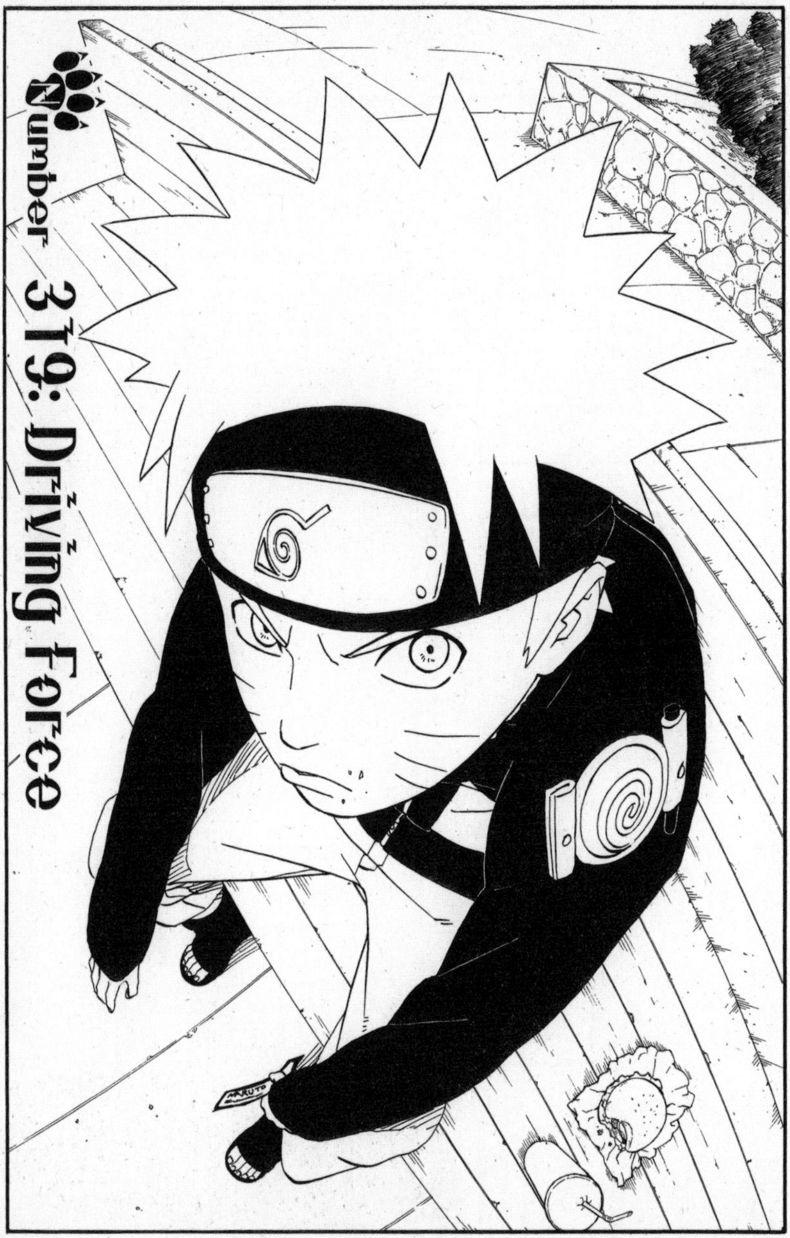
Number 319: Driving Force

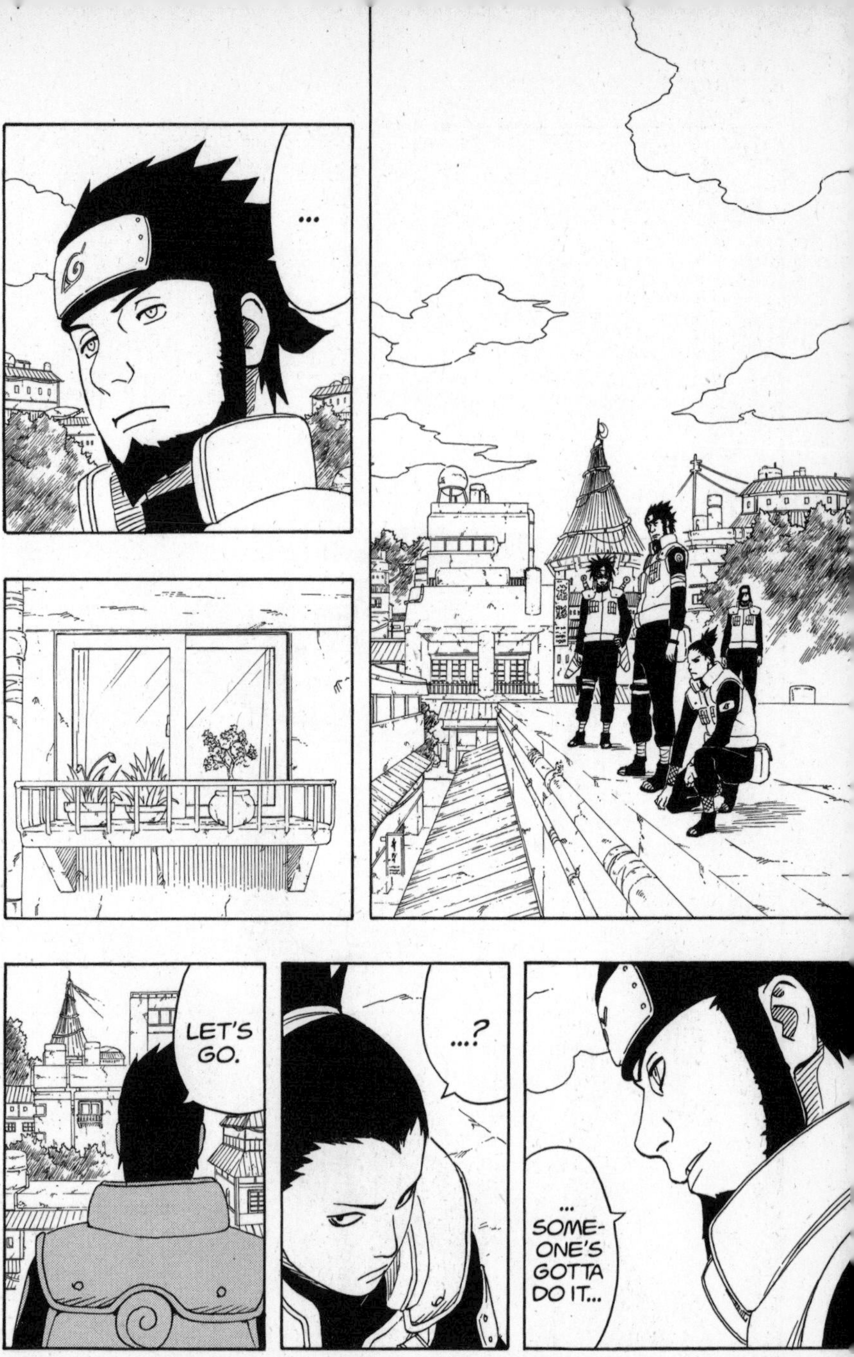
...
... SOME-ONE'S GOTTA DO IT...
...?
LET'S GO.

READ THIS WAY

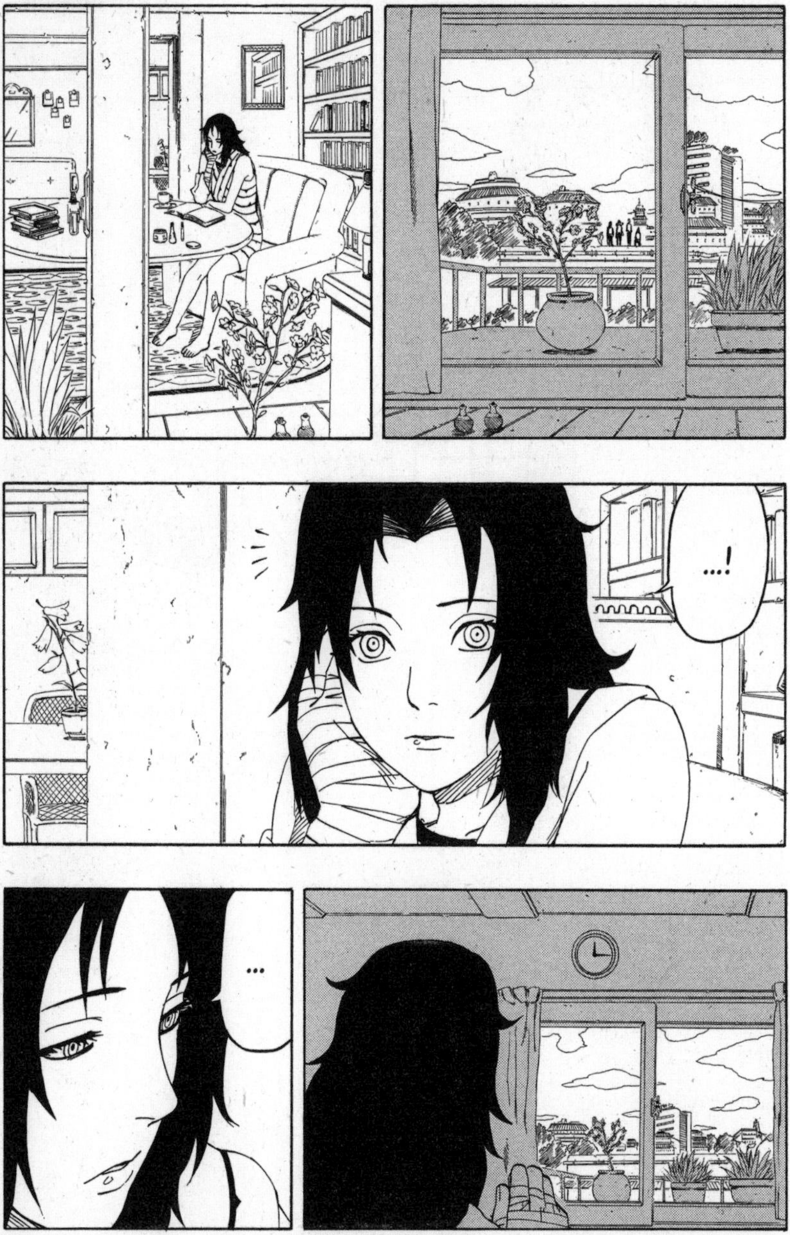

...!
...

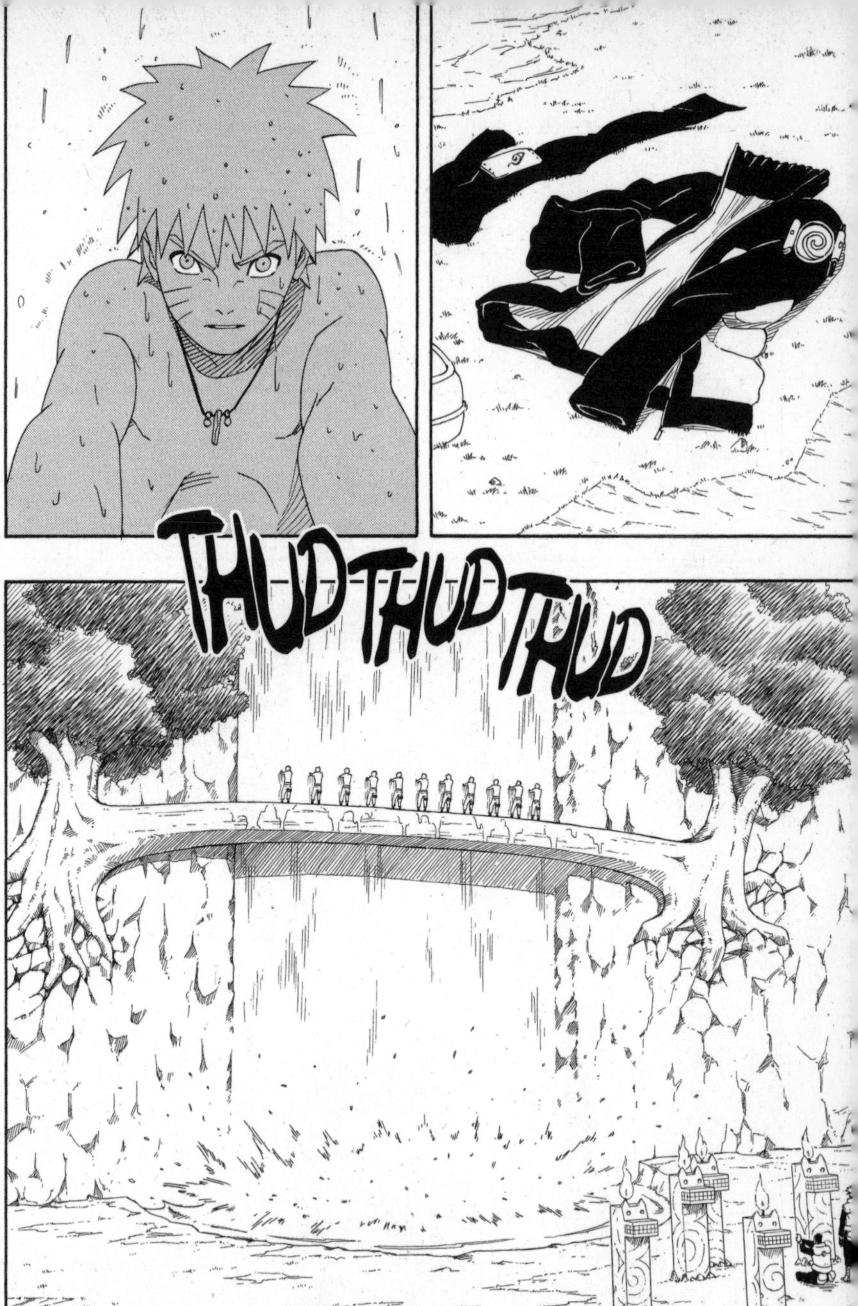
THUD THUD THUD

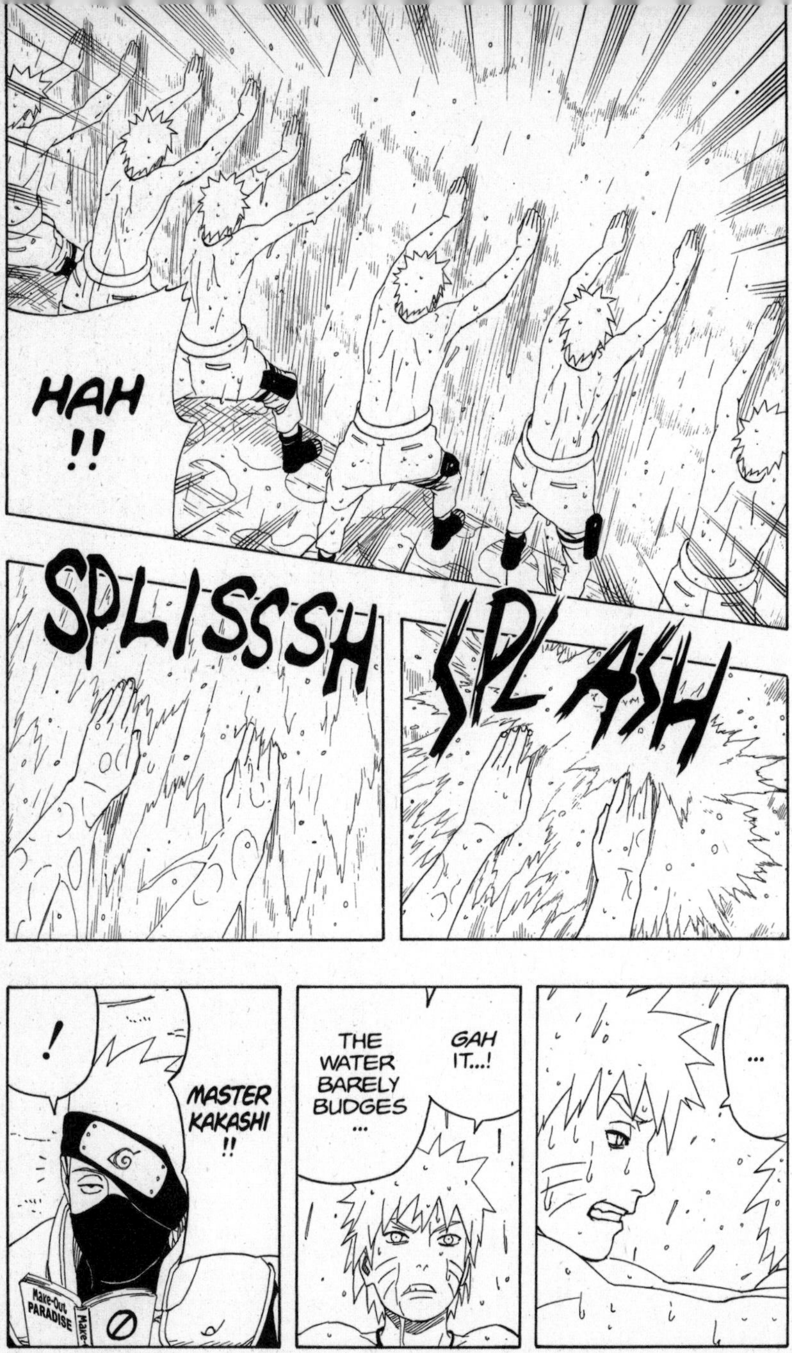
HAH!!
SPLASH
SPLISSSH
...
GAH IT...!
THE WATER BARELY BUDGES...
!
MASTER KAKASHI!!
Make-Out PARADISE

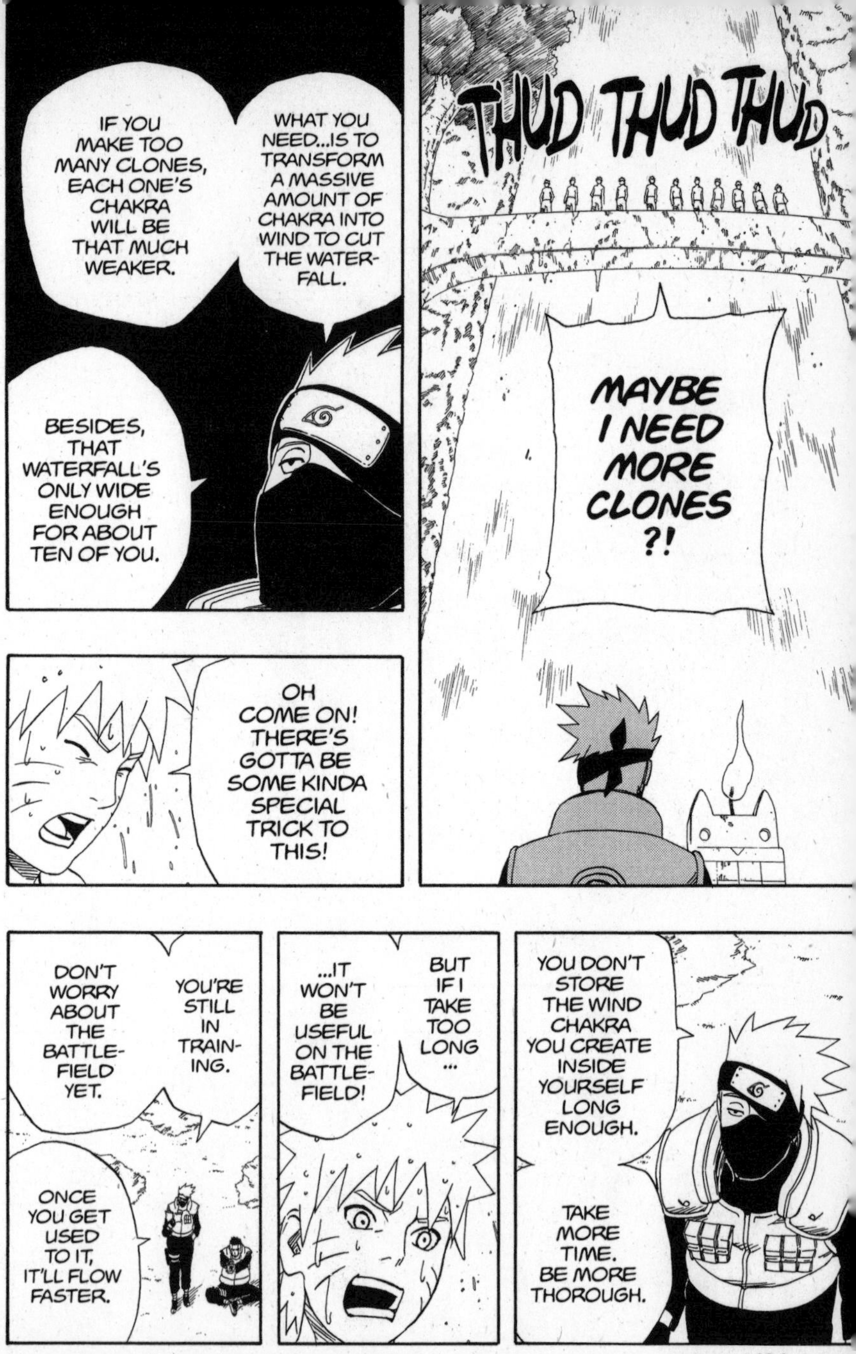
THUD THUD THUD
MAYBE I NEED MORE CLONES ?!
WHAT YOU NEED...IS TO TRANSFORM A MASSIVE AMOUNT OF CHAKRA INTO WIND TO CUT THE WATER-FALL.
IF YOU MAKE TOO MANY CLONES, EACH ONE'S CHAKRA WILL BE THAT MUCH WEAKER.
BESIDES, THAT WATERFALL'S ONLY WIDE ENOUGH FOR ABOUT TEN OF YOU.
OH COME ON! THERE'S GOTTA BE SOME KINDA SPECIAL TRICK TO THIS!
YOU DON'T STORE THE WIND CHAKRA YOU CREATE INSIDE YOURSELF LONG ENOUGH.
TAKE MORE TIME. BE MORE THOROUGH.
BUT IF I TAKE TOO LONG ...
...IT WON'T BE USEFUL ON THE BATTLE-FIELD!
YOU'RE STILL IN TRAIN-ING.
DON'T WORRY ABOUT THE BATTLE-FIELD YET.
ONCE YOU GET USED TO IT, IT'LL FLOW FASTER.

READ THIS WAY

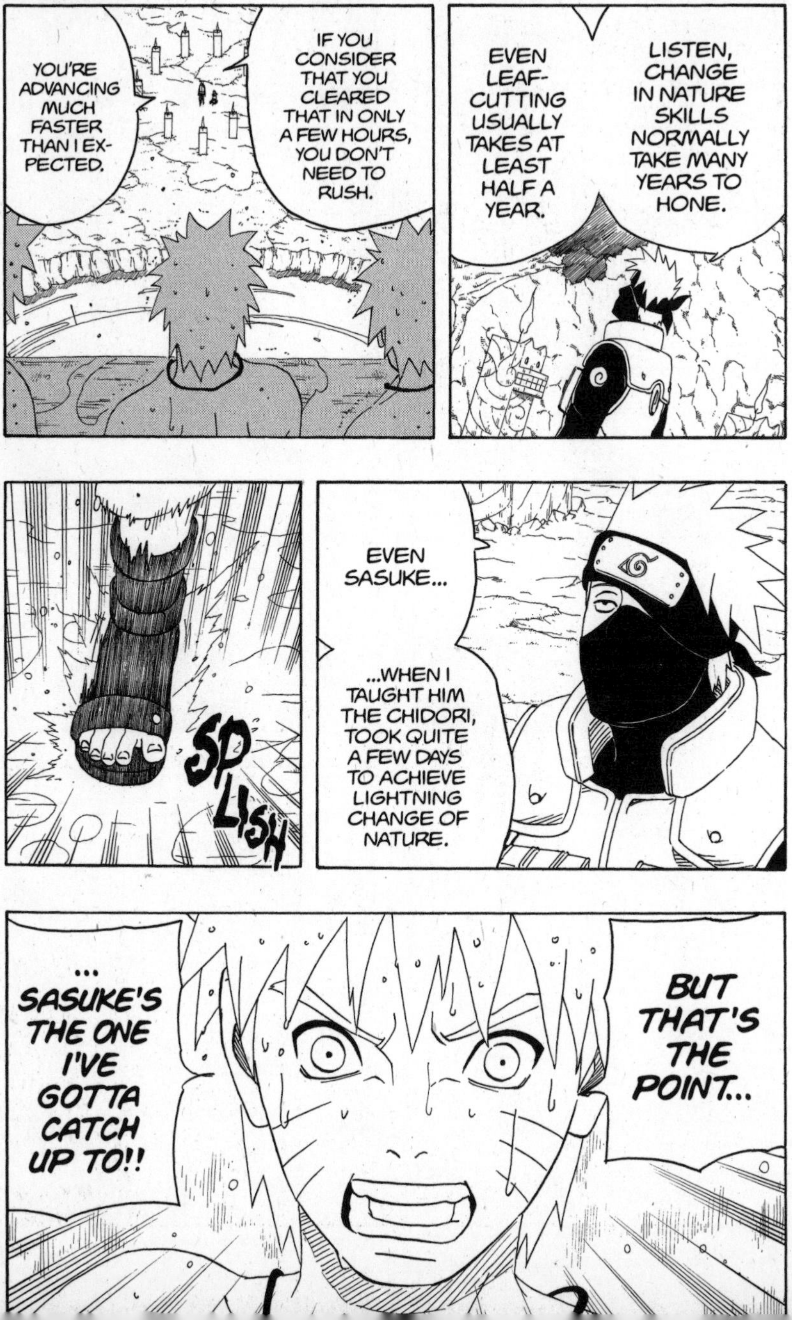
LISTEN, CHANGE IN NATURE SKILLS NORMALLY TAKE MANY YEARS TO HONE.
EVEN LEAF-CUTTING USUALLY TAKES AT LEAST HALF A YEAR.
IF YOU CONSIDER THAT YOU CLEARED THAT IN ONLY A FEW HOURS, YOU DON'T NEED TO RUSH.
YOU'RE ADVANCING MUCH FASTER THAN I EXPECTED.
EVEN SASUKE...
...WHEN I TAUGHT HIM THE CHIDORI, TOOK QUITE A FEW DAYS TO ACHIEVE LIGHTNING CHANGE OF NATURE.
SPLISH
BUT THAT'S THE POINT...
... SASUKE'S THE ONE I'VE GOTTA CATCH UP TO!!

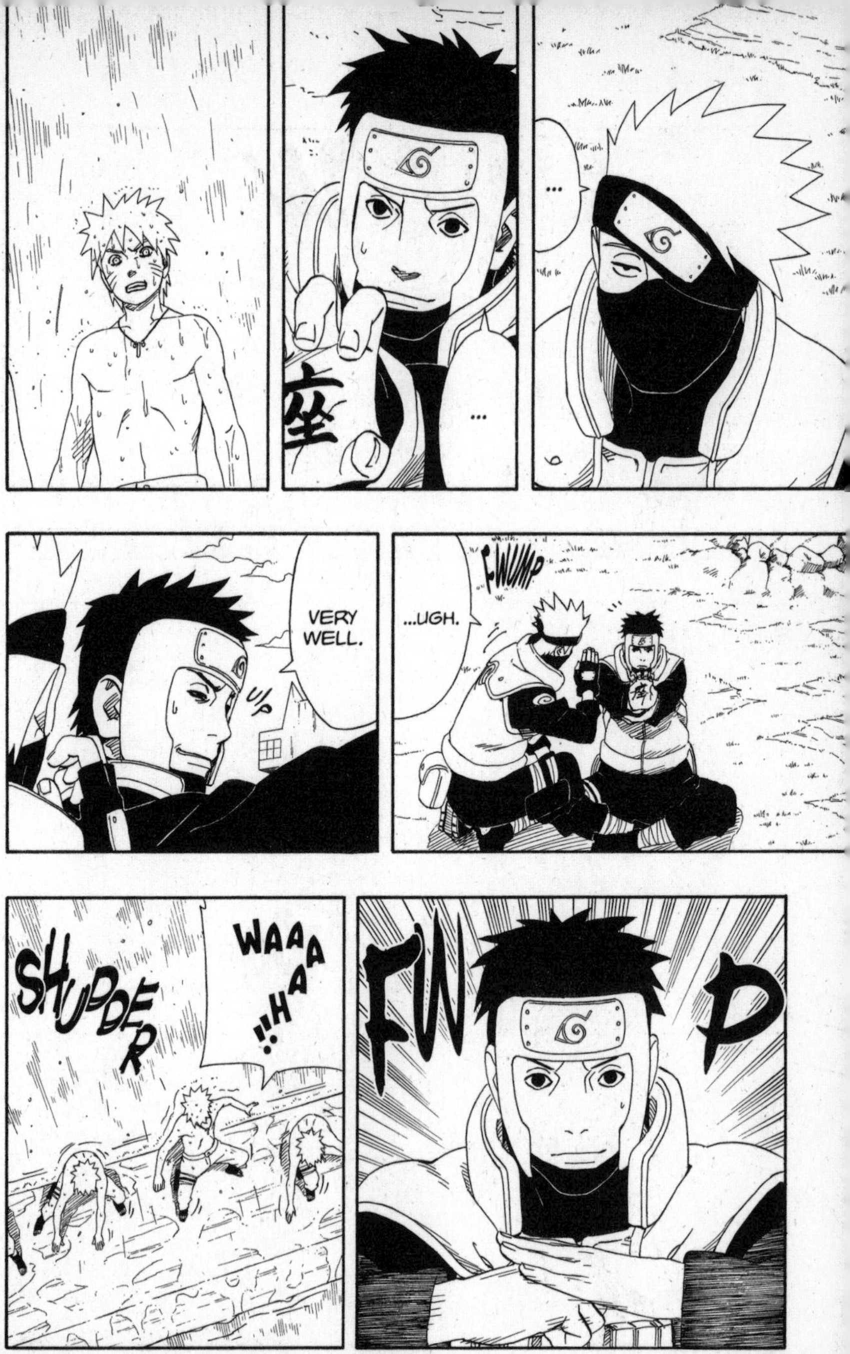
...
...
座
FWUMP
...UGH.
VERY WELL.
FW P
WAAAHA!!
SHUDDER

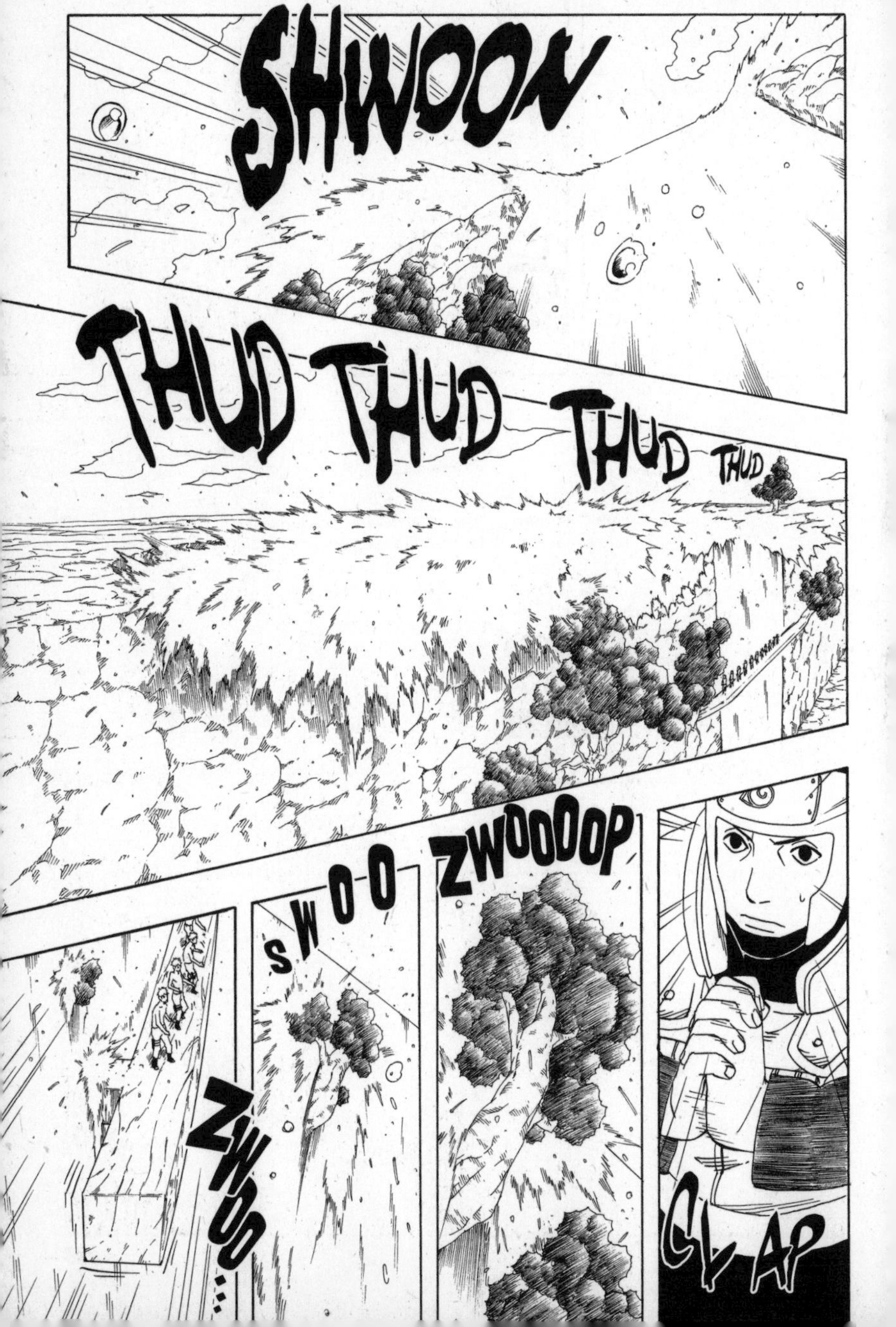
SHWOON
THUD THUD THUD THUD
CLAP
ZWOOOOP
SWOO
ZWOO...

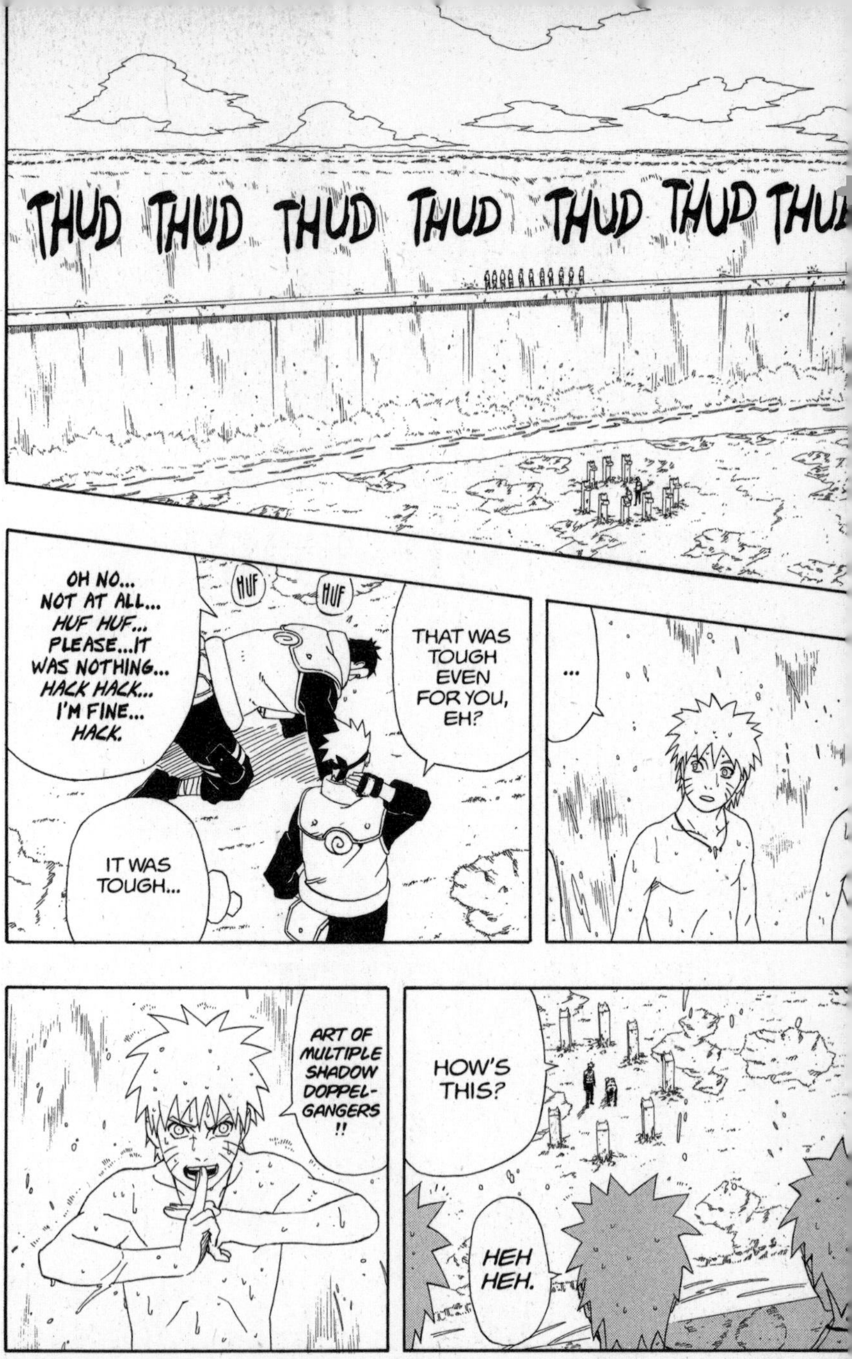
THUD THUD THUD THUD THUD THUD THU
...
THAT WAS TOUGH EVEN FOR YOU, EH?
HUF
HUF
OH NO... NOT AT ALL... HUF HUF... PLEASE...IT WAS NOTHING... HACK HACK... I'M FINE... HACK.
IT WAS TOUGH...
HOW'S THIS?
HEH HEH.
ART OF MULTIPLE SHADOW DOPPEL-GANGERS!!

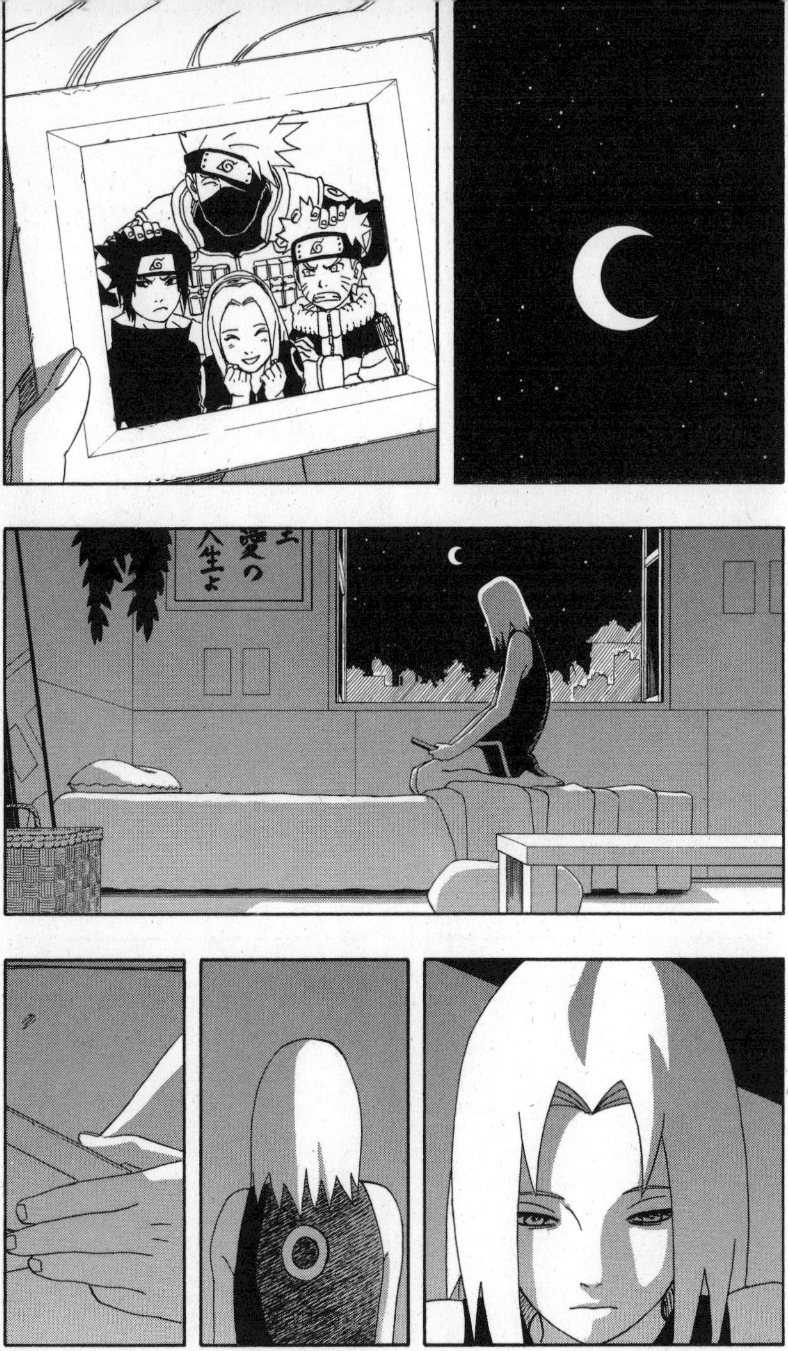
愛の
人生よ

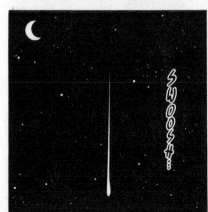

SWOOSH..

A SHOOT-ING STAR... COOL...

SHFF

...SASUKE...

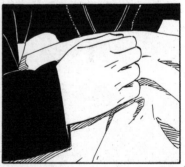

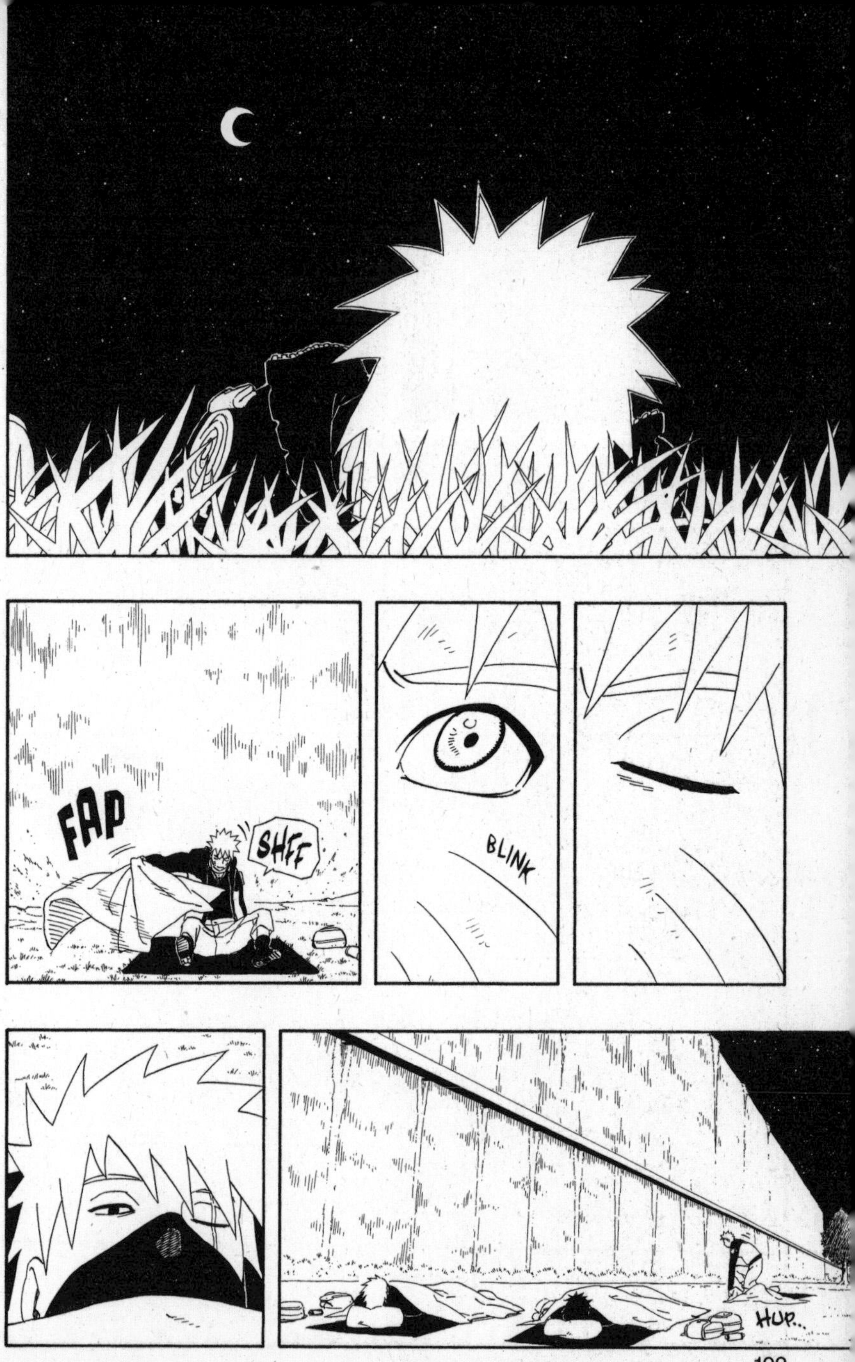
BLINK
FAP
SHFF
HUP...

READ THIS WAY

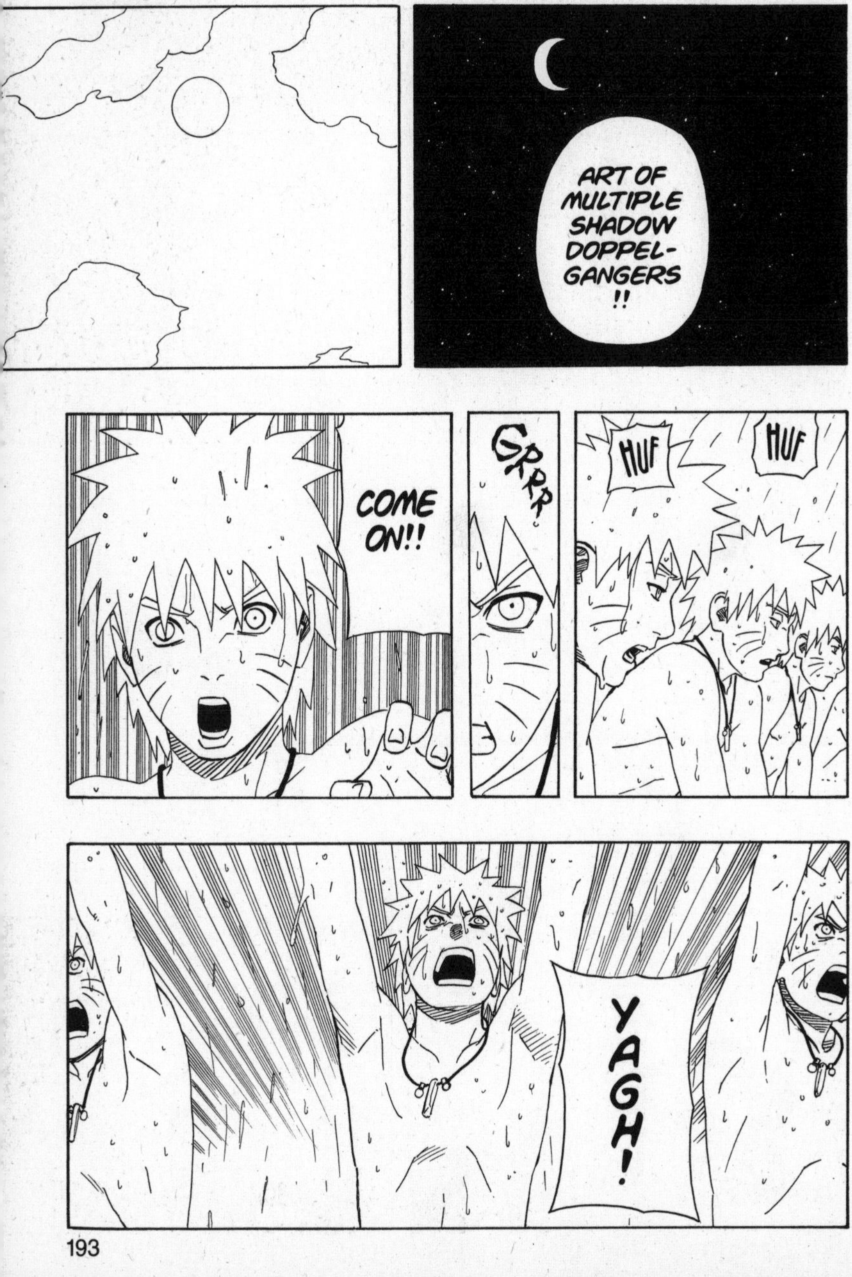
ART OF MULTIPLE SHADOW DOPPEL-GANGERS !!
HUF
HUF
GRRR
COME ON!!
YAGH!

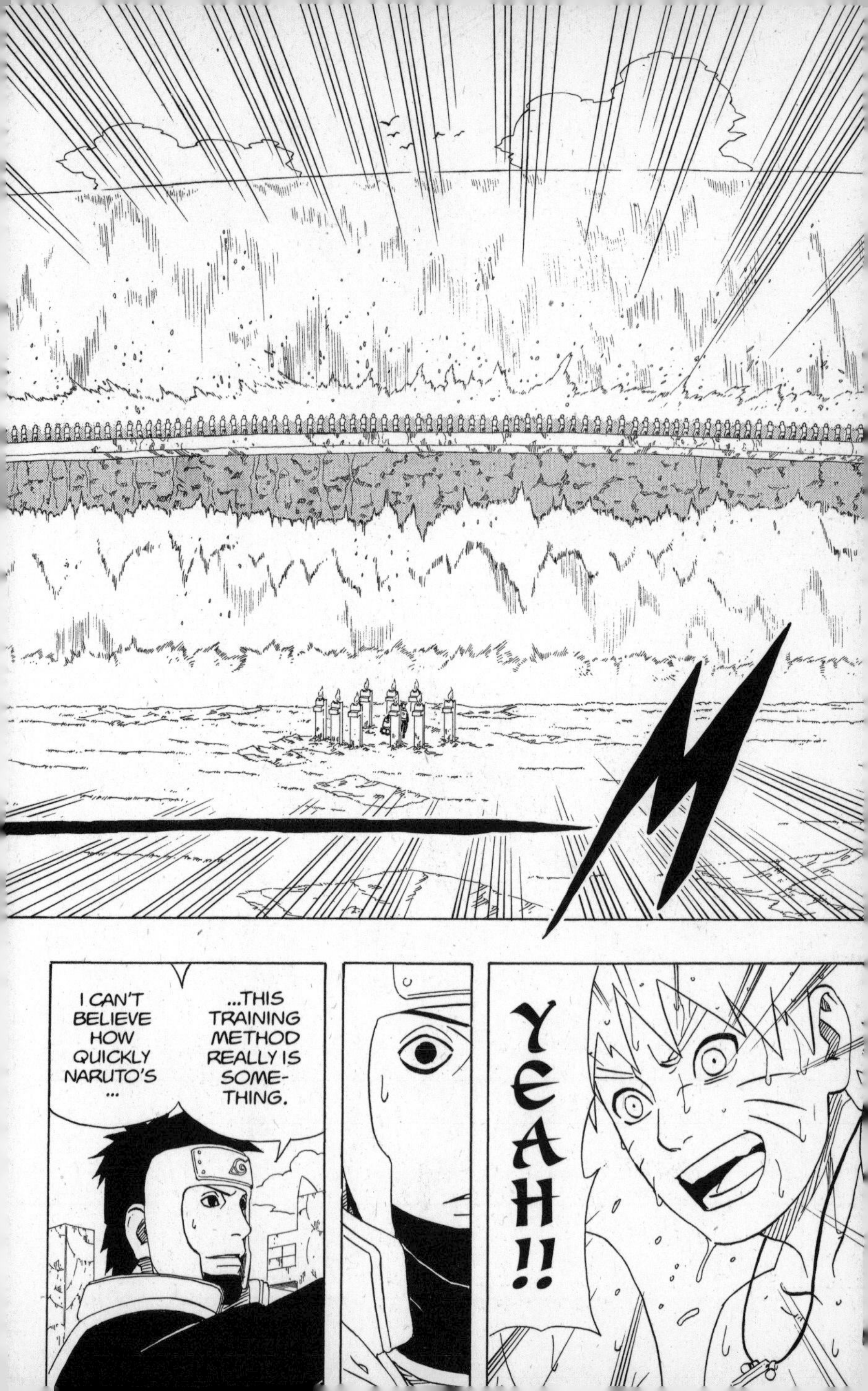
YEAH!!
I CAN'T BELIEVE HOW QUICKLY NARUTO'S...
...THIS TRAINING METHOD REALLY IS SOMETHING.

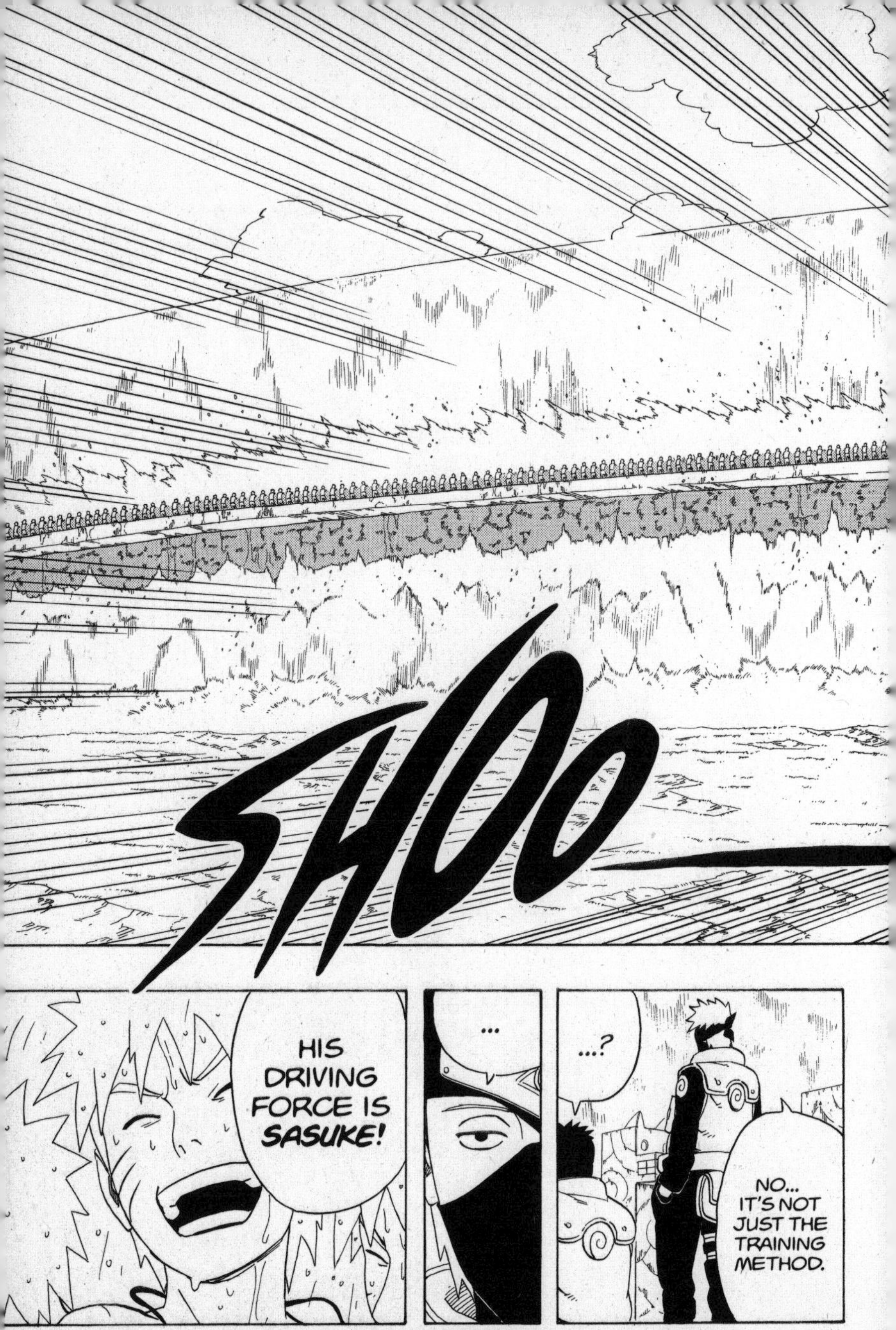
SHOO
...?
NO... IT'S NOT JUST THE TRAINING METHOD.
...
HIS DRIVING FORCE IS SASUKE!

TO BE CONTINUED IN *NARUTO* VOLUME 36!

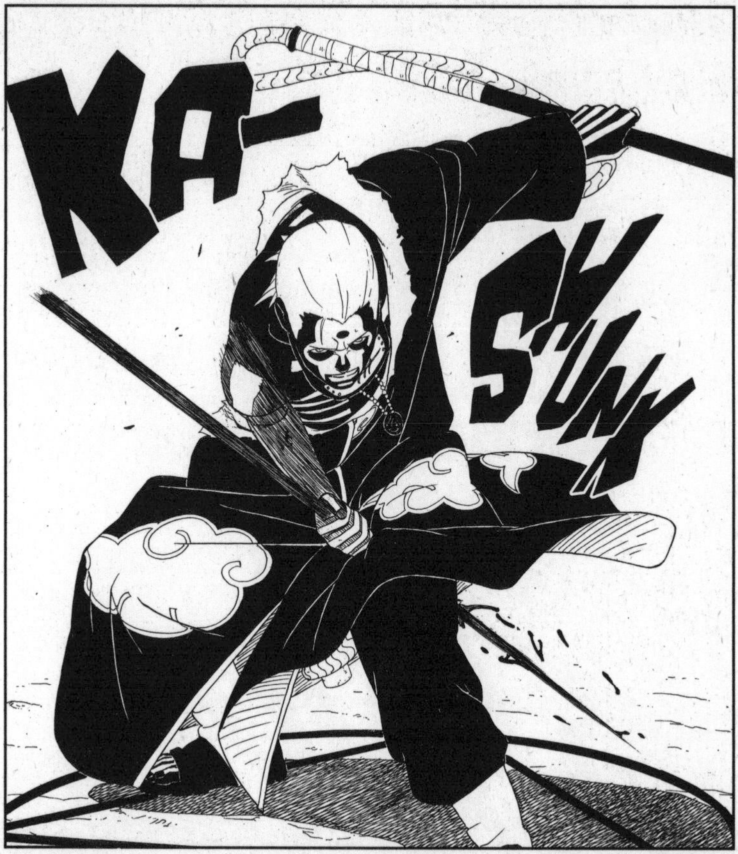
KA-
SHUNK

IN THE NEXT VOLUME...

CELL NUMBER 10

Asuma's new team and the former Cell Number 10 battle Hidan of the Akatsuki, who may be the most unstoppable foe the Konoha ninja have encountered—and who could mean the end for one of Naruto's longest-standing allies. As Naruto prepares for the worst, the Akatsuki reveals its master plan!

AVAILABLE NOW!

Secrets of the Village Hidden in the Leaves Revealed!

Get exclusive insider information on your favorite ninja with these Anime Profile books—complete with:
- Character designs
- Show production information
- Special color illustrations

Episodes 1-37
Plus, creator and voice actor interviews, and an original pinup!

Episodes 38-80
Plus, a fold-out chart connecting all 55 major characters and an original poster!

SHONEN JUMP™
NARUTO
ANIME PROFILES™

Complete your collection with Naruto *manga, fiction, art books, and anime*

Visit **www.naruto.com** for online games, downloads, and more!
© 2002 MASASHI KISHIMOTO

RATED TEEN
ratings.viz.com

ST PROFILES

viz MEDIA
www.viz.com

Tell us what you think about SHONEN JUMP manga!

Our survey is now available online.
Go to: **www.SHONENJUMP.com/mangasurvey**

Help us make our product offering better!

THE REAL ACTION STARTS IN...

SHONEN JUMP
THE WORLD'S MOST POPULAR MANGA
www.shonenjump.com

ADVANCED

VIZ
MEDIA

BLEACH © 2001 by Tite Kubo/SHUEISHA Inc. NARUTO © 1999 by Masashi Kishimoto/SHUEISHA Inc.
DEATH NOTE © 2003 by Tsugumi Ohba, Takeshi Obata/SHUEISHA Inc. ONE PIECE © 1997 by Eiichiro Oda/SHUEISHA Inc.

SHONEN JUMP

THE WORLD'S MOST POPULAR MANGA

12 ISSUES FOR ONLY $29⁹⁵*

THAT'S 50% OFF THE NEWSSTAND PRICE!

Each issue of SHONEN JUMP contains the coolest manga available in the U.S., anime news, and info on video & card games, toys AND more!

SUBSCRIBE TODAY and Become a Member of the ST Sub Club!

- **ENJOY** 12 HUGE action-packed issues
- **SAVE** 50% OFF the cover price
- **ACCESS** exclusive areas of www.shonenjump.com
- **RECEIVE** FREE members-only gifts

Available ONLY to Subscribers!

www.viz.com

RATED T FOR TEEN
ratings.viz.com

3 EASY WAYS TO SUBSCRIBE!

1) Send in the subscription order form from this book **OR**
2) Log on to: www.shonenjump.com **OR**
3) Call 1-800-541-7919

*Canada price for 12 issues: $41.95 USD. including GST, HST, and QST. US/CAN orders only. Allow 6-8 weeks for delivery.
BLEACH © 2001 by Tite Kubo/SHUEISHA Inc. NARUTO © 1999 by Masashi Kishimoto/SHUEISHA Inc.
GINTAMA © 2003 by Hideaki Sorachi/SHUEISHA Inc. ONE PIECE © 1997 by Eiichiro Oda/SHUEISHA Inc.

Save **50% OFF** the cover price!

SHONEN JUMP

THE WORLD'S MOST POPULAR MANGA

Over **300 pages** per issue!

Each issue of SHONEN JUMP contains the coolest manga available in the U.S., anime news, and info on video & card games, toys AND more!

☑ **YES!** Please enter my one-year subscription (12 HUGE issues) to **SHONEN JUMP** at the LOW SUBSCRIPTION RATE of **$29.95!**

NAME

ADDRESS

CITY _____ STATE ____ ZIP

E-MAIL ADDRESS _____ P7GNC1

☐ MY CHECK IS ENCLOSED (PAYABLE TO SHONEN JUMP) ☐ BILL ME LATER

CREDIT CARD: ☐ VISA   ☐ MASTERCARD

ACCOUNT # _____ EXP. DATE

SIGNATURE

CLIP AND MAIL TO →

SHONEN JUMP
Subscriptions Service Dept.
P.O. Box 515
Mount Morris, IL 61054-0515

Make checks payable to: **SHONEN JUMP**. Canada price for 12 issues: $41.95 USD, including GST, HST and QST. US/CAN orders only. Allow 6-8 weeks for delivery.

RATED T TEEN
ratings.viz.com

BLEACH © 2001 by Tite Kubo/SHUEISHA Inc. NARUTO © 1999 by Masashi Kishimoto/SHUEISHA Inc.
ONE PIECE © 1997 by Eiichiro Oda/SHUEISHA Inc.